Domestic Violence Offenders: Current Interventions, Research, and Implications for Policies and Standards

Domestic Violence Offenders: Current Interventions, Research, and Implications for Policies and Standards has been co-published simultaneously as *Journal of Aggression, Maltreatment & Trauma*, Volume 5, Number 2(#10) 2001.

The *Journal of Aggression, Maltreatment & Trauma* Monographic "Separates"

Robert Geffner, PhD, Senior Editor

Below is a list of "separates," which in serials librarianship means a special issue simultaneously published as a special journal issue or double-issue *and* as a "separate" hardbound monograph. (This is a format which we also call a "DocuSerial.")

"Separates" are published because specialized libraries or professionals may wish to purchase a specific thematic issue by itself in a format which can be separately cataloged and shelved, as opposed to purchasing the journal on an on-going basis. Faculty members may also more easily consider a "separate" for classroom adoption.

"Separates" are carefully classified separately with the major book jobbers so that the journal tie-in can be noted on new book order slips to avoid duplicate purchasing.

You may wish to visit Haworth's Website at . . .

http://www.HaworthPress.com

. . . to search our online catalog for complete tables of contents of these separates and related publications.

You may also call 1-800-HAWORTH (outside US/Canada: 607-722-5857), or Fax 1-800-895-0582 (outside US/Canada: 607-771-0012), or e-mail at:

getinfo@haworthpressinc.com

Justice Grant A. Campbell, Justice of the Ontario Superior Court of Justice, Family Court, London, Canada)

Maltreatment in Early Childhood: Tools for Research-Based Intervention, edited by Kathleen Coulborn Faller, PhD (Vol. 2, No. 2 [#4], 1999). *"This important book takes an international and cross-cultural look at child abuse and maltreatment. Discussing the history of abuse in the United States, exploring psychological trauma, and containing interviews with sexual abuse victims,* Maltreatment in Early Childhood *provides counselors and mental health practitioners with research that may help prevent child abuse or reveal the mistreatment some children endure."*

Multiple Victimization of Children: Conceptual, Developmental, Research, and Treatment Issues, edited by B. B. Robbie Rossman, PhD, and Mindy S. Rosenberg, PhD (Vol. 2, No. 1 [#3], 1998). *"This book takes on a large challenge and meets it with stunning success. It fills a glaring gap in the literature . . . " (Edward P. Mulvey, PhD, Associate Professor of Child Psychiatry, Western Psychiatric Institute and Clinic, University of Pittsburgh School of Medicine)*

Violence Issues for Health Care Educators and Providers, edited by L. Kevin Hamberger, PhD, Sandra K. Burge, PhD, Antonnette V. Graham, PhD, and Anthony J. Costa, MD (Vol. 1, No. 2 [#2], 1997). *"A superb book that contains invaluable hands-on advice for medical educators and health care professionals alike . . ." (Richard L. Holloways, PhD, Professor and Vice Chair, Department of Family and Community Medicine, and Associate Dean for Student Affairs, Medical College of Wisconsin)*

Violence and Sexual Abuse at Home: Current Issues in Spousal Battering and Child Maltreatment, edited by Robert Geffner, PhD, Susan B. Sorenson, PhD, and Paula K. Lundberg-Love, PhD (Vol. 1, No. 1 [#1], 1997). *"The Editors have distilled the important questions at the cutting edge of the field of violence studies, and have brought rigor, balance and moral fortitude to the search for answers." (Virginia Goldner, PhD, Co-Director, Gender and Violence Project, Senior Faculty, Ackerman Institute for Family Therapy)*

Domestic Violence Offenders: Current Interventions, Research, and Implications for Policies and Standards

Robert A. Geffner, PhD, ABPN
Alan Rosenbaum, PhD
Editors

Domestic Violence Offenders: Current Interventions, Research, and Implications for Policies and Standards has been co-published simultaneously as *Journal of Aggression, Maltreatment & Trauma*, Volume 5, Number 2(#10) 2001.

HMTP

The Haworth Maltreatment & Trauma Press
An Imprint of
The Haworth Press, Inc.
New York • London • Oxford

Published by

The Haworth Maltreatment & Trauma Press, 10 Alice Street, Binghamton, NY 13904-1580 USA

The Haworth Maltreatment & Trauma Press is an imprint of The Haworth Press, Inc., 10 Alice Street, Binghamton, NY 13904-1580 USA.

Domestic Violence Offenders: Current Interventions, Research, and Implications for Policies and Standards has been co-published simultaneously as *Journal of Aggression, Maltreatment & Trauma*, Volume 5, Issue 2, Number 10 2001.

The development, preparation, and publication of this work has been undertaken with great care. However, the publisher, employees, editors, and agents of The Haworth Press and all imprints of The Haworth Press, Inc., including The Haworth Medical Press® and The Pharmaceutical Products Press®, are not responsible for any errors contained herein or for consequences that may ensue from use of materials or information contained in this work. Opinions expressed by the author(s) are not necessarily those of The Haworth Press, Inc.

Cover design by Thomas J. Mayshock Jr.

Library of Congress Cataloging-in-Publication Data

Domestic violence offenders : current interventions, research, and implications for policies and standards / Robert A. Geffner, Alan Rosenbaum.
    p. cm.
    "Co-published simultaneously as Journal of aggression, maltreatment & trauma, volume 5, issue 2, number 10, 2002."
    Includes bibliographical references and index.
    ISBN 0-7890-1930-2 ((hard) : alk. paper) – ISBN 0-7890-1931-0 ((pbk) : alk. paper)
    1. Family violence. 2. Family violence–Prevention. I. Rosenbaum, Alan. II. Journal of aggression, maltreatment & trauma. III. Title.
HV6626 .D4398 2002
362.82'927–dc21
                                              2002004031

Indexing, Abstracting & Website/Internet Coverage

This section provides you with a list of major indexing & abstracting services. That is to say, each service began covering this periodical during the year noted in the right column. Most Websites which are listed below have indicated that they will either post, disseminate, compile, archive, cite or alert their own Website users with research-based content from this work. (This list is as current as the copyright date of this publication.)

(continued)

(continued)

Special Bibliographic Notes related to special journal issues
(separates) and indexing/abstracting:

- indexing/abstracting services in this list will also cover material in any "separate" that is co-published simultaneously with Haworth's special thematic journal issue or DocuSerial. Indexing/abstracting usually covers material at the article/chapter level.
- monographic co-editions are intended for either non-subscribers or libraries which intend to purchase a second copy for their circulating collections.
- monographic co-editions are reported to all jobbers/wholesalers/approval plans. The source journal is listed as the "series" to assist the prevention of duplicate purchasing in the same manner utilized for books-in-series.
- to facilitate user/access services all indexing/abstracting services are encouraged to utilize the co-indexing entry note indicated at the bottom of the first page of each article/chapter/contribution.
- this is intended to assist a library user of any reference tool (whether print, electronic, online, or CD-ROM) to locate the monographic version if the library has purchased this version but not a subscription to the source journal.
- individual articles/chapters in any Haworth publication are also available through the Haworth Document Delivery Service (HDDS).

Domestic Violence Offenders: Current Interventions, Research, and Implications for Policies and Standards

CONTENTS

NONCONVENTIONAL APPROACHES FOR INTERVENTION IN CASES OF SPOUSE/PARTNER ABUSE

RESEARCH AND EVALUATION CONCERNING DOMESTIC VIOLENCE OFFENDERS

ABOUT THE EDITORS

Robert A. Geffner, PhD, ABPN, is the Founder and President of the Family Violence and Sexual Assault Institute (and Executive Editor of the *Family Violence & Sexual Assault Bulletin*) located in San Diego, California. Dr. Geffner is also Clinical Research Professor of Psychology at the California School of Professional Psychology, Alliant International University in San Diego. He is a licensed psychologist and a licensed marriage and family therapist in California and Texas and was the clinical director of a large private practice mental health clinic in East Texas for over 15 years. Dr. Geffner is Editor-in-Chief of Haworth's Maltreatment and Trauma Press, Editor of the *Journal of Child Sexual Abuse* and the *Journal of Aggression, Maltreatment & Trauma,* and Co-Editor of the *Journal of Emotional Abuse.* He has a Diplomate in Clinical Neuropsychology from the American Board of Professional Neuropsychology. He has edited and authored numerous books, book chapters, journal articles, and research papers concerning family violence, sexual assault, child abuse, family and child psychology, custody issues, forensic psychology, neuropsychology, and diagnostic assessment. Dr. Geffner has also served on several national and state committees dealing with various aspects of family psychology, family violence, child abuse, and family law.

Alan Rosenbaum, PhD, is currently Professor of Psychiatry and Director of Psychology Training at the University of Massachusetts Medical School. He is also Founder and Director of the Marital Research and Treatment Program, which includes one of the largest batterer treatment programs in Massachusetts. The program provides anger management treatment for both men and women. Dr. Rosenbaum's research interests include the contributions of biological factors, such as head injury and serotonergic deficits to relationship aggression, batterer treatment outcome, women's aggression, and the etiology of relationship aggression in both men and women. Much of his work has been funded by grants from the National Institute of Mental Health and has been presented at conferences and universities throughout the United States and internationally.

ABOUT THE CONTRIBUTORS

Audrey L. Begun, PhD, MSW, is currently Associate Professor at the University of Wisconsin-Milwaukee in the Social Work Programs, and is Center Scientist with the Wisconsin Center for Addiction and Behavioral Health Research. As Center Scientist, she has integrated the Stages of Change approach into her teaching, research, and scholarship. Dr. Begun was a principal co-investigator on the Safe At Home collaborative research project. Her latest work is with the National Institutes on Alcoholism and Alcohol Abuse, facilitating the preparation of social work education curriculum materials related to epidemiology, screening, assessment, readiness to change, motivational interviewing, prevention and other interventions in alcohol use problems.

Larry W. Bennett, PhD, is Associate Professor at the Jane Addams College of Social Work, the University of Illinois at Chicago. His research interests include the implementation of evidence-based practice in social service agencies, the relationship between substance abuse and domestic violence, the structure and effectiveness of community based batterers intervention systems, and the developmental/structural links between various forms of men's violence such as bullying, sexual harassment, dating violence, and adult partner abuse. He has served on domestic violence advisory groups of several public agencies including the Illinois Department of Human Services and the U.S. Center for Substance Abuse Treatment. He practices social work in Crystal Lake, Illinois, limiting his practice to court ordered child custody evaluations.

Jacquelyn C. Campbell, PhD, RN, FAAN, is currently the Anna D. Wolfe Endowed Professor and Associate Dean for Doctoral Education Programs and Research at Johns Hopkins University School of Nursing with a joint appointment in the School of Hygiene and Public Health. She is the Principal Investigator of five NIH, DOD, or CDC major funded research studies on battering, and the author or co-author of more than 90 publications on the subject. These include five books: *Nursing Care of Survivors of Family Violence; Sanctions and Sanctuary; Assessing Dangerousness; Ending Domestic Violence;* and *Em-*

powering Survivors of Abuse: Health Care, Battered Women and Their Children. Dr. Campbell has worked with wife abuse shelters and policy related committees on domestic violence for more than 18 years.

Lynn Dowd, PsyD, is a clinical psychologist and a licensed clinical social worker who provides treatment for adolescents and adults in the Ambulatory Psychiatry Clinic at University of Massachusetts Memorial Health Care (UMMHC). She designed the group treatment format for the Women's Anger Management Program at UMMHC, and has led groups and conducted research on partner aggressive women since 1996. Other treatment and research interests include trauma, mood disorders, substance abuse, and developmental issues related to women's aggression.

Paul J. Gearan, MA, is currently the Director of Research for Maguire Associates of Bedford, MA, a research and consulting firm specializing in higher education. He formerly served as the Associate Director of the Marital Research and Treatment Program. In this capacity, he coordinated clinical services for and treated individuals with anger and aggression problems, and conducted several research studies utilizing this population. Mr. Gearan was also affiliated with the University of Massachusetts Medical School while working on his doctorate degree in psychology.

Robert A. Geffner, PhD, ABPN, is the Founder and President of the Family Violence & Sexual Assault Institute (and Executive Editor of the *Family Violence & Sexual Assault Bulletin*) located in San Diego, California. Dr. Geffner is also Clinical Research Professor of Psychology at the California School of Professional Psychology, Alliant International University in San Diego. He is a licensed psychologist and a licensed marriage and family therapist in California and Texas and was the clinical director of a large private practice mental health clinic in East Texas for over 15 years. Dr. Geffner is Editor-in-Chief of Haworth's Maltreatment and Trauma Press, Editor of the *Journal of Child Sexual Abuse* and the *Journal of Aggression, Maltreatment & Trauma*, and Co-editor of the *Journal of Emotional Abuse*. He has co-authored numerous books (including the most recent, *Treatment of Women Arrested for Domestic Violence*), articles, and chapters concerning various areas of family violence. He has a Diplomate in Clinical Neuropsychology from the American Board of Professional Neuropsychology.

Richard J. Gelles, PhD, holds The Joanne and Raymond Welsh Chair of Child Welfare and Family Violence in the School of Social Work at the University of Pennsylvania. He is the Co-Director of the Center for the Study of Youth Policy and Co-Director of the Center for Children's Policy, Practice, and Research. His book, *The Violent Home,* was the first systematic empirical investigation of family violence and continues to be highly influential. He is the author or co-author of 23 books and more than 100 articles and chapters on family violence. His latest books are: *The Book of David: How Preserving Families Can Cost Children's Lives* (Basic Books, 1996) and *Intimate Violence in Families, Third Edition* (Sage Publications, 1997). Gelles was a member of the National Academy of Sciences panel on "Assessing Family Violence Interventions."

Tamara S. Hagar, BA, is a Master of Arts candidate in Couple and Family Therapy at Antioch University Seattle. She is also a clinical assistant at the Harborview Anger Management and Domestic Violence Program at the University of Washington School of Medicine in Seattle.

L. Kevin Hamberger, PhD, is Professor of Family and Community Medicine at the Medical College of Wisconsin, Milwaukee, WI. For the past 15 years, he has conducted a program of treatment and research for domestically violent men and women. He is a member of the Wisconsin Governor's Council on Domestic Abuse, in which he chaired the Treatment Standards Committee from 1994-1996. Dr. Hamberger has authored or co-edited several books, articles, and chapters concerning intimate partner violence, including *Violence Issues for Health Care Educators and Providers.*

Amy Holtzworth-Munroe, PhD, received her doctorate in clinical psychology from the University of Washington in 1988. She joined the psychology department faculty at Indiana University, where she is now Professor. She has been conducting research on the problem of relationship aggression since the mid-1980s. Her recent research has focused on the identification and comparison of subtypes of male batterers. She has published more than 50 journal articles, book chapters, and reviews.

She has led batterer treatment groups and has worked with a local domestic violence taskforce to set up a new batterers' treatment program.

Alyce LaViolette, MS, is a Licensed Marriage and Family Therapist in private practice in Long Beach, CA. She has worked with battered women since 1978, and domestic violence offenders since 1979 when she founded Alternatives to Violence. This was one of the first programs originating in a shelter to work with such offenders. Ms. LaViolette has also developed training programs on various aspects of intimate partner violence. She is a featured keynote speaker, national trainer, consultant, expert witness in various types of court cases, and co-author of *It Could Happen to Anyone—Why Battered Women Stay.*

Penny A. Leisring, PhD, is currently Assistant Professor of Psychology at Quinnipiac University in Hamden, CT. She received her PhD in Clinical Psychology from the State University of New York at Stony Brook in 1999. Her clinical interests focus on the prevention and reduction of aggressive behavior in adults and children. She conducts research examining male- and female-perpetrated relationship aggression, parental discipline styles, and child behavior problems.

Hsin-hua Lin, BS, is a Master of Science candidate in Marriage and Family Therapy at Seattle Pacific University. She is also a clinical assistant at the Harborview Anger Management and Domestic Violence Program at the University of Washington School of Medicine in Seattle.

Roland D. Maiuro, PhD, is Director of the Harborview Anger Management and Domestic Violence Program and Associate Professor in the Department of Psychiatry and Behavioral Sciences at the University of Washington School of Medicine in Seattle. He is currently Editor-in-Chief of the journal *Violence and Victims.* Dr. Maiuro has been involved in research, training, and clinical practice involving family violence for over two decades. He is Co-Editor, with Daniel O'Leary, below, of the recent book, *Psychological Abuse in Violent Domestic Relations.*

Christopher M. Murphy, PhD, is Associate Professor of Psychology at the University of Maryland, Baltimore County. He also coordinates the counseling program for domestic abuse perpetrators at the Domestic Violence Center of Howard County, Maryland. His current investigations involve the link between alcohol problems and domestic abuse, emotional abuse in marriage and dating relationships, and the efficacy of cognitive-behavioral and motivational enhancement approaches in the treatment of domestic violence perpetrators.

K. Daniel O'Leary, PhD, is Distinguished Professor of Psychology, Psychology Department, State University of New York, Stony Brook, NY. He has been conducting research on domestic violence since 1979, and has evaluated risk factors and assessment strategies for evaluating partner abuse. Dr. O'Leary is a clinical psychologist who has specialized in relationship issues and conflict for over two decades. His research focuses on the etiology and treatment of relationship aggression and the marital discord/depression link. He is Co-Editor, with Roland Maiuro, of the recent book, *Psychological Abuse in Violent Domestic Relations.*

Natalie Olson, BA, is a graduate of the University of Washington and a former clinical assistant at the Harborview Anger Management and Domestic Violence Program in Seattle. She is currently Criminal Justice Act Administrator for The Federal Public Defender, Western District of Washington in Seattle.

Charissa Ondovic, BA, received a Bachelor's degree in psychology from the University of MA–Amherst. She received a research fellowship from University of Massachusetts Medical Center in the spring of 1996. She is currently teaching 7th grade math at Shrewsbury Middle School, Shrewsbury, MA where she has been for the past five years.

Alan Rosenbaum, PhD, is currently Professor of Psychiatry and Director of Psychology Training at the University of Massachusetts Medical School. He is also Founder and Director of the Marital Research and Treatment Program, which includes one of the largest batterer treatment programs in Massachusetts. The program provides anger management treatment for both men and women. Dr. Rosenbaum's research interests include the contributions of biological factors, such as head injury and serotonergic deficits to relationship aggression, batterer treatment outcome, women's aggression, and the etiology of relationship aggression in both men and women. He has authored or co-authored numerous articles and book chapters on all aspects of family violence during the past two decades. He was one of the first people to recognize and study the effects of intimate partner aggression on children.

Daniel G. Saunders, PhD, MSSW, is Associate Professor at the School of Social Work, University of Michigan. Dr. Saunders teaches courses on direct practice and domestic violence and focuses his research on victim trauma, offender typologies and treatment as well as the social response to domestic violence. He has authored or co-authored numerous articles and chapters on various aspects of intimate partner violence.

Gene Shelley, PhD, MPH, is currently Behavioral Scientist with the Prevention Development and Evaluation Branch, Division of Violence Prevention, National Center for Injury Prevention and Control at the Centers for Disease Control and Prevention (CDC) in Atlanta, GA. Dr. Shelley has worked as an expert consultant with the International Health Program Office at CDC and teaches cultural and medical anthropology at Georgia State University. Her present work in Prevention Development and Evaluation Branch includes medical anthropology, research methods (quantitative and qualitative), social network research, child maltreatment, intimate partner violence, dating violence, and the interface between ethnicity and attitudes towards violence and abuse.

Lynn Short, PhD, is Executive Director of Analytic Systems Associates, Inc. and Adjunct Faculty at University of North Carolina, Chapel Hill, School of Medicine. Dr. Short was Senior Scientist in the Division of Violence Prevention, National Center for Injury Prevention and Control, Centers for Disease Control and Prevention (CDC) between 1994-2000. She currently serves as a consultant on numerous evaluation research projects provides statistical consultation for several research teams, and works in proposal development for the evaluation of violence prevention interventions.

Terri Strodthoff, ABD, is currently completing her doctoral studies in Political Science at the University of Michigan. She served for four years as the Project Coordinator for the Safe At Home Project at the Milwaukee Women's Center, and then as the Project Evaluator of the Judical Oversight Initiative. She is currently serving as a project consultant to social service programs in Southeast Wisconsin.

Richard M. Tolman, PhD, is Associate Professor at the University of Michigan, School of Social Work. His research focuses on the issue of men who use violence against women and children, and on the effectiveness of interventions designed to change violent and abusive behavior. Dr. Tolman is currently co-Director of the Project for Research on Work, Welfare, and Domestic Violence, which is co-sponsored by the University of Michigan, School of Social Work, Research Center on Poverty, Risk and Mental Health, and the Center for Impact Research of Chicago. His current research includes a study of domestic violence, mental health, substance abuse, and other barriers to work for low-income single mothers.

Neil Vincent, PhD, LCSW, is Assistant Director of Outcome and Program Evaluation, Metropolitan Family Services, in Chicago, IL. Dr. Vincent currently conducts program evaluation research for Metropolitan Family Services in Chicago. While at his current position, he has conducted evaluation research focusing on the effectiveness of multidisciplinary domestic violence programs. He was formerly the Project Director for the Domestic Violence Program Evaluation Project at the Jane Addams College of Social Work at the University of Illinois at Chicago.

INTRODUCTION AND EXISTING STANDARDS FOR THOSE WHO BATTER

Domestic Violence Offenders: Treatment and Intervention Standards

Robert A. Geffner

Alan Rosenbaum

SUMMARY. This article introduces the volume and the various issues covered concerning current interventions, research, and standards for offenders arrested for domestic violence. The controversies that have arisen as many jurisdictions in the United States have established mandatory standards for batterer intervention are introduced, including the type of treatment modality and content permitted, the qualifications of those providing the interventions, the duration of treatment, and the relationship of the various standards to actual research. This volume presents articles concerning recent research, innovative as well as non-conventional intervention approaches, and policies that have often been adopted by legislatures. The present article identifies some of the controversial issues and calls into question the appropriateness of some of the statutes that currently

[Haworth co-indexing entry note]: "Domestic Violence Offenders: Treatment and Intervention Standards." Geffner, Robert A., and Alan Rosenbaum. Co-published simultaneously in *Journal of Aggression, Maltreatment & Trauma* (The Haworth Maltreatment & Trauma Press, an imprint of The Haworth Press, Inc.) Vol. 5, No. 2(#10), 2001, pp. 1-9; and: *Domestic Violence Offenders: Current Interventions, Research, and Implications for Policies and Standards* (ed: Robert A. Geffner, and Alan Rosenbaum) The Haworth Maltreatment & Trauma Press, an imprint of The Haworth Press, Inc., 2001, pp. 1-9. Single or multiple copies of this article are available for a fee from The Haworth Document Delivery Service [1-800-HAWORTH, 9:00 a.m. - 5:00 p.m. (EST). E-mail address: getinfo@haworthpressinc.com].

1

exist. Suggestions for a more inclusive and less rigid process are given for creating standards and policies concerning domestic violence offenders. *[Article copies available for a fee from The Haworth Document Delivery Service: 1-800-HAWORTH. E-mail address: <getinfo@haworthpressinc.com> Website: <http://www.HaworthPress.com> © 2001 by The Haworth Press, Inc. All rights reserved.]*

KEYWORDS. Batterers, domestic violence intervention, mandated standards, spouse abuse, wife abuse

Family violence has been recognized as one of the most serious social, mental health, criminal justice, and public health problems in the United States and other countries for many years. Many terms have been applied to aggression between romantic partners. Early incarnations, such as wife or spouse abuse were problematic as it became clear that although the marriage license might, as Straus (1980) called it, have been a hitting license, there apparently were many "unlicensed" participants. Terms such as intimate partner violence, relationship aggression, and partner abuse have been used almost interchangeably to refer to aggression between adult intimate partners. These terms also convey the realization that couples are not necessarily heterosexual, and perpetrators are not exclusively male. Abuse usually involves a person (termed the primary or dominant aggressor) in the relationship utilizing various forms of aggression (physical, sexual, and emotional) to coerce and control the behavior of his/her partner. It usually involves a pattern of behavior, but it can be a single incident or anything in between.

The term aggression should not be used as a synonym for abuse. Aggression is an action, abuse is a dynamic. Partners may be mutually aggressive, and the evidence overwhelmingly suggests that they are (Straus & Gelles, 1990), but they are rarely mutually abusive. Hitting by either partner is equally unacceptable, but not equally destructive. Women may hit their male partners, but infrequently batter them, because battering or abuse includes a pattern of coercion, intimidation and control, which is less frequently present in female to male aggression. It may, however be present in lesbian relationships. Legally, in many jurisdictions, an aggressive action may constitute the criminal act of domestic violence even if it is the first incident and no intimidation or control is exercised or attempted. Physically aggressive acts involve any form of unwanted or uninvited contact between individuals where the objective is to cause injury or pain, to intimidate, threaten or coerce the recipient. These may range from mild forms of pushing, shoving, and grabbing to more serious forms of punching, physical injury, strangulation, attempted or completed homicide. Regardless of the behaviors, the consequences for the victims and any children exposed to such abuse are usually traumatic.

The initial societal response to intimate partner violence was the development of the shelter movement for battered women. Women's shelters and/or safe houses developed in almost all major population areas throughout the United States and abroad. The goals were to provide a safe environment for abused women and their children, to offer advocacy, counseling, and medical services, and to empower women to leave their abusers. While shelters continue to serve these and other critical needs, and are an essential part of the service delivery system for battered women, they address only part of the problem. Left untreated, batterers often will continue to abuse their partners who leave shelters and return to the relationship. If their partner leaves the relationship, the batterers may find new victims to abuse. The response to this harsh reality was the development of batterer intervention programs.

Numerous intervention approaches and techniques have been developed and implemented in an attempt to reduce and eliminate spouse/partner abuse. These approaches, aimed at promoting attitudinal and behavioral changes in perpetrators, have been collectively subsumed under the heading batterers' treatment or batterers' intervention. The earliest interventions were developed in the 1970s and have been evolving over time, guided by both research findings and clinical experience. The most common approaches to batterer intervention are psychoeducational groups based on both cognitive-behavioral and pro-feminist theory. Almost all incorporate a focus on the power and control issues that are viewed as core elements in abusive relationships (e.g., Decker, 1999; Geffner & Mantooth, 2000; Mathews, 1995; Pence & Paymar, 1993; Sonkin & Durphy, 1997).

Domestic violence offenders have long been recognized to be a treatment resistant population, and in the beginning groups consisting of voluntary participants were small and attrition high. Those most in need of treatment were also the least likely to avail themselves of those services. The most significant change developed slowly as a result of the significant efforts of the battered women's movement to enlighten the legislators, courts, and law enforcement agencies regarding the need to deal seriously with domestic aggression toward women. The policy changes wrought by their efforts led to a proliferation of court mandated batterers' intervention, and dramatically increased the number of offenders participating in these programs. At present, most jurisdictions in the United States permit, urge, or mandate judges to require offenders to attend and complete some type of intervention, either as a pre-trial diversion or as a term of probation following a finding of guilt, or a plea.

Just as we now know batterers to be a heterogeneous population, so too are batterers' intervention programs. These programs may share numerous commonalities but may also vary in terms of length, philosophy, format, and content. The credentials and qualifications of the program leaders and facilitators also vary widely. What should become obvious from the selections in this volume, is the diversity of these programs and the fact that it is as difficult to identify the "typical batterer treatment" program as it is to identify the "typical batterer." Consequently, judges and probation officers many have several different options in choosing programs. In order to provide judges and victims with some quality assurances to guide in the selection of programs, many states and jurisdictions have developed batterer treatment standards and anoint programs meeting those standards with certification.

As with just about everything in the domestic violence area, batterers' treatment and intervention standards have been controversial. Outcome research is plagued by a host of methodological problems, not the least of which is defining and measuring successful outcome. There is evidence that some batterers' intervention programs may be ineffective, or even if somewhat effective, may yield a very small effect size. This would certainly be supported by recent meta-analyses and other research (Davis & Taylor, 1999; Dunford, 2000; Green & Babcock, 2001; Levesque & Gelles, 1998). On the other hand, treatment outcome is dependent on the nature of the interventions and there is evidence that batterer subtypes, stage of readiness for change, and other factors may interact with program philosophy and content to moderate effectiveness. Interestingly, the uncertainty regarding the effectiveness of batterers' treatment has been one of the arguments leveled against treatment standards which attempt to specify appropriate and inappropriate treatment strategies, and suggest that our knowledge of what works and what does not is more certain than would be justified by the research evidence.

There is also controversy regarding whether batterer interventions should be considered "treatment" or "education," and whether those providing such services should be mental health or social work professionals or simply individuals with prior experience with spouse/partner abuse. Some jurisdictions exclude reformed batterers from providing treatment while others do not. The question of whether the intervention is treatment or education has many ramifications. If it is classified as treatment, then providers would require some type of professional training, experience and/or credentials. It might also bring confidentiality and other ethical issues into consideration.

Crafting batterer intervention standards which afford the maximum protection for victims, exclude substandard programs, do not preclude the development of more effective programs, and allow for the conduct of research while remaining flexible, is the challenge confronting all states and jurisdictions engaging in this process. The input of all stakeholders (treatment providers, battered women's advocates, researchers, law enforcement, and the victims themselves) must be solicited and valued. The present volume has been developed to serve as a guideline for the development of sane, safe, and reasonable standards. The articles have been written by experts from all segments of the batterer intervention field. The purpose is not to offer a specific set of model standards, but to raise consciousness regarding the issues that must be considered and to suggest a process for considering them. We will look at what batterers' intervention has historically included as well as more recent modifications and developments. We will explore the problems and the processes that have been employed to solve them.

In this volume, we first explore some of the issues with respect to the creation of standards for domestic violence offender intervention. In his article, Gelles argues that we are not yet ready for such rigid standards, and further suggests that such standards may cause more harm than good. Maiuro, Hagar, Lin and Olson (in this volume) suggest that standards are often not consistent with what is known in the research. They reviewed the standards in 30 states, and summarized the strengths and weaknesses. Rosenbaum and Leisring summarize the literature concerning more traditional batterers' treatment programs and approaches, so that the reader will have a basis for understanding how the novel and non-traditional strategies differ. LaViolette in her article describes some of her experiences working with such offenders for over 20 years.

Alternative and nonconventional programs, including a stages of change approach (see Begun, Shelley, Strodthoff, & Short in this volume; Levesque, 2001), a couples or conjoint approach (Geffner & Mantooth, 2000; O'Leary in this volume), a solution-focused approach (Lipchik, Sirles, & Kubicki, 1997), and a modified 12-step, empowerment-based approach (Decker, 1999) have been developed as options to the standard techniques. However, innovative and alternative approaches have often been received with skepticism. A recent issue of the *Journal of Marital & Family Therapy* focused on this debate and the question of when abuse-specific couples counseling may be indicated, the pre-conditions, and the appropriate procedures to follow (e.g., Bograd & Mederos, 1999). It is important to note that these authors had strongly argued against any type of conjoint approach for many years; many of their recent recommendations have actually been made quite a while ago (e.g., Geffner, Mantooth, Franks, & Rao, 1989; Geffner, Rossman, & Barrett, 1995).

Another issue of more recent concern involves females arrested for domestic violence. It is not clear whether these women are the primary/dominant aggressors in the relationships, the victims who have fought back in self-defense, or those involved in mutual aggression with their partners in heterosexual or homosexual relationships. Anecdotal reports seem to suggest that a combination of all of these types of cases are being referred by courts. Dowd discusses some of these issues in her article in this volume. A recent curriculum focusing on the intervention for women arrested for domestic violence has now been published as well (Koonin, Cabarcas, & Geffner, 2001).

It is important to keep in mind assessment and safety issues when working with and treating abusive or violent behavior. There has been substantial discussion concerning safety planning for battered partners and the issue of lethality or risk assessment for domestic violence offenders (e.g., Campbell, 1995; Kropp & Hart, 2000). Campbell, in her article in this issue, focuses on the use of lethality assessment in safety planning. This is an important step in intervention that is often overlooked. Some have questioned our ability to conduct such assessments for particular offenders at specific times, and whether our knowledge base is sufficient to provide predictiveness. The research focuses on group differences, and as such, it may be possible to make some general statements concerning potential risk factors. However, the state-of-the-science has serious limitations in attempting to make predictions for specific offenders (see Geffner, 2001). Nevertheless, the issues raised by Campbell in this volume are worthy of further consideration.

The important question of whether having standards in place makes any difference has received little empirical attention, despite the fact that many states include a requirement that programs demonstrate their effectiveness. An exception is the recent research concerning the use of the standards in Illinois, which is reported in Bennett and Vincent's article in this volume. They found that the standards may not have been the panacea that some had hoped for. A recent study of battered women's views concerning such policies as mandatory arrest, mandatory reporting, and no-drop prosecution also found that not all of the women supported such procedures (Smith, 2001). Thus, even though some people believe and have perpetuated the idea that certain procedures and policies may be crucial for reducing intimate partner violence, the policies and standards may not have total popular support from the victims and agencies as previously thought.

It is important to consider what we know about recidivism when we are attempting to create standards for intervention or assessment. Rosenbaum, Gearan, and Ondovic (in this volume) studied the effects of court mandated program length and program completion on recidivism in a group of male offenders in a treatment group. This is one of the few research studies to look seriously at these issues. Even though some researchers are attempting to understand the variables that are associated with both attrition and recidivism in the United States and in Canada (e.g., Loza & Loza-Fanous, 1999; Rooney & Hansen, 2001), we still are in need of more studies in this area.

Over a decade ago, the authors of the present article wrote a chapter summarizing the then state-of-the-science concerning domestic violence intervention (Geffner, Rosenbaum & Hughes, 1988). In that chapter, we recognized the heterogeneity of both batterers and batterers' intervention programs and suggested that the field should begin to move away from "one-size fits all" approaches, and instead, take a prescriptive approach to matching batterer subtypes to specific intervention strategies. Research in the last decade has indeed looked at typologies of offenders, and we now have much more empirical information (for a review of this research, see Holtzworth-Munroe, 2001, and also her article in this volume). We still have a long way to go before we have sufficient knowledge and research data to more definitively state which programs should be utilized with which perpetrators. Unfortunately, the methods prescribed by many states and jurisdictions concerning batterer intervention do not even take these issues and recommendations into consideration. Tolman in this volume presents an ecological framework and analysis in looking at the standards, and makes some recommendations based on such an analysis. Finally, Saunders (in his article in this volume) reviews the related research, especially in other fields, to see what we can learn; he also concludes that we do not have sufficient information to create some of the standards that are in place in some states.

MANDATED STANDARDS:
WHERE ARE WE AND WHERE SHOULD WE BE GOING

Many states and jurisdictions in the United States now mandate at least some standards and policies for the type of intervention that is required for those who are convicted or plead guilty to domestic violence. The goal of this volume is to discuss the issues and policies that have been mandated and implemented throughout the United States for such interventions. The authors of the articles in this volume have diverse backgrounds, experiences, philosophies, and areas of expertise. Some are researchers, others are practitioners, and some are both. All are acknowledged experts in the field. Even though there is diversity of opinion regarding treatment approaches and the nature of standards, all agree that policies, standards, and intervention approaches should be viewed cautiously and with significant discussion that includes people in the field with different perspectives and ideas. Unfortunately, this has not always occurred and in many states, standards that are inconsistent with research and clinical findings have been developed and implemented.

The mechanism by which states create standards may be as important as the content of the standards themselves. In this volume, Hamberger describes his experiences as a chair of the Wisconsin committee charged with the task of creating standards, and provides an inside view of that process. Murphy offers an excellent example of how the Maryland committee created standards that were informed by the literature, included input from a diverse set of stakeholders and maintained the flexibility necessary for continued research to flourish. The standards in Maryland seem to have avoided many of the pitfalls that other states have encountered, and their process and results can serve as a model for other states (also see Murphy & Dienemann, 1999).

The goal of batterer treatment standards is to reduce violence directed at women by insuring that states are offering the most effective, state-of-the-art intervention approaches possible. As empirical data accumulate and our knowledge base grows, so will intervention strategies evolve. In order to stay current, batterers' treatment standards will have to remain flexible. Hopefully, this volume can help to inform the process in jurisdictions in which standards are now being contemplated or developed. In those states which already have standards in place, this volume may serve as a guide to the process of standards revision. This endeavor is too important to be a victim of politics as usual.

REFERENCES

Bograd, M., & Mederos, F. (1999). Battering and couples therapy: Universal screening and selection of treatment modality. *Journal of Marital & Family Therapy, 25(3)*, 291-312.

Campbell, J. C. (Ed.) (1995). *Assessing dangerousness: Violence by sex offenders, batterers, and child abusers*. Newbury Park, CA: Sage.

Davis, R. C., & Taylor, B. G. (1999). Does batterer treatment reduce violence? A synthesis of the literature. *Women & Criminal Justice, 10 (2)*, 69-93.

Decker, D. J. (1999). *Stopping the violence: A group model to change men's abusive attitudes and behaviors*. Binghamton, NY: Haworth Maltreatment & Trauma Press.

Dunford, F. W. (2000). The San Diego Navy Experiment: An Assessment of interventions for men who assault their wives. *Journal of Consulting and Clinical Psychology, 68(3)*, 468-476.

Geffner, R. (2001, July). Family violence research: Where are we and where should we be going? Invited plenary session to 7th International Family Violence Research Conference, University of New Hampshire, Portsmouth, NH.

Geffner, R., Barrett, M. J., & Rossman, B. B. (1995). Domestic violence and sexual abuse: Multiple systems perspectives. In R. H. Mikesell, D. D. Lusterman, & S. H. McDaniel (Eds.), *Integrating family therapy: Handbook of family psychology and systems theory* (pp. 501-517). Washington, DC: American Psychological Association.

Geffner, R., & Mantooth, C. (2000). *Ending spouse/partner abuse: A psychoeducational approach for individuals and couples*. New York: Springer.

Geffner, R., Mantooth, C., Franks, D., & Rao, L. (1989). A psychoeducational, conjoint therapy approach to reducing family violence. In P. L. Caesar & L. K.

Hamberger (Eds.), *Treating men who batter: Theory, practice, and programs* (pp. 103-133). New York: Springer.

Geffner, R., Rosenbaum, A., & Hughes, H. (1988). Research issues concerning family violence. In V. B. Van Hasselt, R. L. Morrison, A. S. Bellack, & M. Hersen (Eds.), *Handbook of family violence* (pp. 457-481). New York: Plenum.

Green, C., & Babcock, J. (2001, July). Does batterers' treatment work? A meta-analytic review of domestic violence treatment. Paper presented at the 7th International Family Violence Research Conference, University of New Hampshire, Portsmouth, NH.

Holtzworth-Munroe, A. (2001, July). Examining stability and change in batterer typology. Invited keynote address presented at the 7th International Family Violence Research Conference, University of New Hampshire, Portsmouth, NH.

Koonin, M., Cabarcas, A., & Geffner, R. (2001). *Treatment of women arrested for domestic violence: Women ending abusive/violent episodes respectfully (WEAVER).* San Diego, CA: Family Violence & Sexual Assault Institute.

Kropp, P. R., & Hart, S. D. (2000). The spousal assault risk assessment (SARA) guide: Reliability and validity in adult male offenders. *Law and Human Behavior, 24(1)*, 101-116.

Levesque, D. (2001, July). Transtheoretical model of change processes used in batterer intervention programs. Paper presented at 7th International Family Violence Research Conference, University of New Hampshire, Portsmouth, NH.

Lipchik, E., Sirles, E., & Kubicki, A. (1997). Multifaceted approaches in spouse abuse treatment. In R. Geffner, S. B. Sorenson, & P. K. Lundberg-Love (Eds.), *Violence and sexual abuse at home: Current issues, interventions, and research in spousal battering and child maltreatment* (pp. 131-148). Binghamton, NY: Haworth Maltreatment & Trauma Press.

Loza, W., & Loza-Fanous, A. (1999). Anger and prediction of violent and nonviolent offenders' recidivism. *Journal of Interpersonal Violence, 14(10)*, 1014-1029.

Mathews, D. J. (1995). *Foundations for violence-free living: A step-by-step guide to facilitating men's domestic abuse groups.* St. Paul, MN: Amherst H. Wilder Foundation.

Murphy, C. M., & Dienemann, J. A. (1999). Informing the research agenda on domestic abuser intervention through practitioner-researcher dialogues. *Journal of Interpersonal Violence, 14(12)*, 1314-1326.

Pence, E., & Paymar, M. (1993). *Education groups for men who batter.* NY: Springer.

Rooney, J., & Hanson, R. K. (2001). Predicting attrition from treatment programs for abusive men. *Journal of Family Violence, 16(2)*, 131-149.

Smith, A. (2001). Domestic violence laws: The voices of battered women. *Violence and Victims, 16(1)*, 91-111.

Sonkin, D. J., & Durphy, M. (1997). Learning to live without violence: A handbook for men. Volcano, CA: Volcano Press.

Straus, M. A. (1980). A sociological perspective on the causes of family violence. In M. R. Green (Ed.), *Violence and the family* (pp. 7-31). Boulder, CO: Westview.

Straus, M. A., & Gelles, R. J. (1990). *Physical violence in American families: Risk factors and adaptations to violence in 8,145 families.* New Brunswick, NJ: Transaction.

Standards for Programs
for Men Who Batter?
Not Yet

Richard J. Gelles

SUMMARY. Programs for men who batter their intimate partners were developed in the late 1970s. Since that time, mandatory and presumptive arrest policies have increased the number of men arrested for domestic violence. Diversion into programs for batterers evolved into a standard part of a coordinated community intervention for domestic violence. Recently, a number of states have begun to establish standards for batterers' programs. While having standards makes sense, especially as it could assure quality of programs, this article argues that it is premature to establish such standards. The article reviews evaluation data on programs for men who batter and concludes that we know too little about what types or features of programs are effective for which men under what circumstances. Establishing rigorous standards may actually produce more harm than good. *[Article copies available for a fee from The Haworth Document Delivery Service: 1-800-HAWORTH. E-mail address: <getinfo@haworthpressinc.com> Website: <http://www.HaworthPress.com> © 2001 by The Haworth Press, Inc. All rights reserved.]*

KEYWORDS. Arrest, domestic violence, meta-analysis, standards, treatment programs

[Haworth co-indexing entry note]: "Standards for Programs for Men Who Batter? Not Yet." Gelles, Richard J. Co-published simultaneously in *Journal of Aggression, Maltreatment & Trauma* (The Haworth Maltreatment & Trauma Press, an imprint of The Haworth Press, Inc.) Vol. 5, No. 2(#10), 2001, pp. 11-20; and: *Domestic Violence Offenders: Current Interventions, Research, and Implications for Policies and Standards* (ed: Robert A. Geffner, and Alan Rosenbaum) The Haworth Maltreatment & Trauma Press, an imprint of The Haworth Press, Inc., 2001, pp. 11-20. Single or multiple copies of this article are available for a fee from The Haworth Document Delivery Service [1-800-HAWORTH, 9:00 a.m. - 5:00 p.m. (EST). E-mail address: getinfo@haworthpressinc.com].

An established set of standards for treatment programs for men who batter their wives and partners makes good sense. More than 15 years ago, the U.S. Attorney General's Task Force on Family Violence stated that arrest followed by court-ordered psychotherapeutic treatment offers "great hope and potential for breaking the destructive cycle of violence in intimate relationships" (U.S. Department of Justice, 1984, p. 48). Indeed, in the subsequent years, a coalition of advocates, researchers, and policy-makers succeeded in putting into place a policy of using arrest as a mainstay of the effort to intervene in the problem of domestic violence. With an increase in the number of laws mandating arrest, followed by an actual increase in the number of men (and women) arrested for domestic assault, programs offering psychotherapeutic treatment grew dramatically. The state of Rhode Island offers one small example. In 1980, prior to laws allowing for presumptive arrest for cases of domestic violence, there was a single treatment program for men who battered their partners. The program served approximately 25 men per year. The program was administrated by a men's collective and had no formal administrative structure. Ten years later, in 1994, there were laws encouraging arrest for domestic assault and five different treatment programs. Just two years later there were nearly 17 treatment programs for men who batter. There was no central administrative agency that coordinated the programs, no standards for who could offer the programs, and no requirements regarding the qualifications of the clinicians who treated batterers. There was no oversight whatsoever for the treatment modalities and their effectiveness (or lack thereof). An individual who had not yet completed a bachelor's degree offered one program. This individual, because of good interpersonal relations with the state department of probation, received more than 700 referrals each year for his treatment program. All of this occurred in a state with a total population of less than 1,000,000. The possibility that such an uncoordinated, unregulated, unsupervised system had evolved nationally underscored the apparent need for a system of standards that could provide some coordination and, more importantly, quality control for the growing number of programs serving the growing number of men arrested for domestic assault.

A RATIONALE FOR STANDARDS

The rationale for having standards for programs that treat men who batter is, on the face of it, obvious. First, the potential pool of men who require some form of constraint and intervention is extensive. Although there is some controversy regarding the extent and nature of domestic violence (see for example, Gelles & Loseke, 1993), experts tend to agree that there are between one and four million men who assault, batter, and/or sexually assault their partners each year (see Gelles, 2000 for a review of estimates of the national incidence and prevalence of domestic violence). The U.S. Department of Justice, Federal Bureau of Investigation, and Uniform Crime Reports, indicates that husbands, ex-husbands, or boyfriends kill some 1,200 women each year (U.S. Department of Justice, 1998).

After decades (actually centuries) of criminal justice indifference, the criminal justice system is more involved in efforts to control and treat domestic violence. A study purporting to find that arrest deterred domestic violence offenders (Sherman & Berk, 1984), followed by the U.S. Attorney General's Task Force on Family Violence (1984) recommendation regarding arrest and court-ordered psychotherapeutic treatment, combined with law suits such as Thurman v. City of Torrington, Connecticut, ultimately resulted in the widespread use of arrest to control domestic violence.

Mandatory and presumptive arrest policies dramatically increased the number of men who were arrested for misdemeanor domestic violence. The courts, while wanting to prevent domestic violence, also were reluctant to incarcerate first-time misdemeanor offenders, so the large majority of offenders were ordered to treatment programs.

We have no national figures on the number of treatment programs, or the number of offenders who are served. If the Rhode Island experience can be extrapolated nationally, it is reasonable to assume that there are thousands of treatment programs treating tens, if not hundreds of thousands of men each year.

For various reasons, programs that treat men who batter received no federal funds and few state funds. Rather, the programs sustain themselves on client fees, typically charged on a sliding scale. Requiring clients to pay for their treatment is consistent with having batterers take full responsibility for their own behavior. Furthermore, after spending nearly 30 years seeking to obtain some level of federal, state, or local funding, advocacy groups working on behalf of battered women are reluctant to allow precious and limited fiscal resources to be used for purposes other than helping and assisting victims.

Thus court-ordered treatment created a demand for programs that would be met, not by advocacy groups working on behalf of battered women, but by agencies and individuals. The key to being able to offer services would be receiving sufficient referrals from probation offices and officers, and then receiving sufficient fees to cover expenses and pay salaries. Such a situation rewarded entrepreneurship rather than effectiveness.

Millions of clients could potentially inflict enormous emotional and physical damage on their intimate partners if they are ineffectively or improperly treated; thus, it is conceivable that unregulated treatment programs could create more harm than good. Therefore, having treatment standards makes considerable sense.

Court ordered treatment for men who assault their partners has, in fact, become the treatment of choice (with the exception of a prison sentence) and the only treatment widely available for men. One survey of state policies (a survey that is now out of date, unfortunately), found that eight states had laws mandating treatment of men convicted of domestic assault, or as a condition of deferred sentencing (Zamora, 1995). In 1995, as would be expected, 12 states had already adopted standards for program certification or funding, two states had recommended standards, and 12 states had standards under development (Zamora, 1995). As of the most recent information, the majority of states now have adopted some form of standards for programs that treat men who batter. For more information concerning the standards various states have adopted, see Maiuro, Hagar, Lin, and Olson (2001, in this volume).

A RATIONALE AGAINST STANDARDS

One argument against standards seems counter-intuitive given the above information. How could there be a justification for allowing anyone to hang out a shingle and offer any kind of "treatment" for a social problem that is as widespread and harmful as domestic violence? Clearly the potential for abuse and misuse of the psychotherapeutic treatment of batterers is enormous. Moreover, the incentive for abuse and misuse is substantial, given that men are both required to enter treatment and required to pay for the treatment.

Nonetheless, there are two compelling arguments against the evolving trend of standards for intervention programs for men who batter. The first argument is the simplest and least controversial: We simply do not know enough about which treatment programs are effective, for which men, and under what conditions to mandate standards for such programs. The second argument is more complex and infinitely more controversial: The standards that are being called for, developed, and applied, represent a particular ideological commitment of those who work on behalf of battered women and are less tied to a therapeutic theory or philosophy.

The Effectiveness of Treatment Programs

The U.S. Attorney General's Task Force on Family Violence's recommendation that arrest followed by court-ordered psychotherapeutic treatment offered great hope for breaking the cycle of domestic violence. This hope was based on empirical evidence from the Minneapolis Police Experiment (Sherman &

Berk, 1984) that arrest reduced the likelihood of subsequent domestic assaults. There was no empirical evidence that court-ordered psychotherapeutic treatment would be effective; this portion of the recommendation was probably based on the common sense assumption that psychotherapy is effective for some clients and, even if not effective, produces few adverse consequences.

Subsequent replications of the Minneapolis Police Experiment (Berk, Campbell, Klap, & Western, 1992; Dunford, Huizinger, & Elliott, 1990; Hirshell, Hutchingson, & Dean, 1990; Pate & Hamilton, 1992; Sherman & Smith, 1992) failed to support the findings from Minneapolis that arrest deterred offenders who had committed acts of misdemeanor domestic violence. Arrest, however, was not without some effectiveness. Sherman (1992) reported that arrest did reduce subsequent domestic violence for men who were employed and married. However, unemployed men who were not married to their partners escalated their use of violence after being arrested.

At the time of the U.S. Attorney General's Task Force on Family Violence report (1984), there were no rigorously evaluated studies of treatment programs for men who batter. Subsequent to the report, a number of evaluations were published that claimed widespread effectiveness of treatment programs (Dutton, 1986; Gondolf, 1987; Saunders & Hanusa, 1986; see Davis & Taylor, 1997 for a recent review of this research). These initial evaluations, however, were limited by the typical methodological problems that occur when innovative programs are evaluated. The studies had small samples and no or inappropriate comparison groups. One of the major factors that influenced the results of the studies was the high drop out rate of men in the programs. If the studies focused only on men who completed the programs, their success rate appeared quite high; however, if men who dropped out of the program were included in the denominator, the success rate was quite a bit lower.

When the National Research Council's Committee on the Assessment of Family Violence Interventions searched for evaluations of treatment programs for men, and limited the search to evaluations that included comparison groups, they found eight evaluations, one of which used a randomly assigned control group. There was quite a bit of variation in the eight evaluations. Some studies focused only on physical violence as the dependent variable, while others looked at physical violence as well as verbal and emotional abuse. Some studies examined programs for men court-ordered to treatment, while others examined programs that had broader recruitment patterns. Not surprisingly, there was considerable variation in the outcomes of the treatments that were evaluated. Some studies found no reduction in violence; other studies found no reduction in violence, but a reduction in verbal and emotional abuse. Two studies of programs where men were court-ordered to treatment found reductions in rates of violence while the other two studies of men court-ordered to treatment found no differences in violence after treatment. One consistency in the four studies was the high dropout rate of men ordered to counseling. Between 25 and 37% of offenders mandated to treatment either never showed up or dropped out early in the treatment (National Research Council, 1998).

The most rigorous evaluations provide little consistency, in terms of outcome, prompting reviewers of the research on such studies to opine that little empirical evidence exists to guide the setting of standards for such programs (Edleson & Syers, 1991). In an effort to more rigorously evaluate treatment programs for men who batter, Levesque (1998) conducted a meta-analysis of 38 outcome studies examining partner violence recidivism for men who participated in court-ordered batterer treatment. The sample consisted of published and unpublished studies, doctoral dissertations, master's theses, conference papers, and research reports completed between 1980 and August 1997. The majority of the studies (N = 23) used a single group design, while the remaining studies (N = 15) used between groups design. Studies had to have a sample size of five or greater to be included in the analysis.

The meta-analysis examined the following attributes of the evaluations: study design (outcome only; between groups), method of group assignment, follow-up period, participation rate, data source, publication characteristic, year of publication, and treatment characteristics. The overall effect size from the between group studies was not significantly different from zero. There was a small effect size for studies that relied on official records. For the entire sample, the overall recidivism rate for treatment completers was 21.6%.

Levesque's (1998) meta-analysis found that the effect of treatment was small, at best. Most importantly, when she examined program and intervention characteristics, she found no strong relationship between program characteristic and outcome. Thus, no particular program or program component was superior to another program or program component in terms of reducing subsequent violent behavior among men who completed the programs. Thus, nearly 10 years after Edleson and Syers' (1991) conclusion about the lack of empirical evidence to guide the setting of standards, there still remains no compelling empirical evidence on which to base standards regarding programs or program components for treatment and counseling interventions for batterers.

The Ideology of Treatment and Counseling

Having served on the National Research Council's Committee on Assessing Family Violence Interventions and having supervised Levesque's (1998) meta-analysis of batterer's intervention and counseling programs, I assumed two things. First, I assumed that advocates might be disheartened or disturbed at the findings that failed to show robust effects of treatment and counseling programs. Second, I assumed that the results of the evaluations of treatment and counseling programs would serve as an argument against the widespread setting of standards for such programs. When we presented the National Research Council's findings and the findings from Levesque's research to the Rhode Island Coalition Against Domestic Violence and members of the Rhode Island Attorney General's staff who were advancing legislation that would set standards, they agreed with the study results but noted that the standards would go forward anyway. We repeated Edleson and Syers' (1991) caution about the lack of empirical evidence to support the setting of standards. This was met with understanding, but also with the acknowledgement that the standards would still be set and enforced.

This seemed counter-intuitive and frustrating, at least to a researcher. How could one set standards without knowing what program components were most effective, least effective, and even harmful?

After much discussion, it became clear that the setting of standards was not an empirical exercise, but the continuation of consistent advocacy work on behalf of battered women. A feminist theoretical perspective has always been the underlying conceptual framework of the effort to prevent and treat battered women. The standards that have been, are being, and will continue to be established for counseling and treatment programs are consistent with a feminist action perspective. Thus, standards tend to emphasize a profeminist, psychoeducational curriculum, rather than an anger-management curriculum.

In the absence of empirical evidence, it does seem reasonable that standards reflect the underlying conceptual model of advocates. However, I would argue, there is no evidence that these programs are actually effective.

After much discussion and debate, we learned that advocates for battered women never did expect treatment to be effective. A content analysis of profeminist literature in the field of domestic violence reveals little faith that men who batter will actually change their behavior (Levesque, 1998). Perhaps violence will be reduced, but this will only lead to more verbal violence, emotional abuse, and other forms of coercive control. The patriarchal model of domestic violence is not an individual-level model, but a socio-cultural model that sees change coming from altering the patriarchal social structure, not individual men. Thus, advocates were less surprised than researchers about evaluation research being unable to reject the null hypothesis; they were pessimistic from the start about the ability of therapy, counseling, or treatment to change men.

CONCLUSION

If there is no evidence on which standards to set, does this mean we should not have standards? One point of view is that since we don't know what works, we should be open to a variety of approaches. On the other hand, since we have no reason to believe the other approaches will be any more effective, why not set standards that have face validity? After all, even if the standards do not produce much change or a reduction in violence, what harm could the standards do? Or, as Berk (1993) argued, when supporting the continued use of mandatory arrest policies when empirical research does not demonstrate that such policies reduced recidivism, "although arrest is not superior to a variety of other criminal justice interventions, one can on the average do no better" (p. 332). However, he went on to say that "unless there are legal, ethical, or practical reasons to prefer some other intervention, arrest remains a viable option" (p. 332).

I think there is good reason to believe that adopting standards has the potential for harm and adverse outcomes for victims of domestic violence. Gondolf and Fisher (1988) found that the single best predictor of whether, after a shelter stay, a woman would return to a violent partner was that the batterer sought treatment. While the researchers do not explore why this was an important predictor, it is reasonable to assume that women thought that the act of seeking treatment indicated a willingness to change, and perhaps the treatment would be successful in reducing the partner's use of physical violence. If seeking treatment increased women's willingness to return to a violent partner, it is also reasonable to assume that if a state offered only treatment that met certain standards, women would be as or even more likely to return to a partner who sought or was ordered to go to treatment. Standards, irrespective of what they include, may well be regarded as a "Good Housekeeping Seal of Approval" for treatment programs, a sign that such programs work.

A second important reason to delay the imposition of standards is that standardizing treatment programs before we know what works, for which men, under what circumstances, limits and eliminates the development of novel or innovative approaches to treating violent and abusive men. The second reason may not appeal to advocates who regard socio-cultural change as more important than individual change in terms of reducing violence and abuse. But socio-cultural change is a long-term endeavor and, in the mean time, society needs some kind of response to the millions of acts of violence and abuse each year. No matter whether we want to control abusive men with criminal justice sanctions, or treat them, we still require some means of intervention. If women are going to believe that receiving an intervention reduces the likelihood that their partners will continue abusive behavior, we have a moral and ethical obligation to seek and implement the most effective interventions.

REFERENCES

Berk, R. A. (1993). What the scientific evidence shows: On the average, we can do no better than arrest. In R. J. Gelles & D. R. Loseke (Eds.), *Current controversies on family violence* (pp. 323-336). Thousand Oaks, CA: Sage.

Berk, R. A., Campbell, A., Klap, R., & Western, B. (1992). The deterrent effect of arrest on incidents of domestic violence: A Bayesian analysis of four field experiments. *American Sociological Review, 57*, 698-708.

Davis, R. C., & Taylor, B. G. (1997, June). *A randomized experiment of the effects of batterer treatment: Summary of preliminary findings.* Paper presented at the 5th International Family Violence Research Conference, Durham, NH.

Dunford, F. W., Huizinga, D., & Elliott, D. S. (1990). The role of arrest in domestic assault: The Omaha Police Experiment. *Criminology, 28*, 183-206.

Dutton, D. G. (1986). The outcome of court-mandated treatment for wife assault: A quasi-experimental evaluation. *Violence and Victims, 1*, 163-176.

Edleson, J. L., & Syers, M. (1991). The effects of group treatment for men who batter: An 18-month follow-up study. *Research in Social Work Practice, 1*, 227-243.

Gelles, R. J. (2000). Estimating the incidence and prevalence of violence against women: National data systems and sources. *Violence Against Women, 6*, 88-107.

Gelles, R. J., & Loseke, D. R. (Eds.). (1993). *Current controversies on domestic violence.* Thousand Oaks, CA: Sage.

Gondolf, E. W. (1987). Evaluating progress for men who batter: Problems and prospects. *Journal of Family Violence, 2*, 95-108.

Gondolf, E. W., & Fisher, E. W. (1988). *Battered women as survivors: An alternative to treating learned helplessness.* Lexington, MA: Lexington Books.

Hirshell, J. D., Hutchinson, I. W., III, & Dean, C. W. (1992). The failure of arrest to deter spouse abuse. *Journal of Research in Crime and Delinquency, 29*, 7-33.

Levesque, D. (1998). *Violence desistance among battering men: Existing intervention and the application of the Transtheoretical Model of Change.* Unpublished doctoral dissertation, University of Rhode Island, Kingston, Rhode Island.

Maiuro, R. D., Hagar, T. S., Lin, H.-H., & Olson, N. (2001). Are current state standards for domestic violence perpetrator treatment adequately informed by research? A question of questions. *Journal of Aggression, Maltreatment & Trauma, 5*(2), p. 21-44.

National Research Council. (1998). *Violence in families: Assessing prevention and treatment programs.* Washington, DC: National Academy Press.

Pate, A. M., & Hamilton, E. E. (1992). Formal and informal social deterrents to domestic violence: The Dade County Spouse Assault Experiment. *American Sociological Review, 57*, 691-697.

Saunders, D. G., & Hanusa, D. (1986). Cognitive-behavior treatment for men who batter: The short-term effects of group therapy. *Journal of Family Violence, 1*, 357-372.

Sherman, L. W. (1992). *Policing domestic violence*. New York: Free Press.

Sherman, L.W., & Berk, R. A. (1984). The specific deterrent effects of arrest for domestic assault. *American Sociological Review, 49*, 261-272.

Sherman, L. W., & Smith, D. A. (1992). Crime, punishment, and stake in conformity: Legal and informal control of domestic violence. *American Sociological Review, 57*, 680-690.

U.S. Department of Justice. (1984). *Attorney General's Task Force on Family Violence. Final Report*. Washington, DC: Author.

U.S. Department of Justice (1998). *Uniform crime reports for the United States, 1998.* Washington, DC: U.S. Department of Justice, Federal Bureau of Investigation.

Zamora, E. (1995). *State statutes regarding mandatory treatment for batterers and treatment program standards*. Minneapolis, MN: Criminal Justice Center, Battered Women's Justice Project.

Are Current State Standards
for Domestic Violence Perpetrator Treatment
Adequately Informed by Research?
A Question of Questions

Roland D. Maiuro
Tamara S. Hagar
Hsin-hua Lin
Natalie Olson

SUMMARY. An empirical review and critique of existing state standards for batterer programs in the domestic violence field appeared timely, given the current debate about their status and utility. Although there has been a considerable amount of polemic discussion of the topic, relatively limited data have been reported. The present article surveyed the content of standards developed in 30 states within the United States. Five categories of interest were examined including: (1) the minimum length of treatment specified; (2) specification of treatment orientation, methods, and content; (3) preferred or allowable modalities of treatment; (4) whether research findings were mentioned or endorsed as a basis for development of treatment standards; and (5) methods for developing and revising standards. A related area, the minimum education required for

---

The authors would like to thank Yuriko Kawakatsu, Leah Livesey, Patricia Memmott, Ellen Setteducati, and Shawna Sullivan for their research support and assistance in tracking down the "Woozle."

[Haworth co-indexing entry note]: "Are Current State Standards for Domestic Violence Perpetrator Treatment Adequately Informed by Research? A Question of Questions." Maiuro et al. Co-published simultaneously in *Journal of Aggression, Maltreatment & Trauma* (The Haworth Maltreatment & Trauma Press, an imprint of The Haworth Press, Inc.) Vol. 5, No. 2(#10), 2001, pp. 21-44; and: *Domestic Violence Offenders: Current Interventions, Research, and Implications for Policies and Standards* (ed: Robert A. Geffner, and Alan Rosenbaum) The Haworth Maltreatment & Trauma Press, an imprint of The Haworth Press, Inc., 2001, pp. 21-44. Single or multiple copies of this article are available for a fee from The Haworth Document Delivery Service [1-800-HAWORTH, 9:00 a.m. - 5:00 p.m. (EST). E-mail address: getinfo@haworthpressinc.com].

21

providers, was also included as an area of interest to further describe the current pool of practitioners targeted for regulation. An analysis of the content of these standards was then performed with regard to existing peer-reviewed research in the field. The results are discussed in terms of the strengths and weaknesses of current standards, the areas in which further research is needed, and specific recommendations regarding steps that might be taken to improve existing efforts. *[Article copies available for a fee from The Haworth Document Delivery Service: 1-800-HAWORTH. E-mail address: <getinfo@haworthpressinc.com> Website: <http://www.HaworthPress.com> © 2001 by The Haworth Press, Inc. All rights reserved.]*

KEYWORDS. Domestic violence, perpetrator standards, domestic violence research, state standards, intimate partner abuse

The development of standards, guidelines, or protocols to regulate batterer interventions in the United States has grown in importance as programs for domestically violent men have proliferated across North America. While these services have gained legitimacy within social service and criminal justice circles, a considerable amount of controversy has persisted regarding the causes of battering and how batterer intervention programs should be conducted (Adams, 1988; Dobash & Dobash, 1992; Edleson, 1996; Gondolf, 1997). For example, some practitioners and many battered women's advocates have viewed domestic violence as resulting from patriarchal factors, thus supporting a focus on men's socially reinforced abuse of power and control over their partners. On the other hand, other practitioners have approached the problem from a cognitive-behavioral or psychotherapeutic perspective, thus employing a variety of intervention strategies based on individual psychological or interpersonal dysfunction. These primary viewpoints, to various degrees, have contributed to the development of a variety of protocols, which have dictated preferred or required practice in the field in a significant number of states across the country.

An empirical review and critique of existing state standards for batterer programs in the domestic violence field appeared timely, given the current debate about their status and utility (Bennett, 1998; Geffner, 1995a, 1995b; Gondolf, 1995; Rosenbaum & Stewart, 1994). An important issue relates to whether, and to what degree, currently developed standards are based on scientific research. A review of the literature on standards revealed a considerable amount of polemic discussion of the topic, but relatively limited data in this regard (Austin & Dankwort, 1999). The present article attempts to provide such data by surveying the content of standards developed in 30 states within the United States. An analysis of the content of these standards was then performed with regard to existing peer-reviewed research in the field. The results are discussed in terms of the strengths and weaknesses of current standards, the areas in which further research is needed, and specific recommendations regarding steps that might be taken to improve existing efforts.

METHOD

Standards governing the treatment of domestically violent perpetrators were obtained for 30 states that had completed and implemented written protocols for practice at the time of this writing. Copies of the standards were obtained from the Batterer's Intervention State Committee, a national organization of treatment service providers, as well as through state governmental or provider/advocate coalition channels. The 30 sample states or jurisdictions included Alaska, Arizona, California (San Diego), Colorado, Connecticut, District of Columbia, Florida, Georgia, Hawaii, Illinois, Indiana (Marion County), Iowa, Kentucky (Jefferson County), Maine, Maryland, Massachusetts, Michigan (Wayne County), Minnesota, New Hampshire, New Jersey, New York, Ohio, Oregon, Pennsylvania, Rhode Island, South Carolina, Texas, Utah, Washington, and Wisconsin. States with non-operational or "in development" draft protocols for batterer treatment were not included in the survey.

The standards were reviewed by three domestic violence practitioners. Five categories of interest were identified based upon empirical or face validity. Although many dimensions could have been evaluated, the following criteria for selection of domains were used. The domains had to be (a) clinically relevant or practice related; and (b) designed to limit or direct the basis or type of intervention employed by practitioners in the field. Thus, the resulting domains selected were commonly addressed parameters of practice (e.g., treatment length, orientation, and modality). A related area, the minimum education required for providers, was also included as an area of interest to further describe the current pool of practitioners targeted for regulation. The resulting six domains were operationalized in terms of questions for the reviewers. Because the information necessary to rate the protocols on each domain was explicitly written in the standards for each state, there was no inter-rater variability. Thus, the standards for each of the states were evaluated with regard to the following six questions:

1. Is minimum length of treatment specified?
2. Are treatment orientation, methods, and content dictated or specified?

3. Do standards dictate preferred, or allowable, modalities of treatment?
4. Are research findings mentioned or endorsed as a basis for development of treatment standards?
5. Do state standards for certification require a minimum education at the Bachelor's level?
6. Are there formally documented methods for developing and revising standards?

The results were compiled and descriptive statistics were computed in terms of categories of responses. Excerpts were drawn from the standards from various states for purposes of illustration, critique, and discussion.

RESULTS AND DISCUSSION

Length of Treatment

The survey results indicated that the recommended treatment duration varied from state to state, ranging from a non-specified period of time to one year or more. However, it was noted that the majority of states (74%) surveyed require 16 or more weeks of treatment (see Figure 1). In most cases, the number of weeks specified also referred to the number of sessions of treatment, as a once-a-week schedule was assumed. While some state standards went so far as to specify the number of contact hours that had to be delivered (e.g., 80 hours for Massachusetts), this parameter remained unspecified for most states.

With the exception of Rosenbaum, Gearan, and Ondovic (in this volume), there are few comparative studies that have examined the relative efficacy of domestic violence treatment by number of sessions or by duration of treatment. However, the minimum requirement of 16 weeks would appear to have some basis in research as many of the available outcome studies have used 16 or more sessions (Dutton, 1986; Edleson & Tolman, 1992; Hamberger & Hastings, 1989). Moreover, Edleson and Syers (1991) provided data that raise questions as to whether violence reduction is significantly improved by a more intensive twice-a-week format, compared to a once-a-week briefer treatment format. Similarly, Rosenbaum, Gearan, and Ondovic provide recidivism data that question whether there are additional benefits to be derived from conducting treatment for more than 10 to 20 weeks for many perpetrators. In some cases, perhaps reflecting the dearth of comparative data on this topic, it appears that the pragmatic issues associated with the need to address a minimum set of content areas have dictated treatment length. For example, Florida State requires:

A minimum of two to three sessions (for a total of 24 weeks) must be de-voted to each specific tactic of power and control.

However, there is also a question of how a successful outcome is defined in the treatment of perpetrators of domestic violence. We may find that fewer sessions are required to bring about lasting cessation of physical violence than might be required to impact the entire cluster of psychological and emotional abuse that is usually associated with physical violence. As O'Leary (1999) has effectively argued, the type of psychological abuse that takes place in domestic violence is worthy of attention in its own right. As new assessment and intervention techniques are developed for dealing with psychological abuse in domestically violent relationships (O'Leary & Maiuro, 2001), it will be important to look beyond the issue of recidivism as the sole criterion to determine the range of sessions required to achieve a "successful" outcome.

Specification of Treatment Orientation and Content

Since the paradigm of intervention for perpetrators of domestic violence is still emerging (Hamberger, 1994), it is not surprising to find that most states (75%) have not specified orientation, method, and content with regard to treatment. Although some standards specifically endorsed a particular orientation with respect to the causality of battering or appropriate areas of intervention, none of the standards reviewed went so far as to dictate a particular regimen (e.g., The Duluth Model by Pence & Paymar, 1993).

FIGURE 1. Is Minimum Length of Treatment Specified?

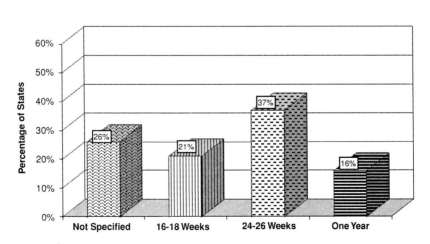

It should be noted that intervention for domestic violence has only recently begun to be embraced and mainstreamed by the traditional health disciplines (Maiuro & Avery, 1996; Maiuro, Vitaliano, Sugg, Thompson, Rivara, & Thompson, 2000). Moreover, since treatment providers tend to be from a number of disciplines, including social work, psychology, counseling, and substance abuse fields, a variety of literatures and theoretical perspectives could very well be emphasized. Without a minimum skill-set dictated and standardized by each social service and health care discipline, it may be difficult to come up with a common set of interventions which can be delivered by different practitioners with different levels of training and backgrounds. Given the current research literature supporting the presence of multiple typologies associated with battering (Gondolf, 1988; Gottman et al., 1995; Hamberger, Lohr, Bonge, & Tolin, 1996; Hershorn & Rosenbaum, 1991; Holtzworth-Munroe & Stuart, 1994; Saunders, 1992; Tweed & Dutton, 1998) and the lack of controlled comparative studies supporting one approach over another in terms of effectiveness, an attempt to develop a "one size fits all" standard for treatment content may be inappropriate.

Nonetheless, the standards of a significant minority of states (25%) provide some direction with regard to treatment orientation and content. Where present, specific directives relate to three primary areas, including: (a) whether treatment should be focused on individual psychopathology and addressed by psychotherapeutic methods, or whether the individual has simply learned a dominant gender role through socio-cultural, political influences which must be modified or relearned through educational methods; (b) generic versus violence-specific treatment, and (c) anger versus power and control as a source of motivation for the abuse of women.

Individual Psychopathology versus Gender-Role/Social-Cultural Models

In some of the states that specify a theoretical orientation, there appears to be an emphasis upon socio-cultural factors and an explicit de-emphasis of individual psychopathological factors. For example, New York standards state:

> *The vast majority of men who batter are not psychologically disturbed in the conventional sense. Their abuse is related to cultural, social, and political practices (Gondolf, 1985). Programs designed to stop battering begin with and focus on that premise.*

Moreover, some standards go so far as to suggest that a focus on individual psychopathology may not only miss the point, but also provide a "sick role" or insanity type of excuse for violence. For example, Massachusetts's standards state:

In his article "Treatment Models of Men Who Batter: A Profeminist Analysis," David Adams, of the Emerge Program in Massachusetts (1988) articulates how some of these clinical approaches fail to adequately address the violence by focusing on individual psychological issues that, although important, are not the cause of the violence. Furthermore, Adams notes that " . . . some of these approaches collude with batterers by not making their violence the primary issue or by implicitly legitimizing men's excuses for the violence." (Adams, 1988)

A review of the literature suggests little in the way of clear direction in these areas. While the early literature on domestic violence emphasized political and socio-cultural influences, the more recent research has emphasized the importance of individual psychological factors as a source of vulnerability or risk for violence toward women (Dutton, 1994; Hamberger, 1994). Despite the tendency for some workers in the field of domestic violence to argue for one viewpoint over another, the existing literature would suggest that both types of factors play an important role as contributing influences to domestic violence (Hamberger, 1994; Hamberger & Hastings, 1990; Rosenbaum & Maiuro, 1989). Furthermore, Hamberger (1994) has observed that socio-cultural variables may operate at a "distal" level, creating the general environmental circumstances, which encourage or condone the behavior, while individual psychological variables operate at a "proximal" level, to precipitate the individual's attitudes, emotions, and behaviors. Other writers provide data to suggest that cultural factors alone may not be sufficient and that individual factors are necessary for domestic violence to occur, thereby emphasizing the necessity of focusing upon both types of factors (see Dutton, 1994, regarding "patriarchal fallacy").

Whether Treatment Should Be Violence Specific or "Generic"

Another theme evident in the standards is an emphasis upon violence specific rather than "generic treatment," with the latter term used to describe more traditional psychodynamic approaches. This emphasis appears to have been developed out of a pragmatic recognition that violent behavior should be prioritized as the focus of treatment rather than the dynamic "symptom" of some other underlying problem. Thus, Kentucky standards state:

The treatment must be violence specific rather than generic.

Based on a review of the literature, Saunders (1996) appears to be the only investigator to have compared violence specific, psychoeducational treatment methods with more traditional psychodynamic methods. In his study, Saunders randomly placed men with histories of domestic violence into either a Feminist-Cognitive-Behavioral or a less structured Process-Psychodynamic treatment program. The psychodynamic treatment focused largely on general counseling and support issues, such as facilitating the participants' personal insight, self-awareness, and understanding of their own victimization within their families of origin. On the other hand, the cognitive-behavioral model focused on issues such as asserting needs, expressing feelings, challenging irrational thought processes, and modifying societal stereotypes of gender roles. Despite the differences in treatment approaches, no evidence was found for the superiority of one approach over the other with regard to the primary outcome of cessation of violence. There was, however, an interaction of treatment with the type of offender. Measured by self-report and partner reports, men with dependent personalities were found to have better outcomes in the process-psychodynamic treatment, whereas men with antisocial personalities had better outcomes in the feminist-cognitive behavioral treatment.

Paradigmatically speaking, some researchers believe the efficacy of intervention in this area has yet to be solidly demonstrated and replicated, let alone the superiority of one theoretical orientation over another. Moreover, in the course of controlled clinical trials, the issue of efficacy generally precedes a component analysis to determine what the key factors are in any regimen. More research is clearly needed in this area before definitive guidelines can be established to direct the "best" course or methods of intervention.

Anger versus Power and Control as a Source of Motivation

Another theme apparent in standards that specify program content is the issue of how much emphasis should be placed upon anger as a target of treatment. Much of the discussion of this topic appears to have taken the form of a debate regarding the motivation for domestic violence, with some feminist proponents suggesting that a focus upon anger detracts from the abusers' abuse of power and control to dominate women. As a result, while some states acknowledge that anger management may be a useful component of batterer's treatment, others explicitly disapprove of such approaches as a primary focus of treatment. For example, according to Florida State standards:

> *. . . Communication enhancement or anger management techniques, which lay primary causality on anger, are prohibited.*

Gondolf and Russell (1986) suggested that anger management approaches were simplistic and ignored important socio-cultural dynamics, such as power and control. However, assuming that the program does not focus solely upon anger, it can be argued that focusing upon anger need not be simplistic, particularly if it is handled within a comprehensive cognitive-behavioral framework. For example, Jefferson County, Kentucky standards state:

> *Components of the individual or group therapy should include cognitive restructuring, anger management, stress management, sex-role stereotyping, power and control issues, conflict resolution, the cycle of violence, chemical abuse/dependency, empathy for the victim's experience, and personal abuse history. The treatment should address cognitive, behavioral, and emotional processes.*

Moreover, when one examines the actual research data, there appears to be fairly strong empirical support for a focus upon anger as a component of intervention in a large percentage of domestically violent men. Significant levels of anger and hostility have been found to be characteristic of domestically violent men across samples and across a variety of different measures (Boyle & Vivian, 1996; Dutton, Saunders, Starzomski, & Bartholomew, 1994; Hanson, Cadsky, Harris & LaLonde, 1997; Hershorn & Rosenbaum, 1991; Maiuro, Cahn, & Vitaliano, 1986; Maiuro, Cahn, Vitaliano, Wagner, & Zegree, 1988; Margolin, John, & Gleberman, 1988).

Some of the debate in this area appears to be due to confusion regarding the differences between "state" anger (situationally provoked or experienced) and "trait " anger (a general tendency to respond to events with anger, regardless of the presence of provocation). In this regard, it is important to note that research data supporting the presence of anger problems in batterers have never been interpreted to suggest that the victim is to blame for this anger by somehow provoking the perpetrator's violent behavior. Rather, current findings have supported the presence of anger as a trait characteristic of the perpetrator; a trait associated with negative emotional reactivity, hostile attitudinal sets, limited coping and conflict resolution skills, and negative family of origin influences such as abuse related trauma. Moreover, as increased attention has focused upon psychological and emotional forms of abuse in domestically violent relationships, few clinical researchers would question the role of anger in the perpetration of psychological and emotional abuse, verbal attacks to self-esteem, and threats to harm.

As is the case with other forms of violence in which vulnerable victims are abused and disempowered, there is a tendency for some domestic violence practitioners to form strong positions of advocacy and to adopt an "either/or" position when it comes to their beliefs about domestic violence. Such thinking can create an artificial dichotomy of "anger" versus "control" models when, in fact, both issues represent two different heads on the same dragon of abuse (see Dutton, 1994). When the research literature is examined, one finds support for multivariate rather than single factor models of domestic violence. This would argue for an inclusive, rather than exclusive, approach to treatment guidelines (Hamberger, 1994; Maiuro & Avery, 1996), if for no other reason, to address the diversity of profiles present in samples of domestically violent men.

Modalities of Treatment

While many modalities of treatment are mentioned in the state standards surveyed, 90% of the guidelines surveyed emphasized group therapy as the primary choice for intervention (see Figure 2). Although there have been no comparative studies of efficacy across individual and group treatment modalities, a number of advantages can be identified in the clinical literature for group methods. These include combating social isolation as a risk factor (Hotaling & Sugarman, 1986), peer support to ventilate acute concerns (Lion, Christopher, & Madden, 1976), the development of a vicarious learning environment, and exposure to coping versus mastery models for change (Rosenbaum & Maiuro, 1989). Many therapists have also recognized the confrontive value of groups for male offenders of various types (Bernard & Bernard, 1984). When supportively guided by a trained therapist, such confrontation can be useful in identifying and modifying interpersonal insensitivity, cognitive distortions, and the type of minimization and denial often evidenced by domestically violent men.

Coping models, which begin with a variety of fears and failings, and then progressively foster the acquisition of skills and positive social judgements, can surpass mastery models in social influence (Rosenbaum & Maiuro, 1989). The use of coping models may be particularly relevant in the case of batterers, as some may have generalized conflicts with authority figures (Fagan, Stewart, & Hansen, 1983). Moreover, those men who present with a "macho" identity may require the social support of other aggressive males in order to let go of their defenses and consider alternatives to their psychological and behavioral weaponry.

Another attribute of group interventions relates to economy and efficiency of service delivery. Although domestic violence occurs across all socio-economic levels, a large proportion of cases come from low socio-economic strata (Hotaling & Sugarman, 1986; Straus, Gelles, & Steinmetz, 1980). By offering relatively less expensive group services, the therapist can decrease financial barriers to treatment for clients who lack comprehensive health insurance, have modest incomes, or partial employment. A related issue deals with the sheer magnitude of domestic violence as a problem. Even though individualized services may be indicated in some cases, such prevalence rates demand efficient service delivery methods to accommodate the needs of the community (Rosenbaum & Maiuro, 1989). Presumably for a combination of these

FIGURE 2. Do Standards Dictate Preferred or Allowable Modalities of Treatment?

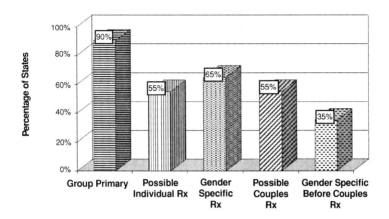

reasons, many states such as Washington endorse a preference for group modalities of intervention over individual ones:

> *The domestic violence perpetrator programs shall require participants to participate in weekly group treatment sessions unless there is a documented, clinical reason for another modality.*

However, in keeping with existing research, there appears to be no reason to exclude individualized approaches, as there are no studies that indicate group therapy is actually superior to one on one intervention. Thus, some states (55%) allow for the substitution of individual therapy for group therapy modalities (see Figure 2).

Gender Specific Treatment

The majority of states (65%) have specifically mentioned that treatment should be conducted in a gender-specific fashion so that male perpetrators are seen in men's groups and female perpetrators are seen in women's groups (see Figure 2). This arises from the belief that the treatment needs of women are different than those of men. The issue of gender-specific groups has received some preliminary support from clinical research, which has documented that the issues and problems of women who perpetrate domestic violence are, in many ways, different than those of men (Hamberger & Potente, 1994; Saunders, 1986).

Although the most important goal in treating either domestically violent men or women is to stop the violence and abuse, Hamberger and Potente (1994) found important gender differences based on the impact of the violence and on the motivation driving the violence. The fear-inducing and injurious impact of male-to-female violence is typically higher than that of female-to-male violence. In addition, the motivations recounted by men who commit domestic violence are more likely to be related to anger, power, and control over their partners, while women tend to be motivated by a cluster of anger, fear, and self-protection (Hamberger & Potente, 1994; Jacobson, 1994; Vivian & Malone, 1997). Thus, men's groups focus on learning to cultivate non-abusive ways of resolving conflict and developing more egalitarian relationships. Women's groups focus on aspects of empowerment, differentiating assertiveness from anger, increasing access to resources, and a variety of safety issues (Hamberger & Potente, 1994).

In addition, Saunders (1986) conducted a survey examining motives of domestically abusive women. Of the 52 women participants studied, 69% indicated they were actually engaging in self-defense or retaliation for violence perpetrated against them. Although the reference to research is not specifically documented and questionable in terms of the figures quoted for the overall percentage of women victimized in domestic violence incidents, Washington State standards appear to have been developed with data on gender differences in mind:

> In light of consistent research findings that a victim of domestic violence is female in ninety-five percent of domestic violence incidents, the program shall give special consideration to a female participant with regard to prior domestic violence victimization.

Couples versus Individual Therapy

An issue related to gender-specific treatment is whether men and women should be seen together. While some states (55%) allow couples therapy when victim safety criteria permit (see Figure 2), many states (43%) explicitly preclude the use of couples therapy in the treatment of perpetrators of domestic violence. Washington State standards are a good example of precluding language:

> Under no circumstances invite or require victims of group participants to attend perpetrator program counseling and education groups.

Other states indicate that couples therapy may be permissible on an ad hoc or an adjunctive basis. For example, the San Diego County Task Force on Domestic Violence states:

A couple's session (as opposed to on-going couple therapy) may be used to elicit information, arrange a separation, arrange visitation for children, or to teach anger management skills such as time out.

In addition, 35% of states surveyed will only allow couples therapy once gender-specific treatment of the perpetrator has been completed (see Figure 2). The reasons commonly cited for limiting the use of couples therapy include: (a) concern that such treatment will endanger or instill fear in the victim, or (b) diffuse responsibility for the violence and abuse from the batterer. The standards for Pennsylvania state:

It is the tendency of couples counselors to equalize responsibility for violence between the man and the woman.

Although research studies have been limited to date, recent studies indicate that couples therapy may be possible with rigorous and careful screening. Dunford's (1997) work with U.S. Navy personnel compared gender specific groups and conjoint groups with an added control condition. Dunford's data revealed no significant difference between the treatment conditions and the control condition. All three conditions had a recidivism rate of approximately 28% and an equal number of incidents during the course of therapy. Interestingly, Dunford's results also indicated that approximately 15% of the batterers accounted for 85% of the recidivism.

Contrary to the concerns raised by some advocates, O'Leary (1996, and in this volume) found that some victims preferred to receive treatment with their partners in a couples format. Moreover, O'Leary found that couples treatment is possible and equally effective if provided under certain conditions. These conditions include safety assessment and screening with regard to prior level of violence and current risk of violence. O'Leary points out that, unlike generic couples therapy, which is often based on systems theory in which both partners assume responsibility for dysfunctional patterns of behavior, violence-specific couples therapy holds the perpetrator accountable and responsible for the abuse.

Although limited, the current data suggest that the exclusion of couples therapy as a modality for domestic violence treatment may be premature. Moreover, some researchers have suggested that mutually occurring violence is more common than previously indicated in the literature (Cascardi, Langhinrichsen, & Vivian, 1992; Morse, 1995; Steinmetz & Lucca, 1987; Vivian & Langhinrichsen-Rohling, 1994) and that certain aspects of treatment for the husband (e.g., time-out techniques) can be more effective if the spouse is involved (Rosenbaum & Maiuro, 1989).

The most reasonable conclusion at this juncture appears to be that further, albeit cautious, investigation of couples modalities is warranted. Detailed protocols now exist for determining whether couples treatment may be safely conducted (Bograd & Mederos, 1999; Gauthier & Levendosky, 1996) and are in need of empirical validation. Of particular interest would be the question of whether there are subtypes of abuse and vulnerability profiles that indicate or contra-indicate the use of such treatment in the presence of willing participants. With proper and ongoing attention to safety issues for the victim, such studies would have merit and should not be precluded on an a priori basis.

Is the Use of Research Findings Formally Documented as a Basis for Developing Standards?

While many states (40%) provide documenting references for the positions taken within the standards, the present survey results also indicated the majority of the states (60%) do not provide any empirical or authoritative references. In the cases in which references are present, the citation is often a book or book chapter based on clinical impressions by early workers in the field. In some cases, these early impressions may have been generalizations or over-simplifications, which have since been modified by more recent findings in empirical research. For example, while some couples counselors may "equalize responsibility for violence between the man and the woman," it may not be accurate to say that all couples counselors have the tendency to do this. Moreover, if the practitioner is a domestic violence treatment provider, it is likely that the practitioner employs a modified form of couples therapy that is violence-specific. In addition, it should be noted that caution regarding the equalization of responsibility for violence between the perpetrator and victim could be reasonably applied to any form of therapy or intervention. Such caution would apply equally to individual and group methods as the diffusion of personal accountability is not necessarily inherent in couples modalities. Thus, what may otherwise be a legitimate concern for practice in general becomes synonymous with a specific modality through a process of overgeneralization.

Although few would question the need for caution in employing certain methods in order to protect the safety of victims, there is a danger of prematurely dismissing potentially effective approaches. This risk is magnified by the fact that such generalizations may become officially codified in standards as a "known" basis for practice and, in some cases, replicated across a number of states. The seasoned observer of the domestic violence movement may recall numerous instances in which a piece of information was promulgated as research based fact (e.g., "domestic violence rates are highest on Superbowl Sunday") in the absence of any such study. Moreover, there are instances in which a particular finding gets quoted and re-quoted, often for dramatic effect, or because it sounds logical, regardless of the reliability or scientific rigor of the original source. This tendency may be affectionately termed the "Woozle Effect" based upon the Winnie-the-Pooh story (Milne, 1926; Himelstein & Mayer, 1995, pp. 5-6) in which Winnie and Piglet set out to find a Woozle by walking around a nearby tree after a snowfall:

At first there was one set of tracks
Then two, then three, then four
We walked around that tree again
And each time there were more
It absolutely, positively
Left a Woozle scent
I wonder where in the world
The Woozle went

Well, it really was a Woozle
Yes it was, was, was
Why it really was a Woozle, yes it was
Of course it was, I'm sure because
I think I saw some Woozle fuzz
It really was a Woozle, yes it was.

Further insight into the apparent gap between current research and existing standards for practice is gained by examining the data on prioritization of program evaluation in current statutes. Only 40% of the states surveyed actually reference research findings. Similarly, only 30% actively endorse program evaluation and applied research as a part of their program missions. Even more remarkable is the fact that only 5% have explicitly specified the inclusion of a qualified researcher on their domestic violence standards development committee.

Education

Some insight into the challenge of creating standards for the treatment of perpetrators of domestic violence is illustrated by the findings on education. Out of the 30 states surveyed, only 20% required a minimum education at the bachelor's level. Furthermore, relatively few states recognize batterer treatment as a specialty that requires training beyond a bachelor's degree. Wisconsin state standards illustrate this point:

The possession or attainment of a formal degree or formal education is viewed as neither necessary nor sufficient for educational qualifications to facilitate batterers treatment groups.

Although some state standards are written in a manner that appears to assume a background in mental health, very few actually require such a background. Of the 80% of the states that forgo a graduate or even a bachelor's degree for batterer treatment, the prevailing practice is to require a given number of hours of specialized training in the areas of domestic violence perpetration and victimization. Colorado state standards, for example, require an:

> *entry level Bachelors Degree in a human service related area or an equivalent combination of college courses and applied experience to include a total of 155-169 clock hours in basic domestic violence and counseling related areas.*

The absence of a requirement for an advanced graduate degree in the social and health sciences may contribute to a lack of familiarity with research methods, findings, and resources. This may contribute to a failure to integrate such findings into practice standards for many states.

Although the presence of a graduate level degree in no way ensures better services or enhanced safety for victims, the lack of a documented minimum education requirement for most states is surprising, given the fact that domestic violence cases routinely involve delicate and complex questions of dangerousness. Such issues are often mandated areas of continuing education for mental health providers. The issue of potential dangerousness alone raises the question of whether it would be appropriate to have minimum credentials similar to those of mental health providers as a basic level of training upon which specialized skills in domestic violence are developed. A variation of this idea has been adopted by San Diego County in California:

> *All treatment providers of domestic violence clients must meet the following criteria: Master's or Doctorate degree in a human services clinical field, currently licensed as a psychotherapist, or for unlicensed persons, agencies may exempt this by providing intense supervision, defined as the ability to have timely and direct access to a supervisor on a daily basis. Supervisors must meet the advanced graduate degree requirement and have at least one year of supervisory experience in domestic violence.*

Method for Developing and Revising Standards

Since the art and science of perpetrator treatment is rapidly expanding, one might expect that existing standards would be revisited often. For example, Colorado standards indicate that:

State standards should undergo continuous review and revision consistent with experiences of new knowledge, skills, and methods. The State Commission is committed to meeting at least twice per year to review the standards and to consider suggestions for improvement.

However, the current survey results suggest that this is not the case for the majority of the states, at least in an explicitly required manner. In this respect, 40% have a formally documented method for developing and revising treatment standards, while the majority (60%) does not.

Moreover, care must be taken in the make-up of committees to determine standards. Although the presence of an established researcher may be of some benefit to ensure that timely, valid, reliable, and representative sources are referenced, it may be of equal or greater importance to include an ethicist to guard against unethical practice or conflicts of interest. These conflicts of interest could include secondary gain in the form of training contracts for a particular intervention approach, or an agenda to put those competitors out of business who do or do not adopt a particular philosophy or offer a specific form of programming. The state of Colorado's standards provide a good example of attention to such issues:

One-half of the board members shall be re-appointed every two years, and the board shall meet at least quarterly. No board member shall have a pecuniary interest in the treatment program or the services provided in connection therewith. The board and its individual members shall be immune from any liability, civil or criminal, and from termination of employment, for the good faith performance of their duties as specified in this subsection.

One method of ensuring balance is a multidisciplinary board as opposed to one solely comprised of advocates and practitioners. Again, the state of Colorado provides a good example of such a protocol:

The chief judge in each judicial district shall appoint a local board, which shall certify and monitor treatment programs for persons convicted of the crime of domestic violence. Said board shall consist of eight members: Two members from the victim services field; one member from law enforcement; one member from a prosecutor's office; one member from the probation department; one member from the community at large; one member from the mental health profession; and one member from the state department of human services or county department of social services. The board should reflect the ethnic composition of the community in which it is located.

CONCLUSIONS

In many ways, the development of standards for treatment of perpetrators of domestic violence represents a positive advancement for the field. Existing standards not only serve to underscore the priority of victim safety but also validate the fact that perpetrator treatment is essential, from a public health perspective (see Maiuro, 1996; Maiuro & Avery, 1996). Moreover, the existence of standards for the assessment and treatment of domestic violence perpetrators also formalizes such intervention as a specialty that requires training and experience not routinely offered within the training curriculum of many social and health care professions. With this recognition, many states have been improving accountability and monitoring of existing, as well as new treatment programs through certification.

Several problem areas also exist. First, most states have unclear and undocumented methods or protocols for the development and revision of standards. Second, many state standards do not appear to be adequately informed by existing research on perpetrators of domestic violence. Third, even in cases in which state standards do make reference to the literature, there are a number of problems. These include: (a) repetition of clinical lore through the "Woozle Effect"; (b) confusion of theoretical orientation with case management methods, as well as unsubstantiated assumptions regarding supposedly inherent attitudes toward violence and victimization; (c) overgeneralization of limited findings to all cases of domestic violence; and (d) premature dismissal of potentially useful, and albeit conditional, treatment strategies on the basis of feared, but empirically unexplored side effects. Fourth, a significant number of states appear to have language that is positively biased toward sociopolitical theories and negatively biased toward individual factors as contributing variables and as valid targets of treatment. Fifth, some states have a rigid, "one size fits all" criteria for conducting treatment, despite: (a) growing evidence of heterogeneity along typological and severity dimensions, and (b) lack of data suggesting "a cure" or the clear superiority of some treatments over others. Sixth, there are some potential ethical problems related to matters of process, representation, and possible conflicts of interest. Specifically, there do not appear to be explicit safeguards to limit or avoid such influences in the development of protocols for most states.

Perhaps the most serious problem lies in the risk of stunting the development of new and alternative interventions for families afflicted with domestic violence. In this respect, more work is needed to assure that existing guidelines truly protect the well-being of victims without inadvertently impeding much needed program development, diversity, innovation, and advances in the field.

RECOMMENDATIONS

As reflected in the title of this article, the issue of whether existing state standards are adequately informed by research is a question of questions. In this regard, the answer depends on how one looks at the standards and what one expects from them. In some respects, there appears to be less than adequate input from empirical research in existing standards and/or the lack of documented protocols to ensure the use of reliable, valid, and representative authoritative sources. The current results also reflect the fact that the field is still young and in need of further research in many areas related to intervention. Most of the research performed to date is descriptive and correlational in nature (e.g., incidence and prevalence studies; studies of the relationship between substance abuse and victimization; assessment of skill deficits and psychological characteristics of battering men) rather than process or outcome related. Only recently have investigators begun to explore attempts to reduce risk factors for domestic violence (Hilton, Harris, Rice, Krans, & Lavigne, 1998) or study what happens when health practitioners take protective action, such as making reports to the police to reduce the risk of further injury (Lund, 1999). Moreover, there is little research focused on treatment failures or methods that increase risk for negative outcomes. Clearly, more research is needed with regard to these critical issues to provide a relevant database for practice and intervention.

However, it is also true that some matters of practice may never be adequately addressed by research and may remain an issue of ethics or "reasonable" standards of care. Due to the complicated and multifaceted nature of standards of care, state development committees might do well to consult respected sources in other fields, such as *Standard of Care: The Law of American Bioethics* for guidance to avoid reinventing the wheel or, in some cases, the flat tire (see Annas, 1993).

Based on the current state of the art and science, few practitioners would argue that the preferred method or cure for domestic violence has been proven or discovered. Given this reality, one might question whether the paradigm for perpetrator treatment is sufficiently developed to warrant detailed dictates regarding preferred modes of treatment or to preclude others. In this sense, one wonders whether the original intent of developing guidelines to help ensure the safety of victims has been overextended to areas of practice that are premature to regulate. If safety permits and until otherwise "known," it may be important to preserve flexibility in methods for purposes of consumer choice, diversity of programming, and creative evolution of treatment technology. The state of Maryland provides a good example of such an approach in that they have opted for assessment guidelines to ensure safety, and a set of operational guidelines, protocols, and principles to facilitate informed and state-of-the art practice, rather than specific theoretical and intervention methods per se (Maryland Family Violence Council Report, 1996).

Given this state of affairs, perhaps the best recommendations are ones that facilitate the development of balanced, informed, and ethical protocol for developing and updating standards of practice. For example, while the current results suggest that the inclusion of an established researcher on the development board has been overlooked in most states and may improve the quality of the database for standards development, one could also argue that a number of other disciplines should be considered. These would include representatives from victim support agencies, a victim agency consumer, perpetrator treatment programs, a perpetrator agency consumer, representative mainstream social and health care organizations, the prosecutor's office, the American Civil Liberties Union or a local public defender agency, as well as a risk management expert and an ethicist.

The issue of providing an explicitly stated protocol for critically reviewing and revising standards also appears to be important. Given the relatively new nature of the field and the significant increase in professional literature on the topic of domestic violence in specialty (e.g., *Family Violence and Sexual Assault Bulletin, Journal of Aggression, Maltreatment & Trauma, Journal of Emotional Abuse, Journal of Family Violence, Journal of Interpersonal Violence, Violence and Victims*) and mainstream journals (e.g., *American Journal of Public Health, Archives of Family Medicine, Journal of the American Medical Association*), frequent updates would appear to be essential. The development of a national blue ribbon panel of "experts" could be developed to provide consultation to state boards and help combat the possibility of untoward local and regional biases.

Another issue is the need to recognize that domestic violence intervention is rapidly becoming a multidisciplinary enterprise. In this regard, there appears to be a need to encourage cross disciplinary education as part of a continuing education requirement so that certain professional perspectives are not dismissed, stereotyped, or vilified due to either historical neglect of the area or differential weighting of contributory factors underlying domestic violence.

If the current standards of care are to develop to their fullest potential, union shop mentalities dictated by philosophy, discipline, or training will need to be tempered by a competent interdisciplinary practitioner base. Each discipline may bring a unique set of knowledge, skills, and technologies to the field. In this regard, it may be that credentialing and certification boards of the future should be discipline-specific. As treatment technologies and methods evolve, such an approach would allow true peer review and monitoring of intervention methods that are commonly, and sometimes exclusively, practiced within a particular profession (e.g., psychopharmacology, psychotherapy, and dual diagnosis treatment of alcohol/substance abuse). With proper attention to process as well as content, the development of state standards for domestic violence intervention could conceivably facilitate the evolution of practice in this direction.

REFERENCES

Adams, D. (1988). Treatment models of men who batter: A profeminist analysis. In K. Yllö & M. Bograd (Eds.), *Feminist perspectives on wife abuse* (pp. 176-199). Newbury Park, CA: Sage.

Annas, G. J. (1993). *Standard of care: The law of American bioethics.* New York: Oxford University Press.

Austin, J. B., & Dankwort, J. (1999). Standards for batterer programs: A review and analysis. *Journal of Interpersonal Violence, 14* (2), 152-168.

Bennett, L. (1998). In defense of batterer program standards. *The Journal of Contemporary Human Services, 79,* 93-97.

Bernard, J. L., & Bernard, M. L. (1984). The abusive male seeking treatment: Jekyll and Hyde. *Family Relations: Journal of Applied Family and Child Studies, 33*(4), 543-547.

Bograd, M., & Mederos, F. (1999). Battering and couples therapy: Universal screening and selection of treatment modality. *Journal of Marital and Family Therapy, 25*(3), 291-312.

Boyle, D. J., & Vivian, D. (1996). Generalized versus spouse-specific anger/hostility and men's violence against intimates. *Violence and Victims, 11*(4), 293-317.

Cascardi, M., Langhinrichsen, J., & Vivian, D. (1992). Marital aggression: Impact, injury and correlates for husbands and wives. *Archives of Internal Medicine, 152,* 1178-1184.

Dobash, R. E., & Dobash, R. P. (1992). *Women, violence, and social change.* New York: Routledge.

Dunford, F. W. (1997). *The research design and preliminary outcome findings of the San Diego Navy Experiment.* Paper presented at the Fifth International Family Violence Research Conference, Durham, NH.

Dutton, D.G. (1986). The outcome of court-mandated treatment for wife-assault: A quasi-experimental evaluation. *Violence and Victims, 1,* 163-175.

Dutton, D. G. (1994). Patriarchy and wife assault: The ecological fallacy. *Violence and Victims, 9*(2), 167-182.

Dutton, D. G., Saunders, K., Starzomski, A., & Bartholomew, K. (1994). Intimacy-anger and insecure attachment as precursors of abuse in intimate relationships. *Journal of Applied Social Psychology, 24,* 1367-1386.

Edleson, J. L. (1996). Controversy and change in batterers' programs. In J. L. Edleson & Z. C. Eisikovits (Eds.), *Future interventions with battered women and their families* (pp. 154-169), Thousand Oaks, CA: Sage.

Edleson, J. L., & Syers, M. (1991). The effects of group treatment for men who batter: An 18-month follow-up study. *Research on Social Work Practice, 1*(3), 227-243.

Edleson, J. L., & Tolman, R. M. (1992). *Intervention for men who batter: An ecological approach.* Newbury Park, CA: Sage.

Fagan, J. A., Stewart, D. K., & Hansen, K. V. (1983). Violent men or violent husbands? In D. Finkelhor, R. J. Gelles, G. T. Hotaling, & M. A. Straus (Eds.), *The dark side of families: Current family violence research* (pp. 49-67). Beverly Hills, CA: Sage.

Gauthier, L. M., & Levendosky, A. A. (1996). Assessment and treatment of couples with abusive male partners: Guidelines for therapists. *Psychotherapy, 33*(3), 403-417.

Geffner, B. (1995a). Standards for batterer intervention: Editor's response. *Family Violence and Sexual Assault Bulletin, 11*(3-4), 29-32.

Geffner, B. (1995b). Standards in the family violence field. *Family Violence and Sexual Assault Bulletin, 11*(1-2), 3.

Gondolf, E. W. (1985). *Men who batter: An integrated approach to stopping wife abuse.* Holmes Beach, FL: Learning Publications.

Gondolf, E. W. (1988). Who are those guys? Toward a behavioral typology of men who batter. *Violence and Victims, 3*(3), 187-203.

Gondolf, E. W. (1995). Gains and process in state batterer programs and standards. *Family Violence and Sexual Assault Bulletin, 11*(3-4), 27-28.

Gondolf, E. W. (1997). Batterer programs: What we know and need to know. *Journal of Interpersonal Violence, 12*(1), 83-98.

Gondolf, E. W., & Russell, D. (1986). The case against anger control treatment programs for batterers. *Response to the Victimization of Women and Children, 9*(3), 2-5.

Gottman, J., Jacobson, N., Rushe, R., Wu Short, J., Babcock, J., La Taillade, J., & Waltz, J. (1995). The relationship between heart rate reactivity, emotionally aggressive behavior, and general violence in batterers. *Journal of Family Psychology, 9*, 227-248.

Hamberger, L. K. (1994). Domestic partner abuse: Expanding paradigms for understanding and intervention. *Violence and Victims, 9*(2), 91-95.

Hamberger, L. K., & Hastings, J. E. (1989). Counseling male spouse abusers: Characteristics of treatment completers and dropouts. *Violence and Victims, 4*(1), 275-286.

Hamberger, L. K., & Hastings, J. E. (1990). Recidivism following spouse abuse abatement counseling: Treatment program implications. *Violence and Victims, 5*, 157-170.

Hamberger, L. K., Lohr, J. M., Bonge, D., & Tolin, D. F. (1996). A large sample empirical typology of male spouse abusers and its relationship to dimensions of abuse. *Violence and Victims, 11*, 277-292.

Hamberger, L. K., & Potente, T. (1994). Counseling heterosexual women arrested for domestic violence: Implications for theory and practice. *Violence and Victims, 9*, 125-138.

Hanson, R. K., Cadsky, O., Harris, A., & LaLonde, C. (1997). Correlates of battering among 997 men: Family history, adjustment, and attitudinal differences. *Violence and Victims, 12*(3), 191-208.

Hershorn, M., & Rosenbaum, A. (1991). Over- vs. under-controlled hostility: Application of the construct to the classification of maritally violent men. *Violence & Victims, 6*, 151-158.

Hilton, N. Z., Harris, G. T., Rice, M. E., Krans, T. S., & Lavigne, S. E. (1998). Antiviolence education in high schools: Implementation and evaluation. *Journal of Interpersonal Violence, 13*(6), 726-742.

Himelstein, M. & Mayer, S. (1995). It really was a Woozle, yes it was. *Winnie-the-Pooh sing-along.* Burbank, CA.

Holtzworth-Munroe, A., & Stuart, G. L. (1994). Typologies of male batterers: Three subtypes and the differences among them. *Psychological Bulletin, 116,* 476-497.

Hotaling, G. T., & Sugarman, D. B. (1986). An analysis of risk markers in husband to wife violence: The current state of knowledge. *Violence and Victims, 1*(2), 101-124.

Jacobson, N. S. (1994). Rewards and dangers in researching domestic violence. *Family Process, 33,* 81-87.

Lion, J. R., Christopher, R. L., & Madden, D. I. (1976). A violence clinic: Three years experience. *American Journal of Psychiatry, 133*(4), 432-435.

Lund, L. E. (1999). What happens when health practitioners report domestic violence injuries to police? A study of the law enforcement response to injury reports. *Violence and Victims, 14*(2), 203-214.

Maiuro, R. D. (1996). Intermittent explosive disorder. In D. L. Dunner (Ed.), *Current psychiatry therapy II* (pp. 528-535). Philadelphia: W.B. Saunders.

Maiuro, R. D., & Avery, D. H. (1996). Psychopharmacological treatment of aggressive behavior: Implications for domestically violent men. *Violence and Victims, 11*(3), 239-358.

Maiuro, R. D., Cahn, T. S., & Vitaliano, P. P. (1986). Assertiveness and hostility in domestically violent men. *Violence and Victims, 1,* 279-289.

Maiuro, R. D., Cahn, T. S., Vitaliano, P. P., Wagner, B. C., & Zegree, J. (1988). Anger, hostility, & depression in domestically violent versus generally assaultive men and nonviolent control subjects. *Journal of Consulting and Clinical Psychology, 56* (1), 17-23.

Maiuro, R. D., Vitaliano, P. V., Sugg, N. K., Thompson, D. C., Rivara, F. P., & Thompson, R.S. (2000). Development of a health care provider survey for domestic violence: Psychometric properties. *American Journal of Preventive Medicine, 19* (4), 245-252.

Margolin, G., John, R. S., & Gleberman, L. (1988). Affective responses to conflictual discussions in violent and nonviolent couples. *Journal of Consulting and Clinical Psychology, 56,* 24-33.

Maryland Family Violence Council. (1996). Abuser intervention programs: Follow operational guidelines and improve effectiveness. *Maryland Family Violence Council Report,* 40-43 & 100-103.

Milne, A. (1926). *Winnie-the-pooh.* New York: Dutton.

Morse, B. J. (1995). Beyond the Conflict Tactics Scale: Assessing gender differences in (intimate) partner violence. *Violence and Victims, 10*(4), 251-272.

O'Leary, K. D. (2001). Conjoint therapy for partners who engage in physically aggressive behavior: Rationale and research. *Journal of Aggression, Maltreatment & Trauma* 5(2), pp. 145-164.

O'Leary, K. D. (1996). Physical aggression in intimate relationships can be treated within a marital context under certain circumstances. *Journal of Interpersonal Violence, 11*(3), 450-452.

O'Leary, K. D. (1999). Psychological abuse: A variable deserving critical attention in domestic violence. *Violence and Victims, 14*, 3-23.

O'Leary, K. D. & Maiuro, R. D. (Eds.). (2001). *Psychological abuse in violent domestic relations.* New York: Springer.

Pence, P., & Paymar, M. (1993). *Education groups for men who batter: The Duluth Model.* New York: Springer.

Rosenbaum, A., Gearan, P. J., & Ondovic, C. (2001). Completion and recidivism among court- and self-referred batterers in a psychoeducational group treatment program: Implications for intervention and public policy. *Journal of Aggression, Maltreatment, & Trauma* 5(2), pp. 199-220.

Rosenbaum, A., & Maiuro, R. D. (1989). Eclectic approaches in working with men who batter. In P. L. Caesar & L. K. Hamberger (Eds.), *Treating men who batter: Theory, practice, and programs* (pp. 165-195). New York: Springer.

Rosenbaum, A., & Stewart, T. P. (1994). Point/counterpoint: Treatment standards for abuser programs. *Violence Update, 5* (1), 9-11.

Saunders, D. G. (1986). When battered women use violence: Husband-abuse or self-defense? *Violence and Victims, 1*(1), 47-60.

Saunders, D. G. (1992). Typology of men who batter women: Three types. *American Journal of Orothopsychiatry, 62*, 264-275.

Saunders, D. G. (1996). Feminist-Cognitive-Behavioral and process-psychodynamic treatments for men who batter: Interaction of abuser traits and treatment models. *Violence and Victims, 11*(4), 393-411.

Steinmetz, S. K., & Lucca, J. S. (1987). Husband battering. In V. B. VanHasselt & R. L. Morrision (Eds.), *Handbook of family violence* (pp. 233-246). New York: Plenum Press.

Straus, M. A., Gelles, R. J., & Steinmetz, S. (1980). *Behind closed doors: Violence in the American family.* Garden City, NY: Doubleday/Anchor.

Tweed, R. G., & Dutton, D. G. (1998). A comparison of impulsive and instrumental subgroups of batterers. *Violence and Victims, 13*(3), 217-230.

Vivian, D., & Langhinrichsen-Rohling, J. (1994). Are bi-directionally violent couples mutually victimized? A gender-sensitive comparison. *Violence and Victims, 9*(2), 107-124.

Vivian, D., & Malone, J. (1997). Relationship factors and depressive symptomatology associated with mild and severe husband-to-wife physical aggression. *Violence and Victims, 12*(1), 3-16.

INTERVENTION TECHNIQUES FOR MALE AND FEMALE DOMESTIC VIOLENCE OFFENDERS

Batterers' Treatment: Observations from the Trenches

Alyce LaViolette

SUMMARY. Group treatments for men who abuse their female partners are relatively recent phenomena. These groups were developed with the encouragement of the battered women's movement, and in the mid- to late-1970s, were seen by advocates as a crucial component in the reduction of violence toward women. In the 1980s, batterer treatment groups often became a mandatory consequence of criminal prosecution, treatment groups proliferated, and their effectiveness was questioned. In the 1990s, the value, form, and success rates of these groups came under scrutiny. This article includes a historical perspective of batterers' intervention programs, a description of the Alterna-

[Haworth co-indexing entry note]: "Batterers' Treatment: Observations from the Trenches." LaViolette, Alyce. Co-published simultaneously in *Journal of Aggression, Maltreatment & Trauma* (The Haworth Maltreatment & Trauma Press, an imprint of The Haworth Press, Inc.) Vol. 5, No. 2(#10), 2001, pp. 45-56; and: *Domestic Violence Offenders: Current Interventions, Research, and Implications for Policies and Standards* (ed: Robert A. Geffner, and Alan Rosenbaum) The Haworth Maltreatment & Trauma Press, an imprint of The Haworth Press, Inc., 2001, pp. 45-56. Single or multiple copies of this article are available for a fee from The Haworth Document Delivery Service [1-800-HAWORTH, 9:00 a.m. - 5:00 p.m. (EST). E-mail address: getinfo@haworthpressinc.com].

45

tives to Violence program, and the experiences, perceptions, and opinions of its founder. *[Article copies available for a fee from The Haworth Document Delivery Service: 1-800-HAWORTH. E-mail address: <getinfo@haworthpressinc.com> Website: <http://www.HaworthPress.com> © 2001 by The Haworth Press, Inc. All rights reserved.]*

KEYWORDS. Abusers, batterers, intervention programs, history, domestic violence

I began my work with battered women in 1978, at WomenShelter in Long Beach, California, during the time when many shelters were feminist collectives. Money to fund these programs was hard to obtain and system support for battered women was virtually non-existent. Arresting an abusive mate was rare. Much has changed in the last 20 years. Shelter staffing is much more eclectic, program budgets have increased exponentially, systems have rallied and changed to provide victims with easier access to services, and arrest is relatively commonplace.

Geraldine Staley, the executive director of WomenShelter at that time, had been collecting data for over 18 months on the women and children who had participated in the program. The findings were both predictable and unsettling. Within a year of leaving the shelter, over 80% of the former residents (who could be tracked and interviewed) had, for a variety of reasons, returned to their abusers. Basic survival needs such as food, shelter, and jobs were ongoing issues for almost every woman in the shelter. Fear of revenge, fear of loss, and fear of the unknown were also consistently embedded in the psyches of women who were part of the residential program. Most shelter advocates failed to recognize that a primary reason for returning to an abusive partner was the woman's attachment to her partner and to her role in the family. In a month-long residential crisis program, belief systems could not be addressed and it was, in large part, these beliefs that drove women back to violent environments.

Another dynamic emerged that provided impetus to the notion of intervening with male perpetrators. Shelters began to form coalitions and advocates began to talk about their cases, looking for common denominators and creative approaches. In some cases, women residing at different emergency facilities shared not only common stories, but also a common perpetrator. The batterer had moved from one relationship to another. A decision was made to begin a counseling program for the male partners of shelter residents.

I had been working at WomenShelter as a volunteer for six months when I was asked if I was interested in becoming the men's services coordinator. The Board of Directors had been looking for a man to fill the position, but could not find a qualified man who would work for 660 dollars a month. Actually, I was not interested either. I had seen the aftermath of the violence directed at women and children, and could only believe that the men who could do such things were evil. However, program development was an interest of mine, and I needed a job.

In 1979, Alternatives to Violence (ATV) was developed as a program of WomenShelter. At that time, we were aware of only three programs that were doing this work. They were willing to share information, however limited, with me. These programs had structured 6 to 16 week formats. There was a heavy emphasis on patriarchy as the single cause of violence toward women by their intimates. That premise developed from the reality that, for centuries, men had beaten and controlled their wives with impunity; that female sexual behavior was strictly regulated in most cultures; and that infidelity and multiple partners were part of male privilege. Marriage basically suspended the individuality of women and made them legally one with their husbands. It was not a quantum leap to view male power and privilege as the root cause of male violence toward women. Program content reflected that perspective.

Because ATV is a program created to address the needs of battered wives, it is rooted in shelter philosophy. Women from the refuge and shelter staff were consulted in the formative stages and in ongoing development of content. Shelter philosophy resonated the "male power and privilege" theme. The women in the program had certainly run head-on into patriarchal problems–with their mates, and with the criminal justice, social service, and religious institutions they encountered when looking for help. However, the women also talked about their partners as emotionally powerless, unable to express feelings, "needing help," and as victims of violent childhoods. Some of these men had substance abuse problems; others did not. Some physically or emotionally abused their children; some tried to be good parents. Some were methodical and employed many forms of abuse; others were impulsive and hit, but were not insidiously and psychologically abusive. The "one size fits all" approach of a one-bullet patriarchal process theory seemed inadequate to address the issues brought to the table by the women in the shelter.

The resocialization process, "after shelter" care and more long-term advocacy that was becoming an ideological foundation of more effective intervention for shelter program participants seemed appropriate for batterer treatment, as well. Introduced as a 12-week program, ATV rapidly expanded to a 6-month program within months. During the next couple of years, the recommended time in group increased to one year. Currently, we view 18 months as a minimal time.

The increased time in group was a practical outgrowth of the participant's ability to change and the change reflected in our goals. In 6-10 months, most of the men in group had just begun to break through their denial. They needed time to feel good enough about themselves in order to look at the harm they had done, and to accept responsibility for their behavior. They needed time to internalize new ways of thinking and to practice new skills. But the really significant changes occurred when they changed their beliefs. The abusers in our programs were becoming "resocialized." They began to believe that their aggressive and controlling behaviors created fear, and that they had to stop. They had to redefine power in terms of their ability to make choices and to be collaborative, without being intimidating. Increased time in the program allowed for this transformation in thinking to occur, which in turn reinforced the behavior change. We met with other group facilitators who reported similar impressions.

Alternatives to Violence was a unique program in 1979 and remains so today. It was one of the first programs to use a female-male co-therapy team. In 1979, the rationale for this particular form of co-leadership was also unusual:

1. Most of the men in group had been in relationships with women. We believed they needed to argue with a woman they were not allowed to hit or psychologically abuse.We believed the men should be exposed to a woman in a significantly different and egalitarian role.
2. A good male facilitator is able to point out the subtleties of oppression and sexist attitudes to the men in the program.
3. An effective male-female team models respectful communication and power sharing.

Since the late 1970s, changes in domestic violence programs have occurred at every level, including those programs targeted to batterers. Spousal abuse has become a cause celebre. Abusers' groups have proliferated across the country. In Los Angeles County, California, the number of programs providing abuser counseling increased from approximately 10 well-known and respected programs to 130 programs of unknown quality within 18 months. Abusers' counseling has become big business for some individuals, and an ongoing issue of the heart for others. With the propagation of programs has come the demand for outcome research, as well as intense scrutiny by battered women's advocates, legislators, and the criminal justice system. Most want to know if batterers can change, and if programs really work and are successful.

What does "work" or "success" mean? What criteria do we use to measure success? Empirical, operationally defined success; clinically-defined success; the battered partner's evaluation; and success defined by the criminal justice system may lead to different conclusions. Criteria for success can range from statistically significant positive change, to nothing short of transformation to an "accountable" man (Hart, 1988). The facilitators of Alternatives to Violence measure success along a continuum of qualitative and quantitative variables. It is important to remember that the success is measured in very different ways for a battered partner than for the group facilitator. For instance, a counselor would view a man in group who stops hitting as a success; however, a battered woman might still feel pain and fear when he raises his voice, calls her a name, gives her the "silent treatment," drives dangerously, or any of a number of overt or covert behaviors. The counselors do not live with their abusive clients.

Given that, some of the criteria used to assess outcome at ATV are:

a. Cessation of physical aggression
b. Recognition of non-physical forms of abuse
c. Changes in attitudes or beliefs
d. Acceptance of responsibility
e. Shorter, less intense outbursts with longer periods between episodes
f. The development of empathy for the victims of their abuse
g. Regular group attendance
h. Cooperation in group and compliance with group rules
i. Redefinition of power as the ability to make choices, and the ability to create change in one's own life without intimidating others
j. Ability to take a time-out
k. Recognition of controlling behaviors

It may be unrealistic to expect a group that meets for approximately two hours once a week to counterbalance the attitudes most men have spent a lifetime acquiring. It would mean that they see their use of power and violence as a problem. For men to address these kinds of issues challenges who they are personally, and in their public lives. It would involve a critique of themselves as a powerful social group.

There is, however, good news. In a synthesis of the literature on batterers' treatment (Davis & Taylor, 1999), there is fairly consistent evidence that batterer treatment works on a variety of dimensions, and that effects of treatment can be substantial. Clinically and anecdotally, these results are echoed over and over again. Group facilitators, as previously mentioned, recognize success in ways that may not be relevant to other agencies or institutions, or the abuse victims themselves. Qualitative changes sought in a counseling environment are measured in baby steps.

CASE EXAMPLE

Jaime achieved dramatic changes in his behavior and belief system while attending ATV classes. Jaime had been a gang member since his childhood and a veteran of domestic warfare since infancy. He carried on a tradition of violence with his own wife and children. He did not want to be in a men's group, but jail had even less appeal. He decided to make the best of it, which was one of the first qualitative changes. After being in treatment for four to six months, other small changes occurred during dinner-time conversations (self-report). His wife openly disagreed with him. His children noticed that "Mommy didn't like what you said," and they felt comfortable laughing about it.

Jaime reported that his wife wanted to take a class and that he was going to stay home with his children. This was a big attitudinal and behavioral change. Jaime told the group that he only had 10 groups left, but brought in a note from his wife requesting an accurate count from the group facilitators. She had counted 12 groups. Jaime was laughing when he gave us the note and said his children told him, "Mommy's not scared of you anymore."

When Jaime was three weeks short of completing his court-ordered 52-week program, he came into group and asked to tell a story. He said he was proud of himself and that he was thinking differently. He had a disagreement with a man at work because of the way he was talking about women. Jaime told the group, "I think that the way we talk about women affects the way we treat them." A fundamental precept of most abusers' programs is that patriarchy is the root cause, or at least a significant causative factor in violence toward women. Given that, Jaime's beliefs changed tremendously.

We quickly saw our work as more than psycho-educational, and our participants as having more than problems of patriarchal entitlement. Our goals became belief, attitude, and perceptual change, as well as behavior change. We used psycho-educational, cognitive-behavioral, Gestalt, insight, psychodynamic interventions, and anything else that worked. We saw our interventions as therapeutic and were willing to say so. Applying the words "treatment" or "therapy" to batterers' intervention has been politically charged. There has been a history of antipathy between peer facilitators, licensed therapists, and victim advocates, which is slowly beginning to change. Peer counselors teaming with psychotherapists are doing wonderful work combining the best of grassroots educational intervention and gender-awareness with creative therapeutic techniques.

Another bit of political contention regarding batterers' treatment involves connectedness. Connection is the alliance, based on trust, empathy, and genuineness created by the facilitator and understood by the group member. It reflects the depth of the relationship and allows meaningful confrontation to occur. There has been a belief that connection means collusion. Connection does not have to mean collusion.

Confrontation is more effective when a connection exists. In fact, confrontation can become more direct because there is trust. A significant purpose for having co-facilitating teams is to provide a check against colluding. ATV was developed with the underlying belief that it is not possible to teach men who abuse power to treat women with respect, to become physically and emotionally non-violent, to value partnerships, and to reevaluate gender roles if group facilitators abuse power. Respectful confrontation is not about browbeating. The following case example demonstrates the use of therapeutic confrontation.

CASE EXAMPLE (CONFRONTATION)

Ralph had a history of violence with women he loved, with friends, and with strangers. He had abused alcohol and drugs, and had spent time in jail for assaultive behavior and drunk driving. He communicated from the beginning of group that he did not want to be there, and that he would not learn anything. "Stupid" was the nicest word he used to describe his weekly meeting.

As time went on, Ralph would talk about his relationships with women, his relationship with his parents, and his on-and-off job history. He would question his motivations, behaviors, and beliefs, and try to use something he had learned in group, but then he would "screw up."

Ralph had a problem that manifested itself in group by his withholding information, failing to pay his agreed-upon fee, and sporadic attendance. He was also developing a connection to the female facilitator in his group and confided a very personal problem to her. He sought her advice. The improvements in his behavior were most significant by his 10th month in the program. He was maintaining a regular job, had not gotten physically violent inside or outside of his relationship, and his attendance at group had improved.

He made a commitment to complete the program (the last 10 weeks) without missing a group. Then he broke that commitment. The female co-facilitator confronted him with his "breach of contract." She also told him that she would report him to his probation officer and request three more months of group (as they had agreed upon when the attendance agreement was made).

Ralph called the female co-facilitator. He was angry and accused her of betraying him. In group the following week, he again told her he was angry and felt betrayed. He took a "time-out," but came back to group. He told the facilitator that he always broke commitments, and asked her what she thought would happen in 3 months. He told her nothing would change; he would not learn a thing. He admitted that he cared about the co-leader and respected her opinions, and that was why he felt betrayed.

The female therapist confronted him with the importance of trust and keeping commitments to strengthen relationships. She was angry at him and let him know it. She told him she felt betrayed. Ralph said, "Well, I guess we both feel betrayed." She said, "You betrayed me by breaking your promise. You believe I betrayed you by keeping mine." By the end of the group Ralph was still upset, but he smiled, and even laughed.

Another unique feature of our program involves the experience of our facilitators and the size of our program. Our program remains small (four groups). This allows us to know the men in group, and it makes follow-up more manageable. The continuity of our work is supported by the continuity of our facilitation team. I do not believe there are many programs that have kept the same staff for over a decade. Our newest facilitator has worked with ATV since 1988.

Many of the programs throughout the state have continual staff turnover. Group participants may not have the experience of developing relationships with the people who facilitate their programs, or to work with seasoned counselors. Experience in the field is an asset when it comes to assessing dangerousness and interpreting subtle cues in language and behavior.

Groups are not time-limited and include men who have just started the program and men who have participated for 18 months and longer. At any given time, 30-50% of the men in group are non-court-ordered. Group size is limited. In Los Angeles County, court-ordered groups with one facilitator are limited to 15 participants. There is a limit of 20 participants when there are co-facilitators. Philosophically, ATV does not support large groups. There are 10-13 men in each group and each group has two counselors. If groups are too large, it is too easy for men to hide in group, there is too little time to practice skills, and too many men for facilitators to connect with effectively and to supervise adequately. The safety of battered women is a primary focus of an ethical batterers' program. It is certainly more cost-effective to have larger groups, and for some agencies, size is a funding contingency, but larger groups also make it more difficult to keep track of the group members, and harder to monitor safety issues.

ATV groups are heterogeneous. Members vary in age, ethnicity, sexual preference, socio-economic status, and educational level. Diversity within the group allows the members to address various forms of oppression (racism, classism, homophobia), as well as sexism. For example, black men in group have been able to relate being "one-down" in a white culture to their partner's status and power in their intimate relationships. Other men in group have been able to understand both oppressions (i.e., racism and sexism) by listening to Black, Hispanic, and Asian men speak about cultural bias. For example, one group met on the night the O.J. Simpson verdict was handed down. Racial tension was very high in Los Angeles. David, an African-American credit union employee, talked about the way he felt when his friends, white employees he had worked with for several years, ostracized him. The men in group were supportive verbally, and decided they would write a letter to the editor of a local newspaper discussing domestic violence and oppression. They were empowered and gave David the gift of empathy, even though the letter was never published.

Empathy is a core issue in the Alternatives to Violence program. Men in the abuser's program generally learn to empathize with themselves before empathizing with anyone else. They often see themselves as victims. Empathy tends to trickle down to the other men in their group, then to their children, and lastly, to their partners.

The ATV contract is short. There are very few rules, and problems with individual members are handled individually. Policy is not created based on a rarely occurring infraction. The idea is to approximate a healthy family. These men are more comfortable in a structured environment than they are in a fluid, flexible, and changing situation. A healthy family is not rigid, and unexpected events occur frequently. ATV groups are places for men to practice living in an ever-changing family.

Victim contact is made at the intake session. The victim and perpetrator are invited to come in together (if they are living together and the abused partner feels comfortable), but interviewed separately. If the partner does not want to attend, she is interviewed by phone or sent a letter. The victim's input is critical. It creates a context for the facilitators, adds vital information about the perpetrator, which lays the foundation to assess dangerousness, often breaks the victim's own isolation (as shelter information is given), and creates a link between the abused partner and her batterer's group facilitator. The information obtained during this process has been more valuable than any other information obtained (e.g., police or medical reports).

We have had no negative feedback or repercussions as a result of this intake procedure. What has resulted, however, is that partners of our clients have felt free to call us with their concerns and we have been able to address them in group. ATV also hosts a picnic or holiday party once a year, which the partners and children of clients are invited to attend. Because more of the partners have contact with the group facilitators, they often choose to attend. This tradition started over 18 years ago and has been successful from a variety of perspectives:

1. The men are seen interacting with their partners and/or children in an informal setting.
2. The partners and children have informal access to the facilitators.
3. The men have responsibility for organizing the event and bringing the food (buying it or preparing it).

4. The family views the facilitators as people who they can trust and are more likely to talk to them when they are in crisis or have concerns.
5. The men believe they are human beings in the therapist's eyes because we are able to see their strengths as well as their weaknesses.
6. We have received very positive feedback from the partners of our clients.

Facilitators in our program have strong community and shelter connections. These connections stem from our shelter origins and the belief that a coordinated community response is the most effective intervention for partner violence. The ability to respond effectively is predicated on a program's ability to know and access community resources. Meeting with city prosecutors, judges, police officers, clergy, children's advocates, battered women's advocates, probation officers, representatives from children's services, etc., makes it possible to intervene in an individual abuser's problems from a holistic perspective. Members of each system know and trust each other, and interventions can be creative and tailored to a specific situation.

For example, one of the men in ATV violated a "no-contact order" with his partner. He also destroyed a piece of property. He reported this action in group. We would not have known about it otherwise, as his partner made no report. We asked him to go to the judge and to admit documenting his honesty, his request for help and his progress. Our relationship with the judge affected her response. She placed him on formal probation, increased his time in group by six months, required him to make restitution, but did not send him to jail. If he had gone to jail, he would have lost his job and been unable to make restitution. According to the other men in group, they would have been hesitant to self-report if this man had gone to jail. Men in these groups must be able to speak honestly in group if we are to protect their partners. Everyone saw this client's logical consequences as fair.

Coalition building is not only a goal for the counselors of our program; it is also an objective for the group itself. Group can expand a man's social network, diffuse the emotional dependency he focuses on his partner, and provide numerous sources of feedback. Most violent men feel guilt and shame about their abusiveness, which tends to escalate their rage at their partners. A working group allows men to disclose their violent thoughts and behaviors, and receive confrontation that supports change. In an environment that supports an honest appraisal of their actions, shame is reduced. When shame is reduced, the men are better able to confront their own abusive behavior, take responsibility for it, and feel empathy for the people they have harmed.

Over the years, an evolution in thinking about batterers has occurred. They are not all just "normal" men acting out their sexism. Dutton describes some batterers as psychopaths, over-controlled, and cyclically/emotionally volatile (Dutton, 1995). Sonkin has described men with affective disorders (e.g., depression, bipolar disorder), and personality disorders (borderline, narcissistic, anti-social) (Sonkin, 1995; see also Holtzworth-Munroe & Stuart, 1994).

The content of most intervention programs is psycho-educational. The implication is that men learn to be violent and controlling and that they can unlearn these destructive patterns. This does not mean that therapy does not happen in group. It does, and it must. Most counselors believe that abused children or those exposed to domestic violence experience some long-term effects. Children in shelters often require therapy. Most batterers are those children as adults. Confronting therapeutic issues and sexism are not mutually exclusive. Both can be done in an abuser's group.

Battering men can and do change as a function of their participation in an intervention group, but their change is not a cure; it is more analogous to recovery. Men who have a pattern of chronic aggression often do not change without relapse. Recidivism of some kind is part of the process.

CASE EXAMPLE

Mitch relapsed in his program, but returned to make significant progress. Mitch came into our program after he was arrested and court-mandated to treatment for an assault on his wife that left her bleeding and unconscious. He was angry, felt remorseful, and blamed his wife almost simultaneously. He did not want to be in the program. He was a young man, and extremely rigid and hostile. He opened up a little at a time, but it was months before he really talked about the night he kicked his wife, literally, into the car. He began to look at his controlling behavior toward his wife: the way he talked down to her, scowled at her, and intimidated her into silence. One night he talked about how his wife had stood up to him that week. He smiled and felt relief. That was a real beginning for him in many ways. This may have been one of the first times he did not feel like the "bad guy." He came to group every week for over two years.

Mitch is back in group now, three-and-a-half years after his first attempt at nonviolence. He did not hit his wife this time. He threatened her and she believed him. He was re-arrested, but he came into group differently than he did the first time. Mitch told the men he should have seen the build-up. His wife had, and she wanted him to rejoin group. He needed a "tune-up." Mitch said that he thought he had really changed because he did not physically attack her. Then he looked at her and saw the fear in her face. He told the men that non-physical violence was just as bad, and how terrible he felt for hurting her again, and betraying her trust. He is working hard again. For Mitch, group will be a touchstone, a safe place. He knows he may need a group on and off throughout his life. He is not unique.

CONCLUSION

Batterers are not a homogenous population and different types may require different approaches. Many batterers can and do make significant changes, but they do not all change, and the changes a batterer makes may not be sufficient for his partner to feel safe and happy in the relationship. Batterers' programs are part of the larger social movement to end violence and the inequitable treatment of women. But such programs are only one part of a much larger network of intervention. They are not cure-alls. They have successes, which certainly keep many of us doing the work. They are links in the chain. They hold out one hope for change.

REFERENCES

Davis, R. C., & Taylor, B. G. (1999). Does batterer treatment reduce violence: A synthesis of the literature. In L. Feder (Ed.), *Women and domestic violence* (pp. 69-93). New York: The Haworth Press, Inc.

Dutton, D. (1995). *The batterer: A psychological profile.* New York: Basic Books.

Hart, B. (1988). Safety for women: Monitoring batterers' programs. Harrisburg Pennsylvania Coalition Against Domestic Violence.

Holtzworth-Munroe, A., & Stuart, G. L. (1994). Typologies of male batterers: Three subtypes and the differences among them. *Psychological Bulletin, 116,* 476-497.

Sonkin, D. J. (1995). *Domestic violence on trial: Psychological and legal dimensions of family violence.* New York: Springer.

Group Intervention Programs for Batterers

Alan Rosenbaum
Penny A. Leisring

SUMMARY. Batterer intervention programs are extremely diverse yet share many common strategies. This article summarizes the relevant issues, and provides an overview of the intervention strategies most commonly included in these programs. Issues discussed include confidentiality, group structure and length, partner contacts, leadership configuration, and program goals. In the second part of the paper, topics and strategies are presented. These include power and control, anger management, time-out, feelings underlying anger, stress reduction, parenting, and the costs of aggression, substance abuse, communication, and cognitions. Finally, brief descriptions of two frequently modeled, pro-feminist programs, Duluth and Emerge, are presented. Similarities and differences between pro-feminist and cognitive-behavioral programs are discussed. *[Article copies available for a fee from The Haworth Document Delivery Service: 1-800-HAWORTH. E-mail address: <getinfo@haworthpressinc.com> Website: <http://www.HaworthPress.com> © 2001 by The Haworth Press, Inc. All rights reserved.]*

KEYWORDS. Batterer, treatment, intervention, domestic violence

Posing questions regarding whether batterer treatment is effective and passing laws, which permit judges to mandate batterers into batterers treatment

[Haworth co-indexing entry note]: "Group Intervention Programs for Batterers." Rosenbaum, Alan and Penny A. Leisring. Co-published simultaneously in *Journal of Aggression, Maltreatment & Trauma* (The Haworth Maltreatment & Trauma Press, an imprint of The Haworth Press, Inc.) Vol. 5, No. 2(#10), 2001, pp. 57-71; and: *Domestic Violence Offenders: Current Interventions, Research, and Implications for Policies and Standards* (ed: Robert A. Geffner, and Alan Rosenbaum) The Haworth Maltreatment & Trauma Press, an imprint of The Haworth Press, Inc., 2001, pp. 57-71. Single or multiple copies of this article are available for a fee from The Haworth Document Delivery Service [1-800-HAWORTH, 9:00 a.m. - 5:00 p.m. (EST). E-mail address: getinfo@haworthpressinc.com].

programs, contributes to the illusion that batterers' treatment is a definable entity. Batterers treatment programs are diverse just as batterers, themselves, are a heterogeneous population. Recognition of the latter point has led to the overuse of the phrase "one size fits all" to describe the illusion that all batterers will benefit from the same type of program. On the other hand, we are only recently beginning to conduct the empirical research to enable prescriptive matching of batterer subtypes to specific treatment regimens. While this notion of prescriptive matching implies a recognition that batterers treatment programs are not all alike, little attention has been paid to how they differ. Descriptive phrases such as psychoeducational, pro-feminist, or cognitive-behavioral belie the many philosophical, structural, and substantive differences between programs, even those with the same categorical designation (e.g., Duluth model). Since there is a lack of research comparing programs, any representation that one approach is superior to another is groundless. The purpose of the present article is simply to describe various treatment issues and approaches to batterers' treatment.

The first issue concerns the term "batterer treatment" itself. Treatment connotes therapy and therapy assumes an underlying psychological problem, which is objectionable to many, especially pro-feminists who insist that battering is exclusively about power and control and not about psychological dysfunction. It is often espoused that battering is a crime and should be punished, not treated. There is also the realistic fear that if battering is seen as a psychological disorder, lawyers will try to take advantage of the diminished capacity defense to secure lighter sentences for their clients. Consequently, it has been argued that the term "batterer intervention" be used in place of "batterer treatment." The controversy is more than semantic. Therapeutic approaches, especially as practiced by professional therapists carry confidentiality considerations that may be inconsistent with the reporting policies of many programs and incompatible with many state standards.

Although there are substantial philosophical differences among programs, there are also many points of agreement. There is little argument that relationship aggression is a crime and should be treated as such by the police and the courts. The fact that it is a crime, however, does not preclude the use of therapeutic approaches to intervention. Criminal behavior and psychological dysfunction are not mutually exclusive. There is general agreement that power and control issues are important and must be dealt with in treatment. One difference among approaches lies in the weight and centrality assigned to power and control issues. Pro-feminist programs see this as the most important topic to be dealt with in treatment; others view this as one of many relevant issues.

Mainstream pro-feminist treaters view protecting the woman/victim as the main objective of batterer treatment. This dictates their behavior vis-a-vis confidentiality issues, such as notifying probation, or the female partner, of missed sessions, drinking, aggressiveness, or even concerns regarding his progress. Many of these programs identify their role as the management and control of batterers. Alternatively, therapeutic programs typically view the batterer as the patient and effective treatment of the batterer as the main program goal. This is consistent with the view that patients will not engage in therapy, nor can they be successfully treated unless they view the treater as an advocate, who has their own best interests at heart. Protection of confidentiality is viewed as essential to the creation of a safe environment where the batterer can discuss his problems, and the therapist can offer suggestions for avoiding such problems in the future, and/or referrals for additional treatment. The value of this is exemplified in the areas of alcohol and substance abuse. If group members are afraid to discuss their use of alcohol or other substances, it impairs the group leader's ability to address the issues and refer for counseling. For therapeutic programs, protection of the victim is achieved as a by-product of the successful treatment of the batterer. They are, of course, also bound by the ethical duties imposed by the Tarasoff decision, which held that therapists have a duty to take whatever steps are reasonably necessary to protect potential victims of their patients' violent acts (Tarasoff v. Regents of the University of California, 1976).

Most commonly, batterers are treated in gender specific groups of determinate length. That is, the groups include only males, and are time limited. Other approaches, for example, the use of couples groups and groups for aggressive females are described elsewhere in this volume and will not be covered in the present article. Although there are groups that are open-ended, they primarily serve self-referred participants and are more similar to standard therapy groups. Groups serving court-mandated batterers are, of necessity, time limited, as judges could not be expected to sentence batterers to programs of indeterminate length. There is considerable inter-program variability regarding group, and session, length.

We recently surveyed the literature and found program length to vary from a low of ten weeks to a high of nine months (see Gondolf, 1997; Palmer, Brown, & Barrera, 1992), and we are also aware of programs lasting longer than one year. Programs employed in research designs may be briefer than those developed solely for clinical purposes. About half of the studies classified length in terms of the number of sessions, while the remainder reported the number of weeks. The length of each session was often unspecified. The Massachusetts standards require 80 hours of treatment. Specifying the number of hours of treatment offers a convention, which more clearly describes program length.

Programs vary in terms of group leadership, with the male-female co-leader team considered by many to be the gold standard. Like gold, however, it is also more expensive and many programs cannot afford the luxury of two group leaders. Groups led by a single male leader and even a single female leader are both common. Dual gender co-leader teams offer opportunities for modeling shared power between males and females, bring a female perspective to the group, and importantly, impede the development of a "good old boys" club atmosphere in the room. On the liability side, maintaining the power balance and avoiding falling into stereotypical patterns of responding (e.g., the male co-leader protecting the female co-leader from group criticism, or worse, the male assuming de-facto leadership of the group) require constant vigilance and can disrupt the normal therapeutic behavior of group leaders. The presence of a female may stifle misogynistic language or beliefs that might otherwise be expressed and processed thus making them unavailable for treatment. Outcome research comparing the various group leadership configurations is needed.

An increasingly common strategy is the use of a two-tiered group structure. The first component is the intake, or informational group. This is usually a shorter term (8 to 12 weeks), highly structured, educational group designed to raise consciousness, provide information, and, in some cases, teach strategies such as the time-out. It may employ rolling admissions since the assumption is that the content is didactic and can be acquired in any order; thus, an individual who enters in session 5 and continues through session 4 will get the same content as the individual who enters in the first session and stays through the last. The objective is primarily educational, consequently, the possibility that changes in group membership will disrupt the development of group process are of no concern. What may be of concern, however, is the possibility that group content may be sequential and therefore learning to use the time out before one has learned to identify anger cues may not be ideal.

The second component of the two-tiered format is the process group. Once the didactic content has been acquired, the assumption is that the group members enter the process component on equal footing with respect to their knowledge of relationship aggression and the strategies that may be employed to eliminate it. The process component is typically much longer and focuses on more complex issues, such as exposure to violence in the family of origin, self-esteem, relationship issues, or their own sexual victimization. Programs vary in terms of whether the process component is also closed- or open-ended. The decision regarding closed/open-endedness is often made on the basis of pragmatic, rather than therapeutic considerations. Many programs lack an insufficient referral base for the closed-ended format to be economically feasible. Others have concerns about waitlisting potentially violent participants even for a short time and open-ended groups allow batterers to enter group more quickly. There are no empirical studies comparing open-ended with closed-ended formats. In general, the open-ended structure is employed for the convenience of the program, rather than for its therapeutic value.

One potential advantage of the two-tiered format, however, concerns recent attempts to apply a transtheoretical model of psychotherapy to batterer treatment (Levesque, Gelles, & Velicer, 1999). There is some evidence and an abundance of speculation that batterers, like other patient populations, can be classified into several stages of readiness for change ranging from pre-contemplative to action and that the use of stage-matched interventions might reduce dropout rates and improve outcomes. If so, the intake group might be viewed as a pre-contemplative, stage-specific group and could be structured to include strategies designed to engage the men in treatment, overcome resistance, and reduce dropout. Similarly, the process group could be targeted at individuals further along the continuum, perhaps in the contemplative, or action, stages. At present, such stage specific interventions have not been published.

There is a great deal of variability among programs regarding both content and emphasis, yet there is also a great deal of commonality in that almost all programs use some combination of the following:

1. Power and control issues: Almost all programs include a presentation and discussion of power and control issues. A mainstay of the pro-feminist model and concretized in the power and control wheel developed by Pence and Paymer (1993), many treaters believe that coercive control underlies all male to female domestic aggression. Batterers are presented with the many forms of aggression and types of control and encouraged to consider the way they use these strategies in their intimate relationships. Much of this is consciousness raising, as batterers are often aware of the wrongness of hitting, but do not consider restricting activities, monitoring behavior, restricting access to money, or treating their partners as servants as abusive. Most programs also discuss alternatives to power and control strategies, for example, Geffner and Mantooth (2000) include these behaviors on an "equality wheel" which was adapted from the Duluth program.

2. Anger cues: Teaching batterers to identify cues that they are becoming angry offers several benefits. There is some evidence that batterers fail to correctly label their emotional states until they become highly aroused, by which time they are impaired in their ability to modulate their emotions or to think clearly regarding alternatives and consequences. Helping them to identify physical, behavioral, and psychological cues earlier in the anger trajectory increases the likelihood that they can preempt the buildup and choose a more reasonable alternative. Situational cues are also presented. Batterers are taught to identify "hot topics" and to avoid replicating trouble spots.

Concrete suggestions, such as remaining seated during arguments, avoiding affect-laden topics while riding in automobiles, and carefully choosing times and places for working out disagreements are often presented.

3. Time out: Most programs teach some variation of the time-out procedure. Batterers are encouraged to identify cues that their anger is building and remove themselves (physically) from the argument until they have calmed down sufficiently to continue the interaction. The combination of identifying cues and using time-out are the foundations of anger management.

4. Feelings underlying anger–the anger funnel: Although some have argued that battering is not about anger, anger management seems to be a feature of many batterer treatment programs. The anger funnel is a metaphor for the idea that men are socialized to suppress all emotions except anger and thus anger becomes the only acceptable way to express feelings. As such, anger becomes a proxy for hurt, fear, sadness, shame, and other painful emotions. Helping batterers get in touch with the actual emotions can be therapeutic in and of itself, but can also be used to get the men to address the emotions they are feeling. For example, telling a partner that they are hurt is potentially more productive than disguising it as anger and gives the partner a chance to respond to the true feeling.

5. Costs of aggression: Most batterer programs take a multifaceted, "whatever works," approach to the problem. Focusing on the many costs of aggression including, financial costs, effects on their own and partner's health, effects on children, effects on career, damage to the relationship, loss of intimacy, loss of freedom, and loss of status in the community increases the likelihood that batterers will learn that the negative consequences of using aggression outweigh any benefits. Discussing the effects on children can be particularly powerful, since many batterers witnessed violence in their own families and have negative feelings about their fathers.

6. Alcohol and substance abuse: Alcohol and aggression are inextricably linked, and although as Kantor and Straus (1990) noted, alcohol is neither necessary nor sufficient for the occurrence of relationship aggression, it is a common accompaniment. Programs differ in their handling of these issues. Some require group members to be in alcohol or substance abuse treatment prior to or during batterers' treatment. Others include a module in which they discuss the relationship between alcohol and aggression, raise consciousness about the problems associated with alcohol and substance use, and provide information and referral.

7. Communication Training: Batterers may have poor communication skills and typically are not good listeners. They tend to be defensive in

discussions and magnify the importance of winning the argument by tying their sense of self worth to being right and having their way. Because they lack good communication skills and may be less articulate than their partners, they sometimes resort to violence as a conflict resolution strategy. Although communication is a dyadic issue, which may be more effectively worked on in a couple counseling environment, some groups include a communication component. This might involve encouraging the men to listen, ask questions, use "I" language, and paraphrase. It also may involve teaching batterers about the different elements of communication, such as tone, posture, facial expression, volume, gestures, content, and the fact that they may send mixed messages, for example, if the tone and content are discrepant.

8. Cognitions: Based on the premise that batterers rile themselves up with inflammatory cognitions in the absence of factual information, many programs include a cognitive component. Presented with the scenario that "your partner is two hours late in coming home and she hasn't called to let you know where she is," many batterers will make the interpretation that she is out "screwing someone" or some other negative attribution. Pressed for alternative possibilities, it often takes a long time (if ever) to get less negative suggestions (e.g., maybe she had an accident or is stuck in traffic). Non-batterers, in contrast, will more often conjure non-inflammatory, or even empathetic, possibilities (Gearan & Rosenbaum, 1997). Batterers may be taught to identify this pattern and to replace the inflammatory cognitions with more calming ones, or at the least, to suspend judgment until they find out what is really going on.

9. Relaxation and stress reduction: Batterers more often come from lower socio-economic strata and report a variety of stressors including financial stress, work stress, parenting stress, and family stress. They often see themselves as helpless in the face of these stressors and take no steps to alleviate them. Programs may take a problem solving approach to reducing stress, teaching batterers to identify specific stressors, generate possible solutions, evaluate pros and cons of each, select the most reasonable alternative, and try it out. Relaxation protocols (deep muscular relaxation, breathing exercises, mental imagery) may be used to provide the men with skills they can use to reduce tension and/or anger. These skills may be used in conjunction with other techniques taught in group. For example, when angered, the men may be taught to take a time-out, relax, identify inflammatory cognitions, and replace them with calming ones.

10. Parenting: In addition to problems with their partners, many batterers have difficulty relating to, and interacting with, their children. Having low self-esteem, many are excessively sensitive to disrespect and view

their children's misbehavior as a personal failure, and/or an embarrassment. Some were brought up with excessive physical discipline and are angered and frustrated by society's recent intolerance of physical discipline. Batterers may be taught how to empathize with the child, the importance of developing a positive parent-child relationship, and the value of non-physical means of child management, such as the "other time out," the use of consistent consequences and positive reinforcement.

11. Future orientation: This is a recent development in our own program and may not be in use elsewhere. It is presented here so that others might consider its utilization in batterer treatment. This begins with the premise that the immediate consequences of aggression are often positive. These include feelings of power or superiority, a release of tension, and the accomplishment of the objective for which the violence was intended (e.g., to silence the other, to get one's way, to hurt the other). On the other hand, the long-term consequences of aggression are mostly negative. These include loss of intimacy, loss of relationship, financial costs, legal consequences, and many others. Combine this with the fact that many batterers have no long-range future orientation. By this, we mean that if you ask a group of batterers how they see their lives going five, or even three, years from now, you will get few responses. You might have to ask what they see themselves doing the next day or even right after group before you get an answer. In short, they do not think of the future, or rather, their future is very contracted. They do not think long term, yet it is the long-term consequences of aggression that are the negative ones. Absent this future orientation, the immediate consequences of aggression take precedence and thus aggression is reinforced. One explanation for this absence of a future orientation may be that many batterers grew up in inner city, or high crime environments. Many witnessed the deaths of friends or family members at an early age and did not expect to reach adulthood themselves. It is not surprising that they live in the present. Helping the men to think about their lives and relationships in a longer time frame might bring some of the longer-range negative consequences to bear on their current behavioral choices.

12. Assertiveness: Batterers are often saddled with traditional male attitudes that they must be strong and self-reliant. In addition to some of the negative consequences that this has for their partner, it also puts a great deal of pressure on the men, themselves. They may be unable to ask for help from their partners. They may also have difficulty admitting they are wrong, giving and receiving compliments, refusing requests by others. There is research indicating that batterers have difficulty with spouse-specific assertion, that is, asserting themselves in their relationships (O'Leary & Curley, 1986; Rosenbaum & O'Leary, 1981).

Teaching proper assertiveness may reduce aggression and is therefore included in many batterers treatment programs.

13. Empathy with the victim: Developing empathy and compassion are excellent ways of reducing aggression both in and outside of relationships. The military, for example, seeks to dehumanize the enemy because they know it will be more difficult for soldiers to fight someone if they think of his wife and children, or the fact that he is someone's son. The use of such terms as "Krauts," "Japs," or "Pit Bulls" serves the function of objectifying the enemy, thereby facilitating aggression toward them. Thinking of women as "bitches"or "whores" serves a similar function. Programs typically focus on the importance of using non-sexist language. Thinking about what it feels like to be abused themselves, and then projecting that onto their partners and/or children helps many batterers. Do they want their families feeling about them the way they felt about their own fathers?

14. Using media: Many programs employ films, videotapes, and printed handouts to convey some of the content of the program. The Duluth Program, for example, has developed videotapes specifically for their program. These tapes are only available to individuals who have completed their training program. In our own program (The Men's Workshop), we use several films including a film on *Battered Women* (Crowley, 1976), a film on alcohol and substance abuse entitled *Alcohol and Cocaine: The Secret of Addiction* (Siedor & Sykes, 1990), and two clips from the *Time-Out* series (O. D. N. Productions, Inc.). Other films and videotapes made specifically for batterers treatment are also available (e.g., *Shadows of the Heart* by Stosny & Garcia, 1991). Intermedia productions (see reference for Stosny & Garcia for contact information) offers a selection of these materials. These films tend to promote discussion about key points and also present issues in a dramatic and often poignant fashion. The use of handouts is also popular as it provides reminders and review of material covered. Geffner and Mantooth (2000) is a workbook containing a variety of worksheets culled from many different programs throughout the United States. The workbooks themselves may be purchased, or batterers and programs may choose to reproduce those sheets they find most appropriate for distribution to batterers.

15. Partner contacts: Partner contacts are employed for several reasons: to provide referral information and to assess whether the woman is aware of shelter and legal services; to dispel illusions regarding the safety of returning to, or staying with, her partner now that he is being treated; to obtain more accurate descriptions of the batterer's behavior vis-a-vis aggression and/or substance use; to inform her of his progress or the lack thereof; to warn her regarding her safety; and to solicit informa-

tion used to make decisions regarding continuation, or termination of treatment. While many programs endorse the importance of partner contacts, in principal, in practice they are difficult to enact, time consuming, expensive, and potentially dangerous. Many partners, especially those who are no longer in the relationship, desire privacy. Others fear that any contact with the program might provoke retaliation from the batterer. Programs that include partner contacts frequently report low contact rates. There is also the question of whether any information provided by the partner, which contradicts information provided by the batterer, can be used in treatment without endangering the partner.

The foregoing is intended to provide a brief overview of many of the more popular techniques and strategies that are in use in various programs throughout the United States. There may be many omissions, since not every program has published its protocols or curricula. It is probably also true that there are few programs that cover all of the material presented. Many of these strategies are not unique to batterers' treatment and have been more than adequately described in the literature. Many programs are willing to share their treatment manuals and materials with others seeking to develop programs of their own; however, some programs do not have such materials, and others (such as Duluth) charge fees for their training and materials.

To illuminate further what batterer treatment programs are like, two feminist programs will be described in more detail, the Emerge program in Cambridge, Massachusetts and the Domestic Abuse Intervention Project (DAIP) in Duluth, Minnesota. Though there are countless other programs that deserve detailed descriptions, these two programs were selected for the purposes of this article because they are commonly used as models for other programs around the country. They will be compared and contrasted with typical therapeutic cognitive-behavioral interventions for batterers to illustrate the similarities and differences between feminist programs and cognitive-behavioral programs.

Emerge, a pro-feminist batterers treatment program, was founded in 1977. Similar to the Duluth program, it places particular emphasis on issues of power and control. The program is comprised of a minimum of 48 two-hour sessions. The groups typically have two co-leaders and 9-12 clients in each. Clients are not allowed into the Emerge program unless they sign releases allowing staff at the program to contact their partners, probation officers, child protective services, and others. The program is an educational service, not psychological treatment, and therefore, confidentiality privileges do not apply (Program Manual, 1998).

The first eight sessions comprise the "First Phase" of treatment. These initial sessions cover definitions of violence and include discussions about psychological, sexual, and economic abuse in addition to physical. Also discussed are positive and negative self-talk, the effects of violence on women and children, communication skills, and quick versus long-term solutions toward repairing relationships (Program Manual, 1998). Sessions start with a 20-30 minute check-in period during which members describe their abusive behaviors, their partner's injuries, their restraining orders, and their use of drugs and alcohol during the week. They are also asked to state their partner's name and the names and ages of their children. Group members are instructed to refer to their partners by their first names to make it less likely that their partners are viewed as possessions or objects (Healy, Smith, & O'Sullivan, 1998). Presentations are then made about specific topics for 60-80 minutes. The last 10 minutes is a check-out period where members make brief comments about the group. The counselors check-out last and summarize the main points of the group or comment on previous statements made by group members (Program Manual, 1998).

Group members must comply with safety plans while in the program. As part of these safety plans they must refrain from engaging in any type of abuse. They must also refrain from using drugs or alcohol 24 hours before or after sessions, they must comply with court orders, they must respect their partners' limits, and they must cease attempts to isolate their partners from others. Clients are expected to report any violations of their safety plans to the program and must accept the consequences for their actions. Clients must pay an extra fee every eight weeks to pay for partner contact or contact with other agencies (Program Manual, 1998). Partners are sent pamphlets entitled "What You Should Know About Your Violent Partner." This pamphlet provides women with answers to commonly asked questions by battered women, a brief description of the Emerge program, and referral numbers for support and counseling services.

In order to successfully move on to the "Second Phase" of treatment, clients must admit having engaged in some type of abuse, they must participate in groups, they must cooperate with program rules, they must pay the fees for the program, and they must adhere to the attendance policy which stipulates that they cannot miss two consecutive sessions, and cannot have more than one unexcused absence (Program Manual, 1998). During the second phase of treatment, attitudes that perpetuate abuse are challenged, men work on establishing goals for change, and participants help other men achieve change by sharing their experiences and insights. During the second-stage groups, men learn to interact in a respectful manner with women and children and learn non-abusive ways to handle conflict. Emerge was in the process of writing a manual for their second-stage groups at the time of this printing and expect to have it completed in the spring of 2000 (D. Adams, personal communication, January 21, 2000). Throughout treatment, counselors at Emerge take an active role in interrupting any devaluation of women and elicit validating interpretations of women's words and actions (Adams, 1988).

Another feminist program, the Domestic Abuse Intervention Project (DAIP) was started after a brutal domestic homicide in Duluth, Minnesota in 1980. This program has become a model for other batterer intervention programs and is now referred to as the "Duluth Model." Consultants involved in the development of the model included activists in the battered women's movement and Joe Morse and Miguel Gil from the Emerge program (Pence & Paymar, 1993). The program involves community-wide coordination among police officers, probation officers, family and criminal court judges, prosecutors, jailers, the women's shelter, and the rehabilitation program (Pence, 1989). The curriculum is based on the premise that violence is used as a means of controlling other people's behavior. Central to the curriculum is the Power and Control Wheel, which was designed by over 200 battered women in Duluth (Pence & Paymar, 1993). It illustrates that physical violence is part of a larger pattern of controlling behavior including intimidation, emotional abuse, isolation, minimization, using children, using male privilege, economic abuse, and coercion.

In the Duluth program, men have an initial intake in groups of six to ten men. The intakes are conducted in a group format for efficiency and because it seems that men are less defensive in the group format, and seem to blame their victims less than men in individual intakes. Men are not allowed into the program unless they sign a release of information. This release allows the program staff to communicate with representatives of the court and corrections department, the partners of the participants, therapists, and chemical dependency counselors. Men attend a group orientation session, which includes introductions, a description of the time-out technique, and an explanation of the group rules, themes of the curriculum, control logs, and action plans. Men are placed the following week in an ongoing 24-week group. Sessions are two hours in length and cover eight themes for three weeks each. The eight themes of the curriculum include nonviolence, non-threatening behavior, respect, support and trust, accountability and honesty, sexual respect, partnership, and negotiation and fairness. Groups are most often led by a male and female co-leader team. As in the Emerge program, group members are asked to refer to their partners by their first name (Pence & Paymar, 1993).

Groups begin each week with a check-in period during which new group members are introduced and old group members report on their action plans and any use of violence or abuse during the previous week (Pence & Paymar, 1993). Action plans are written accounts of goals and concrete realistic steps that can be taken to change controlling and abusive behaviors. Videotaped portrayals of various men engaging in abusive and violent behavior are used to sensitize men to their own control patterns. These are shown to promote accountability and a "keener awareness of the contradiction between the men's stated intentions . . . and the actual consequences" of their behavior (Adams, 1989b, p. 71). Control logs are also a central part of the Duluth curriculum. They are written sheets that assist group members in analyzing abusive incidents. They are used to help men identify abusive actions, intents and beliefs that they use to justify their actions, motivating feelings, the effects of their abusive behavior on others, the relationship between past violence and their partners' current behavior. Further, the logs help men to identify alternative non-controlling behavior (Pence & Paymar, 1993).

Partner contacts are an important part of the Duluth program. Partners of each participant in the program are contacted by phone. Women who can not be reached by phone are contacted by mail. Partners are invited to attend a women's orientation session and an ongoing support group. They are given information about available resources in the community and they are asked to provide the program with a history of their partners' abusiveness (Pence & Paymar, 1993).

Feminist programs like the Duluth Program and Emerge share many similarities with cognitive-behavioral approaches to batterer treatment. Both feminist and cognitive-behavioral programs typically use broad definitions of abuse, which incorporate emotional, verbal, and sexual abuse, in addition to physical abuse. They point out that acts of physical aggression are not typically isolated incidents but rather occur in the context of other intimidating, controlling, and abusive behavior. Issues of power and control are addressed in both types of programs. Skill deficits, such as being able to communicate with others effectively and nonviolently are addressed in cognitive-behavioral programs as well as in some feminist programs, like Emerge. All programs emphasize that using violence to control others and solve problems is unacceptable and program leaders strive to make batterers take responsibility for their actions. Emerge, Duluth, and many other programs use "control logs" to help men become more aware of their behavior (Adams, 1989b). Men are asked to monitor their own actions by using written checklists of violent and controlling behavior (Adams, 1989b).

Feminist programs and cognitive-behavioral programs also differ in critical ways. Though they both place emphasis on power and control issues and skill deficits, historically feminist programs place more emphasis on power and control and less emphasis on skill deficits than cognitive-behavioral programs. It seems that though some feminist programs incorporate the teaching of anger management skills, stress management, and communication skills, they feel that anger management programs are inappropriate because they "misname the problem" (Adams, 1989a). It is thought by some that naming a program "anger management" implies that battering occurs because of anger and not because of power and control. Feminist programs emphasize the importance of confronting the sexist expectations and attitudes, which prevent batterers from utilizing appropriate skills in noncontrolling ways (Adams, 1989a). Typically feminist programs have more contact with partners, are less constrained by confidentiality issues, and have less emphasis on therapeutic rapport than cognitive-behavioral programs. Pence (1989) described the goal of the Duluth program as "the protection of battered women, not the fixing of batterers" (p. 30). Pro-feminist and cognitive-behavioral programs may differ in the amount of information provided to victims and also in the degree to which batterers feel safe divulging information regarding aggression and substance use during group. Despite these differences, it seems that many of the issues and topics covered in the various programs are quite similar.

There are as many different approaches to batterer intervention as there are batterer intervention programs. Many share a common heritage, tracing their philosophies and/or protocols to more established and better known programs, such as Duluth or Emerge. Others based their curricula on published protocols such as Sonkin and Durphy (1982), or Mantooth, Geffner, Patrick, and Franks (1987). Still others modeled their programs on existing programs in their areas, many of which did not have published materials. It is unclear at this time whether any of these programs are more effective than no treatment, and there is no evidence that any particular approach is more effective than any other. Batterer intervention is a work in progress. It is hoped that future research will help refine the process and guide the development of more effective interventions.

REFERENCES

Adams, D. (1988). Treatment models of men who batter: A profeminist analysis. In K. Yllo & M. Bograd (Eds.), *Feminist perspectives on wife abuse* (pp. 176-199). Beverly Hills, CA: Sage.

Adams, D. (1989a). Feminist-based interventions for battering men. In P. L. Caesar & L. K. Hamberger (Eds.), *Treating men who batter: Theory, practice, and programs* (pp. 3-23). New York: Springer.

Adams, D. (1989b). Stages of anti-sexist awareness and change for men who batter. In L. Dickstein & C. Nadelson (Eds.), *Family violence: Emerging issues of a national crisis* (pp. 63-94). Washington, DC: American Psychiatric Press.

Crowley, C. (Director). (1976). *Battered women: Violence behind closed doors* [Film]. (Available from J. Gary Mitchell Film Company, P.O. Box 2438, Sebastopol, CA 95473-2438).

Gearan, P., & Rosenbaum, A. (1997, July). *Cognitive differences between batterers and nonbatterers.* Paper presented at the 5th Annual International Family Violence Research Conference, Durham, NH.

Geffner, R., & Mantooth, C. (2000). *Workbook to accompany ending spouse/partner abuse: A psychoeducational approach for individuals and couples.* New York: Springer.

Gondolf, E. (1997). Patterns of reassault in batterer programs. *Violence and Victims, 12,* 373-887.

Healey, K., Smith, C., & O'Sullivan, C. (February, 1998). Batterer intervention: Program approaches and criminal justice strategies. *Issues and practices in criminal justice.* National Institute of Justice.

Kantor, G., & Straus, M. A. (1990). The drunken bum theory of wife beating. In M. A. Straus & R. J. Gelles (Eds.), *Physical Violence in American Families* (pp. 203-224). New Brunswick, NJ: Transaction Press.

Levesque, D. A., Gelles, R. J., & Velicer, W. F. (1999, July). *Assessing decisional balance among men who batter: An application of the transtheoretical model of change to partner violence cessation.* Paper presented at the 6th Annual International Family Violence Research Conference, Durham, NH.

Mantooth, C., Geffner, R., Patrick, J., & Franks, A. D. (1987). *Family preservation: A treatment program for reducing couple violence.* Tyler, TX: University of Texas at Tyler Press.

O. D. N. Productions, Inc. (Producer and Distributor). (1981). *Time Out* [Film]. (Available from O. D. N. Productions, Inc., 74 Varick Street, New York, NY 10013).

O'Leary, K. D., & Curley, A. D. (1986). Assertion and family violence: Correlates of spouse abuse. *Journal of Marital and Family Therapy, 12,* 281-290.

Palmer, S. E., Brown, R. A., & Barrera, M. E. (1992). Group treatment program for abusive husbands: A long-term evaluation. *American Journal of Orthopsychiatry, 62,* 276-283.

Pence, E. (1989). Batterer programs: Shifting from community collusion to community confrontation. In P. L. Caesar & L. K. Hamberger (Eds.), *Treating men who batter: Theory, practice, and programs.* New York: Springer Publishing Company, Inc.

Pence, P., & Paymar, M. (1993). *Education groups for men who batter: The Duluth model.* New York: Springer.

Program manual: First stage groups for men who batter. (1998). Cambridge, Massachusetts: Emerge.

Rosenbaum, A., & O'Leary, K. D. (1981). Marital violence: Characteristics of abusive couples. *Journal of Consulting and Clinical Psychology, 49,* 63-71.

Siedor, C. (Executive Producer), & Sykes, M. (Producer). (1990). *Alcohol and cocaine: The secret of addiction* [Film]. (Available from Drystar Television, Inc., Atlanta, Georgia).

Sonkin, D. J., & Durphy, M. (1982). *Learning to live without violence.* San Francisco, CA: Volcano Press.

Stosny, S. (Writer), & Garcia, M. (Director). (1991). *Shadows of the heart: A treatment tape for male batterers* [Film]. (Available from Intermedia, 1700 Westlake Ave. N. Suite 724, Seattle, WA 98109).

Tarasoff v. Regents of the University of California, 131 Cal. Rptr. 14, 551 P.2d 334 (1976).

Female Perpetrators of Partner Aggression: Relevant Issues and Treatment

Lynn Dowd

SUMMARY. The topic of female partner aggression has been a contro-versial focus of debate over the past 25 years, and yet we lack a coherent body of literature that effectively describes the phenomenon of female partner violence and guides the treatments we are able to provide. This paper is an attempt to gather and integrate the fragments of data that we do have with related treatment issues, such as substance abuse, trauma, and attachment disorders, that appear to be highly relevant to this popu-lation. A structured cognitive-behavioral group treatment program, de-signed to address women's needs as both victims and perpetrators, is described, and suggestions for further investigation are offered. *[Article copies available for a fee from The Haworth Document Delivery Service: 1-800-HAWORTH. E-mail address: <getinfo@haworthpressinc.com> Website: <http://www.HaworthPress.com> © 2001 by The Haworth Press, Inc. All rights reserved.]*

KEYWORDS. Domestic violence, partner abuse, female batterers, bat-tered women, treatment, gender

Partner violence perpetrated by women has been a taboo topic for much of the past two decades. Despite the rapidly expanding literature on family vio-

---

[Haworth co-indexing entry note]: "Female Perpetrators of Partner Aggression: Relevant Issues and Treatment." Dowd, Lynn. Co-published simultaneously in *Journal of Aggression, Maltreatment & Trauma* (The Haworth Maltreatment & Trauma Press, an imprint of The Haworth Press, Inc.) Vol. 5, No. 2(#10), 2001, pp. 73-104; and: *Domestic Violence Offenders: Current Interventions, Research, and Implications for Pol-icies and Standards* (ed: Robert A. Geffner, and Alan Rosenbaum) The Haworth Maltreatment & Trauma Press, an imprint of The Haworth Press, Inc., 2001, pp. 73-104. Single or multiple copies of this article are available for a fee from The Haworth Document Delivery Service [1-800-HAWORTH, 9:00 a.m. - 5:00 p.m. (EST). E-mail address: getinfo@haworthpressinc.com].

lence and battering that has accumulated in recent years, the investigation of female aggression in domestic violence has been restricted almost entirely to the perpetration of child abuse. Since the initial discussion of data on women's partner aggression by Steinmetz (1977-78), and the publication of the results of the 1975 national survey of family violence by Straus, Gelles, and Steinmetz (1980), there has been lively debate among community activists, researchers, battered women's service providers, and mental health professionals about the meaning of these, and subsequent, findings. In the context of marital violence, women have traditionally been seen exclusively as victims, their own aggression all but ignored (McNeely & Robinson-Simpson, 1987). Acknowledging and investigating female partner aggression has been dismissed as victim-blaming by some (e.g., Kurz, 1993), but as essential to the understanding and prevention of family violence by others (Straus, 1997; White & Kowalski, 1994).

Mandatory arrest policies are gaining popularity in many jurisdictions as a response to the epidemic of domestic violence. In recent years, women have been increasingly prosecuted for assaultive behavior and are often mandated to treatment. While many have expressed concerns about this turn of events (e.g., Hamberger & Arnold, 1990), and the reliance on the judgment and attitudes of the police officers involved (Martin, 1997; Saunders, 1995), it can be seen as an additional opportunity to intervene with violent couples. Unfortunately, little information is available about these women and the circumstances that precipitated their legal involvement. Few services are available, and many of those that are open to women may have been designed based on the assumption that male and female partner aggression have similar dynamics. While there may be some overlap of the relevant issues, it is unlikely that the same interventions will adequately address the women's needs and behaviors. As with male abusers, women who are adjudicated for partner violence are increasingly referred to mental health practitioners, who are unprepared and looking to a sparse literature for guidance in the development of effective treatments. This article is an effort to identify what is known about this population and how treatment is currently conceptualized.

ARE WOMEN AGGRESSIVE?
PARAMETERS OF THE DEBATE

That women engage in partner aggression has been well documented in a number of studies, including samples of dating, cohabiting, and married couples. Findings from two national surveys (Straus & Gelles, 1990b; Straus et al., 1980) and numerous studies of both community (e.g., Bland & Orn, 1986; Kwong, Bartholomew &

Dutton, 1999), clinical (e.g., Cascardi, Langhinrichsen, & Vivian, 1992), and special population (e.g., DeKeseredy & Schwartz, 1998) samples show that women are as likely to be aggressive toward their partners as men are. Nevertheless, female partner violence is often minimized or denied.

A number of reasons have been suggested to account for the underdevelopment of this area in the research and treatment agenda. Methodological differences in sampling and defining abuse in sources such as crime statistics, representative surveys, and battered women's shelters, yield widely varying accounts of the prevalence of female-perpetrated aggression. Those that define abuse in terms of criminal acts or injury to the victim often show extremely low rates of violent acts by women (Straus, 1999), contributing to the impression that women's partner aggression is extremely rare. Straus has suggested that these low rates are a result of underreporting as well as the fact that women's aggression is less likely to result in injury or a call to the police. Furthermore, as a society, we may tend to dismiss male victimization as a result of persistent sexual stereotypes of men as always stronger, more aggressive, and less vulnerable than women. Some studies have demonstrated attitudes among both men and women that minimize the seriousness of female aggression (Arias & Johnson, 1989), or that see women's aggression as causing minor, if any, injury (Fiebert & Gonzalez, 1997).

While traditional sociological explanations of marital violence (often called "feminist") held that the patriarchal organization of society was responsible for husband-to-wife violence and control, a growing literature on lesbian couples that demonstrates high rates of partner aggression (Renzetti, 1992) suggests the need for a more thoughtful and complex analysis. The implication is that partner abuse is not necessarily a gendered phenomenon, and that we need to look beyond patriarchal privilege for a more complete explanation for some, if not all, forms of domestic violence.

Concern has been expressed that a focus on female-initiated or bidirectional aggression would undermine the feminist agenda to end oppression of women as typified by male abuse of women, and possibly jeopardize funding and support for essential battered women's services (Kurz, 1993). There is also apprehension that the information would be misused in court to defend male batterers (Straus & Gelles, 1990b). Finally, a traditional bias by a male-dominated research establishment has resulted in a preference for studying men and men's issues, resulting in the development of male models of behavior (White & Kowalski, 1994). Until recently, gender differences were neglected, or studied as an afterthought (Macaulay, 1985). This has been a significant disadvantage in the advancement of our understanding of female aggression in general, and female partner violence in particular.

To focus on female aggression in intimate relationships is not to deny the overwhelmingly greater damage sustained by women at the hands of male partners. We are all indebted to the women's liberation movement which first identified the role of the patriarchy in making oppression and abuse of women possible and acceptable on a societal level. In the same vein, the shelter movement heightened our awareness of the prevalence and seriousness of the problems faced by abused women, and organized resources to begin to address their needs on an individual and community level. As the academic and mental health communities became more involved in the study and treatment of family violence, a greater focus was developed on the characteristics and behaviors of the male batterer. Concerns about victim-blaming and relieving the batterer of responsibility for his behavior shifted attention away from violence by women. Thus we know little about women who aggress against their mates. Viewing the woman only as "victim," until quite recently we have not routinely asked domestically violent women and their partners the same questions asked of male batterers and their victims. With the advent of mandatory arrest for domestic violence, more women are processed through the court systems for aggressive acts against their partners. In one community, the referral rate of women to mandated counseling increased by 12-fold following implementation of mandatory arrest, as compared to a doubling of the referral rate for men (Hamberger & Arnold, 1990). Both adjudicated women and self-identified aggressive women are in need of services to assist them in non-violent resolution of domestic issues. Our ability to design appropriate treatment and prevention programming is limited by our inadequate knowledge of the etiology of female partner aggression. We cannot address the problem of family violence in a comprehensive way without understanding the phenomenon of female-directed aggression and its meaning in the cultural, familial, and individual contexts. Thus a multidimensional understanding of female partner violence, as called for by a number of investigators for domestic violence in general (Coleman, 1994; Dutton, 1994; Miller, 1994), appears to be the most useful model in guiding our research agenda and the development of treatment strategies. Such a conceptualization would take into account the significance of cultural, subcultural, familial, neurological, physiological, and psychological variables.

DEFINITIONS

Language used in describing violent couples and their acts is often ill-defined, lacking in operational definition, or laden with emotional, judgmental, or political connotation (Hamberger, 1997; Hamberger & Potente, 1994;

Marrugo & Kreger, 1996). For instance, "battering" is a term that is associated with a man's repeated acts that produce physical injury in a female victim. Is this an accurate term for a woman who has been mandated to treatment for a single retaliative episode? Is "mutual battering" an accurate way to describe bidirectional violence in which only one partner sustains serious injury? Hamberger and Potente (1994) offer the term "domestically violent women," and Marrugo and Kreger (1996), in writing about the roles in violent lesbian couples, suggest the use of "participant," as more neutral terms that do not carry the same unspoken and potentially inaccurate assumptions about the nature and meaning of the behaviors under study. "Participant" is seen as distinct from the traditional categories of "perpetrator" and "victim," and is defined as someone who fights back against his or her partner with the intention of causing harm or getting even with the partner. This is not to deny that there are women who do behave in ways that are consistent with the classic male batterer, as can be seen in the accounts of both male (Cook, 1997) and lesbian victimized partners (Renzetti, 1992). However, the use of more neutral and behaviorally based terms seems more appropriate, given how little we know about the nature of women's partner aggression.

Ganley (1981) identified four forms of spousal abuse: physical violence, sexual violence, psychological abuse, and destruction of property and pets. All forms of partner aggression can result in psychological devastation for the victim and witnesses. The literature shows that some women, in both heterosexual and lesbian relationships, do engage in these acts against their partners (Renzetti, 1992; Straus & Gelles, 1990b; Straus et al., 1980). Furthermore, it should be noted that an essential element of partner violence is the presence of coercion and fear, which is more likely, in heterosexual relationships, for women, who are in greater danger of suffering injury at the hands of their male partners (O'Leary & Curley, 1986).

Hamberger and Potente (1994) studied heterosexual women who were court referred for partner assault, and described their sample as largely battered women who used violence as self-defense, retaliation, or in response to fears of imminent attack by their partners. They suggested that "it is appropriate to view domestically violent women, as a group, as battered women who have gotten caught up in a pattern of violence that, most often, they did not initiate and do not control" (p. 128). These authors wrestled with the question of whether such a population should be mandated into treatment, given the context of their violent behavior. They concluded that since these women had not previously accessed battered women's services, mandated treatment constituted another way of intervening to support and empower them. Additional support for this position may be seen in the findings that women suffer more severe injuries than men in bidirectionally violent couples (Cascardi et al.,

1992), and that women's aggressive responding to abuse or provocation may place them at greater risk for injury (Straus, 1993). Thus, intervening with women who are mandated into treatment may reduce their risk of future victimization by their partners. It has been argued that the reduction in female partner aggression may actually be crucial to the reduction of men's assaultiveness toward women (Arias & Johnson, 1989; Straus & Gelles, 1990a), because of the justification it offers men for retaliation.

Another perspective is that women, too, are committing unlawful acts that are harmful to the targeted partner as well as witnessing children (Straus, 1993). However, Hamberger (1997) has advocated for thorough training of police officers and court prosecutors in the dynamics of partner violence, to establish the context of women's aggression, and thus avoid further victimization of battered women who are violent in self-defense.

CURRENT RESEARCH AND LITERATURE

The literature on female human aggression seems meager in comparison to that of female animal species, but nevertheless, a review is beyond the scope of the current paper. The interested reader is referred to Eagly and Steffen (1986), Fishbein (1992), and Macaulay (1985) for discussions of social psychological and psychobiological issues in gender and aggression research. Fishbein posits that generally men are more aggressive than women due to exposure to masculinizing hormones in utero and at puberty. Her analysis of the psychobiology of female aggression attributes "inappropriate and excessive" (p. 101) aggression in women to the interaction of socio-environmental and biological vulnerabilities. Such factors might include abuse and neglect, and neurological and endocrinological abnormalities, such as low IQ, extreme hormonal fluctuations, thyroid disorders, and depression. An early review of social psychological research on gender and aggression (Frodi, Macaulay & Thome, 1977) did not take a position on the existence of biological differences, but focused on socialization and situational factors that might operate to amplify or reduce the possible biological effects. Despite the myriad of variables that were seen as potentially significant, a clear and persistent pattern overall was not identified. However, the authors did state that "if empathy-arousing factors are controlled and if the arousal of aggression anxiety is avoided by justification of aggression, women may act as aggressively as men" (p. 654). A later meta-analytic review by Eagley and Steffen (1986) also found inconsistent differences in aggression across gender, but found that generally, men were more aggressive than women, particularly regarding physical aggression. Their explanation was that aggressive behavior is mediated by differences between the genders in the beliefs they held about aggression. The authors concluded that

> women, more than men, perceived that enacting a behavior would produce harm to the target, guilt and anxiety in oneself, as well as danger to oneself. . . . (A)ggression sex differences are a function of perceived consequences of aggression that are learned as aspects of gender roles and other social roles. (p. 309)

Among the many limitations of the studies reviewed, perhaps the most unfortunate, for the purpose of the present paper, is the lack of research examining aggression between people who were linked by personal or organizational relationship.

Despite the proliferation of domestic violence research, only a minimal number of studies have specifically addressed the narrower topic of women's aggression toward their partners. For the purposes of this paper the reader may assume that studies utilized a heterosexual sample unless otherwise specified, due to the overwhelmingly greater focus on heterosexual aggression research in the literature.

Prevalence

The first major study to collect data on women's partner aggression was the 1975 National Family Violence Survey (Straus et al., 1980), which asked both women and men about their own behavior toward their partner, as well as their partner's behavior toward them. The results indicated that women engaged in both minor and severe relationship aggression as often as did men. In approximately half of the families reporting partner violence, both partners were physically aggressive, and the remainder of the cases were divided evenly between women and men as the sole perpetrator of violence. These results were confirmed in a resurvey in 1985, in which 124 couples per thousand experienced wife to husband aggression, and in 48 couples per thousand, the wife to husband aggression was classified as severe (e.g., kicking, punching, biting, or choking) (Straus & Gelles, 1990a). In addition to equal rates of physical assaultiveness, women and men have been found to engage in equal amounts of verbal or symbolic aggression, such as name-calling, insulting, sulking, slamming doors, and throwing things, against their partners. In one study, 75% of women acknowledged at least one such act of aggression in the past year, with a mean average of 10.3 incidents per year. They also reported a decrease in verbal/symbolic aggression with age, as did men (Straus & Sweet, 1992).

Steinmetz (1977-78) published a discussion of the 1975 findings and re-lated studies entitled "The Battered Husband Syndrome," which touched off an emotional and continuing debate regarding the validity of the findings, the meaning of women's partner violence, and women's responsibility for their roles and behaviors. Some of the issues raised by Steinmetz, and those who challenged her findings, are important for the purposes of conceptualizing treatment issues, conducting assessment, and designing interventions, and will be reviewed below.

Contextual Issues

Early findings about the prevalence of female-directed partner aggression, as well as many subsequent data, were based on the use of the Conflict Tactics Scale (Straus et al., 1980), which focuses on the frequency of minor and severe acts of aggression between partners. The data and the instrument were chal-lenged on the basis that no information was gathered on the contextual issues surrounding the violence, such as the meaning of the abuse, prior history of vi-olence in the relationship, or consequences of the violence between partners, including severity of injuries suffered. Subsequent research, including the 1985 Family Violence Resurvey (Straus & Gelles, 1990a), has attempted to address these issues.

Motivation or Intent. Although the victim's perspective often provides a source of data for determining the perpetrator's motivation in family violence research (Hotaling & Straus, 1990), accounts describing the experience of the victims of female-directed partner aggression are rare, and motivational fac-tors are as yet poorly understood. In a study of unrelated male batterers and battered women (Barnett, Lee, & Thelen, 1997), there were no differences in frequency of violence, but women more often attributed their violence to self-protection than did men, and men were more likely to attribute their be-havior to wanting to show who was boss. Both genders reported the following attributions in descending order of magnitude: letting out violence, getting the other's attention, showing who was boss, teaching the other a lesson, upsetting the other emotionally, being unaware of their intention, protecting self, and just teasing other. On outcome of abuse measures, men more frequently fright-ened the partner and got their own way. In Saunders' (1986) study of motiva-tion for partner aggression among battered women, the women in his sample described the majority of both their severe and non-severe aggressive acts as in self-defense or in retaliation for previous abuse. It appeared that the respon-dents did not distinguish readily between self-defense and "fighting back." Saunders suggested that when a previously assaulted woman is experiencing subsequent abuse, both fear and anger may be expressed in her response. In a study of female college students, both married and unmarried, 29% of the women acknowledged having assaulted their male partners in the past 5 years, for reasons such as the partner's failure to be sensitive to the woman's needs, wishing to gain the partner's attention, and as a response to a partner's verbal abuse (self-defense or retaliation for physical abuse were not included as options on the instrument used) (Fiebert & Gonzalez, 1997). Another study, comparing men and women mandated to domestic violence treatment (Hamberger, Lohr, & Bonge, 1994), found that men tended to report using violence in order to control their partners, whereas women reported using it largely in self-defense or retaliation in a relationship in which they had previously been victimized. In a later study of the same populations (Hamberger, Lohr, Bonge, & Tolin, 1997), a dimensional analysis was performed in an effort to identify major themes underlying perpetrator motivation. Male and female sorters were used to categorize perpetrators' reported motivations for partner aggression. Perpetrators of both genders were described as using violence to control their partners, to express anger or release tension, and to coerce communication. In addition, female perpetrators reported self-defense, escape, and retaliation as reasons for assaultive behavior, while men used violence to punish their partners for unwanted behavior.

The question of who initiates the violence has been considered in determining motivation. In the 1985 National Family Violence Survey, respondents were asked, "Who hit first?" According to men, women struck first in 45% of the cases, and according to women, women landed the first blow 42% of the time (Straus & Gelles, 1990a). Bland and Orn (1986) found in their community sample that 73.4% of women said that they had hit or thrown things first on at least one occasion, and 51% acknowledged having done so more than once. In the Saunders (1986) sample, a "small percentage" of the women acknowledged their role as the primary initiator of violence. It is unclear how many of these assaults were "pre-emptive strikes" by women who felt extremely threatened. However, Straus (1993) has pointed out that in representative community samples, at least 25% of the cases included violence by the female partner that was not enacted in self-defense, because in these families, the woman was the only partner who was violent in the prior 12 months. Clearly, issues of motivation have not been fully explored and resolved, and may be complicated by the fact that reasons for aggression may vary across populations and subgroups studied. Representative samples and clinical samples, such as battered women receiving shelter services, are distinctly different groups, whose members are likely to disclose divergent histories, behaviors, and motivations. Caution must be exercised to avoid making inappropriate assumptions and generalizations across dissimilar populations (Kwong et al., 1999; Straus, 1993, 1999).

Injuries. Contextual studies have also looked at injuries experienced as a consequence of partner violence, in an effort to address the fact that equivalent acts by men and women as measured on the CTS may actually represent different degrees of forcefulness and harm. Throughout the literature, women consistently reported sustaining more physical injuries than men. In one study (Cantos, Neidig, & O'Leary, 1994) of a clinical population, injury rates were significantly greater than those found in the Family Violence Surveys, suggesting a difference in severity of tactics used between community and clinical populations. As in other studies, women sustained the most injuries, despite the similarity in aggressive acts used by both genders. Twenty-one percent of women sustained injuries requiring medical treatment, as compared to 4% of the men. Using a representative community sample, Stets and Straus (1990) found that 3% of the women and .4% of the men sought medical treatment for injuries related to marital assault. Psychological injury has also been investigated, with results indicating that while violence is harmful to both genders when compared with control groups, women report greater distress and higher rates of depression (Cascardi et al., 1992; Stets & Straus, 1990). Several studies have shown that both women and men who are physically victimized by partners report similar increases in depressive symptomology (Stets & Straus, 1990; Zlotnick, Kohn, Peterson, & Pearlstein, 1998).

Additional Studies of Couples

Dating Violence Studies. Sugarman and Hotaling (1998) conducted a recent review of the dating violence literature. As in studies of married and cohabiting couples, the overall findings in studies of dating couples, usually drawn from college populations, are that women were at least as physically assaultive as men toward their partners, and that women reported significantly greater emotional distress related to relationship violence. While women attributed their violence to jealousy, "uncontrollable anger," self-defense, and retaliation, men were likely to be motivated by sexual refusal and to admit the instrumental quality of their behavior in trying to "intimidate," "frighten," or "force the other to give me something" (p. 107).

Violence in Lesbian Couples. The prevalence of partner assault in lesbian couples has been found to equal or exceed that in heterosexual couples. However, it should be noted that studies of same sex couples generally encounter sampling problems because of the difficulty in accessing a largely hidden population. In one study, 47.5% of the lesbian participants reported having been victimized by a female partner, a rate falling within the range of 30% to 75% reported by other studies reviewed (Waldner-Haugrud, Gratch, & Magruder, 1997). Thirty-eight percent of the respondents acknowledged perpetrating violent behavior against their same-sex partner. Dependency, jealousy, imbalance of power, substance abuse, and intergenerational violence were seen as primary contributing factors to violence between lesbian partners (Renzetti, 1992). In addition to physical violence, sexual coercion has been reported as a significant problem. In one study, lesbian participants reported experiencing at least one incident of unwanted sexual activity with a same sex partner, ranging from unwanted penetration (50%) and fondling (32%) to unwanted kissing (18%) (Waldner-Haugrud & Gratch, 1997).

Characteristics of Domestically Violent Women

There has been little systematic research on personality characteristics and other correlates for women who are aggressive toward their partners. Perhaps the most coherent picture has been developed of women who assault their female partners. Margolies and Leeder (1995) described domestically violent lesbians who sought treatment as personable and seemingly verbally skilled, but who perceived themselves as weak, powerless, and vulnerable. They felt unable to express themselves, or to make their needs known. Black and white thinking and exaggeration were typical thinking errors. Overly dependent on the attention and close involvement of their partner, they were unable to tolerate even planned separations. Chronic fear of abandonment and loss led to social isolation of the couple, followed by violence, further isolation, and a repetition of the cycle. Violence was used as distance regulation, to re-engage the partner and to protect the abuser from intimacy. This picture is consistent with the problem of merging, or loss of interpersonal boundaries, often seen as a treatment issue in lesbian couples. It is suggested that lesbian couples may have this vulnerability due to the emphasis in female socialization on maintaining connection, and to the hostile social environment for same sex couples (Burch, 1986). Renzetti (1992) found that substance abuse, dependency, and jealousy were the most significant variables in explaining variations in partner abuse severity in lesbian couples. Individual vulnerabilities in functioning due to early disruptions or failures in attachment, resulting in narcissistic and borderline traits or full-fledged personality disorders were noted by Coleman (1994). The extent to which lesbian abusers are a homogeneous group, and which individual characteristics and couple dynamics are shared across sexual orientation is not known.

Fragments of the heterosexual picture may be embedded throughout in the literature. For example, in a study of the health-related impact of marital violence, women in violent couples reported such elevated depression scores that the average score indicated moderate depression (Cascardi et al., 1992). This finding seems relevant to the population of women arrested for partner abuse because 86% of Cascardi's sample, composed of couples requesting marital therapy, reported bidirectional aggression. Most of these women both perpetrated and sustained partner aggression.

Women Arrested for Domestic Violence. Hamberger and Potente (1994) described their sample of women referred to treatment by the courts for partner aggression as battered women who were arrested for striking back in self-defense or in retaliation for previous abuse. They differentiated these women from the few initiators or primary perpetrators (3 out of 67) "who came from severely dysfunctional and multiabusive families-of-origin" (p. 135).

Hamberger (1997) more recently described 52 participants of a treatment program for women arrested for partner aggression in an effort to understand the contextual factors surrounding the women's violence. In addition to demographic information, some history and relationship data was provided as per the women's report. The women tended to be Caucasian (84%) or African American (14%), married (37.2%) or never married (27.4%), and employed outside the home (56.8%). Two-thirds of the women had completed high school, and they ranged in age from 19 to 51 years, with an average age of 29.5. Nearly half of the women experienced emotional abuse, physical abuse, or both within their families of origin, and over a third reported a history of sexual abuse. Forty-nine percent had been battered in a previous relationship, and nearly 54% had been exposed to father-to-mother violence. Alcohol use may have been an issue for 32% of the participants. Regarding the development of violence in these relationships, while 73% said they had initiated the violence on at least one occasion, 25% reported being the sole initiator, while 37% said their partner was the sole initiator; 55% said their partner initiated the violence on more than half the occasions, and one-third of the women initiated more than half the episodes. When asked who was the first to ever initiate violence in the relationship, 51% said their partner did, compared to 27.4% who said they initiated it themselves (it is unclear how to account for the remaining couples). Reasons given by the women for using aggression were, in descending order of frequency: self-defense/protection; express feeling/tension; stop nagging/get other to shut up; retaliate for previous assault or get partner to talk, attend, listen/do something; assert authority/be "one up"; retaliate for emotional abuse; don't know why. Hamberger points out the necessity of knowing the contexts for these reasons, as a seemingly controlling response may actually be in the service of self-protection. However, it should be noted that male aggression toward female partners is not excused under any of the above circumstances.

The need is clear for the extension of Hamberger's work through the analysis of more samples of women mandated to treatment in order to identify common characteristics and profiles. Since there is so little empirical data on the identity of these women, the following sections should be seen as speculative, but worthy of further investigation. At present, our picture of domestically violent women is still fragmented, but some promising connections are apparent.

The Impact of Trauma. If we assume that a significant proportion of women referred to treatment for partner aggression have been abused by partners themselves, then it is crucial to recognize that battered women are often survivors of both childhood and adult sexual victimization, in addition to the more evident physical and psychological abuse, as suggested by Hamberger's (1997) data. In Walker's (1984) sample of 435 battered women, 48% reported having been sexually assaulted as children, usually repeatedly, and most often by male relatives. The literature generally shows a rate of girls' sexual abuse in community populations of at least 20%. Women who were sexually assaulted as children have been shown to be at higher risk for revictimization of various types, including battering by their partners and unwanted sexual advances (Russell, 1986). Chu and Dill (1990) found that sexual victimization in childhood doubles a woman's risk for revictimization as an adult. There is reason to believe that for many women, the impact of trauma is cumulative. Rather than habituating to the repeated victimization, women exhibit increasing levels of such symptoms as anxiety, depression, dissociation, and sexual problems (Follette, Polusney, Bechtle, & Naugle, 1996). Traumatized women are often diagnosed with Posttraumatic Stress Disorder (PTSD) (American Psychiatric Association, 1994), which includes well-known symptoms such as hypervigilance and intense physiological reactivity when exposed to internal or external cues associated with traumatic events. A number of studies (Houskamp & Foy, 1991; Kemp, Green, Hovanitz, & Rawlings, 1995; Kemp, Rawlings, & Green, 1991; Saunders, 1994) have identified high rates of PTSD in battered women in sheltered and non-sheltered populations.

The sequelae of severe or repeated interpersonal trauma may have implications for women's emotional self-regulation and, therefore, anger and aggression, especially under circumstances that may elicit memories of previous abuse. Van der Kolk (1996) notes that significant changes occur in stress hormone secretion, leading to a condition of chronic hyperarousal for some trauma survivors. This may result in a compensatory emotional shutdown, causing emotions to lose their function of alerting the woman to the need for adaptive action to manage internal or external events. She may then disregard the information, freeze, or overreact (Litz & Keane, 1989). Studies on the effects of anxiety on information processing suggest that traumatic experiences may cause some individuals to exhibit a bias in preferentially attending to threat stimuli, or innocuous stimuli that may resemble a past threat, at the expense of more relevant stimuli. Thus overall perception of the inner and outer environments is distorted (Herman, 1992a; Litz & Keane, 1989), leaving traumatized women vulnerable to aggressive reaction to both real and misperceived threat.

Some researchers are calling for a broader developmental conceptualization of the impact of trauma to account for the myriad symptoms and pervasive problems with self-development and interpersonal functioning (Pynoos, Steinberg, & Goenjian, 1996) often seen in severely or repeatedly traumatized people, and variously called disorders of extreme stress (DES) or complex PTSD (Herman, 1992b). Cloitre, Scarvalone, and Difede (1997) found that while PTSD accounted for the symptoms of a group of women assaulted as adults only, the group that had suffered both childhood and adulthood victimization also exhibited problems in all interpersonal domains, as well as a greater likelihood of alexithymia, dissociative disorders, and suicide attempts. They suggest that these difficulties of self and interpersonal functioning are due to the impact of trauma at an earlier stage of development, and are related to these women's vulnerability to revictimization.

While battered women's behaviors have been understood as temporary coping strategies resulting from male partner abuse, rather than psychopathology (Walker & Browne, 1985), it may be that for some women with extensive trauma histories, significant and longstanding personality and interpersonal distortions in functioning may be evident. This may be the case for many women referred to treatment for partner aggression.

Trauma and Anger Dysregulation. Some work has been done in articulating the relationship between anger dysregulation and trauma, often based on the experiences of combat veterans (Chemtob, Novaco, Hamada, Gross, & Smith, 1997) and childhood sexual abuse survivors (Scott & Day, 1996; Zlotnick et al., 1997). A theory has been advanced, based on Novaco's (1994) work on anger dysregulation, to explain the role of PTSD symptoms in the disruption of cognitive, arousal, and behavioral components in the regulation of anger and subsequent aggression in patients with combat-related trauma (Chemtob et al., 1997). Case illustration was provided to demonstrate the benefit of focusing treatment on the specific deficit(s) identified in the initial assessment. These authors see anger as a core symptom of PTSD, due to its central function in the "survival mode" behavior typical of traumatized patients.

In a study of female survivors of childhood incest (Scott & Day, 1996), women's anger levels assessed through the State-Trait Anger Expression Inventory (STAXI) (Spielberger, 1991) were higher than comparable STAXI norms. Suppression of anger was associated with more extensive incest-related symptoms, while appropriate expression of anger was associated with fewer symptoms.

Trauma, Intimacy, and Anger. It has been suggested that intimacy, rather than marriage, legitimates abuse as a control tactic in relationships (Stacey,

Hazlewood, & Shupe, 1994). In comparing heterosexual relationships with and without sexual intimacy as a regular feature of the relationship, one study found that greater psychological abuse and control tactics were exercised equally by both men and women in relationships with regular sexual intimacy (Rouse, Breen, & Howell, 1988). Related to this premise is the idea that rage and abuse in intimate relationships may be associated with attachment disorders in adults, stemming from chronic attachment needs frustrated in childhood, presumably by incompetent, negligent, or abusive caregivers (Dutton, Saunders, Starzomski, & Bartholomew, 1994). In a study of attachment patterns, anger, jealousy, borderline personality organization, and trauma symptoms in men, Dutton et al. found that assaultive men showed more affective instability and less secure attachment than the control group. Presumably similar attachment problems would have serious implications for women in intimate relationships as well. Some preliminary work has been done in the articulation of relationships among attachment style and psychological adjustment in adulthood among women with a history of sexual victimization as children (Roche, Runtz & Hunter, 1999). Results indicated that a history of incest was associated with a poorer outcome in later psychological adjustment and adult attachment style than a history of extrafamilial sexual abuse. Women who had been subjected to either type of child sexual abuse were less secure and more fearful than women who were not victimized. Similarly, a relationship was demonstrated between positive and negative childhood experiences and attachment style (Henderson, Trinke, Bartholomew, & Kwong, 1999), but a strong link between attachment style and the perpetration or receipt of relationship aggression for women did not emerge. For men, a preoccupied attachment style was strongly associated with both perpetration and receipt, but for women this association was weak. Other attachment styles were associated inconsistently or not at all with perpetration and receipt of aggression for women. Clarifying the relationships among trauma, attachment style, affect regulation processes, and aggression for women will be a major contribution to the understanding the dynamics and potential treatment strategies for female partner aggression.

Substance Abuse. Alcohol and drug use has been considered an important variable associated with aggression. Unfortunately, studies exploring the effect of alcohol use on women's aggression have been largely conducted within the narrow confines of the laboratory, with college students who were supplied with only moderate doses of alcohol. Furthermore, the results of this laboratory-based research are inconclusive. The role of drug use on female aggression is even less well known (Gomberg, 1993).

While we know that there is a complex relationship between substance abuse problems and domestic violence, it has not been well-explored for female perpetrators of partner aggression. Straus and Sweet (1992) found that for both women and men, the incidence of verbal aggression rose with increasing numbers of episodes of drunkenness on the perpetrator's part. For women, the same relationship held with drug use and verbal aggression.

An important relationship has been identified between childhood victimization and subsequent substance abuse problems for women, which may be relevant for domestically violent women, given the strong association between battered women and prior victimization. In fact, substance abuse and PTSD are often comorbid, and are more severe and difficult to treat than when they occur individually (Najavits, Weiss, & Liese, 1996). In one study (Miller, Downs, & Testa, 1993) comparing alcoholic women in treatment, female drinking drivers, and a random female household sample, two-thirds of the alcoholic women were sexually abused as children, as compared with one-fifth of the drinking drivers and one-third of the household sample. Furthermore, the alcoholic women were far more likely to have suffered more severe kinds of sexual abuse, and to have experienced severe father-to-child violence and verbal aggression than the comparison groups. Overall, only 12% of alcoholic women escaped any childhood victimization, most of which was perpetrated by adult males.

The association of female perpetration of partner aggression with childhood trauma histories and substance abuse appeared in Farley's (1996) study of 169 women referred for abusive behavior toward lesbian partners. All reported histories of psychological abuse, 88% said they had been physically abused, and 94% had experienced sexual abuse as children. They also reported high rates of psychological and physical abuse as adults. Nearly all (94%) of the women had been in previous mental health treatment, 38% reported psychiatric inpatient treatment, and at the time of the study, 38% reported being suicidal and 19% said they were homocidal. Almost half (44.5%) reported abusing substances. Sixty-three percent of the women described themselves as "dependent" in their relationships.

INTERVENING WITH FEMALE PERPETRATORS

There is sparse literature on the treatment of women with anger problems, and even less is available on treatment or outcome studies on treatment of domestically violent women. Currently, intervention is most commonly conducted through group, couple, individual, and combined modalities. Generally speaking, elements of the Duluth model (Pence & Paymar, 1993) and anger management techniques are combined with a sensitivity to the status of women as both victims and perpetrators in most treatment approaches. There are similarities to the content and goals of male batterers' treatment programs, but a central theme is the recognition that women's violence is often related to a history of victimization, in either current or past relationships (Hamberger & Potente, 1994). Thus treatment must address the impact of victimization and the need for self-protection. Not surprisingly, given the affect dysregulation apparent in both trauma victims and participants in partner violence, there is considerable overlap in the goals of the initial stage of stabilization in trauma treatment (van der Kolk, McFarlane, & van der Hart, 1996) and the above elements of treatment for spouse abuse perpetration.

As in treatment for male batterers, an effort is made to raise women's awareness about the effects, both positive and negative, of gender-based socialization of women in the general culture. This may include women's ideas about dependency and autonomy, worthiness if she is without a man or partner, and what conflict strategies are permissible for women (Gilligan, 1982). Some programs take the opportunity to place more emphasis on parenting in regard to anger management and the prevention of future family violence (Hamberger & Potente, 1994; Leisring, Dowd, & Rosenbaum, 1999). As in all treatment, the recognition of subcultural differences, both sexual and ethnic, are essential for effective intervention.

Group Interventions

The sole description in the literature of the treatment of heterosexual women arrested for partner assault is a summary of The Kenosha Domestic Abuse Intervention Program (Hamberger & Potente, 1994), which is no longer in operation following a change in the arrest laws that drastically reduced referrals. A melding of classic interventions for battered women and anger management/assertiveness techniques, the group lasted 12 sessions and addressed the development of safety planning and management of stress and reactivity. The primary goals were not only to help the women avoid the situations and triggers leading to rearrest, but more importantly, to develop safe and healthy alternative behaviors for themselves and their children (T. Potente, personal communications, November 8, 1998 and December 1, 1998).

An account of group treatment of lesbian perpetrators of partner assault describes an ongoing group format in which the average length of involvement is approximately a year (Margolies & Leeder, 1995). The peer culture was used to counteract social isolation and the maintenance of secrecy about members' abusive behavior. Group norms were offered as an alternative to norms of the violent lesbian subculture, and expressions of pride about violent behavior were consistently confronted. Women were expected and given opportunities to recognize and express anger, practicing new behaviors with feedback from the group. They were encouraged to recognize the vulnerable emotions beneath their anger, such as fear of abandonment and deprivation. The model uses didactic, support, and process approaches in conveying and reinforcing the learning.

A third program of 36 weeks in length is conducted by Parker, Froyd and Associates in the Denver area. Utilizing many of the didactic themes of the Duluth model as well as experiential and process-oriented interventions, clinicians have made gender-based modifications to the traditional male batterer curriculum to better address behaviors related to female socialization. The program philosophy emphasizes both an acknowledgement of women's past victimization as well as the need for them to be accountable for their own behavior (D. A. Schmidli, personal communication, November 1, 1998).

A fourth program conducted at the University of Massachusetts Medical Center will be described below in detail as a demonstration of the organization and elaboration of some elements of these group designs.

Group interventions for women vary widely in length and focus, and have not been evaluated in published outcome studies. Since we are still in the process of developing a "best practice" model, awareness of other related group interventions, while not specifically targeting female partner aggression, may be useful for the reader to review. These include a 15-week affect management group for childhood sexual abuse survivors in early stages of treatment, which emphasized safety, stabilization, and stress management (Zlotnick et al., 1997). Followup measures indicated a reduction in levels of symptoms of PTSD and dissociation. Another group intervention was anger management treatment for female inmates who had been arrested for unspecified offenses. The group consisted of three sessions of two hours each, covering awareness of anger cues and contexts, self-monitoring, time out, and relaxation exercises. The women scored significantly lower on the Novaco Anger Scale at posttest, but no long-term follow up was attempted (Smith, Smith, & Beckner, 1994). A third group intervention of interest is a 24-session cognitive-behavioral treatment for women with the dual diagnosis of PTSD and addiction (Najavits et al., 1996). The highly structured format emphasizes patient education regarding these disorders, affect management skills, attention to personal safety and self-nurturing, and relapse prevention training. Additional features include urinalysis and close monitoring of attendance and homework completion.

Non-Group Interventions

A psychoeducational conjoint approach is suggested by Geffner, Mantooth, Franks, and Rao (1989) which takes the view that family violence by any member will affect all members negatively. This systems orientation attempts to help all members take responsibility for their behavior. However, family therapy is criticized by some as potentially unsafe, ineffective, and victim blaming (e.g., Bograd, 1984; Ganley, 1989). Renzetti (1992), in discussing treatment for violent lesbians, recommends the use of couples counseling only if requested by the victim, and only if her safety can be assured.

An alternative to group treatment, suggested by Margolies and Leeder (1995), may be useful when sufficient referrals for groupwork are not available, or if the perpetrator is not willing to enter a group. Based on their experience with lesbian perpetrators, their "community model" consists of several stages, including conjoint sessions, individual work for both partners, and an opportunity to bring other significant people into the treatment to break the isolation of the couple and build support systems for both partners. In comparing the two treatment models, they observed that among the group participants, no relationship survived, while in the "community model," all relationships were still intact at the termination of treatment.

INTERVENTION TECHNIQUES

Assessment. In addition to a standard psychiatric intake interview, issues related to family and non-family violence are given close attention. Circumstances of the referral incident, determining the sequence of interactions leading to the violence, how violence is historically initiated, the typical pattern it takes, and injuries inflicted or sustained are all relevant to understanding how to approach the individual within the group. Determining whether any neuropsychological or physiological factors contribute to the individual's difficulties, such as head injury sequelae, endocrine dysfunction, attention deficits, learning disabilities, or medical illness, is also important.

Treatment: A 20-Week Group Model. For the past several years, an anger management program at the University of Massachusetts Medical Center has been treating a heterogeneous group of women who are referred for a variety of behaviors reflecting anger management difficulties, particularly partner aggression and other assaults. Members are both mandated by court as well as self-referred. In a recent study (Leisring, Dowd, & Rosenbaum, 1999) that examined a sample of 68 mandated women in this program, it was found that 31% were court referred due to partner aggression and an additional 20% acknowledged having assaulted a partner in the past. Other primary reasons for court referral to the program included assaultive behaviors towards family members, friends, strangers, and police officers.

After an initial intake, treatment is offered through a 20-week psychoeducational/support group approach, with a strong cognitive/behavioral emphasis. The group is ongoing, incorporating new members once per month, and repeating the didactic material in the same sequence approximately every five months. New members are given an orientation in which they are familiarized with confidentiality, group rules, the philosophy of the program, a program content outline, and the time out technique prior to entering the group.

Weekly meetings keep issues of behavioral and cognitive control before the participants. Members induct new members into the culture of the group, which includes supportiveness, hope for change, expectation of commitment to non-violent behavior and accountability, overcoming social isolation, ensuring one's own safety, and openness about aggressive behavior. Leaders conduct an ongoing assessment for issues that were not identified on intake, such as the need for medication, substance abuse treatment, and adjunct therapies such as individual, family, or additional group interventions. Participants often need referrals for assistance with housing, legal advocacy, parenting skills, and day care. Overall themes of the curriculum include building and using a cognitive structure for the understanding and management of emotional experiences; effective problem solving and conflict management strategies; recognition of individual vulnerabilities and appropriate adaptations, or further specialized treatment for responsible self-management; taking responsibility for one's own thoughts, feelings, behavior, and happiness; learning to participate in healthy and mutually respectful relationships; and development of a positive sense of self, through interpersonal connection and identification of one's own desires and preferences, plans, and resources.

The curriculum is organized into blocks of content of several weeks each in duration. Each 90 minute session begins with 30 to 45 minutes of check-in time, in which members talk about challenges and successes of the previous week, particularly regarding anger management and safety issues. The leaders use the issues raised as opportunities to present or reinforce previously presented material from the curriculum, to facilitate connection and support among members, and to encourage members to offer each other feedback and ideas about resources and options. The remainder of the time is used to present new material either through lecture, video, role play or other activities. Many exercises use brainstorming as a way for women to examine their own experience, and the ideas generated are written on the board and later incorporated into a handout as a visual reminder. The concepts below are presented in sequence as part of a skill-building curriculum, but are continually reinforced throughout the life of the group.

Emotional Education. A new member often arrives with a constricted emotional vocabulary and a diffuse sense of her own emotional experience. She is introduced to the notion of anger as a phenomenon with survival value, and is helped to distinguish between emotion and behavior, particularly anger and aggression. Other emotions that accompany, underlie, or masquerade as anger, such as grief, sadness, hurt, jealousy, fear, humiliation are identified and explored. Anger is explained as an emotional and behavioral response learned through familial and cultural osmosis, and the cognitive aspect of anger, or how we talk to ourselves, is introduced. Many women mandated to treatment are members of cultural minority groups, and may be subject to cultural rules about interpersonal interaction, as women, in addition to the mainstream gender socialization within the patriarchal larger culture. Gender socialization has typically encouraged nurturing and facilitating roles for girls, which emphasize the avoidance of conflict and potential loss of relationship (Gilligan, 1982). Further suppression of the expression of female anger is accomplished through social disapproval of women who express anger, even appropriately, by castigating them as "bitches," shrewish, unfeminine, and other negative labels (Lerner, 1985). This dilemma is explored, as group members have typically had no positive role models for management of intense emotion.

Basic Skills in Self Awareness and Conflict Management. Women are encouraged to become familiar with the psychological, physiological, and behavioral cues that signal the escalation of anger and potentially harmful behavior in themselves and others. They reflect on the times, places, specific people, and types of interactions that tend to be emotional triggers leading to uncontrolled anger and behavior for themselves. The group reviews techniques for keeping conflicts productive and under control, and the time out procedure for terminating a potentially dangerous interaction. The primary goal is the maintenance of safety for the woman and her partner, to prevent further victimization of either party.

Conditions That Undermine Emotional and Behavioral Stability. Through brief lecture, viewing videos, and discussion of their own experiences, women are educated about the nature, effects, and management of a variety of physiological and psychiatric disorders that may have destabilizing effects on their attempts to manage anger and aggression. Included are substance abuse (their own and/or their partner's), mood and anxiety disorders, PTSD and related trauma sequelae, head injury, attentional problems, as well as problems related to endocrine functioning, such as premenstrual syndrome, postpartum depression, menopause, and thyroid disorders. Each topic is explored with specific attention to the relevance to anger management problems. In discussing abuse and its impact on the victim, they are encouraged to think about their own experiences as well as their partners'. Treatment and/or symptom management for these conditions is described, and local resource lists are made available for relevant services.

Relationship Issues. In this unit, the development of appropriate expectations and boundaries in all significant relationships is discussed. Control issues in parenting and partnerships receive particular emphasis.

Most women entering the program are mothers, and often need help with managing their frustration toward their children in regard to disciplinary issues. Setting clear limits, being consistent, and using non-violent consequences are discussed. Many women have had poor parenting models, and may need a referral to focused parenting programs for skill-building and further support. Women are also educated about the powerful impact that witnessing spousal abuse and being victimized by their parents has on their children's behavior and well-being. Most women do not want their children to engage in violent behavior, and are ashamed and worried about what their children have witnessed. This is a major source of leverage in motivating women to work on behavior change, including the difficult step of leaving an abusive relationship. It is known that a significant risk factor for perpetrating family violence (for men) is having a history of childhood victimization by parents or witnessing parental violence (Hotaling & Sugarman, 1986). In addition, children have been shown to exhibit symptomatic behavior whether the violence is physical or involves verbal abuse and property damage (Jouriles, Norwood, McDonald, Vincent, & Mahoney, 1996). Straus (1990) demonstrated that women who are physically assaulted by their partners are twice as likely to abuse their children as women who were not assaulted. Women can be empowered to protect their children from the effects of family violence if they are educated about these connections.

In regard to partner issues, women are asked to identify typical conflicts and problematic interactions. It is acknowledged that couples have difficulty in sharing power, and that it is necessary for the sake of the relationship to identify and restrain the impulse to be over-controlling. The inappropriate use of manipulation, threat, and violence is highlighted. Women are helped to verbalize their expectations, and to evaluate to what degree they are realistic, negotiated or assumed, and stereotypical or appropriate to the situation. They are encouraged to develop the willingness to listen, and the ability to see another point of view while holding their own as valid. A related skill is the resolution of a conflict through agreeing to disagree, or letting go of the need to win. The meaning and the practice of apology and forgiveness is explored. An exercise that is helpful in providing the structure for the discussion of these issues is a brainstorming of the characteristics of healthy and unhealthy relationships.

Communication Skills. Participants are shown examples of effective and ineffective communication through examples and role plays. The importance of "active listening" is presented, and the structure of an "I message" is explained and practiced. The differences between passive, assertive, and aggressive behavior are demonstrated, and the women brainstorm the characteristics of each, including quality of voice, choice of words, physical posture, and overall nonverbal messages. Women often report that while growing up they never observed family members work out a problem through discussion, so the concept and practice of negotiation is presented and then reinforced in later sessions. An increase in assertive behavior on the part of the woman will constitute a challenge to the balance of power in her relationships. It is important to prepare women for potential reactions from others, particularly from potentially violent partners. Women with abusive partners must consider carefully how to negotiate these changes in their relationships, and to have a well-developed safety plan and resources at their disposal if it becomes too dangerous to remain at home with a partner who is threatened by her developing ability to advocate for herself.

Thinking Errors. Women are introduced to the idea that intense emotion can cause thinking errors, and thinking errors can escalate negative emotion. Common types of cognitive distortions, such as mind-reading, jumping to conclusions, overgeneralization, and black-and-white thinking are demonstrated in detail, using the participants' own experiences. Emphasis is placed on examining the evidence and the use of logic in the evaluation of perceptions and behavioral reactions. The technique of reframing is used to demonstrate flexibility in thinking, and to develop alternative and more productive perspectives. The goal of this unit is to assist women in managing borderline functioning through enhanced emotional self-regulation (Linehan, 1993a, 1993b), focusing on accurate labeling of thoughts and feelings, toleration of emotional distress, and overall increased cognitive control over emotional responses.

Stress Management and Relaxation Techniques. This cluster of group sessions focuses the women's attention on identifying sources of stress, recognizing signs of being overstressed, and learning about the physical and psychological responses to stress. They are encouraged to develop ways to set limits on stressful demands, and to manage their responses to events or chronic stressors that cannot be changed. Each woman is assisted in developing an individual stress management and relaxation plan that includes specific activities that work for her. Demonstrations of "the relaxation response" (Benson, 1975), progressive muscle relaxation, guided imagery, and simple biofeedback techniques are given in the group.

RECOMMENDATIONS FOR FUTURE INTERVENTIONS
AND RESEARCH

Additional research is needed to establish the characteristics and needs of the women who seek treatment for partner aggression, as well as the nature of the contextual issues surrounding their behavior. It would be useful to identify risk factors and protective characteristics. To the extent that such issues as trauma, attachment disorders, and substance abuse are identified as relevant for this population, partner aggression interventions may be conceptualized as the first stage of treatment for women who present with multiple issues. Provisions of ongoing assessment, assistance in stabilization, and guidance in accessing immediate or subsequent more specific types of treatments will assist the women in addressing the most salient symptoms and behaviors that contribute to their aggression.

Profiles or typologies of male batterers (Dutton, 1988; Gondolf, 1988; Hamberger, Lohr, Bonge, & Tolin, 1996) and "violent persons" (a unisex model) (Stacey et al., 1994) have been developed, but it is unclear whether these models describe the population of women who are mandated to treatment. Assuming that these women form a heterogeneous group, attempts at treatment matching, based on clinical and behavioral profiles, may increase the effectiveness of interventions. Women may benefit from different treatment strategies based on such characteristics as typical anger expression style, which may dictate the timing and emphasis of the teaching of such skills as self-soothing or assertiveness training (Wilt, 1993). Women are mandated to treatment in various stages of recovery from addiction and victimization, which would also have relevance for the timing of specific interventions.

Treatment outcome studies are needed to evaluate the effectiveness of our interventions. What types of women are able to benefit, and what differentiates them from women who drop out of treatment, or women who complete, but reoffend?

Given the state of our knowledge of this population, it is not surprising that the development of standards for the treatment of domestically violent women is in its infancy. In their recent review of issues related to standards in batterer treatment programs, Austin and Dankwort (1999) question whether and how standards should be developed for women's treatment, as well as how to determine what interventions are appropriate for lesbian offenders. Although several states have begun to develop women's program standards (J. Austin, personal communication, March 29, 1999), it would seem premature to do so without a far more robust literature to guide the process.

Building on existing models of treatment, several suggestions are offered. Women often describe the difficulty of changing their behaviors while their partners continue with old patterns. Therefore simultaneous and parallel groups for women and their partners, or couples groups, may be a more effective intervention for intact couples. In a comparison study of the effectiveness of conjoint groups and parallel gender specific groups with intact couples (O'Leary, Heyman, & Neidig, 1999), both treatments were found to be equally effective in reducing husbands' and wives' mild and severe aggression. The sample included many couples who engaged in bidirectional aggression, but only those in which the wife felt comfortable in participating in the conjoint group, if so assigned. Obviously, the actual and perceived safety of the victim should be paramount in treatment selection decisions, and perpetrators of both genders must be held accountable for their violent behavior.

Another suggestion is to make the didactic part of the teaching as engaging and memorable as possible, particularly because women with addiction and trauma issues may have difficulty with concentration, dissociation, impulsivity, and other characteristics that interfere with learning. Mnemonic devices, visual aids and handouts, rehearsal of skills, and use of creativity and humor are ways to make the material more accessible (Najavits et al., 1996). High quality video presentations specific to issues of anger management and family violence would help participants visually identify dysfunctional patterns and model non-violent options. Unfortunately most available materials address male violence only.

A third suggestion is more systemic in nature. Multidisciplinary efforts to reach parents about the impact of physical and verbal abusiveness on children should be stepped up. Pediatric visits could include education and literature on the relationship between harsh discipline and aggressive behavior, and between witnessing parental violence and future partner aggression. Similarly, parenting courses and training for day care providers could emphasize the danger in failing to commit to non-violent conflict resolution, and the necessity of supporting this value in all settings relevant to children.

Because the various forms of family violence have been demonstrated to be highly interrelated, Straus (1990) states that the only effective approach to the prevention of spouse and child abuse must include strategies to impact all forms of family violence, including sibling violence, harsh discipline, etc. His research demonstrated that men and women who were physically punished or abused as children were significantly more likely to assault their siblings in childhood, and their partners as adults. Women need to know that partner assault by either spouse increases a child's risk of abuse, and the greatest risk is carried by the children of bidirectionally assaultive parents. In addition, these children are more likely to assault siblings, parents, and non-family members (Hotaling & Straus, 1990). Therefore, treatment for perpetration and victimization in women, as perhaps the most pivotal of family members in their roles as mothers and primary caregivers, can be another vehicle for the interruption and reduction of family violence. The woman who initiates, retaliates, or is the sole perpetrator of partner aggression can learn to manage conflict in non-violent and constructive ways, and model these behaviors for her children. If her aggression is in response to her own victimization, she can be supported to increase the level of her safety and that of her children, in whatever ways she is ready to do so. While Ganley (1989) makes a strong case for the necessity of the aggressive man to change in order to improve the lives of women and children, waiting for this to come about is not an empowering strategy for his partner, regardless of her level of aggression or motivation for participation in it. Active engagement in a treatment program that is sensitive to the woman's dual status as aggressor and victim, and which offers the connection with and support of other women and additional community resources, would seem to be a surer path to gaining more control and peace in her life.

REFERENCES

American Psychiatric Association. (1994). *Diagnostic and statistical manual of mental disorders* (4th ed.). Washington, DC: Author.

Arias, I., & Johnson, P. (1989). Evaluations of physical aggression among intimate dyads. *Journal of Interpersonal Violence, 4*(3), 298-307.

Austin, J. B., & Dankwort, J. (1999). Standards for batterer programs: A review and analysis. *Journal of Interpersonal Violence, 14*(2), 152-168.

Barnett, O. W., Lee, C. Y., & Thelen, R. E. (1997). Gender differences in attributions of self-defense and control in interpartner aggression. *Violence Against Women, 3*(5), 462-481.

Benson, H. (1975). *The relaxation response.* New York: Avon.

Bland, R., & Orn, H. (1986). Family violence and psychiatric disorder. *Canadian Journal of Psychiatry, 31*, 129-137.

Bograd, M. (1984). Family systems approaches to wife battery: A feminist critique. *American Journal of Orthopsychiatry, 54*, 558-565.

Burch, B. (1986). Psychotherapy and the dynamics of merger in lesbian couples. In T. S. Stein & C. J. Cohen (Eds.), *Contemporary perspectives on psychotherapy with lesbians and gay men* (pp. 57-71). New York: Plenum Medical Book Company.

Cantos, A. L., Neidig, P. H., & O'Leary, K. D. (1994). Injuries of women and men in a treatment program for domestic violence. *Journal of Family Violence, 9*(2), 113-124.

Cascardi, M., Langhinrichsen, J., & Vivian, D. (1992). Marital aggression: Impact, injury, and health correlates for husbands and wives. *Archives of Internal Medicine, 152*, 1178-1184.

Chemtob, C. M., Novaco, R. W., Hamada, R. S., Gross, D. M., & Smith, G. (1997). Anger regulation deficits in combat-related posttraumatic stress disorder. *Journal of Traumatic Stress, 10*(1), 17-36.

Chu, J. L., & Dill, D. L. (1990). Dissociative symptoms in relation to childhood physical and sexual abuse. *American Journal of Psychiatry, 147,* 887-892.

Cloitre, M., Scarvalone, P., & Difede, J. (1997). Posttraumatic Stress Disorder, self- and interpersonal dysfunction among sexually retraumatized women. *Journal of Traumatic Stress, 10*(3), 437-452.

Coleman, V. E. (1994). Lesbian battering: The relationship between personality and the perpetration of violence. *Violence and Victims, 9*(2), 139-152.

Cook, P. W. (1997). *Abused men: The hidden side of domestic violence.* Westport, CT: Praeger.

DeKeserdy, W. S., & Schwartz, M. D. (1998). *Woman abuse on campus: Results from the Canadian National Survey.* Thousand Oaks, CA: Sage.

Dutton, D. G. (1988). Profiling of wife assaulters: Preliminiary evidence for a trimodal analysis. *Violence and Victims, 3*(1), 5-29.

Dutton, D. G. (1994). Patriarchy and wife assault: The ecological fallacy. *Violence and Victims, 9*(2), 167-182.

Dutton, D. G., Saunders, K., Starzomski, A., & Bartholomew, K. (1994). Intimacy-anger and insecure attachment as precursors of abuse in intimate relationships. *Journal of Applied Social Psychology, 24*(15), 1367-1386.

Eagly, A. H., & Steffen, V. J. (1986). Gender and aggressive behavior: A meta-analytic review of the social psychological literature. *Psychological Bulletin, 100*(3), 309-330.

Farley, N. (1996). A survey of factors contributing to gay and lesbian domestic violence. In C. M. Renzetti & C. H. Miley (Eds.), *Violence in gay and lesbian domestic partnerships* (pp. 35-42). New York: Harrington Park Press.

Fiebert, M. S., & Gonzalez, D. M. (1997). College women who initiate assaults on their male partners and the reasons offered for such behavior. *Psychological Reports, 80,* 583-590.

Fishbein, D. H. (1992). The psychobiology of female aggression. *Criminal Justice and Behavior, 19*(2), 99-126.

Follette, V. M., Polusney, M. A., Bechtle, A. E., & Naugle, A. E. (1996). Cumulative trauma: The impact of child sexual abuse, adult sexual assault, and spouse abuse. *Journal of Traumatic Stress, 9*(1), 25-35.

Frodi, A., Macaulay, J., & Thome, P. R. (1977). Are women always less aggressive than men? A review of the experimental literature. *Psychological Bulletin, 84*(4), 634-660.

Ganley, A. L. (1981). Counseling programs for men who batter: Elements of effective programs. *Response, 4,* 3-4.

Ganley, A. L. (1989). Integrating feminist and social learning analyses of aggression: Creating multiple models for intervention with men who batter. In P. L. Caesar & L. K. Hamberger (Eds.), *Treating men who batter: Theory, practice, and program* (pp. 196-235). New York: Springer Publishing Company.

Geffner, R., Mantooth, C., Franks, D., & Rao, L. (1989). A psychoeducational, conjoint approach to reducing family violence. In P. L. Caesar & L. K. Hamberger (Eds.), *Treating men who batter: Theory, practice, and program* (pp. 103-133). New York: Springer Publishing Company.

Gilligan, C. (1982). *In a different voice: Psychological theory and women's development.* Cambridge, MA: Harvard University Press.

Gomberg, E. S. L. (1993). Alcohol, women, and the expression of aggression. *Journal of Studies on Alcohol, 11*, 89-95.

Gondolf, E. W. (1988). Who are those guys? Toward a behavioral typology of batterers. *Violence and Victims, 3*(3), 187-203.

Hamberger, L. K. (1997). Female offenders in domestic violence: A look at actions in context. *Journal of Aggression, Maltreatment & Trauma, 1* (1), 117-129.

Hamberger, L. K., & Arnold, J. (1990). The impact of mandatory arrest on domestic violence perpetrator counseling services. *Family Violence and Sexual Assault Bulletin, 6*(1), 11-12.

Hamberger, L. K., Lohr, J. M., & Bonge, D. (1994). The intended function of domestic violence is different for arrested male and female perpetrators. *Family Violence and Sexual Assault Bulletin, 10*(3-4), 40-44.

Hamberger, L. K., Lohr, J. M., Bonge, D., & Tolin, D. F. (1996). A large sample empirical typology of male spouse abusers and its relationship to dimensions of abuse. *Violence and Victims, 11*(4), 277-292.

Hamberger, L. K., Lohr, J. M., Bonge, D., & Tolin, D. F. (1997). An empirical classification of motivations for domestic violence. *Violence Against Women, 3*(4), 401-423.

Hamberger, L. K., & Potente, T. (1994). Counseling heterosexual women arrested for domestic violence: Implications for theory and practice. *Violence and Victims, 9* (2), 125-137.

Henderson, A. J. Z., Trinke, S. J., Bartholomew, K., & Kwong, M. (1999, August). *An attachment perspective exploring women's and men's relationship aggression.* Poster presented at the Annual Convention of the American Psychological Association, Boston, MA.

Herman, J. L. (1992a). *Trauma and recovery.* New York: Basic Books.

Herman, J. L. (1992b). Complex PTSD: A syndrome in survivors of prolonged and repeated trauma. *Journal of Traumatic Stress, 5*(3), 377-391.

Hotaling, G. T., & Straus, M. A. (1990). Intrafamily violence and crime and violence outside the family. In M. A. Straus & R. J. Gelles (Eds.), *Physical violence in American families: Risk factors and adaptations to violence in 8,145 families* (pp. 431-470). New Brunswick, NJ: Transaction Publishers.

Hotaling, G. T., & Sugarman, D. B. (1986). An analysis of risk markers in husband to wife violence: The current state of knowledge. *Violence and Victims, 1*, 101-124.

Houskamp, B. M., & Foy, D. W. (1991). The assessment of Posttraumatic Stress Disorder in battered women. *Journal of Interpersonal Violence, 6*(3), 367-375.

Jouriles, E. N., Norwood, W. D., McDonald, R., Vincent, J. P., & Mahoney, A. (1996). Physical violence and other forms of marital aggression: Links with children's behavior problems. *Journal of Family Psychology, 10*, 223-234.

Kemp, A., Green, B. L., Hovanitz, C., & Rawlings, E. I. (1995). Incidence and correlates of Posttraumatic Stress Disorder in battered women. *Journal of Interpersonal Violence, 10*(1), 43-55.

Kemp, A., Rawlings, E. I., & Green, B. L. (1991). Post-Traumatic Stress Disorder (PTSD) in battered women: A shelter sample. *Journal of Traumatic Stress, 4*(1), 137-148.

Kurz, D. (1993). Physical assaults by husbands: A major social problem. In R. J. Gelles & D. R. Loseke (Eds.), *Current controversies on family violence* (pp. 88-103). Newbury Park, CA: Sage Publications.

Kwong, M. J., Bartholomew, K., & Dutton, D. G. (1999). Gender differences in patterns of relationship violence in Alberta. *Canadian Journal of Behavioral Science, 31*(3), 150-160.

Leisring, P., Dowd, L., & Rosenbaum, A. (1999, July). *Characteristics of women mandated to anger management treatment.* Paper presented at the 6th International Family Violence Research Conference, Durham, NH.

Lerner, H. (1985). *The dance of anger: A woman's guide to changing the patterns of intimate relationships.* New York: Harper & Row.

Linehan, M. M. (1993a). *Cognitive-behavioral treatment of borderline personality disorder.* New York: The Guilford Press.

Linehan, M. M. (1993b). *Skills training manual for treating borderline personality disorder.* New York: The Guilford Press.

Litz, B. T., & Keane, T. M. (1989). Information processing in anxiety disorders: Applications to the understanding of posttraumatic stress disorder. *Clinical Psychology Review, 9*, 243-257.

Macaulay, J. (1985). Adding gender to aggression research: Incremental or revolutionary change? In E. E. O'Leary, R. K. Unger, & B. S. Wallston (Eds.), *Women, gender, and social psychology* (pp. 191-224). Hillsdale, NJ: Lawrence Erlbaum Associates.

Margolies, L., & Leeder, E. (1995). Violence at the door: Treatment of lesbian batterers. *Violence Against Women, 1*(2), 139-157.

Marrugo, B., & Kreger, M. (1996). Definition of roles in abusive lesbian relationships. In C. M. Renzetti & C. H. Miley (Eds.), *Violence in gay and lesbian domestic partnerships* (pp. 23-33). New York: Harrington Park Press.

Martin, M. E. (1997). Double your trouble: Dual arrest in family violence. *Journal of Family Violence, 12*(2), 139-157.

McNeely, R. L., & Robinson-Simpson, G. (1987). The truth about domestic violence: A falsely framed issue. *Social Work, 32*, 485-490.

Miller, B. A., Downs, W. R., & Testa, M. (1993). Interrelationships between victimization experiences and women's alcohol use. *Journal of Alcohol Studies, 11*, 109-117.

Miller, S. L. (1994). Expanding the boundaries: Toward a more inclusive and integrated study of intimate violence. *Violence and Victims, 9*(2), 183-194.

Najavits, L. M., Weiss, R. D., & Liese, B. S. (1996). Group cognitive-behavioral therapy with women with PTSD and Substance Use Disorder. *Journal of Substance Abuse Treatment, 13*(1), 13-22.

Novaco, R. W. (1994). Anger as a risk factor for violence among the mentally disordered. In J. Monahan & H. Steadman (Eds.), *Violence and mental disorder: Developments in risk assessment* (pp. 21-56). Chicago: University of Chicago Press.

O'Leary, K. D., & Curley, A. D. (1986). Assertion and family violence: Correlates of spouse abuse. *Journal of Marital and Family Therapy, 12*, 281-290.

O'Leary, K. D., Heyman, R. E., & Neidig, P. H. (1999). Treatment of wife abuse: A comparison of gender-specific and conjoint approaches. *Behavior Therapy, 30*, 475-505.

Pence, E., & Paymar, M. (1993). *Education groups for men who batter: The Duluth model.* New York: Springer Publishing Company.

Pynoos, R. S., Steinberg, A. M., & Goenjian, A. (1996). Traumatic stress in childhood and adolescence. In B. A. van der Kolk, A. C. McFarlane, & L. Weisaeth (Eds.), *Traumatic stress: The effects of overwhelming experience on mind, body, and society* (pp. 331-358). New York: The Guilford Press.

Renzetti, C. M. (1992). *Violent betrayal: Partner abuse in lesbian relationships.* Newbury Park, CA: Sage.

Roche, D. N., Runtz, M. G., & Hunter, M. A. (1999). Adult attachment: A mediator between child sexual abuse and later psychological adjustment. *Journal of Interpersonal Violence, 14* (2), 184-207.

Rouse, L. P., Breen, R., & Howell, M. (1988). Abuse in intimate relationships: A comparison of married and dating college students. *Journal of Interpersonal Violence, 3,* 414-429.

Russell, D. (1986). *The secret trauma: Incest in the lives of girls and women.* New York: Basic Books.

Saunders, D. G. (1986). When battered women use violence: Husband-abuse or self-defense? *Victims and Violence, 1*(1), 47-60.

Saunders, D. G. (1994). Posttraumatic Stress symptom profiles of battered women: A comparison of survivors in two settings. *Violence and Victims, 9*(1), 31-44.

Saunders, D. G. (1995). The tendency to arrest victims of domestic violence: A preliminary analysis of officer characteristics. *Journal of Interpersonal Violence, 10*(2), 147-158.

Scott, R. I., & Day, H. D. (1996). Association of abuse-related symptoms and style of anger expression for female survivors of childhood incest. *Journal of Interpersonal Violence, 11*(2), 208-220.

Smith, L. L., Smith, J. N., & Beckner, B. M. (1994). An anger-management workshop for women inmates. *Families in Society, 75*(3), 172-175.

Spielberger, C. D. (1991). *State-Trait Anger Expression Inventory: Revised research edition.* Odessa, FL: Psychological Assessment Resources.

Stacey, W. A., Hazlewood, L. R., & Shupe, A. (1994). *The violent couple.* Westport, CT: Praeger.

Steinmetz, S. K. (1977-78). The battered husband syndrome. *Victimology, 2,* 499-509.

Stets, J. E., & Straus, M. A. (1990). Gender differences in reporting marital violence and its medical and psychological consequences. In M. A. Straus & R. J. Gelles (Eds.), *Physical violence in American families: Risk factors and adaptations to violence in 8,145 families* (pp.151-165). New Brunswick, NJ: Transaction Publishers.

Straus, M. A. (1990). Ordinary violence, child abuse, and wife-beating: What do they have in common? In M. A. Straus & R. J. Gelles (Eds.), *Physical violence in American families: Risk factors and adaptations to violence in 8,145 families* (pp. 403-424). New Brunswick, NJ: Transaction Publishers.

Straus, M. A. (1993). Physical assaults by wives: A major social problem. In R. J. Gelles & D. R. Loseke (Eds.), *Current controversies on family violence* (pp. 67-87). Newbury Park, CA: Sage Publications.

Straus, M. A. (1997). Physical assaults by women partners: A major social problem. In M. R. Walsh (Ed.), *Women, men, and gender: Ongoing debates* (pp. 210-221). New Haven: Yale University Press.

Straus, M. A. (1999). The controversy over domestic violence by women: A method-ological, theoretical, and sociology of science analysis. In X. B. Arriaga & S. Oskamp (Eds.), *Violence in intimate relationships* (pp. 17-44). Thousand Oaks, CA: Sage.

Straus, M. A., & Gelles, R. J. (1990a). How violent are American families? In M. A. Straus & R.J. Gelles (Eds.), *Physical violence in American families: Risk factors and adaptations to violence in 8,145 families* (pp. 95-112). New Brunswick, NJ: Transaction Publishers.

Straus, M. A., & Gelles, R. J. (1990b). Societal change and change in family violence from 1975 to 1985 as revealed by two national surveys. In M. A. Straus & R. J. Gelles (Eds.), *Physical violence in American families: Risk factors and adaptations to violence in 8,145 families* (pp. 113-131). New Brunswick, NJ: Transaction Publishers.

Straus, M. A., Gelles, R. J., & Steinmetz, S. K. (1980). *Behind closed doors: Violence in the American family.* New York: Anchor Books.

Straus, M. A., & Sweet, S. (1992). Verbal/symbolic aggression in couples: Incidence rates and relationships to personal characteristics. *Journal of Marriage and the Family, 54,* 346-357.

Sugarman, D. B., & Hotaling, G. T. (1998). Dating violence: A review of contextual and risk factors. In B. Levy (Ed.), *Dating violence: Young women in danger* (pp.100-118). Seattle: Seal Press.

van der Kolk, B. A. (1996). The body keeps the score: Approaches to the psychobiology of Posttraumatic Stress Disorder. In B. A. van der Kolk, A. C. McFarlane, & L. Weisaeth (Eds.), *Traumatic stress: The effects of overwhelming experience on mind, body, and society* (pp. 914-941). New York: The Guilford Press.

van der Kolk, B. A., McFarlane, A. C., & van der Hart, O. (1996). A general approach to treatment of Posttraumatic Stress Disorder. In B. A. van der Kolk, A. C. McFarlane, & L. Weisaeth (Eds.), *Traumatic stress: The effects of overwhelming experience on mind, body, and society* (pp. 417-440). New York: The Guilford Press.

Waldner-Haugrud, L. K., & Gratch, L. V. (1997). Sexual coercion in gay/lesbian rela-tionships: Descriptives and gender relationships. *Violence and Victims, 12*(1), 87-98.

Waldner-Haugrud, L. K., Gratch, L. V., & Magruder, B. (1997). Victimization and perpetration rates of violence in gay and lesbian relationships: Gender issues ex-plored. *Violence and Victims, 12*(2), 173-184.

Walker, L. E. (1984). *The battered woman syndrome.* New York: Springer Publishing Company.

Walker, L. E. A., & Browne, A. (1985). Gender and victimization by intimates. *Jour-nal of Personality, 53*(2), 179-195.

White, J. W., & Kowalski, R. M. (1994). Deconstructing the myth of the nonaggressive woman: A feminist analysis. *Psychology of Women Quarterly, 18,* 487-508.

Wilt, D. (1993). Treatment of anger. In S. P. Thomas (Ed.), *Women and anger* (pp. 233-257). New York: Springer Publishing Company.

Zlotnick, C., Kohn, R., Peterson, J., & Pearlstein, T. (1998). Partner physical victimization in a national sample of American families: Relationship to psychological functioning, psychosocial factors, and gender. *Journal of Interpersonal Violence, 13*(1), 156-166.

Zlotnick, C., Shea, T. M., Rosen, K., Simpson, E., Mulrenin, K., Begin, A., & Pearlstein, T. (1997). An affect-management group for women with posttraumatic stress disorder and histories of childhood sexual abuse. *Journal of Traumatic Stress, 10*(3), 425-436.

NONCONVENTIONAL APPROACHES FOR INTERVENTION IN CASES OF SPOUSE/PARTNER ABUSE

Adopting a Stages of Change Approach for Individuals Who Are Violent with Their Intimate Partners

Audrey L. Begun
Gene Shelley
Terri Strodthoff
Lynn Short

SUMMARY. The Stages of Change principles related to individuals' attempts to change problem behaviors provides a useful framework for illuminating the processes by which individuals may be able to successfully eliminate violence directed toward intimate partners. In this article, the five stages and relapse phenomenon are discussed, along with implications for developing standards for violence prevention interventions,

This work and related research has been supported, in part, by the Centers for Disease Control and Prevention grant #U50/CCU511248-01 to the Milwaukee Safe At Home collaboration between the Milwaukee Women's Center, Sojourner Truth House, Asha Family Services and the Center for Addiction and Behavioral Health Research. Dr. Carlo DiClemente's consultations have also proven to be invaluable.

[Haworth co-indexing entry note]: "Adopting a Stages of Change Approach for Individuals Who Are Violent with Their Intimate Partners." Begun et al. Co-published simultaneously in *Journal of Aggression, Maltreatment & Trauma* (The Haworth Maltreatment & Trauma Press, an imprint of The Haworth Press, Inc.) Vol. 5, No. 2(#10), 2001, pp. 105-127; and: *Domestic Violence Offenders: Current Interventions, Research, and Implications for Policies and Standards* (ed: Robert A. Geffner, and Alan Rosenbaum) The Haworth Maltreatment & Trauma Press, an imprint of The Haworth Press, Inc., 2001, pp. 105-127. Single or multiple copies of this article are available for a fee from The Haworth Document Delivery Service [1-800-HAWORTH, 9:00 a.m. - 5:00 p.m. (EST). E-mail address: getinfo@haworthpressinc.com].

105

the potential of stage-matched interventions, and the importance of addressing the ongoing risk of violence. *[Article copies available for a fee from The Haworth Document Delivery Service: 1-800-HAWORTH. E-mail address: <getinfo@haworthpressinc.com> Website: <http://www.HaworthPress.com> © 2001 by The Haworth Press, Inc. All rights reserved.]*

KEYWORDS. Intimate partner violence, stages of change, readiness to change

Intimate partner violence is the threatened or actual use of physical force against an intimate partner that results in or has the potential to result in injury or death. Violence of this type includes physical, sexual, and psychological assault by partners or acquaintances. Terms that are commonly used to describe intimate partner violence include domestic violence, spouse abuse, woman battering, courtship or dating violence, relationship aggression, sexual assault, and date or partner rape. Researchers and those involved with intervention are beginning to develop a consensus that intimate partner violence is a multicausal phenomenon (Eisikovits & Edleson, 1989; Rosenbaum, Cohen, & Forsstrom-Cohen, 1991). In response to the multicausal nature of the problem, numerous intervention and prevention approaches have been developed. Factors such as the psychiatric, bio-physiological, psychological, sociological, and family interaction influences have been emphasized in various programs. While there is no consensus on the single, best approach to helping individuals cease being violent towards intimate partners, some individuals do manage to make positive change towards ending their violent behavior (Edleson & Grusznki, 1989; Gondolf, 1997).

In the domains of (1) multicausality, (2) availability of diverse intervention approaches, and (3) the potential for individual change, the problem of intimate partner violence is similar to other problem behaviors that individuals strive to change (e.g., abuse of tobacco and alcohol, overeating, and engaging in unsafe sexual practices). Therefore, emerging theories and models related to the principles of behavior change also may be appropriate for use with those who are violent toward their intimate partners. In particular, the Transtheoretical Model of Behavioral Change (TMBC) and the Stages of Change principles that have emerged in the field of health psychology (Prochaska & DiClemente, 1984; Prochaska, DiClemente & Norcross, 1992) offer a promising perspective for understanding, preventing, and intervening with the problem of intimate partner violence.

The purpose of this article is to explore the relevance of a Stages of Change approach for individuals who have been violent toward their intimate partners. First, the principles of the model are explained and each stage is presented along with issues related to intimate partner violence behavior. Then, related applications of the approach are discussed, including how the approach may enhance risk assessment, the identification of typologies to improve program matching, enhancing program evaluation, and establishing treatment standards. The paper concludes with a discussion of caveats, cautions, and progress in applying this approach for individuals who are violent with intimate partners, and implications for the development of treatment standards. For clarification, the term "Stages of Change principles" is employed to refer to a theory of how individuals change their behaviors and the term "Stages of Change approach" is used to designate the application of these principles.

THE STAGES OF CHANGE

The most significant contribution offered by the Stages of Change principles to intimate partner violence is a well articulated explanation of the extreme challenges and processes experienced by individuals who are able to replace their undesirable behaviors with more acceptable, healthy ones. The Stages of Change principles address the issue of how individuals engage in the actual process of changing their problem behaviors. The principles have been applied successfully to a variety of health promotion behaviors, including smoking cessation, weight management and exercise participation, alcohol and substance abuse recovery/relapse prevention, and practicing "safe sex" (Grimley, Riley, Bellis, & Prochaska, 1993; Prochaska, 1994). The Stages of Change principles have been relatively consistent across a wide range of behaviors (Prochaska, 1994), including understanding the process of change among women who have been battered (Brown, 1997).

According to the Stages of Change principles, individuals progress through a series of stages while attempting to change their problem behaviors. Each stage is characterized by certain types of thoughts, beliefs, values, and attitudes towards the change process, as well as accompanying behaviors and change strategies. Prochaska et al., (1992) define five stages through which a person progresses. These are labeled precontemplation, contemplation, preparation, action, and maintenance.

Critical to the Stages of Change principles is the developmental, recursive nature of the change process. Not only do the principles suggest that individuals progress through a developmental course of change, but that individuals typically require three to seven "cycles" through these stages before succeeding in long-term maintenance of the desired change. Progress through the stages is often a recursive pattern, as most individuals move part of the way through the stages and periodically spiral back to prior stages before making forward progress again. For example, many individuals who successfully "quit" smoking require between three and five attempts before they finally achieve their abstinence goal; "relapse is the rule rather than the exception . . . " (Prochaska et al., 1992, p. 1104). The Stages of Change principles suggest that such relapses do not necessarily represent failures; instead, they represent a predictable pattern in the change process, one which can be reframed as learning opportunities for refining an individual's future change and maintenance strategies. Furthermore, the model suggests that not all clients in treatment improve: Some drop out of treatment while others relapse following treatment; still others are able to make significant change without professional intervention (Prochaska et al., 1992).

Using the Stages of Change approach with regard to violent behavior represents an innovation in the field. However, Gondolf (1987a) has argued for a stage-development approach to the treatment of men who batter. The arguments are based upon the stages constituting Kohlberg's theory of moral reasoning and on how each successive stage may affect behavior. No clear research evidence has yet emerged to: (1) develop a practical moral reasoning instrument for assessing stages among individuals who are violent with intimate partners, (2) confirm that moral reasoning actually directs behavior and is sufficient to predict future violence or its prevention, and (3) systematically demonstrate that intervention programs have significant life-long developmental impact. On the other hand, Gondolf and Fisher (1991) have indicated that individuals who have ceased their violent behaviors passed through a series of developmental stages. Their work suggests that individuals may initially blame their partners for the violence, normalize or minimize the violence, accuse the criminal justice system of unfairness and over-reaction, etc. Through intervention, the individual may learn to recognize the behaviors which constitute intimate partner violence, and to develop attitudes consistent with the illegal and unacceptable nature of such behavior (Gondolf & Fisher, 1991). Once the need to change violent behavior is recognized, specific skills and strategies may be learned to avoid the behavior and/or the situations in which the individual typically engaged in the behavior. Using the Stages of Change approach, Daniels and Murphy (1997) have proposed suggestions appropriate for each stage for use by clinicians who work in batterer's treatment programs.

One of the most salient implications of the Stages of Change approach is that intervention outcomes could be maximized through appropriate matching of interventions to client characteristics and readiness to change. Proper matching holds promise for enhancing the impact of interventions and for improving program attendance/completion (Rollnick, Heather, Gold, & Hall, 1992); this represents an important set of hypotheses for future research attention. Program matching based on the Stages of Change approach involves assessing and tracking the person's change experiences and internal processes. It also requires selecting interventions that are most likely to promote movement through the stages. Gondolf and Fisher (1991) have also noted, "The leading batterer programs consequently employ a phased approach that moves batterers from didactic sessions of accountability and consequence to social support groups with a focus on service" (p. 287). This progression closely parallels aspects of the Stages of Change approach.

Unfortunately, a vast majority of interventions described in the literature are primarily geared towards working with individuals in the later stages of the cycle (e.g., anger management or social skills training). While it is possible for persons in any stage to benefit from these "taking action" interventions, those who appear to do so most readily and effectively are already prepared to take an active role in changing their behaviors (Velicer, Prochaska, Rossi, & Snow, 1992). However, by relying solely upon this type of intervention approach to intimate partner violence, we are likely to "underserve, misserve, or not serve the majority . . . " (Prochaska et al., p. 1105), since many in need of change are not yet at that stage of readiness to change.

The following discussion presents a description of each of the five stages and the relapse phenomenon, along with intervention implications related to each stage. The sample statements associated with the stages are currently being tested for their appropriateness in a Stages of Change/Readiness to Change assessment instrument.[1]

Stage 1. Precontemplation

Description: Precontemplation, for most individuals, represents the earliest aspects of the change process. At this stage, the individual is not intending to change the particular behavior of concern, and may be either unaware or under-aware that a problem exists. The person in precontemplation may appear for intervention solely because of outside pressures for change. Resistance to recognizing the problem is one hallmark of this stage; any behavioral changes that are made are likely to persist only for as long as the external pressure exists. Many individuals enter into treatment for their violence toward intimate partners through the criminal justice system as nonvoluntary clients (Gondolf, 1990). Others participate in treatment because of threatened losses imposed by their partners, employers, or others important in their lives (Rooney, 1992). Unfortunately, imposing external force on an individual is not guaranteed to stimulate meaningful changes. External controls can be imposed, but should not be mistaken for sustainable, internalized change. Nonvoluntary clients are very likely to be in the precontemplation phase of the change cycle (O'Hare, 1996), although a few may have begun to contemplate change or to prepare for taking positive action (see stages of Contemplation, Preparation and Action below).

The following types of statements are frequently heard from individuals who are in the precontemplation stage related to changing their violence toward intimate partners: "It's not my fault that I act this way"; "I'm not the one who needs to be here, she's the one with the problem"; "She makes me act this way"; "That judge just had it in for me, that's all"; "If she doesn't like the way I act, she can just leave"; "There's nothing wrong with the way I handle conflict"; "I'll come to groups, but I won't talk."

Implications: Interventions designed to provide specific violence prevention skills (action-oriented interventions) are likely to be ineffective at best and, at worst, detrimental for individuals in the precontemplation stage. Because these approaches have little relevance to individuals at this stage, they may serve to reinforce a belief that the problem and its solutions are not "about" themselves, only about other people. More appropriate interventions would support the transition to becoming voluntary clients and moving into the next stages. For example, interventions which address the likely consequences of not changing the behaviors encourage individuals to contemplate and desire the change process for themselves, and to begin shifting the decisional balance toward making change. It is important at this stage to support the individual's development of an awareness, appreciation, and endorsement of the advantages associated with making the change. It is also important at this stage to minimize the use of approaches which unwittingly increase resistance and defensiveness (Murphy & Baxter, 1997).

Additional suitable interventions include helping individuals to assume responsibility and to become accountable for their own actions, because these interventions help the individual prepare for the change process and to recognize that a significant problem exists. Toward these ends, court mandates, in tandem with stage-appropriate intervention programs, may be more effective than either strategy alone in mobilizing the individual to make the desired changes. Legal sanctions currently appear to have a positive impact, however, only among certain types of individuals. The threat of arrest is not likely to have a significant impact upon individuals who do not perceive that there are personally meaningful losses associated with arrest, or who do not believe that the consequences will actually occur (Fagan, 1996; Sherman, Smith, Schmidt, & Rogan, 1992). It is important that well-designed and controlled evaluation studies of the appropriateness of these intervention approaches for individuals in this stage be conducted.

True precontemplators may never appear in the intervention system. They may evade the criminal justice system, may never attend scheduled intake sessions, or may fail to attend intervention sessions assigned after intake. As a result, we know relatively little about the full range of individuals in this stage. As treatment increasingly becomes mandated and enforced, intervention programs should be prepared to address the heightened need for appropriate interventions with the diverse group of individuals in precontemplation. Creative intervention options must be designed to match the precontemplative individual's characteristics, such as including motivational enhancement strategies and "cost/benefit" analysis. Furthermore, it should be recognized that only multi-sourced strategies will be effective in stimulating change at this point in the process. In other words, there may need to be multiple forces acting in concert upon multiple domains of the individual's life. Consistency in messages and significant consequences from interpersonal relationships, family (including children) and peer groups, the criminal justice system, the workplace, the media, mental health professionals, and other potent agents of socialization may be necessary.

Partners of individuals in precontemplation should not expect to see any significant, positive change in the intimate partner violence during this stage, even if the violent individual is attending an intervention program. One responsibility of intervention programs should be to educate partners about the serious risk of ongoing violence from individuals in the precontemplation stage.

Stage 2. Contemplation

Description: Individuals in the contemplation stage recognize the problem and are seriously thinking about overcoming that particular problem, but have not yet made a concrete commitment to take action. People can remain "stuck" in this stage for a very long time, weighing the pros and cons of the problem and of possible solutions. According to Gondolf (1985), the first step in assuming responsibility for exploitative behavior is making the decision that change is desirable. The violent person may have every intention of following through with the promise that "it won't happen again" (Sonkin, 1987). However, without a concrete action plan, even the best intentions may be diverted. The verbalized intent is not so much an intentional deception as an unfinished commitment to change. For some individuals, it may represent preliminary changes in acknowledging the problem; however, the individual has not developed an effective action plan for behavior change.

Statements of recognition or intent to change characterize individuals in the contemplation stage: "The last time I got arrested, I realized that I had a problem"; "Some of what I see and hear about domestic violence seems to apply to me"; "I can't go on this way"; "I need to make a change before something really bad happens."

Implications: Interventions which reinforce the individual's recognition of the problem as "a step in the right direction" are important for contemplation stage individuals. Momentum toward change can be maintained by helping the individual recognize the full range of costs and benefits associated with the change process. According to Bowker (1983), women who remained with their partners but were able to negotiate successfully an end to the violence believed that their partner recognized the high costs associated with not changing violent behaviors and attitudes. Important societal messages about the social and personal costs of violence are provided through court mandates to individuals at the stage of contemplating change (Ganley, 1987). Individuals at this stage are internally debating the costs and benefits of making a change. However, they may not be able to make a convincing argument to themselves because they lack sufficient experience or exposure to the benefits of success. It is important to support the contemplation process by helping the individual to de-emphasize the significance of the "con" arguments that arise in their personal cost-benefit analyses. Individuals in contemplation are often receptive to hearing the personal stories and successful experiences of their predecessors in individuals who can serve as mentors concerning the early change process.

As in the case of precontemplation stage individuals, interventions during contemplation which emphasize the building of nonviolence skills, changing violence attitudes, or taking action to stop violence may be premature. While it is useful to introduce the individual to the range of intervention options available, it may not be useful to begin training the individual to make changes before the person is prepared to make change happen. Without recognition of the problematic nature of their violence with intimate partners, individuals are not likely to respond appropriately to instruction on ways of changing the behavior, or the need to change attitudes, values, and beliefs. Pseudosuccess (Scalia, 1994) is one likely consequence of premature participation in action-oriented interventions. In other words, an individual may simply mimic the appearance of having changed when, in fact, change has not occurred internally.

Individuals at this stage benefit from interventions that provide reinforcement for reasons to change. The extent to which an intervention addresses and responds to the participants' cultural experiences is particularly likely to affect the process of moving from contemplation into the next stage (Williams, 1992, 1994; Williams & Becker, 1994). For example, it has been suggested that rational-emotive therapy is a preferred treatment approach in cross-cultural counseling because it encourages the examination and challenging of cultural assumptions that result in dysfunction without requiring that clients think, feel, or behave like members of the dominant culture in order to effect change (Brownell, 1997). In this way, clients might be supported in their own, culturally-relevant reasons for changing the violence and supported in challenging any culturally-based perceptions concerning barriers to change.

Stage 3. Preparation

Description: Preparation is the stage in which the individual actively develops specific plans for making change. The plans include clearly defined time frames. By definition, the person in preparation intends to take action within the next month and may even have unsuccessfully taken (incomplete) action during the past year (Prochaska et al., 1992). In the preparation stage, individuals may have accomplished some reduction in their problem behaviors, but have not successfully achieved their change goals.

This stage did not appear in early discussions of the Stages of Change principles. Preparation became evident only through complex reanalysis of data, resulting in a discussion of five, rather than four, stages in the change process (Prochaska et al., 1992). This stage has considerable overlap with contemplation and action, the preceding and ensuing stages, because it reflects attitudes common to both.

Implications: Because these individuals are in transition between contemplation and action, interventions related to taking action may be somewhat helpful. The greatest benefit of these interventions, at this stage, is likely to be achieved when coupled with interventions that reinforce the person's commitment to the change effort. Interventions which emphasize the assumption of accountability and responsibility for one's own actions are appropriate at this stage because they are in accord with the person's own thinking about taking responsibility for the change process. It is also important at this stage to support and reinforce a fragile positive decisional balance.

Attendance and drop-out rates may represent significant indicators of the transition from contemplation to action. Making a commitment to regularly attend intervention sessions is considered to be one serious step in the change process. The importance of this commitment is supported by evidence that high attendance rates in violence intervention programs are related to lower rates of recidivism (Shepard, 1992). However, it is important to note that the evidence does not permit causal inference; it is equally likely that commitment to attend results in success or that some other factor affects both commitment and successful outcome in the same fashion.

Stage 4. Action

Description: Action is the stage most recognizable and most often researched because it is marked by overt, observable change efforts and the actual adoption of change strategies. The action-oriented individual is *actively* modifying behavior, revising cognitions, attitudes, values, and belief systems, and regulating the environment in order to overcome the specified problem. Action requires tremendous expenditures of energy, vigilance, and focus in order to control and maintain the changes which are initiated. By definition, this period extends from the first day of successful change through six months of successful effort.

The person in the action stage is likely to make statements that acknowledge the specific change strategies being employed, and to acknowledge the importance of what is being accomplished: "Now when I get upset, I take a time out"; "I know how to recognize my early danger signals"; "I know that I have to avoid certain situations in order to keep control of myself;" "People are noticing the changes in me."

Implications: According to the Transtheoretical Model of Behavioral Change (Prochaska et al., 1992), there may not be any one "best" specific type of action-oriented intervention for overcoming a specific problem behavior. In fact, many individuals are able to change their behaviors satisfactorily without the benefit from professional intervention at all. On the other hand, it may be important for individuals to have available a range of intervention options from which to select. Individuals may differ in their preferences for, and responsiveness to, group versus individual sessions, different locations and hours of service, personalities or gender of the intervention staff, costs and fees, distinct program image and/or philosophy, etc., as well as differing in their need for developing certain skills, attitudes, beliefs, and values.

It may be important with individuals in the action stage to exclude precontemplative individuals from intervention groups, not only because it is not helpful to them, but also because they may be counterproductive influences upon the preparation and action stage group members. Gondolf (1993) describes the manner in which certain individuals who are unprepared to change may, in a group setting, undermine the progress of those who have the potential to change. According to a Stages of Change framework, such exposure to a precontemplative individual may result in the decisional balance, based on personal analysis of the costs and benefits associated with changing versus not changing, being influenced away from decisions that promote change, and toward a decisional balance that discourages change. It is also likely to demoralize and frustrate those who have moved to an action phase, and may result in their abandonment of the treatment group because it is not perceived to be a "good fit" for them.

Motivationally, the person in the action stage is in a prime position to learn from others' experiences and to incorporate new ideas about the problem. However, the person may also be susceptible to fanaticism and a certain amount of superstitious thinking in relation to a specific change strategy. Such superstitions may include feeling compelled to attend meetings only at a specific day and time, fearing that failure to adhere to a strict schedule will result in a failure of self-control, or believing that a chance exposure to a personal violence trigger will automatically instigate a repetition of the violence. While the intervention approaches should have sound theoretical underpinnings and a track record based upon reliable evaluation procedures, successfully matching the person's preferences with the intervention characteristics might improve the chances of successful completion.

Stage 5. Maintenance

Description: After a full six months of action without any recurrence of the undesired behavior, an individual has achieved the maintenance stage. Maintenance is characterized by efforts to sustain the behavioral changes beyond the action period and to avoid relapse. Maintenance involves continuing the changes that were invoked, and consistently engaging in behaviors that are incompatible with the problem behavior. Maintenance should not be characterized simply as an absence of further change. For some behaviors, maintenance may last a lifetime, requiring continued vigilance against relapse. For other behaviors, successful maintenance for a five-year period may permit termination of the change effort. Termination is only valid if the individual no longer experiences any temptation to relapse and has complete confidence in the new behaviors. It is also possible that individuals in maintenance will choose to reinforce their changed status through a commitment to social action and to helping others who struggle to overcome the same problem.

Individuals in the maintenance stage are likely to state: "I've come too far now to end up like that again"; "I don't believe that I'll return to my old ways of treating my partner(s)"; "That's not me anymore, I'm a different person than I was then"; "I worry that my recent changes won't last"; "Sometimes I find that it's very hard for me to avoid my old ways of treating my partner(s)"; "I believe that I have something to offer to others based on my experiences."

Implications: Once a person reaches this stage, it is usually assumed that a permanent change has been effected and that no further intervention is required. But experience with the Stages of Change in smoking, alcohol abuse, or other substance abuse behaviors indicates that relapse may be expected.

Therefore, partners of those who were violent continue to be vulnerable to violence. Those who formerly were violent with intimate partners and who have attained the maintenance stage should not "graduate" out of the intervention system that has helped them to achieve this goal. Instead, programs should plan for continuing reinforcement of recently acquired changes in behavior for an extended period of time. Involving maintenance stage individuals in the interventions with new clients may be an ideal mechanism for both mentoring the earlier stage person and for ensuring the later stage person's ongoing support and validation of the new attitudes and behaviors. Serving as a mentor may help to reinforce a person's sense of confidence and ongoing development of competence in managing unexpected situations and challenges.

Relapse

During relapse, an individual regresses to the behavior and experiences associated with an earlier stage in the change process. Relapse is commonly perceived by others and experienced by the individual as failure. The person becomes demoralized and may resist thinking about attempting to change again (precontemplation). A person in relapse can recycle to contemplation or preparation, where plans for the next action attempt can be informed by what was learned from the recent efforts (e.g., what worked, what didn't work, etc.). "Each time relapsers recycle through the stages, they potentially learn from their mistakes and can try something different the next time around" (Prochaska et al., 1992, p. 1105).

Many individuals repeat their cyclical and escalating patterns of intimate partner violence and abuse (Walker, 1979), despite sincere intentions to avoid becoming violent or abusive again. A number of evaluation reports indicate that there is a relatively high probability that individuals who have been involved in treatment because of their violence toward an intimate partner will repeat the violence, even after completing a treatment program (Edleson & Syers, 1990, 1991; Saunders & Azar, 1989; Shepard, 1992). These individuals are typically considered "treatment failures." However, in adopting a Stages of Change perspective, relapsing individuals have not necessarily failed in their efforts to change, but have moved out of a maintenance stage and back into an earlier stage in the cycle of change. In the longitudinal, developmental perspective associated with the Stages of Change approach, relapses become opportunities to learn to develop more successful action plans, means of avoiding future relapses, and means of continually expanding the period of maintenance. With appropriately matched interventions, the relapsing individual should be able to progress to a point of maintenance once again.

While relapse is an anticipated event in the developmental course of changing behavior, it is clear that all repeated violence is not necessarily a relapse episode. Relapse assumes prior successful progress through the stages of change. Violence from individuals in precontemplation, contemplation, or preparation stages is simply an ongoing expression of the problem. These individuals have not yet taken sufficient steps toward changing the behavior. Relapse is not a failure to make change, but a failure in maintaining the positive change that has been achieved. What is known about the relapse phenomenon, however, has been learned in the study of behaviors that do not necessarily have the magnitude of impact generally associated with violence toward an intimate partner. The "learning opportunities" related to relapse lose significance when viewed within the context of the physical, financial, health, emotional, psychological, legal, and potentially lethal consequences of any repetition of the violence.

The expectation of relapse implied by the Stages of Change principles should not be adopted as an excuse for repeated violence. Excuses imply acceptance or tolerance of the behavior, and at no point in the process of changing intimate partner violence is the violent behavior ever acceptable or tolerable. Regardless of the stage, intimate partner violence remains dangerous, inappropriate, and illegal. At any stage in the process of change, the decision not to act violently remains the responsibility of the individual. Even when an individual has achieved some degree of change, relapse should continue to be accompanied by criminal and social sanctions. Appropriate sanctions provide a means of reinforcing individual accountability for intimate partner violence, and possibly, of reinforcing an ongoing commitment to change.

Intervention programs are very likely to include individuals who have already cycled through the change process at least once. It is likely to benefit the individuals' change process if their prior experiences are addressed and properly framed. The fact that someone was able to change in the past, even for a while, is a positive phenomenon and relapse should not be considered as evidence of failure to make a change. Discussion should address relapse as an aspect of the change process, without appearing to excuse the relapse behaviors or minimize the impact of relapse on partners and others (e.g., children and other family members). Instead, intervention should be directed at helping individuals identify the challenges and barriers that resulted in relapse, and to develop strategies for avoiding them in the future. Strategies for ensuring support for maintaining positive change should also be developed with the relapsing individual. The intervention program may have to return to the beginning of the change cycle with motivating the person to make change (contemplation and preparation stages) before exploring strategies and means of restructuring one's environment to ensure success (action and maintenance stages).

RELATED APPLICATIONS

Enhancing Risk Assessment

The Stages of Change approach offers a set of criteria for developing more refined risk assessment profiles and information essential in advising partners about the risk of ongoing violence, both during and following involvement with an intervention. It also offers a pertinent means of disaggregating the population for purposes of eventually matching intervention approaches to client types. Intervention matching is one means of enhancing intervention impact and effectiveness (Holtzworth-Monroe & Stuart, 1994).

Enhancing Typologies and Program Matching

Studies of intimate partner violence indicate that the problem is not limited to any particular class of people; it occurs across racial, ethnic, social class, age, religious, and gender groups, and "is discouragingly common in every community in this country and in every neighborhood" (Crime and Violence Prevention Center, 1995). While studies may demonstrate differences in relative frequencies of intimate partner violence across various groups, clearly the problem is widespread and diversely distributed across the population. One practical translation of this fact is that there exists tremendous heterogeneity among those who need to change their intimate partner violence behaviors. In light of this observed heterogeneity, it is likely that no standard or uniform approaches to intervention will be universally effective. In an effort to promote the development of targeted interventions, or "treatment matching," a number of social scientists have created systems by which the individuals who are violent with intimate partners can be meaningfully categorized, or "typed."

Typologies are created through the identification of clusters among characteristics, traits, or experiences reported among the individuals who are violent with intimate partners. One typology approach refers to the individual's patterns of aggressiveness: (1) family-only violence, (2) generalized, undercontrolled violence, and (3) the emotionally volatile aggressor (Brisson, 1981; Fagan, Stewart, & Hansen, 1983; Gondolf, 1987b; Hershorn & Rosenbaum, 1991; Saunders, 1993; Shields, McCall, & Hanneke, 1988). Other typologies reflect personality traits and subtypes, as well as dimensions, such as attitudes toward women, intrinsic anger, depression, psychiatric history, and substance abuse patterns (Hamberger, Feuerbarch, & Borman, 1990; Hamberger & Hastings, 1986; Hamberger, Lohr, Bonge, & Tolin, 1996; Holtzworth-Monroe & Stuart, 1994; Saunders, 1992, 1993). The typologies are useful in that they permit enhanced risk assessment and meaningful disaggregation of the heterogeneous population by creating subgroups with greater similarity (Holtzworth-Monroe & Stuart, 1994; Saunders, 1993). It remains to be demonstrated whether the Stages of Change and typology approaches actually interface. The simplest interface would be an observation that, within the types, individuals vary with regard to their stages in the change process. Conversely, it may be found that individuals of certain types are more highly concentrated within certain stages. An interactive relationship between stage and type is currently speculative, and requires the execution of targeted research to confirm or revise.

Enhancing Program Evaluation

Popular approaches to the evaluation of interventions for eliminating intimate partner violence employ pre- or post-intervention comparisons of data about the severity or frequency of violence (Murphy & Cascardi, 1993), using such indices as the Conflict Tactics Scale (Pan, Neidig, & O'Leary, 1994; Straus, 1979; Straus & Gelles, 1990), the Abusive Behavior Inventory (Shepard & Campbell, 1992), the Severity of Violence Against Women Scales (Marshall, 1992), the Violent Behavior Inventory (Faulkner, Stoltenberg, Cogen, Nolder, & Shooter, 1992), or the Psychological Maltreatment Inventory (Tolman, 1989). While these approaches provide important information about intervention outcomes, they do not provide information about the actual process of change experienced by individuals who attempt to cease their violent behaviors. The Stages of Change approach offers an opportunity to enhance current program evaluation practices by generating information about the change process itself. In this way, programs may become more responsive to the diverse change experiences of the individuals enrolled and may become more successful in achieving positive outcomes.

In order to apply the Stages of Change approach to program evaluation, reliable and valid instruments must be developed. There are currently no published instruments specifically designed to assess Stage of Change or readiness to change violence towards intimate partners. However, several are under construction and undergoing psychometric testing at this time (e.g., the Stages of Change measure employed by the Safe at Home[1] project and the stages of change measure developed by Levesque, Gelles, and Vellicer, in press). Generic or universal readiness to change indices are not recommended for evaluating intimate partner violence interventions because the lack of specificity about which behaviors are being addressed may lead to confusion; individuals may be responding about plans to change behaviors unrelated to their violence (e.g., smoking, employment, weight, etc.). The effort to construct reliable and valid evaluation instruments represents an important research objective in the field of intimate partner violence.

Establishing Treatment Standards

The Stages of Change approach has considerable relevance to the development and implementation of batterer's treatment standards. The first, and perhaps, most evident implication is related to creating standards concerning appropriate time frames for treatment. Considerable time is required to make a significant change in entrenched, habitual behaviors. The cumulative behavioral and attitudinal change demands associated with the cessation of intimate partner violence are monumental. The individual must change attitudes and behaviors that have been developed over a lifetime and which are often reinforced by societal norms. Therefore, it is speculated that an extensive amount of time may be needed to ensure lasting change (Jennings, 1990). A single progression through the cycle of change may require a year or more to complete. As relapsing and recycling are factored into the equation, several years may be necessary for successful completion of the change process, even for those motivated to change. Thus, standards must be suitably flexible to acknowledge the nature of the change process, but not so vague as to dilute the impact of setting such standards.

A second implication is the importance of standards evolving in tandem with research discoveries concerning the nature, measurability, and validity of the stages of change principles with respect to changing intimate partner violence behavior. Research is only beginning to confirm that aspects of the approach apply to this category of behaviors; much remains to be determined. Furthermore, the development of reliable and valid instruments for assessing stage development in individuals is in a foundling state. As measurement accuracy improves through continued research, standards should be modified. It is currently premature to establish standards related to specific test scores obtained by individuals on any current stage-related instrument.

The third implication for establishing standards concerns the specific nature of the interventions supported. Again, as in the case of time frames, the stages of change approach suggests that a flexible array of approaches may be most responsive to the true nature of the change process. Key to the concept of an intervention array is the development and testing, through controlled research study, of intervention approaches that match aspects of the change process. For example, an appropriate array may need to have diversity both within stage-typed intervention (e.g., different types of action approaches), as well as between stages (i.e., interventions matched to each stage–precontemplation, contemplation, preparation, action, and maintenance).

CAVEATS, CAUTIONS, AND PROGRESS

The Stages of Change approach to intervention with individuals who are violent toward their intimate partners is not without limitations. For example, this approach does not adequately address the social contexts within which individuals change their behavior. A variety of social factors (e.g., peer group influences, media images, economic stressors, family norms and values) affect the process of individual behavior change. These factors may inhibit or enhance individual behavior change. Thus, an individual's progress through the Stages of Change, or lack of progress, may be closely tied to a host of influencing factors about which little is yet understood.

Adopting a Stages of Change approach to intervention with individuals who are violent toward their intimate partners also has implications that transcend any particular stage. One implication relates to the importance of creating coordinated community response systems. Such coordination may prove helpful to individuals in all stages. To be helpful, however, the system must deliver coherent, non-ambiguous messages about the unacceptable nature of intimate partner violence and must significantly enhance the deterrence power of prescribed consequences by increasing the probability that they will actually occur. In fact, Gondolf (1987a) argued that a major limitation in efforts to effectively change individuals who are violent with intimate partners is the piecemeal, uncoordinated, and competitive nature of intervention programs. He suggests that the literature tends to support one mode of intervention over another, rather than examining the ways in which various approaches might complement one another in producing and maintaining change. Adoption of a developmental perspective about individuals changing their intimate partner violence behaviors results in the implication that,

> interventions for batterers need to be integrated into a series of interventions that correspond to the developmental stage of the batterer and furthers it. As a batterer moves toward a higher stage of development, he may become more responsive to another form of intervention which is more appropriate to that stage. Therefore, one kind of intervention is not sufficient to change batterers, and an intervention that does not correspond to the batterer's stage of development is not likely to be effective. (Gondolf, 1987a, p. 336)

A second, and closely related, implication of adopting a Stages of Change approach for individuals who are violent with intimate partners is related to the importance of integrating cultural competence with the type of "stage competence" elements described above. It is not likely to be sufficient to address matching interventions to stages without regard for multicultural aspects of the clients' situations and interventions; it is possible that research will reveal important interactive relationships between multicultural factors and stage of change.

The third general implication is that, regardless of the stage, it is important to maintain appropriate expectations about the amount of time necessary for the change process, and flexibility in standards related to time frames. Furthermore, if interventions are delivered incrementally, the collective package requires extensive synthesis and assimilation by the individual, especially for those in the earliest stages. Research may eventually suggest that a long-term, single-type intervention approach may be less effective in achieving the end goal, an absence of violence, than a series of stage-appropriate short-term interventions. In fact, it is possible that a single-focus, long-term intervention may exceed a threshold of influence, and may even contribute to a situation of stage-stagnation and seriously diminished returns on the intervention investment. Instead, greater gain might be made and sustained within a series of staged, more diverse intervention approaches. While the total time frame for intervention and monitoring may need to be prolonged and allow for periods of "backsliding" towards earlier stages, the cost of providing this complex array of interventions, tailored to the individual's stage of the change process, may become prohibitive for any one program or agency. It becomes increasingly evident that a synchronized and coordinated community response may be necessary to support the change process over time. This group of speculations, however, requires examination through controlled and thoughtful study.

The fourth key point is related to the profound ethical obligation of intervention personnel to inform partners of their ongoing risks for continued exposure to violence throughout the change cycle. The duty to warn is of greatest concern in situations of high lethality (Sonkin, 1987) or risk of danger. Given the recursive nature of the Stages of Change cycle, it is unwise for clients, victims, or treatment personnel to become too complacent prior to the emergence of long, successful maintenance periods.

Another concern is that adopting a Stages of Change approach might encourage another excuse for continued violence, rather like the (mis)use of diagnoses embraced by "domestic violence admitters" as described by Gondolf (1993). For example, it is feared that relapse might be employed as a rationale for minimizing legal consequences for subsequent violence, despite the fact that intimate partner violence is a criminal act, regardless of the individual's readiness to change or previous efforts to change.

Finally, the development and psychometric testing of emerging instruments will help shed light on the question of whether violence toward an intimate partner is sufficiently similar to other health-related behaviors to warrant application of this approach. It is not entirely clear that the Transtheoretical Model of Behavior Change (Prochaska et al., 1992) adequately explains the process of change in such complex behaviors. Furthermore, some individuals' violence may occur too sporadically for this behavior change model to have reasonable applicability. However, if the violence continuum includes varied forms of psychological, emotional, sexual, and human rights abuses, the violence frequency may be fully adequate for this model (Saunders, 1992). This is a research question of primary significance as a foundation for appropriately applying the Stages of Change approach to the problem of intimate partner violence.

In summary, adopting a Stages of Change approach, derived from a Transtheoretical Model of Behavioral Change (Prochaska et al., 1992) holds promise for those who design and evaluate interventions with individuals who are violent toward their intimate partners. The approach encourages us to more closely examine how individuals successfully change their violence-related attitudes and behaviors. The approach reflects a need to coordinate a range of "stage-matched" interventions within the community. It also reflects a need to develop accurate, systematic, scientifically valid, and reliable instruments for determining stage or readiness to change. The Stages of Change approach provides a useful framework for closely examining the heterogeneous population of individuals who are violent with intimate partners by illuminating the actual processes by which they are able to eliminate this violence successfully.

NOTE

1. Safe At Home is a partnership project developed between three intimate partner violence service agencies in Milwaukee County (Milwaukee Women's Center, Inc., Sojourner Truth House, Inc., and Asha Family Services, Inc.) and the University of Wisconsin-Milwaukee School of Social Welfare and the Center for Addiction and Behavioral Health Research. The community intervention project was funded by a 5-year $1.5 million grant from the Centers for Disease Control and Prevention. The overall goal of the project is to prevent violence against women and girls. Project components include the development, delivery, and evaluation of community education and public awareness campaigns, professional education programs, adolescent education, and interventions with those who are violent toward their intimate partners.

REFERENCES

Bowker, L. (1983). *Beating wife beating*. Lexington, MA: D. C. Heath & Co.

Brisson, N. (1981). Battering husbands: A survey of abusive men. *Victimology, 6*, 338-344.

Brown, J. (1997). Working toward freedom from violence: The process of change in battered women. *Violence Against Women*, 3(1), 5-26.

Brownell, P. (1997). Multicultural practice and domestic violence. In E. P. Congress (Ed.), *Multicultural perspectives in working with families* (pp. 217-235). New York: Springer.

Crime and Violence Prevention Center. (1995, August). *Violence prevention: A vision of hope.* Final report of Attorney General Daniel E. Lungren's Policy Council on Violence Prevention. Crime & Prevention Center, P. O. Box 944255, Sacramento, CA 94244-2550. (916)324-7863.

Daniels, J. W., & Murphy, C. (1997). Stages and processes of change in batterers' treatment. *Cognitive and Behavioral Practice, 4*, 123-145.

Edleson, J. L., & Grusznki, R. J. (1989). Treating men who batter: Four years of outcome data from the domestic abuse project. *Journal of Social Service Research, 12* (1/2), 3-22.

Edleson, J. L., & Syers, M. (1990). The relative effectiveness of group treatments for men who batter. *Social Work Research and Abstracts, 26*(2), 10-17.

Edleson, J. L., & Syers, M. (1991). The effects of group treatment for men who batter: An 18-month follow-up study. *Research on Social Work Practice, 1*(3), 227-243.

Eisikovits, Z. C., & Edleson, J. L. (1989). Intervening with men who batter: A critical review of the literature. *Social Service Review, 63*(3), 384-414.

Fagan, J. A. (1996). *The criminalization of domestic violence: Promises and limits.* National Institute of Justice, U. S. Department of Justice, Research Report.

Fagan, J. A., Stewart, D. K., & Hansen, K. V. (1983). Violent men or violent husbands? Background factors and situational correlates. In D. Finkelhor, R. J. Gelles, G. T. Hotaling, & M. A. Straus (Eds.), *The dark side of families: Current family violence research* (pp. 49-67). Beverly Hills, CA: Sage.

Faulkner, K., Stoltenberg, C. D., Cogen, R., Nolder, M., & Shooter, E. (1992). Cognitive-behavioral group treatment for male spouse abusers. *Journal of Family Violence, 7(1)*, 37-55.

Ganley, A. L. (1987). Perpetrators of domestic violence: An overview of counseling the court-mandated client. In D. J. Sonkin (Ed.), *Domestic violence on trial: Psychological and legal dimensions of family violence* (pp. 155-173). New York: Springer.

Gondolf, E. W. (1985). *Men who batter: An integrated approach for stopping wife abuse.* Holmes Beach, FL: Learning Publications.

Gondolf, E. W. (1987a). Changing men who batter: A developmental model for integrated interventions. *Journal of Family Violence, 2*(4), 335-349.

Gondolf, E. W. (1987b). Who are those guys? Toward a behavioral typology of batterers. *Violence and Victims, 3*, 187-204.

Gondolf, E. W. (1990). An exploratory survey of court-mandated batterer programs. *Response, 13*(3), 7-11.

Gondolf, E. W. (1993). Male batterers. In R. L. Hampton, T. P. Gullotta, G. R. Adams, E. H. Potter, & R. P. Weissberg (Eds.), *Family violence: Prevention and treatment* (pp. 230-257). Newbury Park, CA: Sage.

Gondolf, E. W. (1997). Batterer programs: What we know and need to know. *Journal of Interpersonal Violence, 12*, 83-98.

Gondolf, E. W., & Fisher, E. R. (1991). Wife battering. In R. T. Ammerman & M. Hersen (Eds.), *Case studies in family violence* (pp. 273-292). New York: Plenum Press.

Grimley, D. M., Riley, G. E., Bellis, J. M., & Prochaska, J. O. (1993). Assessing the stages of change and decision-making for contraceptive use for the prevention of pregnancy, sexually transmitted diseases, and Acquired Immunodeficiency Syndrome. *Health Education Quarterly, 20*(4), 455-470.

Hamberger, L. K., Feuerbarch, S. P., & Borman, R. J. (1990). Detecting the wife batterer. *Medical Aspects of Human Sexuality, 24*(9), 32-39.

Hamberger, L. K., & Hastings, J. E. (1986). Personality correlates of men who abuse their partners: A cross-validation study. *Journal of Family Violence, 1*, 323-341.

Hamberger, L. K., Lohr, J. M., Bonge, D., & Tolin, D. F. (1996). A large sample empirical typology of male spouse abusers and its relationship to dimensions of abuse. *Violence and Victims, 11*(4), 277-292.

Hershorn, M., & Rosenbaum, A. (1991). Over- vs. undercontrolled hostility: Application of the construct to the classification of maritally violent men. *Violence and Victims, 6*, 151-158.

Holzworth-Monroe, A., & Stuart, G. L. (1994). Typologies of male batterers: Three subtypes and the differences among them. *Psychological Bulletin, 116*, 476-497.

Jennings, J. L. (1990). Preventing relapse versus "stopping" domestic violence: Do we expect too much too soon from battering men? *Journal of Family Violence, 5*(1), 43-60.

Levesque, D. A., Gelles, R. J., & Vellicer, W. F. (in press). Development and validation of a stages of change measure for men in batterer treatment. *Cognitive Therapy and Research.*

Marshall, L. L. (1992). Development of the Severity of Violence Against Women Scales. *Journal of Family Violence, 7*(2), 102-121.

Murphy, C. M., & Baxter, V. (1997). Motivating batterers to change in the treatment context. *Journal of Interpersonal Violence, 12*, 607-619.

Murphy, C. M., & Cascardi, M. (1993). Psychological aggression and abuse in marriage. In R. L. Hampton, T. P. Gullotta, G. R. Adams, E. H. Potter, & R. P. Weissberg (Eds.), *Family violence: Prevention and treatment* (pp. 86-112). Newbury Park, CA: Sage.

O'Hare, T. (1996). Court-ordered versus voluntary clients: Problem differences and readiness for change. *Social Work, 41*, 417-422.

Pan, H. S., Neidig, P. H., & O'Leary, K. D. (1994). Male-female and aggressor-victim differences in the factor structure of the Modified Conflict Tactics Scale. *Journal of Interpersonal Violence, 9*, 366-382.

Prochaska, J. O. (1994). Strong and weak principles for progressing from precontemplation to action on the basis of twelve problem behaviors. *Health Psychology, 13*, 47-51.

Prochaska, J. O., & DiClemente, C. C. (1984). *The transtheoretical approach: Crossing traditional boundaries of change.* Homewood, IL: Dow Jones, Irwin.

Prochaska, J. O., DiClemente, C. C., & Norcross, J. C. (1992). In search of how people change: Applications to addictive behaviors. *American Psychologist, 47,* 1102-1114.

Rollnick, S., Heather, N., Gold, R., & Hall, W. (1992). Development of a short readiness to change questionnaire for use in brief, opportunistic interventions among excessive drinkers. *British Journal of Addiction, 87,* 743-754.

Rooney, R. H. (1992). *Strategies for work with involuntary clients.* New York: Columbia University Press.

Rosenbaum, A., Cohen, P., & Forsstrom-Cohen, B. (1991). The ecology of domestic aggression toward adult victims. In R. T. Ammerman & M. Hersen (Eds.), *Case studies in family violence* (pp. 39-56). New York: Plenum Press.

Saunders, D. G. (1992). A typology of men who batter: Three types derived from cluster analysis. *American Journal of Orthopsychiatry, 62*(2), 264-275.

Saunders, D. G. (1993). Husbands who assault: Multiple profiles requiring multiple responses. In N. Z. Hilton (Ed.), *Legal responses to wife assault* (pp. 9-34). Newbury Park, CA: Sage.

Saunders, D. G., & Azar, S. (1989). Family violence treatment programs: Descriptions and evaluation. In L. Ohlin & M. Tonry (Eds.), *Family violence* (pp. 481-546). Chicago: University of Chicago Press.

Scalia, J. (1994). Psychoanalytic insights and the prevention of pseudosuccess in the cognitive-behavioral treatment of batterers. *Journal of Interpersonal Violence, 9,* 548-555.

Shepard, M. F. (1992). Predicting batterer recidivism five years after community intervention. *Journal of Family Violence, 7*(3), 167-178.

Shepard, M. F., & Campbell, J. A. (1992). The abusive behavior inventory: A measure of psychological and physical abuse. *Journal of Interpersonal Violence, 7,* 291-305.

Sherman, L. W., Smith, D. A., Schmidt, J. D., & Rogan, D. P. (1992). Crime, punishment, and stake in conformity: Legal and informal control of domestic violence. *American Sociological Review, 57,* 680-690.

Shields, N. M., McCall, G. J., & Hanneke, C. R. (1988). Patterns of family and nonfamily violence: Violent husbands and violent men. *Violence and Victims, 3,* 83-98.

Sonkin, D. J. (1987). The assessment of court-mandated male batterers. In D. J. Sonkin (Ed.), *Domestic violence on trial: Psychological and legal dimensions of family violence* (pp. 174-196). New York: Springer.

Straus, M. A. (1979). Measuring intrafamily conflict and violence: The Conflict Tactics Scales. *Journal of Marriage and the Family, 41,* 75-88.

Straus, M. A. & Gelles, R. J. (1990). *Physical violence in American families: Risk factors and adaptations to violence in 8,145 families.* New Brunswick, NJ: Transaction Books.

Tolman, R. M. (1989). The development of a measure of psychological maltreatment of women by their male partners. *Violence and Victims, 4,* 159-177.

Velicer, W. F., Prochaska, J. O., Rossi, J. S., & Snow, M. G. (1992). Assessing outcome in smoking cessation studies. *Psychological Bulletin, 111,* 23-41.

Walker, L. E. (1979). *Battered women.* New York: Harper & Row.

Williams, O. J. (1992). Ethnically sensitive practice to enhance treatment participation of African American men who batter. *Families in Society, 73,* 588-595.

Williams, O. J. (1994). Group work with African American men who batter: Toward more ethnically sensitive practice. *Journal of Comparative Family Studies, 25,* 91-103.

Williams, O. J., & Becker, R. L. (1994). Domestic partner abuse treatment programs and cultural competence: The results of a national survey. *Violence and Victims, 9*(3), 287-296.

Safety Planning
Based on Lethality Assessment
for Partners of Batterers
in Intervention Programs

Jacquelyn C. Campbell

SUMMARY. This chapter outlines a process of individualized safety planning with the partners of batterers in intervention programs that is based on the principles of empowerment and autonomy, and takes into account the context of the woman's situation. Assessing context is operationalized as considering the potential lethality of the situation from her partner, her relationship and emotional status, available resources, and her children. The safety planning process is described as an opportunity for the abused woman to gain information in order to strategize her responses. It is also a way for the program staff to gain more accurate information about the batterer's level of violence and dangerousness, and to work with women to enhance retention of abusers in the program. *[Article copies available for a fee from The Haworth Document Delivery Service: 1-800-HAWORTH. E-mail address: <getinfo@haworthpressinc.com> Website: <http://www.HaworthPress.com> © 2001 by The Haworth Press, Inc. All rights reserved.]*

This research was supported by NIH NCNR, R29NR01678, NIH NCNR, R01NR02571; CDC/NIJ/NIDA/NIMH, NIH, R01DA/AA11156.

[Haworth co-indexing entry note]: "Safety Planning Based on Lethality Assessment for Partners of Batterers in Intervention Programs." Campbell, Jacquelyn C. Co-published simultaneously in *Journal of Aggression, Maltreatment & Trauma* (The Haworth Maltreatment & Trauma Press, an imprint of The Haworth Press, Inc.) Vol. 5, No. 2(#10), 2001, pp. 129-143; and: *Domestic Violence Offenders: Current Interventions, Research, and Implications for Policies and Standards* (ed: Robert A. Geffner, and Alan Rosenbaum) The Haworth Maltreatment & Trauma Press, an imprint of The Haworth Press, Inc., 2001, pp. 129-143. Single or multiple copies of this article are available for a fee from The Haworth Document Delivery Service [1-800-HAWORTH, 9:00 a.m. - 5:00 p.m. (EST). E-mail address: getinfo@haworthpressinc.com].

129

KEYWORDS. Batterer intervention, battered women, violence, risk factors, danger assessment, homicide

Many comprehensive batterer intervention programs offer or routinely provide some level of contact, assessment, and referral for the partners of batterers. These programs often make use of partnerships with shelter programs or are actually part of a shelter program. Assessment of the batterer's initial and ongoing level of violence is considered more accurate if provided by the partner than by the abuser (Dobash & Dobash, 1997; Gondolf, 1997), and work with partners can be considered important for retention of batterers in intervention and prevention of re-offending after intervention (Chalk & King, 1998; Chez, 1987). In addition, the partners of men (or women) in batterer intervention may never go to a shelter or other service system for help in dealing with the abuse, so that safety planning conducted by batterer intervention program staff may be a partner's only intervention. Batterer intervention program contact can also successfully bridge the abused woman[1] to other services in the mental health, social service and/or criminal justice system(s). Although some programs are concerned about victim safety with partner contact, partner choice in the matter plus using Gondolf's (1997) ongoing program of research as a model for safe contact can minimize these concerns.

Therefore, any batterer intervention program involving partners needs to include safety planning for those abused (far more often women), and for children in the home. The objectives of safety planning are empowerment and the woman's autonomy; it is a dialogic process rather than prescriptive, and cannot guarantee the woman's safety. Rather, it is an opportunity for the abused woman to gain information, thoroughly assess her situation, and strategize her responses. In order to be effective, safety planning cannot be standardized, but instead must be tailored to the individual woman and her situation. The most important aspects of the situation are: (a) the potential lethality or dangerousness from her partner; (b) whether she is planning to stay, is in the process of leaving, or has left; (c) her emotional status; (d) resources offered by her family, job, and community; and (e) her children. Thus, her safety is not only dependent on the personal resources and decision making she brings to the process, but the degree to which the community can be engaged in keeping her safe. By using safety planning as a cornerstone of intervention with battered women, partner advocates who are part of batterer intervention make sure that intervention programs are cognizant of, and involved with the wider community and its resources (or lack thereof) for women and children's safety. This kind of safety planning also needs to take into account ethnic and cultural influences on a partner's responses to the abuse, and the individual and community strategies that can contribute to (or compromise) women and children's safety. Finally, basing such safety planning on relative dangerousness of partners necessitates this dimension to become an ongoing consideration and natural outcome criterion of the intervention program itself.

This chapter outlines a process of safety planning based on the parameters listed above. Generic safety planning for battered women is addressed in many excellent publications (e.g., Dutton, 1992; McFarlane, Parker, Soeken, Silva, & Reel, 1998; Warshaw, Ganley, & Salber, 1998) and will not be repeated here. However, it is recommended that a more comprehensive safety planning, as part of batterer intervention, start with an evaluation of these aspects of context, and then modify suggestions for safety planning accordingly.

ASSESSMENT OF DANGEROUSNESS

Assessment of dangerousness or lethality risk is recommended by most experts working with battered women (e.g., Ganley, 1989; Hart, 1988), but none of the lethality-risk assessment instruments put forth in the clinical and advocate literature have been validated prospectively (Campbell, 1995b). Prediction of lethality or even the more generic term, dangerousness, is an inexact science, and clinicians usually predict no better than chance without some sort of psychometrically evaluated instrument or systematic method improving their assessment (Campbell, 1995a). The following factors are common to all of the means of assessment of risk factors for lethality in battering relationships that have been published: threats of lethality, threats with weapons or use of weapons, presence of a gun in the home, and obsessive jealousy. At the very least, a quick assessment of the presence of these factors in the situation is warranted, both for the woman's information and for the program providers. Sharing them with the woman as risk factors for homicide gives her data upon which she can base a more informed decision making process. Many battered women, especially those severely abused, are acutely aware of the possibility of homicide (Langford, 1996; Stuart & Campbell, 1989), but they have difficulty assessing their degree of risk. Others try not to think about the possibility or purposely minimize possible danger because of the normal anxiety it engenders. Conducting a lethality assessment with women brings these fears into the open and allows the woman to discuss the issue with an informed professional. The process also helps the professional gain a better idea of her degree of risk, what kinds of safeguards are needed from the criminal justice and shelter systems, and how assertive the professional needs to be with both the woman and the systems in order to get her help. Risk assessment also gives the batterer program information upon which to base a more tailored intervention.

A more comprehensive safety planning could be conducted using the Danger Assessment (Figure 1) (Campbell, 1995b). This list of 15 risk factors has been supported by psychometric evaluation in six major studies with acceptable reliability and support for convergent construct validity (with the Index of Spouse Abuse [Attala, Hudson & McSweeney, 1994; Hudson & McIntosh, 1981] and the Conflict Tactics Scale [Straus & Gelles, 1990]), and discriminant group validity (Campbell, 1995b). It has also been used (with appropriate wording modification for gender) with male abusers in criminal justice settings, with one small (N = 53) evaluation providing preliminary support for predictive validity of reoffending (Goodman, Dutton, & Bennett, in press). The Danger Assessment, by using the calendar documentation of severity and frequency of abuse, was designed to be a consciousness raising exercise for the woman. By having the woman mark approximately each time there was an episode of violence during the past year, she is able to put on paper for herself the pattern of violence she has been experiencing. Not only does this give her (and the advocate/professional working with her) a better idea of patterns of increasing severity and/or frequency, it helps her counteract her normal tendency to minimize the abuse (Campbell, 1986).

Another risk factor for homicide commonly recognized is the woman leaving the relationship or making clear to the abuser that she is in the process of leaving for good (Hart, 1988; Wilson, Johnson, & Daly, 1995). However, leaving the abuser is generally a long-term protective factor, although dangerous in the short term. Because of the complexity of this issue, it is not part of the Danger Assessment (DA) per se. The DA was designed for women to fill out by themselves and discuss with a nurse or other advocate afterwards. Because leaving is both a potentially dangerous and life-saving act, it is best addressed in a discussion. Once a woman has left her abuser, the number and frequency of stalking and harassing behaviors has been found to be correlated with the DA using the HARASS instrument developed by Sheridan (Campbell & Humphreys, 1993; McFarlane et al., 1999). Also, based on recent empirical data, the risk factor of presence of a stepchild of the batterer in the home, or his perception that one of her children is not his (parental uncertainty) should be added to the list of risk factors (Campbell et al., 1997; Daly, Singh, & Wilson, 1993). Finally, the importance of the DA item asking women their own perception of the batterer's dangerousness was supported in a recent prediction of reassault study (Weisz, Tolman & Saunders, in press).

FIGURE 1

DANGER ASSESSMENT

Jacquelyn C. Campbell, Ph.D., R.N.

Several risk factors have been associated with homicides (murders) of both batterers and battered women in research conducted after the murders have taken place. We cannot predict what will happen in your case, but we would like you to be aware of the danger of homicide in situations of severe battering and for you to see how many of the risk factors apply to your situation.

Using the calendar, please mark the approximate dates during the past year when you were beaten by your husband or partner. Write on that date how bad the incident was according to the following scale:

1. Slapping, pushing; no injuries and/or lasting pain
2. Punching, kicking; bruises, cuts, and/or continuing pain
3. "Beating up"; severe contusions, burns, broken bones
4. Threat to use weapon; head injury, internal injury, permanent injury
5. Use of weapon; wounds from weapon

   (If **any** of the descriptions for the higher number apply, use the higher number.)

Mark **Yes** or **No** for each of the following. ("He" refers to your husband, partner, ex-husband, ex-partner, or whoever is currently physically hurting you.)

_____ 1. Has the physical violence increased in frequency over the past year?
_____ 2. Has the physical violence increased in severity over the past year and/or has a weapon or threat from a weapon ever been used?
_____ 3. Does he ever try to choke you?
_____ 4. Is there a gun in the house?
_____ 5. Has he ever forced you to have sex when you did not wish to do so?
_____ 6. Does he use drugs? By drugs, I mean "uppers" or amphetamines, speed, angel dust, cocaine, "crack," street drugs or mixtures.
_____ 7. Does he threaten to kill you and/or do you believe he is capable of killing you?
_____ 8. Is he drunk every day or almost every day? (In terms of quantity of alcohol.)
_____ 9. Does he control most or all of your daily activities? For instance: does he tell you who you can be friends with, how much money you can take with you shopping, or when you can take the car? (If he tries, but you do not let him, check here: _____)
_____ 10. Have you ever been beaten by him while you were pregnant? (If you have never been pregnant by him, check here: _____)
_____ 11. Is he violently and constantly jealous of you? (For instance, does he say "If I can't have you, no one can.")
_____ 12. Have you ever threatened or tried to commit suicide?
_____ 13. Has he ever threatened or tried to commit suicide?
_____ 14. Is he violent toward your children?
_____ 15. Is he violent outside of the home?

_____ Total "Yes" Answers

Thank you. Please talk to your nurse, advocate or counselor about what the Danger Assessment means in terms of your situation.

RELATIONSHIP STATUS

Recent research on abuse has made it clear that battered women's relationship status is neither dichotomous (with him versus separated/divorced) nor reflective of traditional marital status (Campbell, Miller, Cardwell, & Belknap, 1994; Campbell, Rose, Kub, & Nedd, 1998; Rosenfeld, 1997). Battered women usually leave the batterer several times and return in a normal progression of first deliberately leaving temporarily "to get his attention in trying to end the abuse" (often extremely effective for a man very invested in attachment and control); then perhaps leaving to bargain with him to force him into intervention either for substance abuse or battering; and then testing how she (and the children) do without him (Campbell, McKenna, Torres, Sheridan, & Landenburger, 1993). When she returns, she monitors the violence and other problems in the relationship, watching and hoping for improvement (Campbell et al., 1998). She often first stays with family or friends and then in later separations may go to a shelter, especially if the violence and threats escalate and she is afraid for her family. Some women live elsewhere but see the abuser occasionally as they decide whether the relationship can be salvaged. Others may make serious plans to leave while staying physically with the abuser. This process has been called *disengagement* by Landenburger (1989, 1993) in her model of Entrapment and Recovery from Abusive Relationships.

In safety planning it is critical to assess whether the woman is planning to stay in the relationship, is in the process of disengaging, or has left for good (establishing a separate domicile as her only living place, filed for divorce, or otherwise symbolically or literally ended the relationship). The range of possibilities of safety planning strategies are different and the types of actions women are willing to take are often dependent on where she is in the process.

When women are planning or hoping to stay in the relationship if the violence ends as the result of intervention, they are clearly still attached to the batterer, invested in the relationship, and have a great deal of hope that the relationship will improve. They are often also characterized by feeling that the violence is just one part of the relationship with other aspects that are either more important or positive enough to make up for the abuse. Because there is empirical evidence that batterers can and do significantly decrease their violence, and in some cases end all aspects of emotional abuse and coercive control, these hopes may not be unrealistic (Feld & Straus, 1989; Jacobson, Gottman, Gortner, Berns, & Shortt, 1996; Quigley & Leonard, 1996). Qualitative analysis of three interviews from 31 battered women over 3 to 4 years demonstrated that women planning to stay also engage in active strategies to address the abuse and other problems in the relationships (Campbell et al., 1998). Many women talked about actively "subordinating themselves" in areas of conflict with their husbands and partners. Although this strategy may lead over time to the disappearance of self and depression that often characterizes battered women (Campbell et al., 1997; Jack, 1991; Landenburger, 1989), women in that sample felt like it was a useful strategy in keeping themselves safe.

Another strategy that women who wanted to stay found useful was negotiating with the batterer around him staying nonviolent and/or getting intervention for substance abuse or battering. They may use leaving temporarily as a way to gain a "level playing field" in these negotiations. In fact, Gondolf, Fisher, and McFerron (1988) found that the most frequent reason that batterers voluntarily entered intervention was when their partners left them. An important safety planning measure (and one that will help the batterer stay in intervention) is to help the partner plan to stay away until intervention has been completed. Since men not completing intervention is one of the biggest problems in batterer intervention, this may help women both to stay safe and increase the rate of success of batterer intervention. Conversely, it is essential (no matter what the relationship status), that the batterer intervention program notify her if he drops out of intervention or actively threatens her in the course of intervention. The intervention program staff will need to get more than one safe address and phone number for her, and a way to leave her a message through a parent, sibling, or best friend in case she moves or her phone becomes disconnected.

If the woman is planning to stay in the relationship, engaging the criminal justice system is probably difficult for her since such action will often jeopardize her husband's future earning capacities and thus their family security. It may also alienate her partner's family, friends, and the community in which she plans for the family to stay (Campbell, 1993). However, she still needs to know her entire range of options through the criminal justice system and how these options can be engaged. Discussion of calling the police, new attitudes on the part of the police, and how to best engage the police, if necessary, are still useful. She may also want to have the abuse documented in her health records so that the evidence is available should she ever need it for a court action. She may not think of herself as needing shelter services at this point but she still needs to know about them, and also about the National Domestic Violence Hotline (1-800-799-SAFE) that provides 24-hour telephone advocacy and information.

If the woman is in the process of disengaging or leaving, reaching out to support systems for help and protection becomes even more important. If she is in a substantial amount of danger based on lethality assessment, or if she has limited family or friends with whom she can stay, or has otherwise limited resources, a wife abuse shelter may be critical to her leaving successfully. Even if she is not planning to go to the shelter, she needs to know that there are a whole range of services available to her through the shelter system, including court advocacy, individual advocacy, support groups, and services for children. Most battered women know about the existence of shelters but not about the full range of services. It is also important for her to know that leaving and returning is part of a normative process and that the professionals at the batterer intervention facility will not consider such ambivalence problematic unless the children are also being abused. It is very important to convey that she can return for support, conversation, and referrals at any time, no matter where she is physically *and* emotionally in the process of leaving. If the children are being abused, the intervention staff needs to have an ongoing relationship with the local child protective services agency for case management.

If she has clearly left physically and emotionally, court action (protection orders) is a necessary safety insurance process, and one that may be helpful in establishing the basis of her claims in any future child custody disputes. If he is part of the probation system, the batterer intervention program can make sure that his probation officer is in touch with her, especially if he drops out of intervention. If he harasses and/or stalks her and seems potentially highly lethal (especially if he drops out or seems resistant to intervention), the shelter system can be helpful in getting her to a safe place away from her current community.

EMOTIONAL STATUS

Given the high (40-50%) rates of serious depression and posttraumatic stress disorder (PTSD) found in samples of battered women (Campbell, Kub, Belknap, & Templin, 1997; Campbell, Kub, & Rose, 1996; Gleason, 1993), it is necessary to assess for these problems as part of the basics of safety planning. If she is depressed, it is difficult for her to be an active problem-solver and good at strategizing ways to stay safe. If she has symptoms of PTSD, she is likely to be hypervigilant and perhaps have exaggerated perceptions of the abuser's ability to control her and the system (Foa, Rothbaum, Riggs, & Murdock, 1991; Herman, 1992). Helping her see that depression and/or PTSD are normal responses, given the difficulties and trauma she has experienced, is as important as helping her access intervention for these problems. Local shelters and advocacy agencies will have lists of therapists who have experience working with battered women. Support groups provided by shelters have been shown to be effective in increasing battered women's self-esteem; and shelter stays (and/or the cessation of violence they engender), useful in addressing depression (Campbell, Sullivan & Davidson, 1995; Trimpey, 1989). Intervention programs for PTSD in sexual assault victims show promise as a method of intervention for domestic violence victims with PTSD as well (Foa et al., 1991; Resnick, Kilpatrick, Dansky, Saunders, & Best, 1993).

It is equally important to assess and share with the battered woman the professional's impressions of the strengths she brings to the safety planning process. Her sense of self-efficacy or self-care agency (ability to take care of her own health), ability to resist, concerns about her children, existing resources, and support systems are all important as protective mechanisms against emotional problems, and as strengths that can be built upon in safety planning (Campbell et al., 1998; Lempert, 1996).

RESOURCES OFFERED BY FRIENDS, FAMILY, JOB AND COMMUNITY

The resources available to the battered women through both informal and formal support systems are also important to include in safety planning. She may have been isolated by the batterer as one aspect of control, or isolated herself from family and friends because of shame. If she is isolated from family and friends, she may need encouragement to re-establish contact. Part of what may be isolating her is that family and friends don't know what to say to her or how to help. She can be encouraged to tell them what would be the most helpful. Conversely, she may continue to have close ties with extended family and friends, a situation that may be especially true for women from ethnic minority groups (Campbell, 1993; Campbell, Misaki, & Torres, 1997; Jacobson et al., 1996; Torres, 1991). Extended family, especially when the cultural group norms are tolerant of wife beating, can be non-supportive of her safety. Therefore, it is necessary to assess, not only for the presence of informal support systems, but also for her perception of their helpfulness in this situation.

Her job may also be an important resource, not only of financial support, but also for safety. Many employee assistance, occupational health, and work place security systems have been trained in domestic violence and have policies and procedures that are helpful to battered women (Campbell & Campbell, 1996; Ganley, 1989; Klein, Campbell, Soler, & Ghez, 1997). An analysis of harassment in one sample of battered women, revealed that 24% of the women who had left their partners experienced work related tactics by their ex-husbands and boyfriends, such as phone calls at the job site, trying to get her fired, and damaging her car so that she could not get to work. Particularizing protection orders to cover such actions, and enlisting job place security to help enforce these orders can be enormously helpful to women in this situation. Employee assistance can provide counseling and special absentee or work hours considerations. Occupational health can document domestic violence related health problems and arrange more extensive counseling if needed. Contact with these professionals by batterer intervention staff can often make these systems more accessible and supportive for the battered woman.

Finally, the community may vary in its support for battered women. The criminal justice, health, governmental, mental health, social service, private business, and batterer intervention sectors can all be part of an active coordinated community response or a fragmented non-supportive system. The public awareness of domestic violence and sanctions against battering are important cornerstones for prevention and amelioration of abuse (Klein et al., 1997). Batterer intervention staff needs to be aware of how helpful the criminal justice system is to victims in that community, how likely domestic violence calls are to be screened out in the 911 system, what documentation is necessary for a protection order, how helpful the health system is likely to be for her, and so forth. If she is a member of a particular ethnic or cultural group, it is necessary to have referral sources that are specific to her community and also knowledgeable about domestic violence. The program needs to have a list of translators available for local immigrant groups or migrant workers. The domestic violence advocacy community can work together to provide training in intimate partner violence issues, especially confidentiality; it is also important to know what the local cultural norms are related to domestic violence and how supported she (and her partner) will be in their cultural group for him completing batterer intervention.

THE CHILDREN

The final area of context necessary to assess is the children. Because of the significant overlap of child and wife abuse, as well as the possibility of the children being hurt inadvertently in a violent episode, the safety of the children is also of paramount concern. According to the National Family Violence survey (Straus & Gelles, 1990), as many as 77% of children are abused when there is severe wife abuse, with the abusing father committing the most severe abuse but battered women also abusing the children. Child abuse by the batterer is also a risk factor for potential lethality for the woman and is therefore an item on the DA shown on page 135 in this article. The question about child abuse on the DA needs to be preceded by an explanation that the staff person is a mandated reporter of child abuse, and that if there is child abuse in the home, the staff will work with the woman so they can engage the help of Child Protective Services (CPS) together. The staff at batterer intervention programs need to have good working relationships with their local CPS so that these cases can be handled with minimum perceptions of punitiveness, maximum safety for the child, and improved parenting.

Even if there is no physical child abuse, the children are at risk for a variety of mental and physical health problems, as well as perpetrating violence in the future as a result of being a witness to the abuse (Campbell & Humphreys, 1993; Campbell & Lewandowski, 1997). Children may also be hurt by trying to protect their mother or accidentally getting in the middle of a violent episode. Battered women are seriously concerned about their children and generally are trying very hard to protect them (Humphreys, 1995a; 1995b; Sullivan et al., in press). Concerns about the children are often critical to women's decisions to leave (Ulrich, 1991), although they also may decide to stay because they believe it is in the best interests of the children. One of the most important interventions in terms of the children's safety is to help women think through the potential effects of the abuse on the children, and to encourage them to talk with the children (in an age-appropriate manner) about what is happening. Otherwise it may be too easy for women to hope that the children are not being affected or do not know about the abuse. The shelter system can help women communicate with their children on the subject and access further help for them if needed. Meanwhile, there are some basic safety measures she can talk about with the children. These are:

1. escape, don't get in the middle of it;
2. run to neighbors, family, or friends;
3. don't get cornered (e.g., hide in closets);
4. mommy will be ok (to alleviate their anxiety); and
5. mommy will talk with you about it afterwards.

In this way communication between the battered women and their children is being fostered. The staff can discuss various age appropriate communication techniques with the children, depending on their age(s). If the mother wants the neighbor or friend to call the police in these situations, she should tell the neighbor or friend to do so, if the children come over saying there is fighting at home. In this way, the onus of responsibility for calling the police on their father does not rest with a child.

PROCESS OF SAFETY PLANNING

Once the context is assessed, the batterer intervention staff can proceed with an informed safety planning process. The DA items will give the professional good information on specific dangers (e.g., any guns), as well as information about the degree of danger, and therefore, how assertive to be. If there is a high risk of lethality, calling in criminal justice or shelter services can be urged more strongly. Guns can be removed under the Violence Against Women extension of the Brady Bill if the perpetrator has been convicted of domestic violence, and again the staff can be helpful in mobilizing the criminal justice system to take that action. Another approach to the gun is to have the woman take home a pamphlet on gun safety for children that urges locking the gun and ammunition up separately, thus appealing to her partner's concerns as a parent. The woman can identify other times and situations of particular danger and she and the professional can brainstorm ways to address them. In addition, having some money, children's toys, and copies of important documents and phone numbers hidden away is an important safety precaution (see Warshaw, Ganley & Salber, 1998 for details and check lists).

CONCLUSIONS

A framework of safety planning is an important intervention approach because it engages battered women without imposing solutions. The process can result in increasing her conscious awareness of the extent and danger of the situation, while at the same time, providing her with relevant information, supporting her resistance, reinforcing her sense of agency, and capitalizing on her concerns for her children. Appropriate and interactive lethality assessment is a cornerstone of the approach that can also provide important information for batterer intervention.

NOTE

1. Although men are also abused, relatively little clinical or research background is available upon which to base safety planning for them. Since the vast majority of batterers in intervention programs are men, the rest of the article will assume the partner is female.

REFERENCES

Attala, J. M., Hudson, W. W., & McSweeney, M. (1994). A partial validation of two short-form partner abuse scales. *Women & Health, 21*(2/3), 125-139.
Campbell, D.W. (1993). Nursing care of African-American battered women. *AWHONN's Clinical Issues In Perinatal and Women's Health Nursing: Domestic Violence, 4,* 407-415.
Campbell, D. W., Misaki, B., & Torres, S. (1997). "Water on rock": Changing domestic violence perceptions on the African American, Asian American, and Latino communities. In E. Klein, J. C. Campbell, E. Soler, & M. Ghez (Eds.), *Ending do-*

mestic violence: Changing public perceptions/Halting the epidemic (pp. 64-87). Thousand Oaks, CA: Sage.

Campbell, J. C. (1986). Nursing assessment for risk of homicide with battered women. *Advances in Nursing Science, 8*(4), 36-51.

Campbell, J. C. (1995a). *Assessing dangerousness: Violence by sexual offenders, batterers, and child abusers.* Newbury Park, CA: Sage.

Campbell, J. C. (1995b). Prediction of homicide of and by battered women. In J. C. Campbell (Ed.), *Assessing the risk of dangerousness: Potential for further violence of sexual offenders, batterers, and child abusers* (pp. 96-113). Newbury Park, CA: Sage.

Campbell, J. C., & Campbell, D. W. (1996). Cultural competence in the care of abused women. *Journal of Nurse-Midwifery, 41*(6), 457-462.

Campbell, J. C., & Humphreys, J. (1993). *Nursing care of survivors of family violence.* St. Louis: Mosby.

Campbell, J. C., Kub, J., Belknap, R. A., & Templin, T. (1997). Predictors of depression in battered women. *Violence Against Women, 3*(3), 276-293.

Campbell, J. C., Kub, J., & Rose, L. (1996). Depression in battered women. *Journal of the American Medical Women's Association, 51*(3), 106-110.

Campbell, J. C., & Lewandowski, L. (1997). Mental and physical health effects of intimate partner violence on women and children. *Psychiatric Clinics of North America, 20*(2), 353-374.

Campbell, J. C., McKenna, L., Torres, S., Sheridan, D., & Landenburger, K. (1993). Nursing care of abused women. In J. C. Campbell & J. Humphreys (Eds.), *Nursing care of survivors of family violence* (pp. 240-289). St. Louis, MO: Mosby.

Campbell, J. C., Miller, P., Cardwell, M. M., & Belknap, R. A. (1994). Relationship status of battered women over time. *Journal of Family Violence 9,* 99-111.

Campbell, J. C., Ryan, J., Campbell, D.W., Torres, S., King, C., Stallings, R., & Fuchs, S. (1999). Physical and nonphysical abuse and other risk factors for low birthweight among term and preterm babies: A multiethnic case control study. *American Journal of Epidemiology, 150,* 714-726.

Campbell, J. C., Rose, L., Kub, J., & Nedd, D (1998). Voices of strength and resistance: A contextual and longitudinal analysis of women's responses to battering. *Journal of Interpersonal Violence, 14,*743-762.

Campbell, J. C., Sharps, P., Webster, D., McFarlane, J., Campbell, D., Ulrich, Y., & Sachs, C. (1997, November). *Risk factors for femicide in intimate relationships: Preliminary data.* Paper presented at the American Society of Criminology, San Diego, CA.

Campbell, R., Sullivan, C. M., & Davidson, W. S. (1995). Depression in women who use domestic violence shelters: A longitudinal analysis. *Psychology of Women Quarterly, 19,* 237-255.

Chalk, R., & King, C. (1998). Panel on the Evaluation of Family Violence Interventions, Committee on Children and Families, & National Research Council. *Evaluation of family violence interventions.* Washington, DC: National Academy Press.

Chez, R. A. (1987). If you suspect a patient is a victim of abuse. *Contemporary OB/GYN, 6,*132-47.

Daly, M., Singh, L., & Wilson, M. (1993). Children fathered by previous partners: A risk factor for violence against wives. *Canadian Journal of Public Health, 84,* 209-210.

Dobash, R. P., Dobash, R. E., Cavanagh, K., & Lewis, R. (1998). Separate and intersecting realities: A comparison of men's and women's accounts of violence against women. *Violence Against Women, August,* 382-414.

Dutton, M. A. (1992). *Empowering and healing the battered woman.* New York: Springer.

Feld, S. L., & Straus, M. A. (1989). Escalation and desistance of wife assault in marriage. *Criminology, 27*(1), 141-161.

Foa, E. B., Rothbaum, B. O., Riggs, D. S., & Murdock, T. B. (1991). Intervention of posttraumatic stress disorder in rape victims: A comparison between cognitive-behavioral procedures and counseling. *Journal of Consulting and Clinical Psychology, 59,* 715-723.

Ganley, A. (1989). Integrating a feminist and social learning analysis of aggression: Creating multiple models for intervention with men who batter. In P. L. Caesar & L. K. Hamberger (Eds.), *Treating men who batter: Theory, practice, and programs* (pp. 196-235). New York: Springer.

Gleason, W. J. (1993). Mental disorders in battered women: An empirical study. *Violence and Victims, 8,* 53-68.

Gondolf, E. W. (1997). Patterns of reassault in batterer programs. *Violence and Victims, 12,* 373-387

Gondolf, E. W., Fisher, E., & McFerron, R. (1988). Racial difference among shelter residents. *Journal of Family Violence, 3,* 39-51.

Goodman, L. A., Dutton, M. A., & Bennett, M. A. (2000). Predicting repeat abuse among arrested batterers: Use of the danger assessment scale in the criminal justice system. *Journal of Interpersonal Violence, 15,* 63-74.

Hart, B. (1988). Beyond the "duty to warn": A therapist's "duty to protect" battered women and children. In K. Yllo & M. Bograd (Eds.), *Feminist perspectives on wife abuse* (pp. 234-248). Newbury Park, CA: Sage.

Herman, J. (1992). *Trauma and recovery.* New York: Basic Books.

Hudson, W. W., & McIntosh, S. R. (1981). The assessment of spouse abuse: Two quantifiable dimensions. *Journal of Marriage and the Family, 43,* 873-885.

Humphreys, J. (1995a). Dependent care by battered women: Protecting their children. *Health Care for Women International, 16,* 9-20.

Humphreys, J. (1995b). The work of worrying: Battered women and their children. *Scholarly Inquiry for Nursing Practice: An International Journal, 9*(2), 126-145.

Jack, D. C. (1991). *Silencing the self.* New York: Harper Perennial.

Jacobson, N. S., Gottman, J. M., Gortner, E., Berns, S., & Shortt, J. W. (1996). Psychological factors in the longitudinal course of battering: When do the couples split up? When does the abuse decrease? *Violence and Victims, 11,* 371-392.

Klein, E., Campbell, J. C., Soler, E., & Ghez, M. (1997). *Ending domestic violence: Changing public perceptions/Halting the epidemic.* Thousand Oaks, CA: Sage.

Landenburger, K. (1989). A process of entrapment in and recovery from an abusive relationship. *Issues in Mental Health Nursing, 3,* 209-227.

Landenburger, K. (1993). Exploration of women's identity: Clinical approaches with abused women. In *AWHONN'S Clinical Issues in Perinatal and Women's Health Nursing* (pp. 378-384). Philadelphia: Lippincott.

Langford, D. R. (1996). Predicting unpredictability: A model of women's processes of predicting battering men's violence. *Scholarly Inquiry for Nursing Practice, 10*(4), 371-385.

Lempert, L.B. (1996). Women's strategies for survival: Developing agency in abuse relationships. *Journal of Family Violence, 11*(3), 269-290.

McFarlane, J., Campbell, J. C., Wilt, S. A., Sachs, C., Ulrich, Y., & Xu, X. (1999). Stalking and intimate partner femicide. *Homicide Studies, 3* (4), 300-316.

McFarlane, J., Parker, B., Soeken, K., Silva, C., & Reel, S. (1998). Safety behaviors of abused women after an intervention during pregnancy. *Journal of Obstetric Gynecology in Neonatal Nursing, 27*(1), 64-69.

Quigley, B. M., & Leonard K. E. (1996). Desistance of husband aggression in the early years of marriage. *Violence and Victims, 11*, 355-370.

Resnick, H., Kilpatrick, D., Dansky, B., Saunders, B., & Best, C. (1993). Prevalence of civilian trauma and posttraumatic stress disorder in a representative national sample of women. *Journal of Consulting and Clinical Psychology, 61*, 984-991.

Rosenfeld, R. (1997). Changing relationships between men and women: A note on the decline in intimate partner homicide. *Homicide Studies, 1*(1), 72-83.

Stuart, E. P., & Campbell, J. C. (1989). Assessment of patterns of dangerousness with battered women. *Issues in Mental Health Nursing, 10*(3-4), 245-260.

Straus, M. A., & Gelles, R. J. (1990). *Physical violence in American families: Risk factors and adaptations to family violence in 8,145 families.* New Brunswick, NJ: Transaction Publishers.

Sullivan, C. M., Nguyen, H., Allen, N., Bybee, D., & Juras, J. (in press). Beyond searching for deficits: Evidence that physically and emotionally abused women are nurturing parents. *Journal of Emotional Abuse.*

Torres, S. (1991). A comparison of wife abuse between two cultures: Perceptions, attitudes, nature and extent. *Issues in Mental Health Nursing, 12*, 113-131.

Trimpey, M. L. (1989). Self-esteem and anxiety: Key issues in an abused women's support group. *Issues in Mental Health Nursing, 10*, 297-308.

Ulrich, Y. (1991). Women's reasons for leaving abusive spouses. *Women's Health Care International, 12*(4), 465-473.

Warshaw, C., Ganley, A. L., & Salber, P. R. (1998). *Improving the health care response to domestic violence: A resource manual for health care providers (newly revised).* San Francisco: Family Violence Prevention Fund.

Weisz, A., Tolman, R., & Saunders, D. G. (2000). Assessing the risk of severe domestic violence: The importance of survivor's predictions. *Journal of Interpersonal Violence, 15*, 75-90.

Wilson, M., Johnson, H., & Daly, M. (1995). Lethal and nonlethal violence against wives. *Canadian Journal of Criminology, 37*, 331-362.

Conjoint Therapy
for Partners Who Engage
in Physically Aggressive Behavior:
Rationale and Research

K. Daniel O'Leary

SUMMARY. Debates have appeared in professional journals and conferences about which interventions/treatments are appropriate and effective for men and women in physically aggressive relationships. Gender specific and conjoint treatments have been the most frequently discussed interventions, and they are the focus of this review. At present, there is a need to recognize that physical aggression in intimate relationships is very common, especially in young individuals, and that the very commonly observed physical aggression in young people has different causes than the severe, longstanding aggression that engenders fear in women. It is also important to recognize that whatever the intervention, a therapist needs to be concerned about safety planning. Finally, given that there is increasing recognition of different types of partner abuse and causes thereof, it is time to address the need for multiple interventions in certain cases, e.g., gender specific, conjoint, substance abuse. Arguments and data are presented regarding the circumstances in which conjoint treat-

Portions of this paper were presented at the Fifth Family Violence Conference, University of New Hampshire, July 1997 and at the American Psychological Association, Chicago, Illinois, August 1997. Kenneth Chase, Richard Heyman, Yuen Tung, and Dina Vivian provided helpful commentary on an earlier version of this manuscript.

[Haworth co-indexing entry note]: "Conjoint Therapy for Partners Who Engage in Physically Agressive Behavior: Rationale and Research." O'Leary, K. Daniel. Co-published simultaneously in *Journal of Aggression, Maltreatment & Trauma* (The Haworth Maltreatment & Trauma Press, an imprint of The Haworth Press, Inc.) Vol. 5, No. 2(#10), 2001, pp. 145-164; and: *Domestic Violence Offenders: Current Interventions, Research, and Implications for Policies and Standards* (ed: Robert A. Geffner, and Alan Rosenbaum) The Haworth Maltreatment & Trauma Press, an imprint of The Haworth Press, Inc., 2001, pp. 145-164. Single or multiple copies of this article are available for a fee from The Haworth Document Delivery Service [1-800-HAWORTH, 9:00 a.m. - 5:00 p.m. (EST). E-mail address: getinfo@haworthpressinc.com].

145

ment is associated with marked reductions in psychological and physical ag-gression. *[Article copies available for a fee from The Haworth Document Delivery Service: 1-800-HAWORTH. E-mail address: <getinfo@haworthpressinc.com> Website: <http://www.HaworthPress.com> © 2001 by The Haworth Press, Inc. All rights reserved.]*

KEYWORDS. Partner abuse, psychological aggression, gender spe-cific interventions, shelter movement, power, control, marital discord, responsibility

There has been considerable debate over the last five years about the utility, feasibility, and even the ethics of conducting conjoint therapy with men and women in which there has been aggression by one or both partners. The issue has been debated in professional journals (e.g., McMahon & Pence, 1996; O'Leary, 1996), at professional conferences (e.g., Campbell, 1997; Dunford, 1997; Maiuro, 1997), and at the Department of Defense Policy Planning Meet-ing (Lloyd, 1997). Given the extent of recent attention to the issue of conjoint treatment, it is important first to describe the prevalent treatment formats uti-lized to address issues of partner abuse. By far, the most commonly used treat-ments or educational formats are gender specific. That is, men are seen by male therapists or mixed sex co-therapy teams, and women are seen by female therapists. Within this format, gender segregation is considered paramount, and it is rare for the males' therapists and the females' therapists to have any communication–often because relatively few of the partners receive treatment from the same facility. On the other hand, many treatment facilities have con-tact with the female partners of males in mandated treatment programs (per-sonal communication, October 13, 1998, Drs. Christopher Murphy, Baltimore, MD & Alan Rosenbaum, Wooster, MA). In the case of women in shelters, there is not generally any contact with the male abuser, since there is a need to have secrecy about the woman's location, and often the agency is helping the woman to extricate herself from the relationship. These traditions just de-scribed may be understood better if one considers the background and context of treatments for domestic violence.

It is important, however, to emphasize first that physical aggression in an intimate relationship varies greatly depending on the type and severity of ag-gression (e.g., a shove versus a beating), the frequency (e.g., one shove versus repeated shoving), and the impact of the aggression (e.g., does the aggression from one partner make the other fearful or not?). Further, while typologies of partner aggression have not yet been related to treatment outcome, there is enough data available to indicate that different types and/or frequencies of physical aggression should not be regarded as having the same etiology and meaning (see Holtzworth-Munroe & Stuart, 1994; O'Leary, 1993). Consequently, as has been emphasized recently, the means of addressing physical aggression should depend at least in part on the type and impact of the aggression (Boyle & Vivian, 1996; Holtzworth-Munroe & Stuart, 1994; O'Leary, 1993; O'Leary, Neidig, & Heyman, 1995; Vivian & Heyman, 1996). For example, conjoint therapy should not be attempted if the violence is severe enough to elicit substantial fear or serious injury to the female partner; if the female is afraid for her life; if she is afraid of participating in therapy with her partner; if she desires to leave the relationship; and if both partners do not want to participate in a program that makes aggression the primary target of treatment.

Given the status of treatment outcome evaluations, researchers and legislators who are in policy-making roles should recognize that there is not one way that has been documented as the best method of treating partner aggression (Brannen & Rubin, 1996; Gondolf, 1997; Saunders, 1996). At the same time, it is clear that different types of services are contracted and preferred by individuals in problematic intimate relationships where physical aggression is present. An illustration of the numerous services utilized by men and women in marital and family relationships generally characterized by some level of abuse, and the frequencies with which those services are used can be seen in a sample of 1,464 Air Force personnel who came in contact with the Family Advocacy Program. Those varied services are noted in Table 1 (Brewster, 1996).

The Department of Defense mandated that each of the Military Services establish programs for the prevention, reporting, investigation, assessment, treatment, and follow-up of child abuse and neglect, and spousal abuse. The programs and services addressing these problems are referred to as the Family Advocacy Program and they are provided under the authority of the Department of Defense Directive 6400.1, Family Advocacy Program. It is this author's opinion that the military has done far more than the civilian sector in terms of providing a coordinated response to problems of partner and child abuse. As illustrated by the US Air Force Family Advocacy Program, many options are available to individuals in need, and fortunately, service members utilize a diversity of those services.

As can be seen from Table 1, marital therapy for couples is frequently found in the blend of services sought by Air Force personnel, although marital therapy is not mandated by the Air Force. It is possible that some women feel cajoled into marital treatment, but the 1997 Department of Defense Policy indicates that "Couples counseling occurs only after all victim safety issues

TABLE 1. Most Frequent Services Utilized

Service	%
Marital Therapy	60.4%
Anger Management	48.9%
Individual Therapy	38.1%
Conflict Containment	26.2%
Communication Skills	13.8%
Alcohol Counseling	11.3%
Group Therapy	10.2%
Stress Management	7.1%
Abuser Removed from the Home	6.2%

Note: Percentages do not add to 100 because clients may use more than one service.

have been addressed, and is tied to continuous separate assessment of the abuser and of the victim. Assessment should never be joint" (Lloyd, 1997, p. 7). It should be recognized that the manner in which individuals come in contact with the Family Advocacy Program varies widely, with the top two referral sources being medical and the military commander–each providing approximately 25% of the referrals. Victim contacts make up approximately 12% of the referrals, while police contacts make up only 2% of the referrals. In brief, the types of individuals in aggressive relationships who contact the Family Advocacy Program and the types of services they use vary widely, and presumably the blend of services is customized for each family according to the severity and frequency of aggression in the intimate relationship. Importantly, it should be noted that many Air Force personnel use a mixture of the services provided.

Ideally, policy planning to address partner abuse should range from preventive strategies to provision of a range of services, to legal sanctions against the abuser. In addition, the types of services offered should vary depending upon the presenting and comorbid problems, as well as whether one is voluntarily seeking service, or whether one is mandated to a service. Broadly, interventions addressing partner abuse may be categorized under four headings: (1) prevention, (2) educational and psychological treatments, (3) social services (e.g., shelter and financial support), and (4) legal sanctions. Since there is little research data to support the view that one particular approach or program within any one of these categories is better than another, alternatives from all four categories should be provided and matched or customized to various client needs.

It is this author's opinion that there are a wide variety of factors that must be considered if one is to adequately solve the problem of partner aggression.

Those factors include services such as prevention programs in junior and senior high schools, individual support services, conjoint therapy, group and individual therapy, advocacy programs, adjunctive substance abuse programs, and shelters. Because the purpose of this article is to present the reasons why conjoint interventions should be one of the service options provided, the arguments for and against such treatment are presented. Before doing so, a brief historical context of interventions for women and men in physically abusive relationships are presented.

DEVELOPMENT OF INTERVENTION PROGRAMS

The impetus for treatment of women began in the 1960s and early 1970s with shelters for battered women and their children (e.g., Haven House, Pasedena, California, 1964, and Chiswick Women's Aid in England, 1971; see Barnett, Miller-Perinn, & Perrin, 1997). The shelters, which grew out of grass roots concerns, provided an important respite and safe haven for physically and psychologically abused women. Mental health professionals were relatively uninvolved in the development of shelters, and, consequently, shelters are not typically staffed by mental health professionals. In addition, parallel to the treatment for alcoholism, formerly physically abusive men often provided support and educational groups for fellow men who were abusive. Hence, in almost all cases, the interventions were gender specific (i.e., men saw men and women saw women for support, therapy, and guidance). Initially, some believed that the purpose of shelters and women's support groups was to provide the necessary sustenance and guidance to enable the women to leave their relationships. Schechter (1982), in an early account of the feminist battered women's movement, noted, "As a collective effort, the shelter movement not only saves lives, but also inspires women to organize together and help one another" (p. 315). She also pointed out that the movement had a fierce commitment to women's self-determination, self-organization, and democratic participation. The feminist movement deserves central credit for addressing problems of battered women, and for, among other things, providing them with shelter. As it turned out, however, the majority of women who used the services of a shelter returned to their partners (Strube, 1988). It is clear that many women return to abusive partners because of economic, familial, religious, and psychological reasons. Unfortunately, at the same time, their male partners received little or no help in dealing with their aggression (Strube, 1988).

A number of years after the shelter movement began, groups for men who battered their wives were formed (for a review of these programs, see Edelson &

Tolman, 1992; Gondolf, 1997; Rosenbaum & Maiuro, 1989). Presently, men who are arrested and prosecuted for aggression toward their female partner are commonly mandated to batterers treatment programs (both in the civilian and military sectors of society). While there are a few programs for women arrested for domestic violence, according to Hamberger and Potente (1994), most of these women are motivated by the need to defend themselves, or are retaliating for previous battering. The majority of court-mandated batterer programs for men emphasize two major interrelated issues: (1) misuse of power over women, and (2) the patriarchal structure of society. However, there is no evidence that these types of programs lead to greater reductions in wife abuse than any other type of program, and it is unclear how well men in these programs fare in comparison to men not mandated to treatment (Dunford, 1997; Fagan, 1996; Gondolf, 1997; Rosenfeld, 1992). Actual success rates, sometimes defined as cessation of aggression against a partner, vary between approximately 40% and 80%. However, these rates are difficult to interpret because the dropout rates for men's programs are approximately 50%, even when the men are court-mandated to treatment (Edleson & Tolman, 1992). In a large study of treatment dropout, self-referred men had even higher dropout rates than court-mandated men (Rosenbaum, Gearan, & Ondovic, 1997).

Despite the concerns about the effectiveness of men's treatment programs, most professionals conducting such programs believe that the programs help a significant percentage of the men who attend (e.g., Edleson & Tolman, 1992; Gondolf, 1997; Rosenbaum & Maiuro, 1989; Saunders, 1996). Yet some experts point to the high drop-out rate from these programs and question whether the treatment programs, as they are sometimes formatted, are so critical of the men that they simply refuse to attend, despite the fact that they are court-mandated (Murphy & Baxter, 1997). In addition, there is also a question about the efficacy of the substantive content common to the majority of programs, namely, power and control, and an emphasis on the patriarchical nature of our society. Research demonstrates that one psychodynamically-based program which offers a very different content appears to work as well as the programs addressing behavioral skills, cognitive skills, and cultural norms and structures that support male violence (Saunders, 1996). As the author stated, "Rates of violence did not differ significantly between the two types of treatment nor did reports from the women of their fear level, general changes perceived in the men, and conflict resolution methods" (Saunders, 1996, p. 393). However, men with dependent personalities had better outcomes in the psychodynamic intervention, whereas those with antisocial traits had better outcomes in the cognitive-behavioral group. Such research should be encouraged, as this is one of the only studies that addresses client interactions with different types of treatments.

REASONS FOR THE USE OF CONJOINT PROGRAMS

In the 1980s, marital therapists began to publish accounts of treating couples that were physically aggressive (e.g., Deschner & McNeil, 1986; Harris, 1986; Lindquist, Telch, & Taylor, 1983; Neidig & Friedman, 1984). Although these programs were often theoretically at odds with the perspective of those who worked in shelters and treatment programs for physically abusive men, it became clear that physical aggression was engaged in by both men and women and was initiated by women at approximately equivalent rates in representative community and nonclinical samples (e.g., Mihalic, Elliot, & Menard, 1994; O'Leary et al., 1989; Schulman, 1979; Straus, Gelles, & Steinmetz, 1980). It became more apparent that the occurrence of women's physical aggression could not be denied, even though it has been repeatedly found that the physical aggression by men has more deleterious psychological and physical effects (O'Leary, 1993).

O'Leary, Vivian, and Malone (1992) found that approximately one half of the wives presenting at a marital therapy clinic reported the occurrence of physical aggression in their relationship in the past year. This result was surprising, as few men or women over the years since our clinic opened in 1976 presented with primary complaints of physical aggression in the marriage. In fact, only 6% of women reported that their partner's aggression was a problem when they were asked to write down the major problems in their marriage (O'Leary et al., 1992), even though approximately one half of these women reported that their partner engaged in some acts of physical aggression during the past year. Similar results were found by Holtzworth-Munroe et al. (1992). In addition, using a structured interview, Ehrensaft and Vivian (1996) found that only 14% of the clinic females reported that aggression was a problem, even though 55% of these women reported on a modified form of the Conflict Tactics Scale (Straus & Gelles, 1990) that their husbands had engaged in physical aggression. Clearly, the frequency of physical aggression by men *and* women in marital clinic samples was so high as to merit attention. Surprisingly, the physical aggression in these couples was empirically reported to have been engaged in by both members of the couple.

It should be noted here that the field does not have extensive data about the extent of mutual physical aggression in relationships characterized by very severe injuries and/or extensive fear and intimidation tactics. However, it seems likely that aggression by both members of the dyad would be significantly less severe than in the couples who request to be treated conjointly. Moreover, one would expect that some of the aggression by women in cases where the husband is severely aggressive would be in self-defense.

It has long been observed by clinicians and clients that physical aggression starts in the context of an argument between partners (Cascardi & Vivian, 1995; Dobash & Dobash, 1984; O'Leary, 1993). While "out of the blue" acts of physical aggression do occur, they are infrequent. In fact, in longitudinal research, even for couples that have never been physically aggressive, high levels of psychological aggression and arguing predict later use of physical aggression by both men and women (Murphy & O'Leary, 1989). Indeed, our path model of the etiology of partner abuse involves a central link of psychological aggression occurring at one time that leads to physical aggression at a later time (O'Leary, Malone, & Tyree, 1994). Given that the physically aggressive behaviors often occur in the context of arguments, it makes sense that a reduction in arguments and concomitant psychological aggression might lead to a reduction in physical aggression.

As previously mentioned, power and control tactics have been described as the primary explanatory factors accounting for wife abuse (Martin, 1981; Schechter, 1982), and these factors have been incorporated into many treatment programs for men (e.g., Pence & Paymar, 1993). In fact, most programs, including our own gender specific and couples programs, address power and control issues in the intervention. However, when we turn to research, it becomes unclear whether men who engage in physically aggressive behavior actually use more power and control tactics than men who are in discordant, nonaggressive marriages. Two studies address this issue. In a sample of physically aggressive men who were still with their partners, scores on the Tolman Psychological Maltreatment of Women Inventory (PMWI; Tolman, 1989) measure of dominance and isolation did not differ from a control group of men matched for levels of marital discord (Rathus, O'Leary, & Meyer, in press). As expected, the two clinic groups (the discordant/violent and the discordant/nonviolent) differed from a group that was happily married. On the other hand, when Tolman (1999) compared PMWI scores from a group of discordant women who were also physically abused with women who were discordant but not physically abused, he found that the physically abused women reported a higher psychological dominance/isolation score for their husbands than the discordant, nonabused women. However, when he re-analyzed the data, breaking down the physically abused women into service-seeking and nonservice-seeking, he found that the nonservice-seeking women did not differ from the discordant, non-physically abused women.

It should be noted that the populations of men who engaged in physical aggression against their wives differed significantly in the Rathus et al. (in press) study and in the Tolman (1999) study. In the Rathus et al. study, subjects in the violent clinical group responded to notices in the newspaper for "men seeking treatment for relationship problems" who were in turn selected for having marital discord and violence. The criteria for selection were that the men had to have at least two mild to moderate acts or one severe act of physical aggression within the past year. Subjects in the Tolman study were selected from diverse sources, including an agency for battered women, social service agencies providing counseling, parenting classes, and public service announcements regarding a study on relationships. One interpretation of the data from these two studies is that dominance/isolation is not the key discriminating variable of physical aggression in some men. That is, some men who use dominance/isolation tactics also engage in physically aggressive behaviors against their partners but there are also groups of men who engage in dominance and isolation but do not engage in physically aggressive behaviors. It is possible that power and control tactics differentiate the more severely aggressive men from the men who engage in the moderate levels of physical aggression. In any case, it seems clear from these two studies that power and control tactics are critical discriminating variables for some types of aggressive men, but not for all aggressive men. Such research highlights the need to recognize that different types of men engage in physically aggressive acts against their partners for different reasons.

Marital discord is one of the strongest correlates/predictors of physical aggression against a partner. Rosenbaum and O'Leary (1981) found that abused women reported a mean Locke Wallace Marital Adjustment Test score of 41; a non-physically abused discordant group had a mean of 67; a satisfactorily married group had a mean of 117. Among a number of variables (e.g., violence in the family of origin, alcohol abuse, sex-role beliefs), marital discord was the most important discriminator between the groups. In recent work involving the prediction of mild and severe husband to wife physical aggression with 11,870 randomly selected military personnel, Pan, Neidig, and O'Leary (1994) also found that marital discord was the most important predictor of physical aggression against a partner. More specifically, they found that for every 20% increase in marital discord score, the odds of being mildly aggressive increased by 102%, and the odds of being severely aggressive increased by 183%. Although other variables, such as having a drug or alcohol problem, having a low income, and being younger also increased the odds of being physically aggressive toward a wife, marital discord was the best predictor of such aggression. Since marital discord is such a strong predictor of physical aggression toward a partner, it would seem logical that a reduction in marital discord would make partner abuse less likely. Moreover, it would seem that failure to address marital problems at some point in the treatment of men and/or women would make it more likely that physical abuse/aggression would occur.

My colleagues and I have not advocated conjoint treatment for all couples in physically aggressive relationships (O'Leary et al., 1995; O'Leary, Heyman, &

Neidig, 1999). Rather, we have compared gender specific and conjoint treatments under the following conditions: (a) when the couple is choosing to remain intact; (b) when the violence is not severe enough to elicit substantial fear or serious injury to the female partner; and (c) when both members of the couple acknowledge that aggression is a problem and they are willing to participate in a program that makes it the primary target of treatment. Participants were recruited through notices in the local newspaper for spouses whose "arguments led to throwing, pushing, shoving, etc." Husbands did not meet criteria for alcohol dependence.

Men's gender specific treatment (GST) groups comprised 6-8 men and a male therapist. The major focus of the gender specific treatment for men was to help them to: (a) decrease their use of psychological and physical aggression; (b) accept responsibility for their aggression; (c) understand the negative effects of violence on every member of the family; (d) learn to recognize the cycle of violence and to control their anger; and (e) learn how to communicate requests rather than give orders. The women's gender specific treatment involved groups of 6-8 women and a female therapist. The focus of the treatment was to help women: (a) recognize the characteristics of abusive relationships; (b) understand the emotional effects of violence; (c) learn ways to control their emotional reactions to negative events; and (d) evaluate the status of the marriage, including advantages and disadvantages of staying in the marriage.

The conjoint treatment (Physical Aggression Couples Therapy; PACT) involved groups of 6-8 couples plus male and female co-therapists. The focus of the treatment was to help spouses: (a) eliminate psychological and physical violence in the home; (b) accept responsibility for escalation of angry interchanges and the resulting violence; (c) recognize and control self-angering thoughts; (d) communicate more effectively; (e) increase caring and mutually pleasurable activities; and (f) understand that each partner has a right to be treated with respect (see Table 2 for a comparison of the two treatments).

In both treatments, the male partner is held responsible for his physical aggression in the marriage. In GST, a greater emphasis is placed on having the male stop psychological and physical aggression. In PACT, the wife is held responsible for her own aggression, and both partners are encouraged to accept responsibility for their contribution to the escalation of conflict. Both treatments emphasize the greater impact of both physical and psychological aggression on women (Cantos, Neidig, & O'Leary, 1994; Cascardi, Langhinrichsen, & Vivian, 1992). In GST, greater emphasis is placed on power and the influence of societal/patriarchal factors on wife abuse than in PACT. Both treatments produced significant reductions in both physical and psychological aggression, but neither proved superior to the other (O'Leary et al., 1999).

TABLE 2. Session by Session Summaries of Group Treatments for Wife Abuse

Session	GST-Men	GST-Women	PACT
1	Introducing the program; recounting violent incident	Introducing the program; telling your story; safety plan	Introducing the program; recounting violent incident
2	Accepting responsibility for violence	Characteristics of abusive relationships; impact of societal characteristics of spouse abuse	Walker's cycle of violence; discriminating different levels of anger
3	Walker's cycle of violence; Time Out	Determining what you can change	Discriminating different levels of anger (cont.), Time Out procedures
4	Cognitive-Behavioral (ABC) Model of anger	Emotional effects of violence; self-esteem	Cognitive-Behavioral (ABC) Model of anger
5	Anger control techniques; challenging hot thoughts	Cognitive-behavioral model of depression; combating depression	Anger control techniques; challenging hot thoughts
6	Irrational thoughts	Emotional arousal: anger; responsibility for emotional arousal	Stress-Abuse connection; Irrational beliefs
7	Midterm Progress Evaluation; Review	Midterm Progress Evaluation; Review	Midterm Progress Evaluation; Review
8	Family-of-origin lessons about anger; self-esteem	Human rights; assertiveness training	Communication principles and skills; positive behaviors
9	Gender roles; identifying feelings	Constructive communication; barriers to effective communication	Gender differences in communication; expressing feelings; empathy
10	Power/control vs. equality tactics; characteristics of an equitable relationship	Increasing support resources; helping others help you	Assertion versus aggression; equality in rights and decision making
11	Relaxation training	Dealing with criticism; taking constructive action	Conflict escalation process; principles of conflict containment
12	Assertiveness training	Power/control vs. equality tactics; evaluating your marriage	Dirty fighting techniques
13	Constructive communication; empathizing with others	Marriage as a choice	Sex; jealousy; expanding social support network
14	Wrap-up; maintaining gains	Wrap-up; maintaining gains	Wrap-up; maintaining gains; expressive versus instrumental violence

The above treatment outcome study is described in detail elsewhere (O'Leary et al., 1999), but a few comments are in order about the need for therapists who work in a conjoint setting. All therapists should assess for violence in relationships. They should be aware of the extent to which it is underreported, especially by men (Heyman & Schlee, 1997). Unfortunately, as illustrated by Hansen and Harway (1993), professionals often overlook the problem of physical abuse. Even after becoming aware of a lethal outcome in a case, only 50% indicated that the intervention of choice would have been protection for the wife.

In addition to the above criteria for selection into conjoint treatment, clinical experience suggests that the level of anger toward a spouse and the inability to control such anger should also be considered in the selection of clients for marital treatment, regardless of whether physical aggression has occurred. More specifically, in a number of cases, this author has found that repeated anger directed toward a partner, especially in the context of angry blaming, has interfered so much with conjoint therapy that conjoint treatment had to be terminated in preference for individual treatment. In such cases, conjoint treatment should only be reinstated when the individual's anger is modified enough to allow for productive couple therapy.

It should be emphasized that when conjoint or marital treatment is being offered to couples that are in relationships characterized by some level of physical aggression, generic marital therapy is *not* the treatment of choice. Regardless of the particular theoretical slant that one has toward conjoint treatment, the focus must be on reducing psychological and physical aggression.

In addition to our own treatment evaluation, there is a study by Brannen and Rubin (1996) with couples that were referred for treatment by the courts in Dallas, Texas. They compared gender specific and couples interventions for batterers mandated to treatment by the criminal justice system in San Antonio, Texas. The population was comprised mostly of low-income couples. This study used a couples treatment program very similar to ours, which was developed by Neidig and Freidman (1984). Brannen and Rubin's gender specific treatment was based on a model developed at the Domestic Violence Abuse Project (DAP) in Minneapolis, Minnesota (Rusinoff, 1990). Brannen and Rubin randomly assigned 49 couples to either the gender specific treatment or the couples treatment. Both treatments were associated with significant reductions in physical aggression, as assessed by the wife's report at both post-treatment and at six-month follow-up. These findings are complementary to research by O'Leary et al. (1999), as they focused on a volunteer population of couples, whereas Brannen and Rubin utilized a mandated population.

The results of the Brannen and Rubin (1996) study are very impressive in terms of cessation of violence, as reported by the partner (92%); a review of cessation rates indicates a range between 53% and 85% (Edleson & Tolman, 1992). Thus, the success rates for both types of treatment are superior to those generally found in the treatment outcome literature. The positive outcomes may have been due to several factors, such as the close relationship the judge maintained with the treatment program (S. J. Brannen, personal communication, September 1995), close surveillance by the probation department, follow-up assessments by the principal investigator to establish whether any further episodes of physical violence had occurred in the six months subsequent to the termination of the program, and the fact that follow-up contact was only possible with 62% of the couples that completed the program. In brief, the Brannen and Rubin study provides some indication that conjoint intervention can be used successfully with men and women in abusive relationships.

In addition, the conjoint approach was superior for couples with a history of alcohol problems. Also, the conjoint approach was superior in terms of dropout prior to treatment. Of the seven dropouts prior to initiating treatment, six were from the gender specific treatment, suggesting that some couples preferred conjoint treatment to gender specific treatment. In short, both comparative outcome studies, using random assignment to both treatments, and six-month to one year follow-up, indicate that conjoint treatment can result in significant reductions in psychological and physical aggression.

Another program using a conjoint format for partner abuse was described by Lipchik, Sirles, and Kubicki (1997) in their depiction of a solution-focused therapy that makes safety a priority. This program selects partners who show some evidence of the capacity for empathy and mutuality, and who both must agree that they want no further violence, that they want to preserve the relationship, and that there is one small change they want to work on. They argue that, as a rule, the less chronic the abuse, the better the progress. The thrust of the treatment focuses on both partners making choices that are good for the relationship. In 15 years of using this model, Lipchik et al. reported that there has been almost no recurrence of violence during treatment.

REASONS THAT CONJOINT TREATMENT PROGRAMS HAVE BEEN QUESTIONED

Given the theoretical arguments for conducting conjoint treatment, as well as recent data indicating its effectiveness, one may wonder what arguments are made against the use of conjoint therapy. As mentioned earlier, one of the most important ones is that discussions in the conjoint therapy sessions may lead to arguments after the session, and, in turn, these arguments may lead to physical abuse. This position has some plausibility because, as many marital therapists have observed, a therapeutic setting often provides an environment in which an individual who has been fearful of speaking openly and critically will become very negative. As a result, an argument often ensues in the therapy session. The concern is that the argument may continue outside the therapy session and erupt into physical violence. As previously stated, it is the responsibility of the therapist to diffuse highly explosive situations if they arise. We ask our therapists to spend time with clients after a session in which one or both members of a party appear very angry. In addition, we ask the therapists to call the client(s) after they get home from a session if they still feel that the anger level is too high following a post-session discussion.

Although perhaps less likely, it is also possible that anger from an individual session could escalate into an argument that in turn would lead to physical aggression. However, in this author's experience, individual sessions do not usually get as "heated" as conjoint sessions. Gender specific group sessions, on the other hand, sometimes involve anger outbursts and support of that anger from group participants. Indeed, some men's and women's sessions have the quality of "I can top that story!" Reports of partners' negative behaviors are common in the beginning of a session when participants describe problems from the prior week. Thus, this author believes that any therapist working with abusive men has a major responsibility to "talk down" or defuse strong anger experienced by men following *any type of therapy session* to minimize the likelihood of a continuing argument or hostile eruption at home.

Another argument against conjoint treatment is that women may assume more responsibility for the physical aggression than they might in gender specific treatments. Similarly, it is argued that men in conjoint treatment may feel less responsibility for the physical aggression than if they had been in gender specific treatment. A central tenet of our conjoint treatment is that both partners have responsibility for arguments that can escalate, but that each individual is responsible for controlling his/her own physical aggression. Whether there are changes in perceived responsibility that occur as a function of type of treatment is an empirical question that has been tested. This author and colleagues (O'Leary et al., 1999) found that husbands in both groups reported significant increases in taking responsibility for their own aggression, both at the end of treatment and at a one-year follow-up. In addition, husbands in both treatment conditions reported significant decreases in their perceptions that their aggression was caused by their wives. Women's perceptions of the causes of their physical aggression did not change significantly in either treatment. While there was considerable variability, they had a mean score at post treatment that reflected an attitude that the husband to wife physical aggression was not caused by them.

An additional concern is that conjoint treatment may limit the wife's ability to express herself in treatment. We (O'Leary et al., 1999) addressed that concern by seeing each partner individually before accepting them into either our conjoint or gender specific treatment, and by asking the wife if she felt comfortable participating in treatment with her husband. We measured wives' fear of their husbands at pre- and post-treatment, and found that women's fear of their husbands declined significantly. These reductions were not different across the different treatments. It is our contention that fear of a partner will be reduced if the wife sees that her partner's physical aggression declines or ceases. However, it is possible that the wife's fear of her partner could increase during treatment, and it is important for therapists to be alert to this possibility.

A further argument raised against conjoint treatment is that mental health professionals and marital therapists often believe that the cause of the physical aggression is due to psychopathology, communication problems, anger control problems, and/or marital discord. McMahon and Pence (1996) argue that if physical aggression against a partner is seen as due to some underlying problem,

> This characterization of domestic violence undermines the years of struggle by battered women and their advocates to get the police, the judiciary, and the public to finally recognize wife assault as *violence,* as no longer tolerable, and as being a crime rather than simply a personal or domestic problem. On an individual level, it may represent a form of collusion with an abusive man when it fails to make his violence the primary issue and by compromising his responsibility to change. (p. 454)

In our treatment programs, the primary goal is the elimination of violence. We believe that many different kinds of programs which vary in their conceptualization of the causes of violence can have a primary goal of eliminating violence (e.g., feminist/cognitive behavioral programs; psychodynamic programs [Saunders, 1996]; conjoint programs [Geffner, Mantooth, Franks, & Rao, 1989]; eclectic approaches [Rosenbaum & Maiuro, 1989]). This diversity in approaches is consistent with the increasing recognition of the heterogeneity in batterer types and underlying causes of physical aggression in intimate relationships (Holtzworth-Munroe & Stuart, 1994; O'Leary, 1993). The fact that the conceptualizations vary, however, does not mean that the primary goal of the program cannot be the reduction of violence. Variations in conceptualizations do not preclude legal interventions in concert with, or as alternatives to, some treatment programs. To use a medical analogy, conceptualizations of the causes of cancer have varied for years, but these conceptualizations do not preclude the primary goal of eliminating the cancer. In brief, violence can be *and is* the primary treatment goal in diverse treatment programs.

RECOMMENDATIONS

1. Clinicians, researchers, and policy makers all need to keep an open mind about alternative treatments that might help reduce psychological and physical aggression in relationships (psychodynamic, educational, mediational, conjoint, power and control). No treatment has been empirically demonstrated to be superior to all others.
2. Couple or conjoint treatments *tailored to address psychological and physical aggression* have demonstrated some efficacy, as evidenced by the work of Brannen and Rubin (1996), and the work described here at Stony Brook. Related promising conjoint work was described by Lipchik, Sirles, and Kubicki (1997). These programs are not generic marital therapy programs; they are targeted to reduce psychological and physical aggression. Overall, the effects of the conjoint programs have not been different from gender specific treatments; both were associated with reductions in physical aggression.
3. Responsible therapists of all orientations must consider the safety of the client to be of paramount importance, but safety issues need to be considered in the larger context of the relationship, if the relationship is likely to continue. Because relationship factors are major predictors of violence, it seems potentially dangerous not to address relationship issues at some point while providing services to the victim and/or aggressor, even if the marital problems receive attention *after* the male has ceased being physically aggressive.
4. We need to stop seeing all aggression/violence by men as the same; there are different types and levels of aggression, and they do not easily fit into one rubric with the same etiology and with the same kind of treatment. Dropout rates from treatments for problems of partner abuse are considerably higher than for many other individual psychological problems, and "one size fits all" treatments are not very likely to be effective for everyone.
5. General fear of partner (husband) as well as the specific fear of participating with the husband was assessed in our own research (O'Leary et al., 1999), both in an interview and self-report format to screen out women who had fears of their partner. The specific assessments we used were pragmatic and not based on well-developed measures of fear. Such instruments should be developed and evaluated with diverse populations ranging from dating to shelter samples. Moreover, measurement of

fear of partner(s) across various assessment instruments and treatment points is needed with both self-report and interview methodology to monitor the possibility of initial denial or minimization during the assessment period.

6. Various studies have found that men and women seeking marital therapy do not identify physical aggression as a problem in their marriage (O'Leary et al., 1992). Further, the reasons for not reporting such physical aggression have begun to be examined systematically (e.g., Ehrensaft & Vivian, 1996). Regardless of the reasons for minimization and denial of partner aggression, it is important for therapists not to collude with clients in this minimization (Hansen & Harway, 1993; Harway, 1994).

REFERENCES

Barnett, O. W., Miller-Perrin, C. L., & Perrin, R. D. (1997). *Family violence across the lifespan: An introduction.* Beverly Hills, CA: Sage:

Boyle, D. J., & Vivian, D. (1996). Generalized versus spouse-specific anger/hostility and men's violence against intimates. *Violence and Victims, 11,* 293-317.

Brannen, S. J., & Rubin, A. (1996). Comparing the effectiveness of gender specific and couples groups in a court mandated spouse abuse treatment program. *Research on Social Work Practice, 6,* 405-424.

Brewster, A. L. (1996). *United States Air Force Family Advocacy Program.* Department of Defense Conference on Domestic Violence, Washington, DC.

Campbell, J. (1997, July). *Prediction of batterer dangerousness: State of science.* Paper presented at the 5th International Family Violence Research Conference, Durham, New Hampshire.

Cantos, A. L., Neidig, P. H., & O'Leary, K. D. (1994). Injuries of women and men in a treatment program for domestic violence. *Journal of Family Violence, 9,* 113-124.

Cascardi, M., Langhinrichsen, J., & Vivian, D. (1992). Marital aggression, impact, injury, and health correlate for domestic violence. *Archives of Internal Medicine, 152,* 1178-1184.

Cascardi, M. A., & Vivian, D. (1995). Context for specific episodes of marital aggression. *Journal of Family Violence, 10* (3), 265-293.

Deschner, J. P., & McNeil, J. S. (1986). Results of anger control training for battering couples. *Journal of Family Violence, 1,* 111-120.

Dobash, R. E., & Dobash, R. P. (1984). The nature and antecedents of violent events. *British Journal of Criminology, 24,* 269-288.

Dunford, F. (1997, July). *The research design and preliminary outcome findings of the San Diego Navy experiment.* Paper presented at the 5th International Family Violence Research Conference, Durham, New Hampshire.

Dutton, D., & Starzomski, A. J. (1993). Borderline personality in perpetrators of psychological and physical abuse. *Violence and Victims, 8,* 327-337.

Edleson, J. L., & Tolman, R. M. (1992). *Intervention for men who batter: An ecological approach.* Newbury Park, CA: Sage.

Ehrensaft, M. K., & Vivian, D. (1996). Spouses' reasons for not reporting existing physical aggression as a marital problem. *Journal of Family Psychology, 10* (4), 443-453.

Fagan, J. (1996). The criminalization of domestic violence: Promises and limits. *National Institute of Justice Research Report.* Washington, DC: U.S. Department of Justice.

Geffner, R., Mantooth, C., Franks, D., & Rao, L. (1989). A psychoeducational, conjoint therapy approach to reducing family violence. In P. L. Caesar & L. K. Hamberger (Eds.), *Treating men who batter: Theory, practice, and programs* (pp. 103-133). New York: Springer.

Gondolf, E. W. (1997). Batterer programs: What we know and need to know. *Journal of Interpersonal Violence, 12*, 83-98.

Hamberger, L. K., & Potente, T. (1994). Counseling women arrested for domestic violence: Implications for theory and practice. *Violence and Victims, 9*, 125-137.

Harris, J. (1986). Counseling violent couples using Walker's model. *Psychotherapy, 23*, 613-621.

Hansen, M., & Harway, M. (Eds.). (1993). *Battering and family therapy: A feminist perspective.* Newbury Park, CA: Sage.

Harway, M. (1994). Marriage and family therapists working with family violence: Strained bedfellows or compatible partners? A commentary on Avis, Kaufman, & Bograd. *Journal of Marital and Family Therapy, 20*, 204-205.

Heyman, R. E., & Schlee, K. A. (1997). Toward a better estimate of the prevalence of partner abuse. Adjusting rates based on the sensitivity of the Conflict Tactics Scale. *Journal of Family Psychology, 11*, 332-338.

Holtzworth-Munroe, A., & Stuart, G. L. (1994). Typologies of male batterers: Three subtypes and the differences among them. *Psychological Bulletin, 116*, 476-497.

Holtzworth-Munroe, A., Waltz, J., Jacobson, N. S., Monaco, V., Fehrenbach, P. A., & Gottman, J. M. (1992). Recruiting non-violent men as control subjects for research on marital violence: How easily can it be done? *Violence and Victims, 7*, 79-88.

Lindquist, C. U., Telch, C. F., & Taylor, J. (1983). Evaluation of a conjugal violence treatment program: A pilot study. *Behavioral Counseling and Community Intervention, 3*, 76-89.

Lipchik, E., Sirles, E. A., & Kubicki, A. D. (1997). Multifaceted approaches in spouse abuse treatment. *Journal of Aggression, Maltreatment, & Trauma, 1*, 131-148.

Lloyd, D. W. (1997, February 5-7). *Conference summary: Department of Defense Policy Conference on Spouse Abuse.* Office of the Assistant Secretary of Defense, Washington, DC.

Maiuro, R. D. (1997, July). *Are current standards for the treatment of domestically violent perpetrators adequately informed by research? A question of questions.* Paper presented at the 5th International Family Violence Conference, Durham, New Hampshire.

Malamuth, N. M. (in press). An evolutionary-based model integrating research on the characteristics of sexually coercive men. In J. G. Adair, K. W. Dion, & D. Belanger, (Eds.), *Advances in Psychological Science* (Vol. 2): Personal, social, and developmental aspects (pp. 151-184). Hove, UK: Psychology Press.

Martin, D. (1981) *Battered wives*. San Francisco: Volcano Press.

McMahon, M., & Pence, E. (1996). Replying to Dan O'Leary. *Journal of Interpersonal Violence, 11*, 452-455.

Mihalic, S., Elliot, D., & Menard, S. (1994). Continuities in marital violence. *Journal of Family Violence, 9*, 195-226.

Murphy, C. M., & Baxter, V. A. (1997). Motivating batterers to change in the treatment context. *Journal of Interpersonal Violence, 12*, 607-619.

Murphy, C., & O'Leary, K. D. (1989). Psychological aggression predicts physical aggression in early marriage. *Journal of Clinical and Consulting Psychology, 57*, 579-582.

Neidig, P. H., & Friedman, D. (1984). *Spouse abuse: A treatment program for couples*. Champaign, IL: Research Press.

O'Leary, K. D. (1993). Through a psychological lens: Personality traits, personality disorders, and levels of violence. In R. J. Gelles & D. R. Loseke (Eds.), *Current controversies on family violence* (pp. 7-30). Newbury Park, CA: Sage.

O'Leary, K. D. (1996). Physical aggression in marriage can be treated within a marital context under certain circumstances. *Journal of Interpersonal Violence, 11*, 450-452.

O'Leary, K. D., Barling, J., Arias, I., Rosenbaum, A., Malone, J., & Tyree, A. (1989). Prevalence and stability of physical aggression between spouses: A longitudinal analysis. *Journal of Consulting and Clinical Psychology, 57*, 263-268.

O'Leary, K. D., Heyman, R. E., & Neidig, P. H. (1999). Treatment of wife abuse: A comparison of gender-specific and conjoint approaches. *Behavior Therapy, 30*, 475-505.

O'Leary, K. D., Malone, J., & Tyree, A. (1994). Physical aggression in early marriage: Prerelationship and relationship effects. *Journal of Consulting and Clinical Psychology, 62*, 549-602.

O'Leary, K. D., Neidig, P. H., & Heyman, R. E. (1995). Assessment and treatment of partner abuse: A synopsis for the legal profession. *Albany Law Review, 58*, 1215-1234.

O'Leary, K. D., Vivian, D., & Malone, J. (1992). Assessment of physical aggression in marriage: The need for a multimodal method. *Behavioral Assessment, 14*, 5-14.

Pan, H. S., Neidig, P. H., & O'Leary, K. D. (1994). Predicting mild and severe husband to wife physical aggression. *Journal of Consulting and Clinical Psychology, 62*, 975-981.

Pence, E., & Paymar, M. (1993). *Education groups for men who batter: The Duluth Model*. New York: Springer.

Rathus, J., O'Leary, K. D., & Meyer, S. L. (in press). Attachment, coercive control, and wife abuse. *Journal of Family Violence*.

Rosenbaum, A., Gearan, P., & Ondovic, C. (1997, August). Completion and recidivism among court-referred and self-referred batterers in a psychoeducational group treatment program. In A. Rosenbaum (Chair), *Batterers treatment: Strategies, issues, and outcomes*. Symposium conducted at the annual meeting of the American Psychological Association, Chicago, IL.

Rosenbaum, A., & Maiuro, R. (1989). Eclectic approaches in working with men who batter. In P. L. Caesar & L. K. Hamberger (Eds.), *Treating men who batter: Theory, practice, and programs* (pp.165-195). New York: Springer.

Rosenbaum, A., & O'Leary, K. D. (1981). Children: The unintended victims of marital violence. *American Journal of Orthopsychiatry, 51*(4), 692-699.

Rosenfeld, B. D. (1992). Court ordered treatment of spouse abuse. *Clinical Psychology Review, 12,* 205-226.

Rusinoff, J. S. (1990). *Men's treatment handbook (2nd ed.)*. Minneapolis, MN: Domestic Abuse Project.

Saunders, D. G. (1996). Feminist-cognitive-behavioral and process-psychodynamic treatments for men who batter: Interaction of abuser traits and treatment models. *Violence and Victims, 11,* 393-414.

Schechter, S. (1982). *Women and male violence: The visions and struggles of the battered women's movement*. Boston: South End Press.

Schulman, M. A. (1979). *A survey of spousal violence against women in Kentucky* (Study No. 792701). Washington, DC: Law Enforcement Assistance Administration, U. S. Government Printing Office.

Straus, M. A., & Gelles, R. J. (1990). *Physical violence in American families: Risk factors and adaptations to violence in 8,145 families*. New Brunswick: Transaction Publishers.

Straus, M. A., Gelles, R. J., & Steinmetz, S. K. (1980). *Behind closed doors: Violence in the American family*. Garden City, NY: Anchor Books/Doubleday.

Strube, M. J. (1988). The decision to leave an abusive relationship: Empirical evidence and theoretical issues. *Psychological Bulletin, 104,* 236-250.

Tolman, R. M. (1989). The validation of the psychological maltreatment of women by their male partners. *Violence and Victims, 4,* 159-178.

Tolman, R. M. (1999). The validation of the Psychological Maltreatment of Women Inventory. *Violence and Victims, 14,* 25-37.

Vivian, D., & Heyman, R. E. (1996). Is there a place for conjoint treatment of couple violence? *In Session: Psychology and Practice, 2,* 25-48.

RESEARCH AND EVALUATION CONCERNING DOMESTIC VIOLENCE OFFENDERS

Standards for Batterer Treatment Programs: How Can Research Inform Our Decisions?

Amy Holtzworth-Munroe

SUMMARY. The development of batterer treatment program standards was a well-intentioned and reasonable step, given the increasing number of batterers being court-referred to treatment, the poor quality of some treatment programs, and the move toward a coordinated community response to domestic violence. While treatment standards were derived from the understanding of husband violence, as it existed at the time, newer research data do not validate many of the assumptions underlying current standards. This point is illustrated by considering four such assumptions: (1) conjoint treatment is never appropriate, (2) we know the best length, content, and process of treatment, (3) in treatment, one size fits all, and (4) doing something is better than doing nothing. Recent research data relevant to each assumption is also considered. Given the lack of empirical support for these assumptions, it is too early to impose standards mandating one type of treatment. In fact, doing so may stifle what is needed most at this time–the development of new intervention

[Haworth co-indexing entry note]: "Standards for Batterer Treatment Programs: How Can Research Inform Our Decisions?" Holtzworth-Munroe, Amy. Co-published simultaneously in *Journal of Aggression, Maltreatment & Trauma* (The Haworth Maltreatment & Trauma Press, an imprint of The Haworth Press, Inc.) Vol. 5, No. 2(#10), 2001, pp. 165-180; and: *Domestic Violence Offenders: Current Interventions, Research, and Implications for Policies and Standards* (ed: Robert A. Geffner, and Alan Rosenbaum) The Haworth Maltreatment & Trauma Press, an imprint of The Haworth Press, Inc., 2001, pp. 165-180. Single or multiple copies of this article are available for a fee from The Haworth Document Delivery Service [1-800-HAWORTH, 9:00 a.m. - 5:00 p.m. (EST). E-mail address: getinfo@haworthpressinc.com].

approaches that may increase treatment efficacy. However, with the freedom to develop new interventions comes the responsibility to empirically validate these approaches. Thus, it is recommended that all batterer treatment programs strive to conduct research on the effectiveness of their interventions and to make public their findings. *[Article copies available for a fee from The Haworth Document Delivery Service: 1-800-HAWORTH. E-mail address: <getinfo@haworthpressinc.com> Website: <http://www.HaworthPress.com> © 2001 by The Haworth Press, Inc. All rights reserved.]*

KEYWORDS. Domestic violence, perpetrators, treatment standards, conjoint treatment, couples treatment, research

TREATMENT STANDARDS: A REASONABLE AND WELL-INTENTIONED DEVELOPMENT

Until the past 10-20 years, male violence against intimate female partners received little attention from either the criminal justice system or the psychotherapeutic community. The major impetus for changing this situation was undoubtedly the efforts of battered women's advocates who brought attention to the problem of male violence, although other influences likely played a role also (e.g., publication of prevalence data from the first nationally representative survey–Straus, Gelles, & Steinmetz, 1980). Of particular importance were early study findings suggesting that arrest of male batterers deterred further violence (Sherman & Burk, 1984). In response to such data and the efforts of advocates, many jurisdictions around the U.S. implemented policies encouraging the arrest of male batterers. As a result, an increasing number of batterers came to the attention of the criminal justice system. In many such cases, however, judges and others in the system were reluctant to impose jail sentences for domestic violence, particularly in cases involving misdemeanor charges. Yet, they also did not want to see batterers get off "scott free," and they hoped that batterers could be helped to become nonviolent. Thus, it became increasingly common for batterers to be court-referred to participate in therapy and psychoeducational intervention programs.

With this new pool of clients referred by the courts, many new treatment programs were established. In some areas, this growth was rapid. For example, as recently as 1988, there was only one batterer treatment program in Indianapolis. Ten years later, there were over 12 such programs! While many of these new programs around the country are excellent, other are not; perhaps as an unfortunate consequence of the rush to develop programs, some are of poor quality. For example, in some cases, while clinicians have good intentions, they are not familiar with basic data on husband violence and have no training in interventions designed to address this issue or related problems (e.g., aggression, antisociality, gender issues). This lack of training can result in inadequate, unethical, or even dangerous care (e.g., agreeing with a man that his wife "provoked" his violence, yelling at a man in group who did not agree with the leader). The establishment of inadequate treatment programs has been one factor leading to the development of standards for batterer programs.

Another factor that likely underlies the development of batterer treatment standards is the move toward community coordination of services in response to domestic violence cases. In many communities, domestic violence taskforces have been established to help relevant sectors of the community (i.e., battered women's shelters, police, prosecutors, judges, probation officers, and therapists) work together to provide a less piecemeal, more unified, and more consistent approach to the problem of husband violence. Efforts at community coordination are generally supportive of the development of treatment standards, as such standards should help ensure consistency across various programs within a community.

Considering these factors, the move to establish standards of care for batterer treatment programs (e.g., mandating the format, length, content, or method of treatment) can be viewed as a reasonable and well-intentioned step. The development of standards resulted from the actions of community members concerned about the poor quality of some programs and from those hoping to develop consistent interventions within the framework of a coordinated community response to violence.

In addition, the standards adopted generally reflected theories of husband violence as they existed at the time the standards were created. For example, the fact that conjoint couples therapy is considered inappropriate in many state standards reflects the general consensus in the field that more harm than good will result from seeing spouses together in treatment (e.g., see O'Leary article in this volume for details regarding that assumption). In other words, most of the standards were not capricious or arbitrary, but rather were derived from the experts' then-current understanding of husband violence. From this historical perspective, the adoption of such standards is not only understandable but also admirable.

THE PROBLEM WITH EXISTING STANDARDS

Unfortunately, however, many of the assumptions used to create standards have no empirical basis and have never been directly tested in methodologically sound research studies. Similarly, this author is unaware of any studies demonstrating that treatment programs that follow the standards are more effective than treatments that do not. Thus, while most existing standards are commonsensical, they have not been proven effective. In addition, a problem with standards is that they tend to reify certain theoretical assumptions and treatment approaches. As a result, they can cut off further research and exploration of alternative approaches that, ultimately, might prove more effective than existing interventions in eliminating male violence.

The present article was written to illustrate this point, by highlighting new research data suggesting that some of the basic assumptions involved in batterer treatment standards are not valid. To make this point, the author has chosen a few example assumptions, reflected in standards adopted in many areas of the country, that are not supported by the available research data; research relevant to each assumption is reviewed. This is not a thorough review of all the assumptions underlying existing standards or of all the available data. Rather, it is a selective review of newer research, designed to illustrate that our increasing understanding of husband violence requires us to re-examine some of the existing batterer treatment standards currently in place around the country.

EXAMPLE 1:
WE KNOW THE BEST TREATMENT FORMAT, OR CONJOINT TREATMENT IS NEVER APPROPRIATE

Many standards for batterer treatment programs mandate that certain treatment formats can or cannot be used. In particular, many standards recommend that batterers be treated in groups of men and indicate that conjoint treatment of the couple is inappropriate. For example, Section 4.5 of the Massachusetts state standards states, "Any form of couples or conjoint counseling or marriage enhancement weekends or groups are inappropriate initially . . . couples counseling shall not be considered a component of batterer treatment"[1] (Massachusetts Guidelines and Standards, 1994 p. 13). As noted above, and as explained in more detail in O'Leary's article in this volume, the assumption that conjoint therapy will be harmful in cases involving husband violence was originally based on reasonable assumptions about such therapy (e.g., conjoint treatment may increase the risk of violence, imply that the woman is responsible for the violence, and lead the woman to be afraid to express herself). At this time, however, existing empirical data suggest that outcome from conjoint treatment is comparable to outcome from men's groups.

In the most recent study, O'Leary, Heyman, and Neidig (in press) carefully selected couples to be randomly assigned to participate in either group conjoint therapy (i.e., couples seen together in a group) or gender specific therapy (i.e., the husband seen in a men's group and the wife seen in a women's group). Study participants responded to a newspaper advertisement offering free therapy to couples experiencing low levels of physical aggression. To be included in the study, the man had to acknowledge at least one act of violence; the wife could not have sustained injuries requiring medical attention, had to be comfortable being assigned to conjoint treatment, and had to report no fear of living with her husband; men with alcohol dependence were screened out. Thus, this was a study of mildly to moderately violent couples in which the wife was not fearful of her partner and was willing to attend couples therapy; obviously, the results from this study will not be generalizable to all couples. In addition, it is important to note that the conjoint therapy employed was not standard marital therapy but rather focused directly on the problem of marital violence.

A total of 75 couples were randomly assigned to one treatment condition or the other; only 37 couples completed treatment. While both treatment approaches (i.e., conjoint and gender specific) resulted in statistically significant changes in men's violence and psychological abuse, neither was particularly effective (i.e., over 70% of the men engaged in violence during the follow-up period); these high rates of recidivism, relative to other therapy outcome studies, may be due to the fact that the researchers were able to obtain wives' reports of husbands' violence. Regarding the comparison of conjoint and gender specific treatments, there were no differences in outcome across treatment format. In addition, women in the conjoint treatment did not report fear of their husbands and did not report that therapy discussions led to physical aggression.

In an earlier study, Brannen and Rubin (1996) recruited a sample from which it is easier to generalize to existing treatment programs; specifically, their sample included couples referred to batterer treatment by the court system who had indicated a desire to remain in their current relationship. Couples were randomly assigned to either a couples group treatment or a gender-specific group intervention. Of the 49 couples who began treatment, 42 completed it. As in the O'Leary et al. study (in press), the conjoint therapy was designed to address husband violence and was not standard marital therapy. While both treatments resulted in a decrease in male physical aggression, there were few differences in outcome across the two types of treatment. Among men with no history of alcohol abuse, neither treatment was more effective than the other. Surprisingly, among men with a history of alcohol abuse (all of whom were involved in a court-monitored Antabuse program), the couples treatment was more effective than the gender specific treatment. As in the O'Leary et al. study, there was no evidence that the conjoint treatment increased risk of physical or emotional abuse.

Similar results were found in the earliest published study on this issue (Harris, Savage, Jones, & Brooke, 1988), which involved over 70 couples who had experienced husband violence and were requesting therapy at a family service agency; the woman had to indicate a wish to continue her relationship and had to say that she did not feel endangered by her partner's knowledge that she had discussed his violence with a counselor. Random assignment was used. As in the two studies just reviewed, some couples were assigned to a couples counseling program which explicitly addressed violence as the primary relationship problem; in this study, however, it appears that a group format was not used. Differing from the other two studies reviewed, the other treatment condition in this study involved a combination of gender-specific groups and couples groups (i.e., after the gender specific group meeting, a couples meeting was held each week). The attrition rate was high, particularly in the couples counseling condition; 35% of the sample never began treatment and, at follow-up, only 28 women could be interviewed! Given these limitations and the resulting problems of data interpretation, the follow-up results indicated that there were no differences in levels of husband abuse reported by women who had received couples counseling versus those who had received the gender-specific/couples group treatment.

Thus, across these studies, no difference in outcome favored gender-specific therapy. All of the studies involved couples who were interested in remaining together and willing to enter conjoint therapy; thus, the generalizability of these samples is potentially limited (e.g., Dunford, 1997,[2] invited the wives of batterers to attend therapy sessions with their husbands but very few accepted this offer). In all of the studies, a specialized couples treatment addressing the man's violence directly was used; in two of the studies (Brannen & Rubin, 1996; O'Leary et al., in press), a group format was used for the couples therapy. Thus, these data do not support the use of standard marital therapy, applied to individual couples, in reducing male violence. These data do suggest, however, that batterer treatment standards, which explicitly rule out the possibility of conjoint therapy, need to be re-examined.

EXAMPLE 2:
WE KNOW THE BEST LENGTH, CONTENT, AND PROCESS OF TREATMENT

In addition to addressing the format of treatment (e.g., no conjoint therapy), many standards implemented around the country also mandate the content, length, and/or process of batterer treatment programs. The basic assumption that appears to underlie these standards is that we know which therapy approach is the most effective in decreasing male violence. Interestingly, the currently available empirical data do not support this assumption.

For example, most standards support the implementation of programs using techniques from feminist and/or cognitive-behavioral interventions. However, in a recent study, Saunders (1996) found that these approaches are no more effective than another approach that is usually considered unacceptable. Specifically, Saunders randomly assigned over 200 men who had engaged in partner abuse to either a feminist-cognitive-behavioral didactic group treatment (i.e., similar in content and psychoeducational structure to many programs across the country), or to a process-psychodynamic group treatment. This new treatment focused on helping men to "re-experience childhood traumas, grieve their losses, give up control over others, and learn to empathize with others" (p. 395). As noted by Saunders, such programs have been criticized as not being confrontational enough and for allowing abusers to maintain their rationalizations for their violence. Indeed, these programs are rarely used for batterer treatment; for example, psychodynamic therapy is explicitly labeled as an "inappropriate method" for batterer treatment in the Massachusetts state standards (Massachusetts Guidelines and Standards, 1994). Despite such theoretical controversies, there was no main effect for type of treatment on the men's violence at follow-up; men in both treatment conditions had similar recidivism rates. Such findings suggest that it may be too early to dictate, via standards, the content (e.g., feminist-cognitive-behavior vs. psychodynamic) or the process (e.g., didactic vs. process) of group interventions with batterers.

Several other studies also suggest that varying treatment length, intensity, and content may have relatively small, if any, effects on treatment outcome. In one, Edleson and Syers (1990) randomly assigned over 280 batterers to one of three treatment approaches (i.e., an educational group, a self-help group, or a combined educational/self-help group). Within each of these three approaches, treatment length and intensity was varied (i.e., each program involved either 12 sessions over 12 weeks or 32 sessions over 16 weeks). Due to attrition, follow-up assessments conducted with victims and/or batterers six months after treatment could only be conducted with 92 cases. The resulting data, while potentially affected by this limitation, revealed no significant differences across the treatment approaches or treatment lengths/intensities, with one small exception (i.e., men in the education groups were the least likely to use terroristic threats).

In a more recent study, Gondolf (1999) compared treatment outcome across batterer programs at four sites around the country. These programs were selected to range in comprehensiveness/intensiveness of services, from the least comprehensive (i.e., a program with pre-trial referrals, three months of weekly sessions, and referral for court-identified substance abuse or mental problems) to the most comprehensive (i.e., a program with mandatory sentencing to counseling as part of conviction, nine months of weekly meetings, extensive clinical evaluation, in-house management of alcohol and mental health problems, and women's case management). In addition, the programs varied in their therapy process, with some being didactic and others involving process, discussion-oriented groups. While all of the sites shared some basic content (i.e., all complied with their respective state standards and included such goals as holding the batterer responsible for his behavior, and identifying abuse as a means of power and control), it is likely that they differed in other content. Thus, this study contrasted programs varying in length, comprehensiveness of services, process, and content.

Among over 800 men participating in the study, there were few differences in outcome across the sites. A few analyses showed trends suggesting that the most comprehensive program yielded better results than the less comprehensive programs, but these differences usually did not reach statistical significance and may or may not be clinically significant (i.e., 8% fewer re-assaults at the most comprehensive program than at the least comprehensive program). For men without additional problems (i.e., alcohol or other criminal arrests), there were even fewer differences across the four sites.

Other similar studies are currently being conducted, although the final results from these studies are not yet available. For example, Davis and Taylor (1997) are conducting a study that involves a comparison of treatment intensity; men are randomly assigned to 40 hours of treatment administered over either an 8-week or a 26-week period. In another recent study, from which preliminary data have been presented, Dunford (1997) compared treatment outcome across four interventions among batterers in the Navy. One treatment condition involved weekly meetings, for six months, of a men's group; another was similar, but wives were invited to attend the sessions. The third intervention involved no therapy sessions, but careful, monthly monitoring of the men to check for, and deal swiftly with, any further instances of domestic violence. The final control condition involved contact with the female victim/partner to provide her with safety information and encourage her to report further violence. The findings from this study may not be applicable to a civilian population (e.g., men could face severe consequences, including discharge from the military, if they engaged in further violence). Keeping this in mind, the findings were remarkable in that there were no differences in outcome across these four treatment conditions.

Taken together, the results of these studies clearly demonstrate that, at this time, no one intervention approach (e.g., content, process, length, intensity or comprehensiveness of services) has been demonstrated superior to any other approach. The findings also suggest that even minimal interventions may have a positive impact on decreasing men's violence. While further systematic study is necessary, it is already clear that the adoption of treatment standards mandating one type of therapeutic approach is premature.

EXAMPLE 3:
STANDARD PROGRAMS, OR IN TREATMENT, ONE SIZE FITS ALL

Traditionally, batterers referred to a treatment program are all provided with the same intervention (i.e., they all enter the same therapy group), with a few exceptions (e.g., providing batterers with substance abuse problems interventions for addiction). At this time, treatment standards essentially require this, by mandating that certain approaches be used with all batterers. Underlying this approach is the implicit assumption that all batterers are the same, or at least similar enough to be helped by the same treatment.

In stark contrast to this assumption is a growing body of evidence demonstrating that all batterers are not alike; rather, batterers are a very heterogeneous group, perhaps comprised of some clearly identifiable subgroups. For example, in a review of 15 previous batterer typologies (e.g., Gondolf, 1988a; Hamberger & Hastings, 1986; Saunders, 1992), Holtzworth-Munroe and Stuart (1994) suggested that three subtypes of violent husbands (i.e., family only, dysphoric/borderline, and generally violent/antisocial) could be identified using three descriptive dimensions (i.e., severity/frequency of husband violence, generality of violence, and psychopathology/personality disorder). Family only batterers engage in low levels of marital violence and violence outside the home, and evidence little or no psychopathology. Dysphoric/borderline batterers engage in moderate to severe marital violence, low to moderate levels of general violence, and evidence psychological distress and borderline personality disorder characteristics. Generally violent/antisocial batterers engage in moderate to severe marital violence, high levels of general violence, and evidence antisocial personality disorder characteristics. Holtzworth-Munroe and Stuart (1994) also proposed that these subtypes of batterers would differ in a theoretically consistent manner on measures of correlates of violence (e.g., borderline/dysphoric batterers would evidence the most insecure attachment and jealousy/dependency; generally violent/antisocial batterers would evidence the most psychopathy, substance abuse, and criminal behavior). A recent study designed to test this typology has generally supported it (Holtzworth-Munroe, Meehan, Herron, Rehman, & Stuart, under review). Thus, it appears that meaningful subgroups of violent husbands can be identified.

The potential clinical implications of these findings are evident in the results of several initial studies suggesting that interventions may have differing effects on different subtypes of men. For example, in the study reviewed above, Saunders (1996) found that men who scored high on a measure of anti-social tendencies (e.g., generally violent/antisocial men) did better in the structured feminist-cognitive-behavioral treatment, while men who scored high on a measure of dependency (e.g., borderline/dysphoric men) had better outcomes in the process-psychodynamic group, consistent with the notion that the violence of this subtype of men is, in part, a result of their insecure attachment resulting from childhood traumas. These study findings suggest that better treatment outcomes might be achieved by developing varying interventions for different types of batterers.

In contrast with Saunders' (1996) finding that men high in antisociality were helped by a feminist-cognitive-behavioral intervention, other studies suggest that, irrespective of type of intervention, this subtype of batterer (i.e., the generally violent/antisocial batterer) may not do well in any currently available intervention. For example, reanalyzing data from a series of studies on the effects of arrest on batterers, Sherman (1992) proposed that arrest has differing effects on different groups of men, with socially marginal men (e.g., unemployed, previous arrest records) being less deterred by arrest than socially bonded men. Indeed, Sherman et al. (1992) found that arrest deterred violence among men who were employed or married, but that it escalated violence among men who had a prior record of arrest, were unemployed, had less than a high school education, were not married, or were black.

Similarly, in the Navy batterer treatment outcome study introduced above, Dunford (1997) found that, while there were no outcome differences across treatment conditions, there were differences in outcome across men. Six months following the end of therapy, approximately 80% of men were not engaging in any further violence, and 10% of the men accounted for 85% of the continuing violence. Predictors of continuing violence included such factors as initial severity of violence and drunkenness, suggesting that men resembling generally violent/antisocial men were the least likely to be helped by any treatment.

Similar findings have emerged in smaller studies. For example, Hamberger & Hastings (1990) found that, relative to violence-free treatment completers, recidivists had higher levels of substance abuse and higher scores on measures of narcissism and aggression (e.g., similar to generally violent/antisocial batterers). Data gathered by Dutton, Bodnarchuk, Kropp, Hart, and Ogloff (1997) from men seeking batterer treatment at two different agencies, suggested that perhaps not only generally violent/antisocial batterers, but also borderline/dysphoric men, do more poorly than other batterers in treatment. In this study, men with high scores on measures of borderline, avoidant, and antisocial personality had less positive treatment outcome than other men in therapy.

In conclusion, research demonstrates that batterers are not a homogeneous group, but rather differ in systematic ways that are theoretically coherent (e.g., Holtzworth-Munroe & Stuart, 1994). Thus, it may not make sense for standards to mandate that one intervention approach be used with all batterers sent to treatment. Rather, there are initial clues in the data that suggest that the majority of violent men who are not severely violent or antisocial may be helped by a wide variety of interventions. Other men (e.g., men high on dependency in Saunders' study, 1996) may do best in new forms of treatment (e.g., psychodynamic process groups). Finally, other batterers (i.e., generally violent/antisocial batterers, men engaging in the most severe violence) may not be deterred from violence by either arrest or currently available treatments. Regarding this group, it is important for workers in the area of husband violence to begin a dialogue with professionals who have experience with related populations (e.g., juvenile delinquents, criminal individuals with antisocial personality disorder, generally aggression populations) to generate ideas about what interventions may be developed to help the most severely violent men.

EXAMPLE 4:
WE NEED TO DO SOMETHING, OR DOING SOMETHING IS BETTER THAN DOING NOTHING

By definition, the existence of treatment standards implies that treatment intervention programs should be offered to batterers; the obvious underlying assumption is that what we are doing is working. Unfortunately, however, there are no strong and consistent data to support this assumption. Some reviewers believe that examination of a handful of methodologically sound studies provides evidence that batterer treatment works (e.g., Davis & Taylor, 1999). Other reviewers, however, have concluded that either we do not know whether batterer treatment works, given the methodological weaknesses in most batterer treatment outcome studies (e.g., Hamberger & Hastings, 1993), or that batterers' treatment is not very effective (e.g., Rosenfeld, 1992).

One might still argue that even if we have not proven that batterers' treatment is effective, it is better to offer such interventions than to do nothing therapeutically; the assumption underlying this assertion would be that at least our interventions do no harm. However, a study by Gondolf (1988b) could lead one to question this assumption. Gondolf asked over 6,000 women leaving battered women's shelters whether they intended to return to the batterer or to leave him. The best predictor of the women's decisions was whether or not the batterer was in treatment. If the man was in treatment, 53% of the wives planned to return to him; if he was not, only 19% of the women planned to return to him. Given the current lack of evidence demonstrating the efficacy of batterer treatments, these data suggest that the very existence of such programs may actually increase a wife's risk, by leading to a false sense of security among battered women whose husbands have sought treatment.[3]

FUTURE DIRECTIONS AND EMPIRICAL VALIDATION OF TREATMENTS

A lack of empirically sound data from batterer treatment outcome studies means that there are little, if any, data on which to firmly base the drafting of treatment standards. Indeed, the lack of data demonstrating the efficacy of currently available programs suggests that certain treatment approaches should not be mandated, as such standards tend to become reified and thus may stifle the development of new, hopefully more effective, interventions. The field of batterer treatment is nowhere near the stage where one can conclude, "Here is what works, and thus everyone should use this approach." Instead, the data suggest that this is a time to be developing new treatments, and experimenting with new approaches and ideas to design treatments that may be more effective than those currently available.

In doing so, however, it is necessary that we empirically test the efficacy of any new therapies. Otherwise, we risk returning to the days before treatment standards were adopted, when any clinician could try anything, regardless of whether or not it made theoretical sense, was ethical, or was potentially endangering to women. To avoid a return to this state, treatment programs should empirically examine the outcome of their interventions.

Attending to the empirical validation of batterer treatment programs would be consistent with developments in the field of clinical psychology in general and with the demands of managed health care that programs demonstrate the efficacy of their interventions. For example, a taskforce formed by Division 12 (clinical psychology) of the American Psychological Association, has set up guidelines for designating treatments as "empirically validated" (Chambless & Hollon, 1998). To do so requires the following: (1) At least two high quality between-group design experiments demonstrating superior efficacy of the treatment, either relative to a placebo or another treatment, or demonstrating efficacy equivalent to an already established treatment in experiments with adequate sample sizes; or (2) A large number (e.g., more than 8) of single-case design experiments demonstrating efficacy in experiments using good designs and compared to another treatment; (3) Experiments must be conducted with treatment manuals; (4) Characteristics of client samples must be clearly specified; and (5) Effects must have been demonstrated by at least two different investigating teams. While meeting such criteria is unlikely to occur in the near future in the field of batterer treatment, these criteria are goals toward which clinicians and researchers in this area should strive.

Of course, currently, there are often practical impediments to the suggestion that clinicians conduct outcome research on the effectiveness of their batterer treatment programs. Many clinicians are already overworked, devoting long hours to providing direct services and dealing with administrative issues at their agencies. They often have little training in treatment evaluation research methods, and incentives for conducting such work are missing in many settings. In addition, it is unclear who will pay for such research. Even if such a suggestion became part of state standards, states may not have the resources to monitor such efforts.

While acknowledging that such constraints make it difficult to implement research on treatment outcome, three local examples of treatment outcome research efforts in Bloomington, Indiana suggest that such work can be done and can have its own rewards. First, derived from domestic taskforce meetings, the local mental health center is offering a new batterer treatment program; they have collaborated with graduate students in the local psychology training program, asking for consultation regarding treatment outcome evaluation. The findings will be used to shape future community decisions about the batterer treatment program (e.g., should it be continued). Around the country, in many communities with colleges and universities, there are students and faculty who are eager to form such alliances. As a second example, at a local center for behavioral health, one program administrator has established an anxiety treatment program that uses only empirically validated treatments, and she gathers outcome data on how effective these programs are when used in a community, rather than an academic setting. She has found that insurance companies are very interested in her work and will often approve insurance coverage for patients whose mental health coverage has been exhausted, because she is able to provide figures showing the effectiveness rates of her interventions. As a final example, a local judge recently obtained a small grant to examine the relative outcomes resulting from dealing with alcohol/drug cases within the general court system versus within a newly established drug/alcohol court. None of these individuals work in settings that have traditionally encouraged empirical research on treatment outcome. All have convinced their administrators that, ultimately, being able to demonstrate treatment effectiveness will benefit the program (e.g., by providing a competitive edge when negotiating for managed care contracts and court referrals; by increasing reimbursement from insurance companies, etc.). All also are willing to learn from their results, modifying or even ending programs that are not effective. None are using perfect research methods (e.g., random assignment), but each has made an effort to take responsibility to provide information on program effectiveness.

CONCLUSIONS

Much of the empirical data reviewed in this article directly contradict assumptions underlying existing batterer standards. The lack of correspondence between standards and empirical data demonstrates that it is premature to have established, rigid treatment standards for batterer programs. No data suggest that we are ready to mandate one treatment approach over others. In fact, to do so risks stifling the very effort that may be necessary to improve treatment efficacy–the development of new ideas and interventions. Thus, freedom from standards is recommended, so that individuals in this field will be encouraged to develop a variety of interventions, and to examine how varying subtypes of batterers fare in these differing treatments.

To keep unethical, irresponsible, and potentially dangerous programs from being developed, however, this recommendation to encourage the development of new therapeutic approaches would, ideally, be tied to another requirement–that all programs, existing and new, include a research component to systematically evaluate treatment outcome. In other words, each agency should examine the efficacy of their offered batterer intervention program; how else can one justify mandating men to attend a particular program? In short, it is recommended that jurisdictions consider encouraging programs to conduct, to the best of their ability, research on their treatment effectiveness. Support and resources for doing so should, ideally, be provided. Programs should then be required to make public their research data on treatment effectiveness.

NOTES

1. I wish to thank one of the editors, A.R., for providing information about the Massachusetts State Guidelines and Standards for Batterer Treatment.

2. Note that the Dunford San Diego Navy experiment, comparing the relative efficacy of several types of batterer treatments, is briefly discussed at several points throughout this article. It is important to note that this is the only treatment outcome study discussed that is not yet published or in press; thus, it has not yet met standards for publication. Indeed, it is a controversial study, given its setting (e.g., findings from a military sample may not generalize to a civilian setting). Yet, it is one of the few large-scale studies that have compared various types of batterer treatments to one another. Thus, it is cited in this paper; but readers are urged to use caution in drawing conclusions from it until they can read the findings for themselves in future publications.

3. Note that the Gondolf (1988b) findings could be interpreted in other ways. For example, directionality may be reversed, as many battered women ask their partners to get therapy as a condition for returning to their relationship. As another example, perhaps the fact that a man is in batterers' treatment indicates that he is more devoted to his relationship, more willing to take responsibility for his behavior, or some other condition exists that may account for his female partner's intention to return to their relationship. (I thank the editor, A.R., for making these points.)

REFERENCES

Brannen, S. J., & Rubin, A. (1996). Comparing the effectiveness of gender-specific and couples groups in court-mandated spouse abuse treatment program. *Research on Social Work Practice, 6*, 405-424.

Chambless, D. L., & Hollon, S. D. (1998). Defining empirically supported therapies. *Journal of Consulting and Clinical Psychology, 66*, 7-18.

Davis, R. C., & Taylor, B. G. (1997, June-July). A randomized experiment of the effects of batterers' treatment: Summary of preliminary research findings. Paper presented at the 5th International Family Violence Research Conference, Durham, NH.

Davis, R. C., & Tayor, B. G. (1999). Does batterer treatment reduce violence? A synthesis of the literature. In L. Feder (Ed.), *Women and Domestic Violence* (pp. 69-93). Binghamton, NY: The Haworth Press, Inc.

Dunford, F. (1997, June-July). The research design and preliminary outcome findings of the San Diego Navy experiment. Paper presented at the 5th International Family Violence Research Conference, Durham, NH.

Dutton, D. G., Bodnarchuk, M., Kropp, R., Hart, S. D., & Ogloff, J. P. (1997). Client personality disorders affecting wife assault post-treatment recidivism. *Violence and Victims, 12*, 37-50.

Edleson, J. L., & Syers, M. (1990). Relative effectiveness of group treatments for men who batter. *Social Work Research and Abstracts, 26*, 10-17.

Gondolf, E. W. (1988a). Who are those guys? Toward a behavioral typology of batterers. *Violence and Victims, 3*, 187-203.

Gondolf, E. W. (1988b). The effect of batterer counseling on shelter outcome. *Journal of Interpersonal Violence, 3*, 275-289.

Gondolf, E. W. (1999). A comparison of four batterer intervention systems. *Journal of Interpersonal Violence, 14*, 41-61.

Hamberger, K. L., & Hastings, J. E. (1986). Personality correlates of men who abuse their partner: A cross validation study. *Journal of Family Violence, 1*, 323-341.

Hamberger, K. L., & Hastings, J. E. (1990). Recidivism following spouse abuse abatement counseling: Treatment program implications. *Violence and Victims, 5*, 157-170.

Hamberger, K. L., & Hastings, J. E. (1993). Court-mandated treatments of men who batter their partners: Issues, controversies, and outcomes. In Z. Hilton (Ed.), *Legal response to wife assault* (pp. 188-229). Newbury Park, CA: Sage.

Harris, R., Savage, S., Jones, T., & Brooke, W. (1988). A comparison of treatments for abusive men and their partners within a family-service agency. *Canadian Journal of Community Mental Health, 7*, 147-155.

Holtzworth-Munroe, A., Meehan, J. C., Herron, K., Rehman, U., & Stuart, G. L. (in press). Testing the Holtzworth-Munroe and Stuart batterer typology. *Journal of Consulting and Clinical Psychology*.

Holtzworth-Munroe, A., & Stuart, G. L. (1994). Typologies of male batterers: Three subtypes and the differences among them. *Psychological Bulletin, 116*, 476-497.

Massachusetts Guidelines and Standards for the Certification of Batterers' Treatment Programs (1994, May revision).

O'Leary, K. D., Heyman, R. E., & Neidig, P. H. (in press). Treatment of wife abuse: A comparison of gender-specific and conjoint approaches. *Behavior Therapy*.

Rosenfeld, B. D. (1992). Court-ordered treatment of spouse abuse. *Clinical Psychology Review, 12*, 205-26.

Saunders, D. G. (1992). A typology of men who batter women: Three types derived from cluster analysis. *American Journal of Orthopsychiatry, 62*, 264-275.

Saunders, D. G. (1996). Feminist-cognitive-behavioral and process-psychodynamic treatments for men who batter: Interaction of abuser traits and treatment model. *Violence and Victims, 11*, 393-414.

Sherman, L. W. (1992). The influence of criminology on criminal law: Evaluating arrests for misdemeanor domestic violence. *Journal of Criminal Law and Criminology, 83*, 1-45.

Sherman, L. W., & Berk, R. A. (1984). The specific deterrent effects of arrest for domestic assault. *American Sociological Review, 49*, 261.

Sherman, L. W., Schmidt, J. D., Rogan, D. P., Smith, D. A., Gartin, P. R., Cohn, E. G., Collins, D. J., & Bacich, A. R. (1992). The variable effects of arrest of criminal careers: The Milwaukee domestic violence experiment. *Journal of Criminal Law and Criminology, 83*, 137-1609.

Straus, M. A., Gelles, R. J., & Steinmetz, S. K. (1980). *Behind closed doors: Violence in the American family*. New York: Doubleday/Anchor.

Standards for Batterer Programs: A Formative Evaluation of the Illinois Protocol

Larry W. Bennett
Neil Vincent

SUMMARY. Our article reports data from a three-year formative study of the *Illinois Protocol for Domestic Abuse Batterers Programs*. This evaluation research is guided by three questions: (1) How do standards affect the way batterer programs deliver services to men who batter? (2) How do standards impact community efforts to prevent violence? and (3) How do standards affect judicial referral for domestic violence intervention? Data include: (1) surveys of 50 victim service agencies, 63 batterer programs, and 823 men in 27 batterer programs, and (2) structured interviews with 146 key informants, including judges and prosecutors, battered women's advocates, and batterer program staff. Results suggest that standards meet the goals set for them, although with some unintended consequences. The primary effects of the Illinois standards are providing a structure for programs working with men who batter,

---

The authors wish to thank their anonymous reviewers for comments on an earlier version of the paper, as well as the numerous agencies and practitioners who participated in the evaluation.

This project is funded by a grant from the Illinois Department of Human Services. An earlier version of this article was presented at the 6th International Conference on Family Violence Research, Durham, NH, July 1999.

[Haworth co-indexing entry note]: "Standards for Batterer Programs: A Formative Evaluation of the Illinois Protocol." Bennett, Larry W., and Neil Vincent. Co-published simultaneously in *Journal of Aggression, Maltreatment & Trauma* (The Haworth Maltreatment & Trauma Press, an imprint of The Haworth Press, Inc.) Vol. 5, No. 2(#10), 2001, pp. 181-197; and: *Domestic Violence Offenders: Current Interventions, Research, and Implications for Policies and Standards* (ed: Robert A. Geffner, and Alan Rosenbaum) The Haworth Maltreatment & Trauma Press, an imprint of The Haworth Press, Inc., 2001, pp. 181-197. Single or multiple copies of this article are available for a fee from The Haworth Document Delivery Service [1-800-HAWORTH, 9:00 a.m. - 5:00 p.m. (EST). E-mail address: getinfo@haworthpressinc.com].

181

structuring collaboration between batterer programs and victim service agencies, increasing judicial confidence that batterers are being served appropriately, and forcing victim programs to think about batterer programs. *[Article copies available for a fee from The Haworth Document Delivery Service: 1-800-HAWORTH. E-mail address: <getinfo@haworthpressinc.com> Website: <http://www.HaworthPress.com> © 2001 by The Haworth Press, Inc. All rights reserved.]*

KEYWORDS. Domestic violence, spouse abusers, program evaluation

Standards for batterer programs evolved out of a concern for the safety of domestic violence victims. At their best, standards provide a structure for programs working with men who batter, a means of holding programs accountable to the community, support for delivering the best interventions available, and a mechanism for extending court control to domestic violence offenders. Twenty-five states in the United States have instituted standards for batterer programs (Austin & Dankwort, 1999).

Standards vary according to the governmental units involved and the means of regulation, which might be a local judicial board (e.g., in Colorado), another criminal justice body (e.g., in Iowa), or a state code agency such as public health (e.g., in Massachusetts), child protection (e.g., in Washington), or Human Services (e.g., in Illinois). While Gondolf (1990) suggests that a great deal of variation exists in batterer programs nationally, a report by the Battered Women's Justice Project (1995) found much similarity in batterer program standards, despite variations in government supervision.

Standards for batterer programs have proponents (e.g., Adams, 1994; Gondolf, 1995; Hessmiller-Trego, 1991) and critics (e.g., Geffner, 1995a, 1995b; Goldman, 1991; Rosenbaum & Stewart, 1994). We have summarized this discussion elsewhere (Bennett & Piet, 1999). For the most part, critics of standards have not opposed the development of standards, only the process of their development and the restrictive nature of some standards. Criticism of standards have included suggestions that: (1) Battering is a mental health issue, and a mental health professional should, if not provide direct services, at least provide supervision and set service standards; (2) Since there is no empirical evidence that one intervention works better than another, standards which favor one intervention are based on ideological rather than scientific considerations; and (3) Standards inhibit free enterprise in service of a feminist agenda.

We believe that both objections and support for standards would be better framed if informed by research. Research on standards has been minimal and entirely descriptive. The Battered Women's Justice Project (1995) compared standards from Colorado, Iowa, three California municipalities, Minnesota, Pennsylvania, Massachusetts, New York, Florida, Idaho, Texas, and Washington. Austin and Dankwort (1999) described standards in the U.S. and Canada. A recent study by Maiuro and his colleagues is in this current volume.

Regardless of government or organizational auspices, typical elements of batterer program standards include: (1) ethical expectations for staff, (2) program-level sanctions for violation of standards, (3) some indication and reminder of staff duty to report violence and to warn victims, (4) an outline of accountability plans for the batterer, (5) logistics of the intervention delivery, (6) treatment approaches which may or may not be utilized, (7) fee policy, (8) criteria for program completion, and (9) information which must be collected on each batterer. As we suggested, the purpose of these standards elements is to enhance victim safety, accountability, punishment and program performance. It is standard area number 6 above, the specification or restriction of treatment approaches, which has elicited most of the criticism of batterer program standards. At present, there is no empirical evidence that standards achieve the aim their designers set for them. This article describes a preliminary appraisal of the effects of one state's standards.

ILLINOIS STANDARDS

Under the auspices of the Illinois Department of Human Services (DHS) and the DHS Domestic Violence Advisory Council, a multi-disciplinary committee crafted the Illinois Protocol for Domestic Abuse Batterers Programs and implemented these standards in January, 1995. The committee utilized several existing state standards as models. According to its authors, the Illinois standards are

> . . . intended to be used by programs working with men who, because of their abuse, were convicted of a crime, or would be if their actions were known. . . . The purpose of this protocol is to guide new and existing programs toward the development and delivery of services which are safe, effective and accountable. (Illinois Protocol, 1994, p. 5)

The Illinois Protocol provides direction to prospective batterer programs in the following areas: (1) Declaration of principles (e.g., the primary goal of batterers programs is cessation of woman abuse); (2) Service coordination, a directive that "Services for batterers shall not exist in isolation" (a key component in these standards is that battered women's organizations must not disapprove of batterers intervention programs); (3) Program approaches (including suggestions about goals, format and structure, content, and components; couples counseling is prohibited except under certain strict conditions); (4) Core Standards (including ethics, confidentiality, reporting, accountability, and fees); (5) Staff selection and training recommendations; (6) Maintenance of a 22-item database.

Since the Illinois standards were not the result of legislation, the regulating mechanism is indirect. The way these standards are designed to affect services for batterers is best characterized as a peer review/judicial influence process. Applicant batterer programs are reviewed for compliance with the standards by a committee of peers appointed by the DHS. This committee of about 20 individuals is selected from a pool of batterer program directors, victim service agency representatives, government officials, and academics. If the review committee finds the applicant agency in compliance with the standards, this compliance is signified by a letter from the DHS to the agency. Three times annually, the DHS provides a list of compliant programs to the Administrative Office of Illinois Courts, which in turn distributes the list statewide to judges. Since Illinois standards are not written in statute, the way standards influence batterer programs is primarily economic. Without judicial referral, the program will not receive referrals from the court. The effect of this compliance list on judicial referral to batterer programs and on batterer program survival is unknown. Strictly speaking, since there is neither law nor empirical evidence supporting the *Illinois Protocol for Domestic Abuse Batterers' Programs*, this document should be referred to as a guideline rather than a standard; however, we will continue to refer to the Protocol as standards to remain consistent with popular terminology.

METHODOLOGY

The current article is based on data from a three-year study of the Illinois standards. This evaluation research is guided by three questions: (1) How have the standards effected the way batterer intervention programs (BIPs) deliver services to men who batter? (2) How have the standards impacted community efforts to prevent violence? and, (3) How have the standards effected judicial sentencing for domestic violence? The Illinois standards apply only to batterer programs serving men; consequently, the current report is applicable only to BIPs serving men.

The theoretical perspective used in this evaluation research is ecological. It is assumed that there exists a local domestic violence community centered on services to victims and justice for perpetrators of domestic violence. This domestic violence community is influenced by state and local systems, which influences individual programs, which in turn influences program participants. Mechanisms for victim safety and program accountability built into state standards ought to be observable at both program and community levels. As defined in this study, the domestic violence community is anchored on the local victim services program, the local court, and the local batterers program(s).

The methods in this study are both qualitative and quantitative. Because we know so little about standards, batterer programs, and domestic violence ecologies, the primary task of this report is description and narrative. This evaluation is viewed as a step toward a statewide evaluation of domestic violence prevention effectiveness.

Data collection for the project includes interviews, surveys, and analysis of archival records. Data reported in this article are based on: (1) interviews with 146 victim service staff, batterer program staff, judges, and other criminal justice staff, (2) survey data from 50 Illinois victim services programs, (3) first-stage surveys from 60 batterers intervention programs and second-stage survey of 23 batterer intervention programs, and (4) surveys from 823 participants in 27 batterer programs. Sampling frames for the surveys varied by the population of interest.

Measures

All measures used in this evaluation research were developed by the authors. Most quantitative measures simply requested numbers (e.g., number of groups, staff, program completion rate). Two variables asked the key informant to make estimates on an ordinal scale:

RELATIONSHIP TO AGENCIES asked program informants to rate the quality of the working relationship between the batterers program and each of the following systems as a whole using a 6-point scale ranging from 0 (No Relationship) to 5 (Excellent Relationship), with 3 being an adequate relationship. The systems rated were: Substance Abuse Agencies, Medical Institutions, Prosecutors, Police, Corrections Officers, Judges, Mental Health Agencies and the Domestic Violence Victim Program. TIME SPENT IN BATTERER GROUP was evaluated from the participant's perspective using a 5-point ordinal scale for each of six themes. The scale was (1) none, (2) very little, (3) some, (4) quite a bit, and (5) all the time. The six themes rated were: Learning to control anger, Issues of power and control, Relationship problems of group members, Personal problems men bring to group, Legal problems of group members, and Issues in men's and women's relationships.

Procedure

The first stage of the project was identification and survey of batterer programs. A sampling frame of batterers programs was constructed from (1) current programs included in the DHS "approved" list, (2) programs who had applied for approval under the standards but were denied, (3) programs pending approval under the standards, and (4) programs identified by victim service agencies and other key informants as providing services to men who batter. Fifty-two Illinois victim service programs were surveyed, and 50 returned the survey. Using the above method, 92 batterer programs were identified for the first-stage sampling frame. A questionnaire was mailed to each program, and 60 (65%) responded. The second-stage sampling frame for a more detailed questionnaire was the 60 agencies who responded to the first-stage survey. Twenty-three agencies (38%) responded to this detailed questionnaire.

The second stage of the project consisted of key informant interviews and batterer program participant surveys in twenty communities statewide. The twenty targeted domestic violence communities were selected using three criteria: (1) at least one batterer intervention program is operational in the area with a DHS-funded victim services agency, (2) director and contact persons at the victim services agency and batterers program agree to participate in the study, and (3) geographic diversity, with proportionate representation of rural, suburban and urban programs. We identified key informants for interviewing as follows: The researcher sent a letter to the director of victim service agencies and each batterer program in the target community, soliciting their assistance in the project. All victim service and batterer program directors in the targeted communities agreed to cooperate. Because the batterer program participation involved a full day of activity, including case review and providing curricula, they were given between $250 and $500 for their participation, depending on how many programs participated in each area. The directors were asked to identify key informants in each community to be interviewed. In addition to the two directors, the Chief Judge in each relevant judicial district was asked to nominate the judges who were most involved in domestic violence cases. These judges were contacted and their participation solicited. A purposive sample of batterers was identified by the BIP director as all men in batterers group during a specified week. Non-identifying surveys were distributed and returned anonymously. The surveys consisted of six questions about how time was spent in the group, and no identifying or demographic information was collected. Due to the anonymity procedures, we have no way of knowing what proportion of surveys were returned.

RESULTS

Illinois Batterer Programs

Using a variety of identification methods, including DHS lists and information provided by battered women's programs throughout the state, we identified 92 batterers programs operating in Illinois. Of these 92 programs, 67 (73%) returned a preliminary questionnaire. Of the 67 programs returning the questionnaire, seven indicated they no longer had a batterers program. The 60 active programs enrolled a total of 7,115 different batterers in their programs in the previous fiscal year, and had a total of 3,714 different batterers enrolled in their programs at the time of the survey (1998). Two programs accounted for 2,338 (33%) of the total batterers seen last year by these 60 agencies. Of the 60 agencies who actually had an operating batterer program, 30 (50%) were listed on the DHS compliance list at that time, 25 (42%) were not listed as compliant, and five (8%) had applied for inclusion under the standards but were rejected. The median number of batterers seen by the BIPs in their last fiscal year and at the time of the survey are listed in Table 1. From Table 1, we may conclude that two-thirds of Illinois batterers are served by standards-compliant programs. Using all available data, we estimate that, in 1998, approximately 12,000 different batterers were enrolled annually in Illinois programs. By comparison, this figure illustrates about one-third of the number of battered women served in Illinois by DHS-funded agencies each year.

The second-stage questionnaire provided a more detailed questionnaire, permitting us to develop baseline information for some of the questions we would ask later in interviews. Of the 60 active agencies, 23 (38%) completed the second questionnaire. Of the 23 agencies, 15 (65%) were on the Illinois list of agencies in compliance with the standards. Eleven (48%) were proprietary agencies, 10 (44%) were non-profits, and two (9%) were public agencies. Table 2 describes the staffing and service patterns of these 23 batterers programs. The data indicate that these programs are, on the average, functioning at about half their projected service capacity, suggesting under-utilization.

Relationship to Agencies. The mean values of relationships across agencies are displayed in Table 3. As we see from Table 3, the strongest relationships perceived by these batterers programs are with domestic violence agencies and judges, and the weakest relationship is with medical institutions. This is not a surprising result, since batterer programs usually have little need of relating to medical institutions unless those institutions provide collateral mental health services. However, the fact that one in seven batterer programs report a less-than-adequate relationship with victim programs should be a matter of some concern.

TABLE 1. Median Number of Batterers Per Program by Compliance Status

	In Compliance	Program Status Not In Compliance	Rejected
Median Number of Batterers	(n = 30)	(n = 25)	(n = 5)
Last Year	83	30	20
At Present	40	12	7

TABLE 2. Service Characteristics of 23 Batterers Programs

	Median	Range
Number Full Time (FTE) Staff	4.0	1 to 19
Assessment Hours Per Week	3.5	0 to 40
Group Hours Per Week	7.0	0 to 30
Individual Counseling Hours Per Week	2.0	0 to 205
Couples Counseling Hours Per Week	0.0	0 to 4
Total Direct Service		
Hours per Week	17.0	5 to 305
Batterers in Program Past Year	80	10 to 1,542
Batterers in Program at Present	26	3 to 1,706
Program Capacity	45	3 to 1,706
Current Load-to-Capacity (%)	58%	0 to 99 %

Accountability. Illinois standards specify that approved programs must document means by which they hold their agency accountable to the larger domestic violence community and to the criminal justice system. It is assumed that such accountability improves the safety of victims. Specifically, the Illinois standards list 11 mechanisms, which programs can utilize to maintain accountable relationships with the community. In order to describe methods of accountability used by batterers programs, we asked key informants to indicate which of the 11 methods of accountability described in the standards they utilized in their program. Methods of demonstrating accountability for 23 batterer programs are listed in Table 4. As we see from Table 4, a large majority of sampled programs stated that they held meetings with battered women's advocates, used male-female co-facilitation teams, had telephone contact with victims, and had written policies for communicating non-compliance with the court. A distinct minority of programs used advocates for supervision or case staffing, and all the programs which did so were in-house programs of victim services agencies. About half of the batterer programs involved advocates at

TABLE 3. Quality of Program Relationships (Self-Rated) with Select Community Agencies and Institutions

	Quality of Relationship		
Institution	M	SD	Percent Adequate or Better
Substance Abuse	3.3	1.7	83 %
Medical	2.2	1.9	57
Prosecutor	3.5	1.0	91
Police	3.3	1.3	82
Corrections	3.1	1.8	70
Judges	4.0	0.8	95
Mental Health	3.2	1.5	86
DV Program	3.9	1.6	86

TABLE 4. Methods of Accountability Utilized by 23 Illinois Batterer Programs

Method	Percent Using
Batterer program has policy for communication of non-compliance to court	100%
Periodic meetings are held with BWAs	83
Batterer program has policy to communicate with non criminal justice referrals	83
Batterer program staff have telephone contact with victims	74
Male-female facilitation model employed in majority of groups	72
Batterer program has written procedures for managing court referrals	65
Batterer program staff have written contact with victims	57
BWA are solicited on program decisions	56
Batterer program has orientation or special program for victims	44
BWAs monitor batterers groups	27
BWAs review cases and attend staffings	26

Note: BWA = Battered Women Advocates

the level of program development, but the link between batterer programs and advocates does not extend to involvement in Illinois batterer programs at the level of program staffing or monitoring.

Participant Views of Program Themes. Participating agencies surveyed their current participants about how much time was spent in their groups on each of six themes: (1) anger issues and anger management, (2) issues of power and control, (3) marital issues, (4) personal issues, (5) legal issues, and

(6) relationship issues between men and women. These were rated on a five-point scale: (1) None of the time, (2) Very little time, (3) Some of the time, (4) Quite a bit of time, (5) All the time. Table 5 lists the mean, standard deviation, and one-way ANOVA statistic (f) for each theme across 23 programs. As Table 5 indicated, time in groups is spent primarily on anger management, power/control, and gender relationship issues, a distribution entirely consistent with expectations of the Illinois standards. Little (but some) time is devoted to participants' personal problems, their legal dilemma, or marital conflict issues. Table 5 also suggests that Anger Management is the one theme which does not vary between programs.

Interviews with Batterer Programs. To date, extensive interviews have been conducted with 146 key informants from 20 communities, including 45 staff from 27 batterer programs. All interviews were taped, and form the basis of this section, and the following two sections of the paper. In open-ended questions, staff described models or orientations employed in their programs of the structured questions on this evaluation asked participants in an open-ended manner about the model or theoretical perspective utilized in their program. Seven of 21 programs (33%) identify their orientation as the Duluth model, and an additional 4 (19%) articulate a modified Duluth perspective, bringing to over half (52%) the proportion of Illinois BIPs who have adopted some version of the Duluth model. One of the concerns often voiced by critics of standards is that standards often prescribe or prohibit certain models. While half of the programs say they utilize some variation of the Duluth approach, from the staff perspective, there appears to be a modest amount of variation between programs. The fact that anger management is the invariant theme of Illinois batterer programs suggest that the Duluth model may be invoked symbolically as much as programmatically, at least if we can believe the perspective of the male participants. Some program directors we interviewed voiced a concern that the standards were too narrow in their prescription, or favor a particular approach to batterer intervention. Among many agencies, the Illinois standards are synonymous with the Duluth model despite the fact that the standards do not make such a recommendation. The Duluth approach utilizes the batterers program as one element in a community-based domestic abuse intervention program, including the justice system and other human service providers. Since domestic violence is viewed as a man's use of socially supported power and control, intervention is both educational and systematic, and emphasizes individual, programmatic, and community accountability. However, the cognitive behavioral approach of anger management appears even more ubiquitous in both program curricula and participant reports.

For the most part, informants from batterer programs believe Illinois standards are a useful tool. Most informants believe standards bring credibility and

TABLE 5. Mean, Standard Deviation and Difference[1] Between 23 Batterer Programs for Six Program Foci

Program Focus	N	Mean	Standard Deviation	F
Anger Control	815	4.11	.77	1.34
Power & Control Issues	813	3.93	.84	1.50*
Men & Women's Relationships	810	3.93	.80	3.43*
Personal Problems	812	3.49	.88	2.85*
Relationship Problems	814	3.22	.92	2.18*
Legal Problems	812	2.64	.96	3.21*

N = 823 men participating in 23 Batterer Intervention Programs
[1] 5-point Index: None = 1, Very Little = 2, Some = 3, Quite a Bit = 4, All the Time = 5
*$p < 0.01$

competence to batterer programs. The most often cited response to probes about how standards had influenced their program were comments that standards influenced programs to alter policies and practice for linkage to other community-based violence prevention efforts, particularly battered women agencies. As we shall see later, this change may not be as appreciated by battered women's programs, but for these batterers programs it was viewed as helpful.

A number of concerns with standards were raised during the interviews. The peer-review approval and compliance process was viewed as a mystery by a number of programs, especially those mental health and substance abuse agencies accustomed to more formal certification and approval processes. The DHS does not disclose the identity of the peer reviewers and many of the informants were very curious about these reviewers, their qualifications, their investment in the review process, and how their decisions were made. A second issue, raised by both batterer program directors from non-approved agencies, is an apparent "catch-22" in the Illinois standards, which demands that a program be operational before it applies for approval under the standards. This is most often a problem for developing programs that are unable to get judicial referrals before they are approved.

A third issue is program length and the marketplace. Illinois standards call for a minimum program of 16 weeks, but a number of batterer programs are 26 to 52 weeks in duration, and several are longer. These longer term programs are usually more established, associated with victim programs, or using the Duluth model. These longer-term programs are finding that batterers and attorneys are selecting the shortest program possible. In communities with several batterer programs, short-time programs advertise publicly as such. Criticism that standards impair a free market of batterer programs would seem to miss the mark in Illinois.

Interviews: Victim and Community Programs

We interviewed 43 staff from 15 community agencies, including domestic violence agencies. An important part of our study is the effects of Illinois standards on community violence prevention agencies, primarily the effects on victim service agencies and advocates. In the Illinois standards, the batterers program is conceptualized as a local node in a (hopefully coordinated) community-based violence prevention effort. To this end, one of the key features of the standards is its requirement that batterers programs have a working relationship with victim programs. Almost all staff of battered women's agencies we interviewed knew there were published standards for batterer programs. They believed that the mechanism of agency accountability to standards helped hold batterers accountable for their behavior. The advocates we interviewed saw standards as useful not only for batterer programs, but also for battered women's agencies. Specifically, the standards provided a vehicle for BWAs to interact with the batterer program and hold them accountable for their actions. The standards also provided advocates with a concrete tool with which to talk to battered women about what to expect from a batterer program. In general, staff of these agencies was enthusiastic about standards, but also voiced several concerns.

One theme of particular concern was the increased pressure on victim programs to interact with batterer programs, which interviewees felt was a direct result of the standards. We found this theme expressed more often in moderate-sized cities which had a large enough population for a battered women's agency and more than one batterers program. Agency directors in particular were concerned that resources were being diverted in order to attend to the requests of incipient batterer programs. Moreover, battered women's agencies who communicated to the state their linkage agreement with a batterer program often felt that such a communication implied their approval of that batterer program, which they had neither the resources nor the inclination to offer. At least two battered women agencies have turned this concern into a means of generating income by consulting with batterers programs about gaining program compliance. A related issue is the conflict of interests now facing some victim programs when an incipient batterers program tries to negotiate linkage with a battered women's program which has an in-house batterers program. Approval of the new batterers program could threaten the victim agency's income, while groundless disapproval could threaten the victim agency's credibility.

A second effect of Illinois standards on community agencies is the rapid increase in batterer programming by substance abuse agencies. Through concerted efforts by the Department of Human Services, which houses both the

Office of Alcohol and Substance Abuse and the Bureau of Domestic Violence Prevention and Intervention, the two primary funding sources for substance abuse and domestic violence agencies respectively, a structural incentive has brought Illinois domestic violence and substance abuse agencies into closer working proximity than before. In addition to the standards and the structural motive, substance abuse agencies have become aware of increasing focus on the co-occurrence of these two problems (Center for Substance Abuse Treatment, 1997). Cash-strapped addictions programs have been attracted by the court-ordered clients who look and act very much like the substance abusers with whom they are familiar.

Interviews: Judges and Prosecutors

We interviewed 28 judges and 11 prosecutors in 16 judicial circuits. It must be recalled that the judges selected were those most likely to hear domestic violence cases in criminal court, and therefore, most qualified to comment on matters related to batterer program standards. Interviews with key judges suggest that they are familiar with the existence of the Illinois standards. All the judges we interviewed were aware that the list of standards-approved programs was published periodically. Furthermore, all judges were familiar with at least one standards-approved program by name. Prosecutors were also aware of state standards for batterer programs, and all could identify by name at least one local batterer program.

We identified several key beliefs held by judges about batterer program standards. First, most judges believed approval under the standards amounts to state certification of the batterer program, a clearly erroneous belief. With neither a legal mandate for the standards, nor a means of enforcement, Illinois does not 'certify' batterer programs. Second, almost all judges believed standards-approved programs were more effective than non-approved programs. This belief suggests an empirical question, but one which will not be tested for some time, if ever. Third, about half the judges we interviewed believed a substantial number of the batterers, before their bench, could not be helped by the available criminal justice, educational, or therapeutic interventions. These judges wanted a way to better identify those unreachable men and seemed confident that such an assessment tool either existed or could be developed.

CONCLUSION

The current study is a preliminary attempt to describe the effect of batterer program standards on batterer programs, on victim services and other community programs, and on the criminal justice system. The study is limited in a number of ways, not the least being its role as a funded evaluation in a single, Midwestern state. It is saddled with the usual flaws of formative evaluation research, including: a dependence on impression, interviews, and surveys; lack of comparison, either historical or concurrent; use of untested and single-item measures; and small samples. Moreover, this evaluation was restricted to batterers who were men, and programs serving those men. The standards we evaluated are not seen as applicable to programs serving women arrested for domestic violence, nor for men and women arrested for battering in a gay or lesbian relationship. While there are approaches to batterer intervention which argue that a single approach is applicable to all forms of partner aggression (e.g. Stosny, 1995), the single approach argument is outside the main stream of thinking in batterer intervention, which suggests that people come to violence in a variety of ways and require multiple approaches to intervention (Healy, Smith, & O'Sullivan, 1998). Despite the limitations of our study, we believe we have provided both a statewide evaluation and some new information about batterers programs. While some of our information is parochial, more useful to programs and policy-makers in Illinois, other information provides a comparison for researchers to examine batterer programs and standards elsewhere.

We have documented that one state's standards do, in fact, affect the way batterers programs deliver services to men who batter. The primary mechanism by which Illinois standards affect batterer programs is through facilitating formal linkage to victim service agencies and the court system. This is a beneficial effect, consistent with the emergent trend away from singular batterer program efforts and toward a broader community response to the prevention of violence (Hart, 1995; Witwer & Crawford, 1995). Coordinated community responses to family violence seek to provide unified, coordinated, and accountable approaches to domestic violence.

An interesting finding in these data is that the men in different batterer intervention programs do not report much difference in how time is allocated. While there may be, as Gondolf (1990) suggests, a great deal of variation in batterer programs nationally, this difference may not be discernable to the consumers of these programs. It may be that the state standards in Illinois are homogenizing batterer programs, and there is not a substantial difference in this state. Alternately, our measures may not capture the true differences, which do exist. One of the key concerns about standards is that they stifle creativity in programming, retarding the application of unpopular approaches and inhibiting the development of new approaches. In fact, this concern was voiced by several of the program directors we interviewed. The balance between program innovation and victim safety is an issue which needs to be addressed in evaluation of state standards, but we are unable to address this important matter in the current evaluation.

We have documented the means by which batterer programs in one state attempt to hold themselves accountable to their communities. We have also documented that the mechanisms of accountability do not include, for the most part, a case-level working relationship with victim service agencies. We have also documented that victim service agencies support standards for batterer programs, believing that standards improve victim safety. Whether standards actually make programs safer to the victims of batterers is a matter of concern, and should be the focus of future evaluation. Gondolf (1988) found that the best predictor of a battered woman leaving a shelter and returning to her abuser was his participation in a batterers program. This finding links the issue of victim safety to batterers program, and by extension, to the standards, which govern them.

Several unintended consequences of standards impact the working relationships of batterer programs and victim service agencies. While forcing batterer programs to work closer with victim agencies, standards may impinge on those same victim agencies, both in terms of the time demanded for collaborative work, and on the problem of supporting a batterer program that they have no actual ability to supervise or control. For victim services agencies, which also have batterers programs, standards, which require victim agency approval put these agencies in an untenable position when they are asked to endorse a batterers program which competes for resources with their own in-house batterers program. Standards which support coordinated community efforts look good on paper, but the reality of these efforts vary widely and impact communities in different ways. Developers of standards should look closely at the effects of standards on victim services programs. If these effects are desirable (we believe they are very desirable), mechanisms should be developed to support the additional, unintended role of victim service agencies in batterer program standards.

A second consequence of standards, at least in Illinois, is their lending support to substance abuse and mental health providers who wish to develop batterer intervention programs. The deployment of mental health and substance abuse providers to the domestic violence field has both positive and negative effects. The problem of co-occurring domestic violence with substance abuse and mental health disorders may be aided by new partners from the mental health and addictions professions. On the other hand, the predominant paradigms upon which domestic violence has been built conflicts with those of the substance abuse and mental health fields (Bennett & Lawson, 1994). While this may herald a new era of collaboration and synthesis, it may also signal an erosion of domestic violence programs and a threat to victim safety. In Illinois, victim service agencies are again being pressed into unfunded service as gatekeepers for these substance abuse and mental health agencies that have little experience in domestic violence.

Further formative evaluations of state standards would be useful, including evaluation of need, implementation, context, characteristics, and cost. We do not expect there to be consistent findings across states because the auspices of standards vary widely. Comparative studies across states would be very useful, but represent a methodological challenge. Once a substantial number of formative evaluations have been reported, evaluators need to examine the outcome of standards. Standards are one of a number of macro-level interventions designed to prevent domestic violence, and should, ultimately, increase public safety. Whether they do so remains a matter for further research and discussion.

REFERENCES

Adams, D. (1994). Point/Counterpoint: Treatment standards for abuser programs. *Violence Update*, 5(1), 5-9.

Austin, J., & Dankwort, J. (1999). Standards for batterer programs: A review and analysis. *Journal of Interpersonal Violence*, *14*, 152-168.

Battered Women's Justice Project. (1995). *State batterers programs*. Unpublished manuscript, 4032 Chicago Avenue South, Minneapolis, MN 55407.

Bennett, L., & Lawson, M. (1994). Barriers to cooperation between domestic violence and substance abuse programs. *Families in Society*, *75*, 277-286.

Bennett, L., & Piet, M. (1999). Standards for batterer intervention programs: In whose interest? *Violence Against Women*, *5*, 6-24.

Center for Substance Abuse Treatment. (1997). *Substance Abuse Treatment and Domestic Violence*, Treatment Improvement Protocol Series No. 25, Rockville, MD: United States Department of Health and Human Services.

Geffner, R. (1995a). Standards in the family violence field. *Family Violence and Sexual Assault Bulletin*, *11*, (1-2), 3.

Geffner, R. (1995b). Standards for batterer intervention: Editor's response. *Family Violence and Sexual Assault Bulletin*, *11*, (3-4), 29-32.

Goldman, J. (1991). Protect us from the protectors. *Family Violence and Sexual Assault Bulletin*, *7* (3), 15-17.

Gondolf, E.W. (1988). The effect of batterer counseling on shelter outcome. *Journal of Interpersonal Violence*, *3*, 275-289.

Gondolf, E.W. (1990). An exploratory study of court-mandated batterer programs. *Response to the Victimization of Women & Children*, *13*, 7-11.

Gondolf, E. (1995). Gains and process in state batterer programs and standards. *Family Violence and Sexual Assault Bulletin*, *11* (3-4), 27-28.

Hart, B. (1995, March). *Coordinated community approaches to domestic violence*. Paper presented to the Strategic Planning Workshop on Violence Against Women, National Institute of Justice, Washington DC.

Healy, K., Smith, C., & O'Sullivan, C.O. (1998). *Batterer intervention program approaches and criminal justice strategies*. U.S. Department of Justice, National Institute of Justice, NJC168638.

Hessmiller-Trego, J. (1991). Letter to the editor. *Family Violence and Sexual Assault Bulletin, 7* (4), 24-25.

Illinois Protocol for Domestic Abuse Batterers Programs. (1994). Illinois Department of Human Services, 300 Iles Park Place, Springfield, IL 62762.

Pence. E. & Paymar, M. (1993). *Education groups for men who batter: The Duluth model*. New York: Springer.

Rosenbaum, A., & Stewart, T.P. (1994). Point/counterpoint: Treatment standards for abuser programs. *Violence Update, 5*(1), 9-11.

Stosny, S. (1995). *Treating attachment abuse: A compassionate approach*. New York: Springer.

Witwer, M.B., & Crawford, C.A. (1995). *A coordinated approach to reducing family violence: Conference Highlights*. U.S. Department of Justice, NCJ155184.

Completion and Recidivism Among Court- and Self-Referred Batterers in a Psychoeducational Group Treatment Program: Implications for Intervention and Public Policy

Alan Rosenbaum
Paul J. Gearan
Charissa Ondovic

SUMMARY. Batterers treatment has become a central component in efforts to curb relationship aggression. However, debate continues over the relative effectiveness of batterers treatment both independent of, and in concert with, legal interventions. The present study examined the relationship between referral source (i.e., self-referred vs. court-mandated), participant characteristics, treatment length (i.e., 7, 10, and 20 weeks), treatment completion, and recidivism in a sample of 326 men who had completed at least one session of a batterers treatment program. Results indicated that court-referred men had a significantly higher treatment completion rate than self-referred men in the 20-session condition, but not in either of the shorter treatment lengths. Men who were exposed to

---

This research and preparation of the manuscript were supported in part by an NIMH grant (MH44812) to Alan Rosenbaum. The conclusions and opinions expressed herein are solely the responsibility of the authors.

[Haworth co-indexing entry note]: "Completion and Recidivism Among Court- and Self-Referred Batterers in a Psychoeducational Group Treatment Program: Implications for Intervention and Public Policy." Rosenbaum, Alan, Paul J. Gearan, and Charissa Ondovic. Co-published simultaneously in *Journal of Aggression, Maltreatment & Trauma* (The Haworth Maltreatment & Trauma Press, an imprint of The Haworth Press, Inc.) Vol. 5, No. 2(#10), 2001, pp. 199-220; and: *Domestic Violence Offenders: Current Interventions, Research, and Implications for Policies and Standards* (ed: Robert A. Geffner, and Alan Rosenbaum) The Haworth Maltreatment & Trauma Press, an imprint of The Haworth Press, Inc., 2001, pp. 199-220. Single or multiple copies of this article are available for a fee from The Haworth Document Delivery Service [1-800-HAWORTH, 9:00 a.m. - 5:00 p.m. (EST). E-mail address: getinfo@haworthpressinc.com].

199

their fathers' physical abuse of their mothers and men who have been aggressive in past relationships had significantly lower completion rates. Recidivism was lowest for men who had been court-referred and completed treatment. Treatment completion was associated with significantly lower rates of recidivism for court-referred but not self-referred participants. Participants in the 10- and 20- session treatment programs had significantly lower rates of recidivism than those in the seven-session program, but were not significantly different from one another. No participant characteristics were found to be significantly associated with recidivism. Implications of these findings for the structure of batterers treatment and public policy are discussed. *[Article copies available for a fee from The Haworth Document Delivery Service: 1-800-HAWORTH. E-mail address: <getinfo@haworthpressinc.com> Website: <http://www.HaworthPress.com> © 2001 by The Haworth Press, Inc. All rights reserved.]*

KEYWORDS. Relationship aggression, batterer's treatment, treatment outcome, partner violence, recidivism, court mandated treatment, group therapy

Relationship aggression, including dating violence, exacts high costs not only on the affected individuals and their families, but on society as well. These costs include the physical and emotional consequences for victims and their children, medical expenses, time lost from the work force, law enforcement, judicial, and penal system expenses, sheltering of victims and their children; and treatment of both victims and perpetrators. These costs are further dramatized by the magnitude of the affected population, which by conservative estimates is 16% of the married population in the United States alone (Straus & Gelles, 1990). Include dating violence and relationship aggression between homosexual partners and the enormity of the problem demands attention. The societal response has progressed in three directions. First was the development of a shelter system, generally accompanied by supportive counseling and advocacy services for victims. The objective was to rescue the victim from the abusive environment, and provide her with the support, skills, and resources necessary to enable her to leave the abuser. The second objective, aimed at the legal/judicial system, was to raise consciousness among law enforcement and the judiciary, to compel the arrest, prosecution, and punishment of perpetrators, and to employ the police and the courts to protect victims (Klein & Orloff, 1999). It was also possible that the criminalization of domestic aggression would serve a preventive or deterrent function. The third direction was the development of batterers treatment programs. Of the three, batterers treatment holds the most promise for the ultimate reduction of violence against women, however, there is an urgent need for effective intervention strategies. Sheltering is necessary for the immediate protection of victims, but does little to reduce levels of violence in the home. Even if the victim is successfully extricated from the abusive environment (and all too frequently this will not be successful), the perpetrator, deprived of his current victim will most likely victimize subsequent girlfriends and/or wives.

Legal remedies, arrest and incarceration, may also play a role but are themselves inadequate unless combined with batterers treatment. Initial enthusiasm that arrest alone was an effective deterrent (Sherman & Berk, 1984) has been moderated by numerous attempts at replication that have not supported the initial claims of success (Dunford, Huizinga, & Elliott, 1990; Hirschel, Hutchison, & Dean, 1992). In practice, batterers are rarely given sentences exceeding a few months, and it is hard to imagine how spending time in so misogynistic an environment as jail or prison would lead to a reduction in either anger or aggression toward women after they are released.

Treatment programs for abusive males began to emerge in the mid 1970s. Initially, and until recently, these were voluntary programs serving self-referred batterers. Consequently, groups were typically small and programs were brief. Participants were technically voluntary but in reality, most were responding to the threatened loss of the relationship. These men were often characterized as spouse mandated. Victims motivated their partners to participate by going to shelters and refusing to return unless he "got help." Too often, batterers dropped out of treatment as soon as the relationship was restored. More recently, owing largely to the efforts of the battered women's movement to lobby for legislation protective of victims, judges have been empowered to require batterers to complete treatment programs as a condition of probation. In many programs, court-mandated batterers now comprise a substantial proportion of treatment participants. As treatment programs for batterers have proliferated and courts become increasingly empowered to mandate treatment, the question of whether batterers treatment is effective has been raised. While asking if batterers treatment works is a valid question, the more important questions are: What are the effective components of batterers treatment and how can it be made more effective? The present study represents an effort to view batterers treatment more microscopically, by looking at the effects of treatment length and referral source on treatment compliance and recidivism.

Batterers treatment programs are characterized by both diversity and uniformity. Perhaps the major defining difference between programs is whether the focus is on management/control, or on therapeutic change. Batterers treatment is conducted individually, with couples (Mantooth et al., 1987) and in groups, with gender specific group treatment being the most popular. Several recent surveys of batterers treatment programs shed light not only on whether these programs are useful, but also on their structure and content. Gondolf (1990) examined 30 programs via telephone interview. He classified programs as psychoeducational (47%), therapeutic (27%), and didactic/confrontational (27%). The majority of the programs were six months or less in length (60%), while 40% were seven months or longer.

Among therapeutic/psychoeducational programs, the most popular theoretical orientation is cognitive-behavioral (Gondolf, 1990), although there are reports of the successful use of psychodynamic group therapy with this population (Saunders, 1996). Cognitive-behavioral programs are generally time limited and include skill training and anger management components. Most programs, regardless of orientation, address power and control issues. Didactic/confrontational programs are often self-described as pro-feminist, focus on power and control issues, are non- or even anti-therapeutic, and view protection of the victim as their primary objective (Adams, 1989). Much of the available outcome research evaluates cognitive-behavioral programs because they are time limited, shorter, more easily described, and more likely to be consonant with the theoretical orientations of researchers.

There are some philosophical and structural differences between programs, but within the major conceptual groups, differences are mainly cosmetic (for example, the number of sessions, length of sessions, group size and leadership). Even across philosophically different programs, there are many commonalties (for example, almost every program deals with power and control, differing along the dimension of the primacy of the issues).

Outcome research on batterers treatment is problematic for several reasons. There is little agreement regarding both how to define successful outcome and how to measure it. Successful outcome has been defined in terms of violence elimination (Edleson & Grusznski, 1988), violence reduction (Feldman & Ridley, 1995; Petrik, Gildersleeve-High, McEllistrem, & Subotnik, 1994), non-recidivism (Dutton, 1986), as well as by changes on instruments measuring variables associated with aggression, including anger, depression, attitudes about women, and jealousy (Saunders & Hanusa, 1986). Follow-up intervals are also variable ranging from immediately post-treatment to more than three years, with six months to a year being most common. The fact that couples experiencing aggression, even if untreated, often experience long violence-free periods, would argue for longer follow-up intervals in evaluating outcome.

Finally, there is variability regarding the source of the outcome data. The most popular sources are the batterer, the victim, and the batterer's criminal record. There are problems associated with each of these. Perpetrators may be motivated to underestimate their use of aggression post-treatment, just as many either deny or minimize their aggression during treatment. This may be especially true for court-mandated batterers who are engaging in treatment against their will and who may fear feedback to the courts. This is not unfounded, since few programs would certify that a batterer had completed treatment if aggression was ongoing. Even at longer-term follow-up, there may be some fear that such information might have adverse legal implications for him.

Those studies that have compared perpetrator report to victim report have found that victims report more aggression than perpetrators (Hirschel et al., 1992; Jouriles & O'Leary, 1985). As Hirschel et al. (1992) note, however, victim reports are seldom validated and there is no empirical support for the bias that they are any more accurate than perpetrator reports. Additionally, victims are often unavailable, or unwilling to participate, as informants. Participation rates for victims range from a low of about 30% (Palmer, Brown, & Barrera, 1992) to a high of 76% (Dunford, 1992) with higher response rates corresponding to shorter follow-up intervals. At best, reliance on victim report injects a substantial sample selection bias into outcome research. It might be noted that this is also a problem for perpetrator reports. Edleson and Syers (1990) were only able to obtain six-month telephone follow-up assessments on 47% of their batterers. Palmer et al. (1992) were able to follow-up with 50% at 16-18 months post treatment, and Faulkner, Stoltenberg, Cogen, Nolder, and Shooter (1992) were only able to collect data on one-third of their batterers at six month follow-up.

Recidivism, as indexed by official criminal record, allows for inclusion of all subjects. It is also somewhat more impartial than the report of either perpetrator or victim. One problem with this method of assessing recidivism, however, is that it only reflects offenses significant enough to provoke a call to the police, and an arrest. It is likely that many instances (of both physical aggression and emotional abuse) go unreported. Not surprisingly, batterers treatment studies utilizing criminal records to assess outcome, report the highest success rates. However, this method may be useful in making comparisons such as whether one treatment strategy, or treatment length, is superior.

Another problem for outcome research on batterers treatment concerns the danger of using no-treatment, or waitlist, controls. Victim safety issues generally discourage the use of such designs and as a result, the comparison groups most often utilized are dropouts from treatment. It also makes sense that if treatment programs are effective, treatment completers should show more positive outcomes than non-completers. On the other hand, treatment dropouts may systematically differ from completers in other significant ways, such as motivation or incentive to complete, which may also produce increased rates of recidivism.

Given the inconsistencies in how successful outcome is defined and assessed, it should not be surprising that the empirical outcome literature is inconsistent and inconclusive. Feldman and Ridley (1995) reviewed the outcome literature on batterers treatment and divided the 30 studies surveyed into three methodological categories. The largest of the three, single group pre-post studies, included 20 studies which they characterized as: (1) defining the sample as males having perpetrated at least one physical act of aggression against a female partner, as indexed either by the CTS (Straus, 1979), interview, or police report; (2) utilizing a psycho-educational, cognitive-behavioral treatment approach (10-32 weeks in length); and (3) having a follow-up interval of 6-12 months. They concluded that these studies suggest that group treatment of batterers has a positive impact: "between one half and two-thirds of participants appear to cease acts of inter-partner violence completely, while others substantially reduce their frequency and range of aggressive acts" (p. 335). The factors most consistently associated with recidivism were a history of alcohol and substance abuse problems, violence experiences in the family of origin (either as a victim or witness), and a previous criminal record (nonviolent).

The second category included six quasi-experimental, nonequivalent control group studies. These studies used either treatment dropouts or untreated controls. Results of the three studies comparing treatment completers to treatment dropouts were inconsistent, with one showing no differences in rates of recidivism (Edleson & Grusznski, 1988; note, this reference contained two separate studies which produced different results), one showing completers to have a minimally lower rate of recidivism (Edleson & Grusznski, 1988), and one showing moderate differences (Hamberger & Hastings, 1988). Three studies compared treatment completers to untreated controls (Chen, Bersani, Meyers, & Denton, 1989; Dutton, 1986; Waldo, 1988) and found significant and substantial improvement in the recidivism rates of treated, as compared to untreated, subjects.

The third category included two experimental designs (employing control groups). In the first, Edleson and Syers (1990) compared three treatment models (education, self-help, and combined) and reported that based on partner reports at 6 month follow-up, the structured education and combined models both demonstrated significantly lower recidivism rates than the self-help group. In the second study (Harris, Savage, Jones, & Brooke, 1988) both conjoint group treatment and individual couples treatment demonstrated significant gains but did not differ from each other. These results were confirmed by O'Leary and Neidig (1993) who reported that both gender specific treatment and conjoint group treatment demonstrated significant reductions in physical and psychological aggression, marital distress, and depressive symptomatology.

While most of these studies offer hope that treatment of relationship aggression can be effective, our optimism must be tempered by the fact that these studies contain numerous methodological weaknesses, and few represent experimental designs with random assignment to groups (including a no-treatment control group). The inherent dangers in relationship aggression preclude the use of such designs; however, Harrell (1991) approximated such a comparison. She utilized a sample of batterers who had been adjudicated and either mandated into a batterers treatment program or not. Although the decision rules utilized by the judges in making the dispositions was unknown, thus increasing the likelihood of a Berksonian bias, Harrell opined that the primary factor in referral decisions "appeared to be judicial approval of batterer treatment" (p. 3) and further that the two groups did not differ on severity of incident, the use of arrest, age, and alcohol/substance abuse. However, offenders referred to treatment were "more likely to be married to the victim, less likely to have a prior criminal record, and less likely to be unemployed" (p. 3). The results of this study were that there were no differences between treated and untreated offenders in rates of recidivism. There are several possible explanations for this in addition to the sampling problems. Several different programs were involved, differing in program length and content. Harrell also notes inconsistencies and delays in program operations. Further, as DeMaris and Jackson (1987) note, there are greater opportunities for recidivism if the couple remains together and as noted above, the treated group in this study was more likely to be married. Nevertheless, this is not the only study to cast doubt on the superiority of batterers treatment over no treatment. Rosenfeld (1992) concludes in his review of the existing treatment outcome studies that "with or without psychotherapeutic treatment, legal-system responses to domestic violence appear to significantly reduce future violent behavior. It is unclear whether fines, incarceration, or even psychotherapeutic treatment add any deterrent effect to that achieved by arrest alone" (p. 223). Proponents of batterers treatment are obliged to empirically demonstrate the value of the services they provide.

Although relatively little attention has been given to the intra-personal or program characteristics predictive of either treatment completion or recidivism, there are a few studies that have addressed this issue. Hamberger and Hastings (1989) found that treatment dropouts, when compared to completers, were more likely to be unemployed, have more pretreatment alcohol and drug offenses, be voluntary rather than court-mandated into treatment, and evidence severe personality disorder as measured by the Millon Clinical Multiaxial Inventory (MCMI; Millon, 1983). Grusznski and Carillo (1988) were able to discriminate completers from noncompleters on several factors including completers being more educated, more likely to be employed, more likely to have been exposed to interparental violence, but less likely to be victims of abuse themselves. In examining videotaped behavioral samples from violent couples, Brown, O'Leary, and Feldbau (1997) found that the wives' greater use of humor and the husbands' lack of empathy were associated with lower treatment completion. Palmer et al. (1992) found that men who had higher rates of depression prior to a 10-session group treatment program had lower rates of recidivism up to one year post-treatment. In their review of outcome research, Feldman and Ridley (1995) identified a history of alcohol and substance abuse problems, exposure to interparental violence, being a victim of child abuse, and having a previous nonviolent criminal record as the most commonly identified risk factors for post-treatment recidivism.

Several investigators have examined the relationship between treatment length, treatment completion, and recidivism. Pirog-Good and Stets (1986) reported an inverse relationship between treatment length and treatment completion. Increasing program length by 10 weeks produced reductions in completion rate of between 1.3% and 9.9%. Edleson and Syers (1990) compared 12 session groups to 32 session groups and found 10% less recidivism in the 12-session format. They also noted higher completion rates (i.e., attended at least 80% of sessions) in the shorter program.

The impact of treatment length on outcome is relevant because of economic considerations and also because it is one of the factors that is often incorporated into state imposed treatment standards. Massachusetts, for example, stipulates 80 hours of treatment for certified programs. Shorter programs are more cost effective and result in shorter waiting times for treatment. Many batterers are financially challenged and it is not clear whether treatment dropout may be tied to program costs. Many of the studies cited above call into question whether increasing treatment length produces corresponding reductions in aggression.

The present investigation evaluated short-term, psycho-educational group treatments of three different lengths, included both court-mandated and self-referred participants, and utilized both group completion and recidivism (as indexed by post-treatment re-offenses on the criminal record) as dependent variables. The relationships between treatment completion and recidivism, as well as the association of several demographic, intra-personal, and experiential factors with both treatment completion and recidivism were also assessed. It was hypothesized that increases in group length would produce decreases in completion rates. It was further hypothesized that the presence of a court mandate would increase completion rates. No hypotheses were made regarding the effects of these variables on recidivism.

METHOD

Participants

The intake interviews and criminal records of 326 men who attended at least one session of the Men's Educational Workshop, a psychoeducational batterers treatment program, were included. These men were either self-referred (n = 82) or court-mandated for batterers treatment (n = 244). The men ranged in age from 18 to 66, with a median age of 30. Seventy-six percent of these men were white; 9% were African-American; 9% were Hispanic; 1% were Asian; 1% were assigned other; and 4% could not be identified from the information in the intake report.

Program Description

Originally, the Men's Educational Workshop (MEW) was comprised of an intake interview followed by a six-session psychoeducational group treatment program. The first three sessions were intended to alter the attitudes of abusive men, which contribute to their aggression against women (e.g., violence toward heterosexual partners is acceptable; patriarchal views of power and equality in relationships, etc.). The last three sessions taught intervention techniques for the prevention of aggression toward female partners (e.g., "Time-out," stimulus control, relaxation and stress reduction, cognitive restructuring, etc.). In 1988, the program was expanded to seven sessions to include one session for group members to invite their partners to attend for the purpose of allowing the partners exposure to the principles of attitude and behavior change presented in the program, and to give them a chance to provide feedback to the group regarding their partner's progress.

In 1991, the program was expanded to 10 sessions in response to larger group sizes (due to increasing numbers of court referrals) and the need to allow for more treatment hours to cover the attitudinal and behavioral change components of the program. In 1993, the MEW was expanded to 20 sessions because 10 sessions did not allow enough time to sufficiently explore many issues raised in treatment or allow group members to build trust and comfort with one another. Five of the additional sessions were designated to explore belief and attitudinal systems in greater depth, develop more interactive and protracted coverage of intervention techniques, and add video materials to exemplify many of the topics presented. Because of the need for greater attention to alcohol and drug use issues with this population, five sessions were added which addressed substance abuse issues (e.g., the role substance abuse plays in aggression; assessment of problematic substance use; the physical, social, financial, and familial impact of substance abuse; and presentation of community and therapeutic resources available to address substance abuse).

Procedures

An undergraduate research assistant extracted the data for this study from the written reports of the intake interviews. As a check on reliability, variables requiring judgment (i.e., the non-demographic variables) on 20 randomly selected intake reports were also coded by the second author. Cohen's Kappas ranged from .78 (history of aggression toward men) to 1.0 (inter-parental aggression by mother toward father), with an average of .87. The intake reports included demographic information, family history, relationship history, medical history, and violence history. Variables selected for examination in this study were: (1) type of referral (court/self); (2) relationship to victim (married/nonmarried); (3) history of aggression in past relationships (yes/no); (4) history of aggression toward men (yes/no); (5) parents' marital status (intact/non-intact); (6) interparental aggression by father to mother (yes/no); (7) interparental aggression by mother to father (yes/no); (8) education (did not complete high school/high school or beyond); (9) employment (unemployed, part-time employment, full-time employment); (10) history of depression (yes/no); (11) history of head injury (yes/no).

Batterers had participated in a group treatment program of 7, 10, or 20 sessions in duration. Group treatment records indicated whether the participant satisfactorily completed treatment, operationalized as attendance at a specific number of sessions. Attendance requirements for completion for each treatment length respectively were: 6 out of 7 sessions; 8 out of 10 sessions; and 17 out of 20 sessions.

Recidivism was obtained from examination of the participants' criminal records. Recidivism was defined as at least one arrest, within 20 months of a participant's last group session, for either a violation of the abuse prevention act, or an assault and battery with violation of the abuse prevention act. These offenses were selected because they could be clearly identified as acts of violence toward women and not general violence.

RESULTS

Completion by Court Referral

Of the 326 men who attended at least one session of the MEW, 74.9% were court-mandated and 25.1% were self-referred. Court-mandated men had a completion rate of 79.5%. Self-referred men had a completion rate of 58.5%. The chi-square analysis for completion rate by mode of referral was highly significant (χ^2 = 14.11, df = 1, p < .001). Table 1 presents the overall completion rates broken down by group length.

Individual analyses for each treatment length indicated that the only significant difference in completion rates between court- and self-referred men occurred in the 20-session program where court-mandated participants were significantly more likely than self-referred participants to complete treatment.

Other Factors Associated with Treatment Completion

Several variables were examined to determine whether they were associated with completion. Table 2 lists the categorical variables examined along with the results of the chi-square analyses for the entire sample. The results indicated that only three variables were significantly associated with treatment completion. Non-completers were more likely to have been aggressive in past relationships (χ^2 = 10.18, df = 1, p < .01), to have been exposed to inter-parental aggression by father to mother, (χ^2 = 7.97, df = 1, p < .05), and to have reported a history of depression (χ^2 = 4.79, df = 1, p < .05).

A logistic regression was conducted to determine the relative contributions of the variables significantly associated with completion (i.e., court referral, aggression in past relationships, father physical abuse toward mother, and depression). Only depression did not contribute significantly when the variables were entered simultaneously into the equation. Court referral was the most significant predictor of completion, followed by father's abuse of mother, and finally aggression in past relationships. Court-mandated participants were more than 2 1/2 times more likely to complete treatment than those who were self-referred.

Since court referral was the most significant factor associated with completion, data for self-referred and court-mandated men were analyzed separately for the variables listed in Table 2. None of these factors were significantly related to program completion for self-referred men. However, four variables were associated with completion by court-mandated men. These results are presented in Table 3. Court-mandated men were significantly more likely to complete if they finished high school (χ^2 = 5.75, df = 1, p < .05), they were married to their victim (χ^2 = 4.21, df = 1, p < .05), their father had not been aggressive toward their mother (χ^2 = 4.48, df = 1, p < .05), and they had not been aggressive in previous relationships (χ^2 = 8.22, df = 1, p < .01).

Logistic regression analysis, when the four variables significantly associated with treatment completion for court-mandated men were entered simulta-

TABLE 1. Completion as a Function of Court Referral and Treatment Length

Group Length	Non-Completers	Completers	Percentage	Chi-square
All groups combined				
Court	50	194	79.5%	14.11*
Self	34	48	58.5%	
7 session				
Court	4	15	79%	.65
Self	8	17	68%	
10 session				
Court	20	100	83.3%	.94
Self	6	18	75%	
20 session				
Court	26	79	75.2%	14.52*
Self	20	13	39.4%	

*p < .001

TABLE 2. Variables Associated with Completion–All Subjects

Variable	Non-Completers	Completers	Percentage	Chi-square
Relationship to victim				
Wife	32	111	77.6%	1.16
Nonmarried	46	120	72.3%	
Aggression in past relationships				
Yes	39	66	62.8%	10.18**
No	41	161	79.7%	
Aggression toward men				
Yes	36	110	75.3%	.01
No	31	97	75.7%	
Parents' marital status				
Intact	45	147	76.5%	1.89
Non-intact	36	82	69.5%	
Father abusive to mother				
No	44	168	79.2%	7.97*
Yes	36	65	64.4%	
Mother abusive to father				
No	69	207	75%	.38
Yes	11	26	70.3%	
Education				
DNC H.S.	33	79	70.5%	1.06
H.S. or beyond	51	160	75.8%	
Employment				
Unemployed	32	89	73.6%	.86
Part-time	2	11	84.6%	
Full-time	45	121	72.9%	
Depression				
No History	42	156	78.8%	4.79*
History	41	87	68%	
Head Injury				
No History	56	149	72.7%	.32
History	32	69	75.8%	

*p < .05; **p < .01.

TABLE 3. Variables Associated with Completion–Court Referred Only

Variable	Non-Completers	Completers	Percentage	Chi-square
Relationship to victim				
Married	12	79	86.8%	4.21*
Nonmarried	33	103	75.7%	
Aggression in past relationships				
Yes	21	43	67.2%	8.22**
No	26	139	84.2%	
Aggression toward men				
Yes	19	82	81.2%	.56
No	24	80	76.9%	
Parents' marital status				
Intact	23	116	83.5%	3.46
Non-intact	25	69	73.4%	
Father abusive to mother				
No	27	137	83.5%	4.48*
Yes	20	50	71.4%	
Mother abusive to father				
No	40	167	80.7%	.65
Yes	7	20	74.1%	
Education				
DNC H.S.	27	68	71.6%	5.75*
H.S. or beyond	23	124	84.4%	
Employment				
Unemployed	22	74	77.1%	.89
Part-time	1	9	90%	
Full-time	25	91	78.5%	
Depression				
No History	29	130	81.8%	1.05
History	20	64	76.1%	
Head Injury				
No History	39	130	76.9%	.86
History	11	52	72.5%	

*p < .05; **p < .01.

neously into the equation, indicated that only aggression in past relationships and father abusive to mother significantly predicted completion. Court-mandated participants who had been abusive in past relationships were twice as likely not to complete treatment as those who had not been previously aggressive. Similarly, men whose fathers were aggressive toward their mothers were twice as likely to not complete treatment as men whose fathers were not aggressive.

Recidivism

Subjects were not randomly assigned with respect to group length. This not only made the data vulnerable to historic change, but also resulted in differing lengths of follow-up. Seven-session groups occurred several years ago, while the 20-session format is current and only has a history of five years. Participants in the seven session groups have had more than seven years in which to recidivate, whereas the 20-session participants have had less than five, with the 10-session participants somewhere in between. In order to control for this, a recidivism period of 20-months was used for each treatment length, since all subjects were at least 20-months post-treatment [i.e., treatment participation, not necessarily treatment completion]. Recidivism, as defined by post-treatment arrests for domestic assault and battery within 20 months of treatment participation, was significantly higher for self-referred men (13.4%) than for court-mandated men (4.9%) ($\chi^2 = 6.76$, $p < .01$).

Because, as we have already shown, court-mandated participants had higher rates of program completion, we examined recidivism as a function of completion. This was analyzed for all subjects, and then separate analyses were conducted for court-mandated and self-referred participants. Table 4 presents the results of these analyses. Indeed, for the full sample, non-completers had significantly higher rates of recidivism than completers ($\chi^2 = 6.30$, df = 1, $p < .02$). When separate analyses were conducted for court-mandated and self-referred participants, differences in recidivism as a function of completion were found only for the court-mandated group. Court-mandated completers were six times more likely not to recidivate than were court-mandated non-completers.

Recidivism as a Function of Treatment Length

Recidivism rates for group completers decreased [from 15.6% for the seven-session group, 4.2% for the 10-session, 2.2% for the 20-session group] as group length increased. Both the 10-session and 20-session lengths produced significantly lower rates of recidivism than the seven session format [Fisher's

TABLE 4. Recidivism as a Function of Court Referral and Completion

Variable	Non-Recidivists	Recidivists	Percentage	Chi-square
Referral source				
Court	232	12	4.9%	6.76**
Self	71	11	13.4%	
All subjects				
Completers	230	12	5.0%	6.30*
Noncompleters	73	11	13.1%	
Court referred only				
Completers	189	5	2.6%	11.09***
Noncompleters	43	7	14.0%	
Self-referred only				
Completers	41	7	14.6%	0.13 (ns)
Noncompleters	30	4	11.7%	

*p < .05; **p < .01; *** p < .001

Exact p = .037 and p = .012, for 10-session and 20-session groups, respectively]; however, differences in recidivism between the 10- and 20-session groups were not significant. Other than referral source, group completion, and treatment length, no other factors were significantly associated with recidivism.

A Note on Effect Sizes

Phi coefficients were generated for each of the significant findings as a measure of effect size. These ranged from a low of 0.12 (depression in the full sample) to a high of 0.32 (completion by referral for the 20-session group). These are presented in Table 5. The strongest effect sizes were for completion by referral source for the full sample (.21), recidivism by completion for court-mandated subjects (.21) and completion by referral source for the 20-session length of treatment (.32). These are all in the low-moderate range for effect sizes. Other Phi coefficients were smaller than .20 indicating relatively small effect size.

DISCUSSION

Overall, the results of this investigation demonstrated that men who were required by the courts to attend a batterers treatment program had significantly lower rates of recidivism than men who attended voluntarily. Participants who

TABLE 5. Effect Sizes

Variable	Phi Coefficient
Completion by referral source	
All groups	.21
20 sessions	.32
Variables associated with completion–All subjects	
Aggression in past relationships	.18
Father abusive toward mother	.16
Depression	.12
Variables associated with completion–Court referred only	
Relationship to victim	.14
Aggression in past relationships	.19
Father abusive toward mother	.14
Education	.15
Recidivism by completion	
Referral source	.14
All subjects	.14
Court referred	.21

were self-referred had a rate of recidivism (over a period of 20 months post-treatment) of 13.4% compared to a rate of 4.9% for men who were court-mandated to participate.

The literature suggested that treatment completion was a predictor of successful outcome (Chen et al., 1989; Pirog-Good & Stets, 1986). The results of this investigation partially support this hypothesis. Indeed, participants who completed treatment (defined as attending at least 80% of sessions) had significantly lower rates of recidivism than participants who failed to complete. However, closer examination showed that this was only true for court-mandated participants. Court-mandated completers had a lower rate of recidivism (2.6%) than court-mandated non-completers (14.0%), self-referred non-completers (11.7%), and even self-referred completers (14.6%).

The difference between court referred completers and self-referred completers is perhaps the most surprising finding. We might expect self-referred completers to be the most highly motivated to change of the four groups. There are several possible explanations for this result. Self-referred men may have a variety of reasons for participating, some less altruistic and mature than others. Ideally, the self-referred batterer has seen the light, taken responsibility for his aggression, and sought treatment for the good of himself and his family. In reality, many self-referred batterers are responding to a different, externally imposed mandate such as his partners threat to call the police, or leave the relationship, unless he agrees to seek help. In some cases, the partner may have already left the relationship, and may be in a shelter. Her return may be predicated on his participation in treatment. On the other hand, although the court mandate to attend may seem an external motivation, for many men (especially those not previously court involved) the legal involvement may serve as a wake-up call that there are serious consequences for their aggression.

In terms of the effective components of the intervention, court-mandated completers have experienced both the treatment program and the legal consequences (arrest, threat of incarceration, police record, etc.), whereas the three other groups have experienced only one of the components, or neither (self-referred non-completers). Clearly, neither court mandate nor treatment completion alone reduce recidivism, but rather it is a combination of these two factors which produces the best outcome. This finding is consistent with research by Dunford et al. (1990), Hirschel et al. (1992) and Sherman et al. (1991) showing that arrest alone is an insufficient deterrent to relationship aggression.

The optimal length of batterers treatment is currently a hotly debated issue. In the present investigation, group lengths of 7, 10, and 20 sessions were compared. The results indicated that for group completers, recidivism decreased as group length increased. The 20-session groups showed the lowest rate of recidivism (2.2%) at 20 weeks post-treatment. However, this was not significantly better than the 10-session group (4.2%) but both 10 and 20 sessions of treatment produced significantly lower rates of recidivism than the 7-session group (15.6%). Unfortunately, these results are confounded by the fact that the seven-session groups also had the highest proportion of self-referred to court-referred participants, which, as we have seen, is inversely related to recidivism. The very small numbers of recidivists, especially in the 20-session groups, precluded any finer analysis of this confound. Of interest is the fact that in the 7-session groups only, non-completers had lower rates of recidivism than did completers. In the 10-session groups, however, treatment completion was associated with significantly lower rates of recidivism. Again, in the 20-session groups, there was insufficient recidivism for meaningful analyses. While this may be an anomalous finding, it is also possible that 7 sessions of treatment allows enough time to open up important issues and expose vulnerabilities, but insufficient time for their adequate resolution. In either case, these findings suggest that treatment length may be a relevant variable and further research is indicated.

The very small differences between the 10- and 20-session program suggests the possibility of diminishing returns as treatment length increases beyond approximately 10 sessions. This would be consistent with the Edleson and Syers (1990) finding that 12-session groups resulted in lower rates of recidivism than did 32 sessions of intervention. Treatment length is relevant for several reasons. Longer treatment is more costly and the battering population is largely financially challenged. Increased cost may serve as a deterrent to many men who would otherwise participate in treatment. Unless longer lengths of treatment are demonstrated to significantly reduce recidivism (or are otherwise shown to be more effective), it is difficult to justify the additional expense. Longer treatment length may also produce longer waiting lists for treatment since programs can run fewer cycles, other factors (such as numbers of staff and space) being held constant. With this population, treatment delayed may be treatment denied. It has also been suggested that longer lengths of treatment might adversely affect completion rates.

In the present investigation, there was no overall relationship between program length and completion. Although not significantly different, completion rates for the 10-session groups were the highest. While these results would appear to dispel concerns that increasing treatment length will reduce completion rates, we again must be concerned with the relationships between the various factors, in this instance, treatment length and referral source. The overall results indicated that court-mandated participants completed treatment significantly more often than did self-referred participants. However, closer examination revealed that this was only true for the 20-session groups. Thus, for self-referred participants, completion rates drop precipitously as length of treatment is increased from 10 to 20 sessions. In the 20-session groups, court mandate nearly doubles the completion rate. Again, the results emphasize the importance of court involvement in the treatment process.

A caveat seems in order here. These results could easily be interpreted to support shorter treatment lengths for self-referred batterers and to suggest that programs dealing exclusively with self-referred batterers will be unable to keep a substantial number involved in treatment beyond 10 or 15 sessions. It is possible that these poor results for self-referred batterers may be due to the fact that our program includes both self-referred, and court-referred, batterers in the same groups. At least in the early sessions, court-mandated batterers express more anger towards the police and courts, and accept less responsibility for their aggressiveness than do self-referred batterers. The large amount of time devoted to "court bashing" and its remediation, may be discouraging to self-referred batterers, especially if they have taken responsibility for their aggression and are looking for help in making positive changes. We have wondered if self-referred batterers would do better in a homogenous group. Unfortunately, our referral rate for self-referred batterers is too low and the wait for treatment would be too long for us to experiment with this concept. We would not be surprised, however, to hear that groups comprised exclusively of self-referred batterers were more successful both in terms of completion rates, and recidivism rates than the present data would predict.

In addition to referral source, the present investigation examined whether any additional social/psychological factors were associated with treatment completion. Univariate analyses indicated that three other variables were significantly associated with treatment completion for the entire sample. Completers were less likely to have been aggressive in past relationships, less likely to have been exposed to inter-parental aggression by father toward mother, and less likely to report a history of depression. When these variables (including court mandate) were entered into a logistic regression, only the history of depression was excluded. Interestingly, when the logistic regressions were run separately for court-mandated and self-referred participants, none of the variables predicted completion for the self-referred group.

In the court-referred group, however, two factors were significantly associated with completion. Court-mandated completers were less likely to have been exposed to inter-parental aggression by father toward mother, and less likely to have been aggressive in previous relationships. It is noteworthy that once again exposure to inter-parental aggression, especially by father toward mother, emerges as a significant predictor of treatment completion, just as it has so consistently been shown to be a risk marker for relationship aggression (Sugarman & Hotaling, 1989). One explanation for this relationship is that men who have grown up in a violent home environment may see aggression in relationships as normative and have lower motivation for change. In fact, it has been our clinical experience that participants for whom aggression toward women is culturally sanctioned, are particularly resistant to treatment. Men who have been aggressive in prior relationships may see themselves as chronically abusive and have less confidence in their ability to make changes.

CONCLUSION

The development of strategies that reduce aggression in intimate relationships is a societal imperative. As with other undesirable behaviors, interventions targeting the perpetrator would appear to have the most direct impact. The strategy of empowering courts to mandate treatment for batterers has widespread support. It seems a sensible strategy, as well, because of the large number of domestic violence cases and the shortage of jail space, as well as because it offers an opportunity to intervene with minimal disruption to the batterer's ability to support his family. Paradoxically, it may also increase the willingness of victims to involve the police, whereas they might be reluctant if they feared the partner would be incarcerated. The utility of this intervention, however, is predicated on the effectiveness of batterers treatment programs. The question of whether batterers treatment is effective seems an unanswerable question. Batterers treatment is not a specific treatment. It is defined not by the intervention, but by the population for whom the intervention is targeted. It is a class of treatments, some of which may work better than others. Because batterers are also a heterogeneous population, we have suggested that the more appropriate question is which interventions, or treatment components are effective, and for which batterers?

The present investigation raises as many questions as it answers. The clearest finding is that court involvement is a critical component of batterers treatment, but is by itself, an insufficient intervention. Court-mandated batterers have lower rates of recidivism. Treatment completers also have lower rates of recidivism, but only if they are court-mandated. Court mandate also increases the rates of treatment completion, but only when the length of treatment exceeds 10 weeks. This investigation had several limitations with the most serious threat to internal validity being the fact that subjects were not randomly assigned to groups of different length and, perhaps more importantly, that the treatment lengths changed over time and were thus vulnerable to historic change, and especially to changes in the program referral base. The fact that the 7-session groups were comprised predominantly of self-referred participants, whereas the 10- and 20-session groups were comprised predominantly of court-mandated participants, prohibits us from independently evaluating the contributions of treatment length and referral source.

Despite this concern, we can still learn something about the impact of length of treatment. Differences in recidivism between 10- and 20-session groups were not significant. It cannot be argued, therefore, that more treatment is necessarily better. It is, however, more expensive and time consuming. As more states begin to institute standards for batterers treatment, or make changes in existing standards, and given that many of those states will dictate the minimal length of treatment required to meet certification standards, the importance of this finding, and the need to replicate and extend it, increases. In Massachusetts, for example, the committee charged with establishing standards for State Certified batterers intervention programs recently and arbitrarily raised the minimum length of treatment from 40 hours to 80 hours, the logic apparently being that if 40 hours is good, 80 hours must be twice as good. The results of the present investigation would suggest that such actions may not be justified and further that much more research is needed before effective treatment can be defined, let alone legislated.

REFERENCES

Adams, David. (1989). Feminist-based interventions for battering men. In P.L. Caesar, L.K. Hamberger et al. *Treating men who batter: Theory, practice, and programs*, (pp. 3-23). New York: Springer.

Brown, P.D., O'Leary, K.D., & Feldbau, S.R. (1997). Drop-out in a treatment program for self-referring, wife abusing men. *Journal of Family Violence, 12*, 365-387.

Chen, H., Bersani, C., Myers, S.C., & Denton, R. (1989). Evaluating the effectiveness of a court sponsored abuser treatment program. *Journal of Family Violence, 4*, 309-322.

DeMaris, A., & Jackson, J.K. (1987). Batterers' reports of recidivism after counseling. *Social Casework, 68*, 458-465.

Dunford, F.W. (1992). The measurement of recidivism in cases of spouse assault. *The Journal of Criminal Law and Criminology, 83*, 120-136.

Dunford, F.W., Huizinga, D., & Elliott, D. (1990). The role of arrest in domestic assault: The Omaha experiment. *Criminology, 28*, 183-206.

Dutton, D.G. (1986). The outcome of court-mandated treatment for wife-assault: A quasi-experimental evaluation. *Violence and Victims, 3*, 5-30.

Edleson, J.L., & Grusznski, R.J. (1988). Treating men who batter: Four years of outcome data from the domestic abuse project. *Journal of Social Service Research, 12*, 3-22.

Edleson, J.L., & Syers, M. (1990). Relative effectiveness of group treatments for men who batter. *Social Work Research and Abstracts, 26*, 10-17.

Faulkner, K., Stoltenberg, C.D., Cogen, R., Nolder, M., & Shooter, E. (1992). Cognitive-behavioral group treatment for male spouse abusers. *Journal of Family Violence, 7*, 37-55.

Feldman, C.M., & Ridley, C.A. (1995). The etiology and treatment of domestic violence between adult partners. *Clinical Psychology: Science and Practice, 2*, 317-348.

Gondolf, E.W. (1990). An exploratory survey of court-mandated batterer programs. *Response to the Victimization of Women and Children, 13*, 7-11.

Grusznski, R.J., & Carrillo, T.P. (1988). Who completes batterer's treatment groups? An empirical investigation. *Journal of Family Violence, 3*, 141-150.

Hamberger, L.K., & Hastings, J.E. (1988). Skills training for treatment of spouse abusers: An outcome study. *Journal of Family Violence, 3*, 121-130.

Hamberger, L.K., & Hastings, J.E. (1989). Counseling male spouse abusers: Characteristics of treatment completers and dropouts. *Violence and Victims, 4*, 275-286.

Harrell, A. (1991). *Evaluation of court-ordered treatment for domestic offenders: Final report*. Paper prepared for the State Justice Institute.

Harris, R., Savage, S., Jones, T., & Brooke, W. (1988). A comparison of treatments for abusive men and their partners within a family-service agency. *Canadian Journal of Community Mental Health, 7*, 147-155.

Hirschel, D.J., Hutchison, I.W., & Dean, C.W. (1992). The failure of arrest to deter spouse abuse. Special issue: Experimentation in criminal justice. *Journal of Research in Crime and Delinquency, 29*, 7-33.

Jouriles, E.N., & O'Leary, K.D. (1985). Interspousal reliability of reports of marital violence. *Journal of Consulting and Clinical Psychology, 53*, 419-421.

Klein, C.F. & Orloff, L.E. (1999). Protecting battered women: Latest trends in civil legal relief. In Feder, L. (Ed.) *Women and domestic violence: An interdisciplinary approach.* New York: The Haworth Press, Inc, 29-47.

Mantooth, C., Geffner, R., Patrick, J., & Franks, A.D. (1987). *Family preservation: A treatment program for reducing couple violence.* Tyler, TX: University of Texas at Tyler Press.

Millon, T. (1983). *Millon Clinical Multiaxial Inventory Manual.* Minneapolis, MN: Interpretive Scoring Systems.

O'Leary, K.D., & Neidig, P.H. (1993, November). *Treatment of spouse abuse.* Poster presented at the Annual Convention of the Association for Advancement of Behavior Therapy, Atlanta, Georgia.

Palmer, S.E., Brown, R.A., & Barrera, M.E. (1992). Group treatment program for abusive husbands: Long term evaluation. *American Journal of Orthopsychiatry, 62*, 276-283.

Petrik, N.D., Gildersleeve-High, L., McEllistrem, J.E., & Subotnik, L.S. (1994). The reduction of male abusiveness as a result of treatment: Reality or myth? *Journal of Family Violence, 9*, 307-316.

Pirog-Good, M.A., & Stets, J. (1986). Programs for abusers: Who drops out and what can be done. *Response to the Victimization of Women and Children, 9*, 17-19.

Rosenfeld, B.D. (1992). Court-ordered treatment of spouse abuse. *Clinical Psychology Review, 12*, 205-226.

Saunders, Daniel G. (1996) Feminist-cognitive-behavioral and process-psychodynamic treatments for men who batter: Interaction of abuser traits and treatment models. *Violence & Victims, 11*, 393-414.

Saunders, D.G., & Hanusa, D. (1986). Cognitive-behavioral treatment of men who batter: The short-term effects of group therapy. *Journal of Family Violence, 1*, 357-372.

Sherman, L., & Berk, R.A. (1984). The Minneapolis domestic violence experiment. *Police Foundation Reports, April*, 1-8.

Sherman, L., Schmidt, J., Rogan, D., Gartin, P., Cohn, E., Collins, D. & Bacich, A. (1991). From initial deterrence to long-term escalation: Short-custody arrest for poverty ghetto domestic violence. *Criminology, 29*, 821-850.

Straus, M.A. (1979). Measuring intrafamily conflict and violence: The Conflict Tactics (CT) Scales. *Journal of Marriage and the Family, 41*, 75-88.

Straus, M.A. & Gelles, R.J. (1990). How violent are American families? Estimates from the National family violence resurvey and other studies. In M.A. Straus & R.J. Gelles (eds.). Physical Violence in American Families. New Brunswick, NJ: Transaction, 95-112.

Sugarman, D.B. & Hotaling, G.T. (1989). Violent men in intimate relationships: An analysis of risk markers. *Journal of Applied Social Psychology. 19*, 1034-1048.

Waldo, M. (1988). Relationship enhancement counseling groups for wife abusers. *Journal of Mental Health Counseling, 10*, 37-45.

IMPLICATIONS
FOR POLICIES AND STANDARDS
IN DOMESTIC VIOLENCE
OFFENDER INTERVENTION

An Ecological Analysis
of Batterer Intervention Program Standards

Richard M. Tolman

SUMMARY. Many states and local jurisdictions have drafted and implemented standards for batterer intervention programs. This article first presents a review of the arguments for and against the current standards. The author argues that the extant empirical research on batterer intervention is, at best, a limited source of knowledge for setting standards. The author then uses Bronfenbrenner's (1972, 1975) ecological framework to analyze existing standards, and to guide recommendations for future research on batterer intervention. *[Article copies available for a fee from The Haworth Document Delivery Service: 1-800-HAWORTH. E-mail address: <getinfo@haworthpressinc.com> Website: <http://www.HaworthPress.com> © 2001 by The Haworth Press, Inc. All rights reserved.]*

[Haworth co-indexing entry note]: "An Ecological Analysis of Batterer Intervention Program Standards." Tolman, Richard M. Co-published simultaneously in *Journal of Aggression, Maltreatment & Trauma* (The Haworth Maltreatment & Trauma Press, an imprint of The Haworth Press, Inc.) Vol. 5, No. 2(#10), 2001, pp. 221-233; and: *Domestic Violence Offenders: Current Interventions, Research, and Implications for Policies and Standards* (ed: Robert A. Geffner, and Alan Rosenbaum) The Haworth Maltreatment & Trauma Press, an imprint of The Haworth Press, Inc., 2001, pp. 221-233. Single or multiple copies of this article are available for a fee from The Haworth Document Delivery Service [1-800-HAWORTH, 9:00 a.m. - 5:00 p.m. (EST). E-mail address: getinfo@haworthpressinc.com].

221

KEYWORDS. Domestic violence, abusers, partner violence, arrest, battered women

THE CONTEXT FOR STANDARDS

The emergence of batterers programs as a component of efforts to end domestic violence is often traced to the day in 1977 when Emerge, a Boston men's collective, first opened its doors. Once the province of a few dedicated male profeminists and some pioneering practitioners of various orientations, the marketplace for batterer intervention programs continues to grow at a pace rivaling coffee franchises and bagel shops. While increasingly seen as a legitimate and important component of community attempts to end domestic violence, concerns about the quality of batterers programs have been raised since the very beginning and continue unabated to the present. The rapid proliferation of programs has only exacerbated the concerns, and made the worries about the potential negative effects of batterer programs more widespread.

Courts across the nation now routinely refer thousands of batterers to treatment as a sanction–often the sole sanction–for conviction or diversion, in lieu of prosecution for the crime of domestic violence. The possibility of a steady stream of clients and profit, in an era of managed care and a shrinking private client base, has no doubt encouraged at least some practitioners, with no real background in domestic violence intervention, to enter the market and hang up their shingles as batterer intervention programs. Beyond concerns about untrained, or unscrupulous practitioners entering the batterer intervention field, there remain numerous concerns about batterer intervention, including the core concerns of the battered women's movement about batterer programs: Do batterer programs share a similar philosophy with providers of service to survivors? Will batterer programs blame battered women for the violence they experience or somehow put them at risk? Will batterer programs collude with male batterers, out of ignorance, or worse, out of shared misogynist values? (See Pence, 1989.)

Out of these concerns, a movement toward establishment of state standards emerged. Some form of standards has now been adopted in numerous states. According to Austin and Dankwort (1999), as of September 1997, 29 jurisdictions, including the District of Columbia, had completed standards. Eight others had drafts of standards, and 11 states were in the process of developing standards. A report by the National Institute of Justice (Healy, Smith, & O'Sullivan, 1998) put the total at 28 states with standards or guidelines, and 13 states in the process of development. Whether compliance with standards is mandatory, and the degree to which compliance with standards is enforced, varies widely from state to state.

WHY STANDARDS HAVE BEEN DRAFTED

One primary function of standards is to promote safety and a coordinated response to domestic violence (Bennett & Piet, 1999). Austin and Dankwort (1999) report that 81% of standards documents identify victim safety as an essential primary focus of batterer programs, and 92% identify a coordinated community effort as necessary to end domestic violence. Standards purport to ensure that programs offered to men who batter address safety issues for battered women and use methods consistent with other components of coordinated community responses. Related to the coordinated response, collaboration has increased among programs, not only because they share some minimal common expectations about philosophy and overall approach, but also because standards themselves can clarify roles and expectations among the collaborating agencies. For example, standards may spell out the role of programs in reporting abuse to the court system, and what response can be expected. With the rapid pace of proliferation of batterer programs, standards provide a starting point for new programs. To the extent that they simplify the development process, clear guidelines will bring programs to a greater level of competence more quickly.

Another major purpose of standards is to promote accountability of programs (Austin & Dankwort, 1999; Bennett & Piet, 1999). This can be accomplished in a number of ways. Standards may formalize consultation or reporting procedures. For example, Illinois standards require programs to consult with shelters concerning issues of safety to survivors. While it may not yet be clear what specific practices are most effective, standards can make it more difficult for those using potentially dangerous or capricious approaches. Standards define a range of practice that is minimally acceptable to a community. Most standards define some practices as unsafe and proscribe their use (e.g., conjoint counseling).

Standards can be viewed as an attempt to legitimize the specialized knowledge and skills required to effectively implement a program for abusers. Standards, in essence, create a practice specialty by certifying only those programs or practitioners who comply with special requirements and procedures. In addition to the legitimization of professional practice, the formal regulation of programs may promote public confidence in batterer programs. For better or worse, batterer intervention programs are often the primary sanction used by courts for those convicted of domestic violence charges. Failure to regulate and monitor closely this widely used sanction potentially erodes confidence in the legal process. Of course, the mere drafting of standards does not ensure that programs are worthy of public trust. If adhering to standards does not actually improve practice, then public confidence would be unfounded.

The process of drafting standards itself may help to promote collaboration among diverse stakeholders. Program staff working with perpetrators and survivors, as well as lawyers, judges, police, and political figures, must come together to draft standards. This contact may increase networking of programs and collaboration among others concerned about standards. With some limitations, broader participation in drafting standards should result in standards that are more likely to be adopted, assuming meaningful consensus can be reached. This consensus should also lead to greater compliance with standards by programs.

CRITICISMS OF STANDARDS

Whatever the intended advantages of standards, there are inevitable costs to the endeavor. A number of arguments have been raised against standards. Several authors (Geffner, 1995; Moore, Greenfield, Wilson, & Kok, 1997; Rosenbaum & Stewart, 1994) have noted that premature prescriptions and proscriptions of techniques may inhibit the development of innovative approaches, as well as established approaches that may be effective for some batterers. Nothing in the research literature to date supports unassailable prescriptions of specific techniques and approaches. On the contrary, there is not yet convincing evidence for the effectiveness of any approach to batterer intervention (Saunders, 1996; Tolman & Edleson, 1995). Yet some state standards restrict practice to one model (e.g., Iowa mandates the use of only the Duluth model of intervention) and many proscribe other models entirely (e.g., couples counseling). Even if the research literature did support some specific practices or models as effective, it may be that untried or untested approaches could be more effective. In addition, setting standards without empirical support for the prescriptions may be sending a false message that programs that meet those standards will be effective, when in fact they may not.

Some authors (Geffner, 1995; Goldman, 1991) have charged that some state standards have been drafted by committees lacking diverse viewpoints, with relatively little involvement from professional associations and researchers. While having relatively narrow involvement in drafting standards may lead to a more ready consensus among drafters, the limited process may produce standards that exclude important considerations from being incorporated into standards. When standards are drafted with insufficient input, practitioners may be less willing to fully comply with the regulations.

While standards that have broad consensual support may be more likely to gain compliance, standards may still be ignored or subverted in everyday practice. Monitoring compliance becomes a critical but potentially costly endeavor. However, without such procedures, standards may become meaningless or misleading, implying quality or conformity of programs that does not exist in practice. Even with monitoring, programs that do not comply with standards may put on a good face during a site visit, or in their submitted written materials. In addition, most states have insufficient funding to support adequate monitoring procedures (Austin & Dankwort, 1999). When standards are low and compliance is relatively easy, irresponsible programs may actually gain stature from the approval process associated with treatment standards.

Because they often obtain the official imprimatur of state governments and agencies, standards hold greater political legitimacy, and may lead to some level of meaningful enforcement of the standards. Successful collaboration may lead to the establishment of meaningful standards that fit the current consensus of stakeholders. However, regulations may be modified by legislatures or administrators in a manner unacceptable to the original drafters.

KNOWLEDGE BASE FOR STANDARDS

As discussed above, some critics of current standards cite the lack of research support for specific interventions as an argument against the setting of rigid state standards, especially those that mandate use of specific models or techniques. Clearly, the research knowledge base about batterers is growing. However, while useful insights can and will be gathered from empirical research, they may be inadequate for the purpose of setting quality control guidelines for batterer intervention projects. First, research on batterer programs is still in its early stages. On the whole, the studies completed to date are methodologically weak (Tolman & Edleson, 1995). Few models have been tested, and even fewer have been subjected to rigorous evaluation in multiple settings. Even as rigor increases, research is likely to be inadequate as a sole source of information for decision-making about standards because of the limitations of evaluation science. As Sherman et al. (1999) pointed out in a report to Congress, "Science is in a constant state of double jeopardy, with repeated trials often reaching contradictory results. Fulfilling the mandate to evaluate will always result in an uneven growth of evaluation results, not permanent guidance" (p. 9).

In regard to the limitations of evaluation research as the sole guideline for setting practice standards, studies of domestic violence arrest policies funded by the National Institute of Justice (NIJ) have provided instructive lessons. In the early 1980s, researchers in Minneapolis evaluated the deterrent effect of arrest using a randomized field experiment design (Sherman & Berk, 1984). Results of the study supported arrest as more effective than ordering the suspect away from the scene of the assault for eight hours, giving advice, or mediating the dispute. In 1986, the NIJ funded six replications of Sherman and Berk's Minneapolis experiment. Police interventions varied somewhat from city to city, but all the experiments essentially replicated the random assignment of subjects to conditions (Sherman, 1992). Results varied, with evidence of a deterrent effect of arrest in some cities, but not in others (Garner, Fagan, & Maxwell, 1995). Arrest also appeared to deter subsequent violence for some groups of offenders (e.g., employed men), but may have increased the risk of subsequent violence by other groups (Berk, Campbell, Klap, & Western, 1992; Pate & Hamilton, 1992; Sherman, Smith, Schmidt, & Rogan, 1992).

The results of the replications highlighted the lack of generalizability of findings from jurisdiction to jurisdiction. The lack of conclusive and broadly generalizable results can be seen as evidence for the need to hold back on setting standards. Given the results of subsequent replications, it appears to have been premature for police departments around the country to mandate the arrest practices of the Minneapolis Police Department following the positive results of Sherman and Berk (1984), although that is exactly what occurred in many jurisdictions (Fagan, 1995; Sherman, 1992). However, as Berk (1994) subsequently argued, the lack of replication of arrest as a superior sanction does not preclude the adoption of proarrest policies for domestic violence. Berk argues that, even if it is shown to be no more effective than non-arrest, justice is among the reasons for adopting proarrest policies. Moral criteria and other values also must inform the selection of approaches.

The NIJ replications also highlighted the local variations and contextual differences in the cities studied. For example, the communities studied differed in key aspects, such as rates of prosecution following arrest, and the time suspects spent in custody following arrest. Local variations in effectiveness support the proposition that decisions about standards may be made best by those with an understanding of the specific contexts, using available evidence, which includes, but is not limited to, research.

Another issue which illustrates the limitations of dependence on empirical data concerns conjoint counseling for batterers and victims. Austin and Dankwort (1999) report that most standards (73%) have proscribed the use of conjoint approaches as an initial intervention for battering. When examining the extant data on conjoint work, one cannot make a conclusive case that couples counseling is inferior to other forms of intervention for domestic violence (Saunders, 1996; Tolman & Edelson, 1995). However, there are other reasons that standards might proscribe the intervention anyway. One is a moral argument: It is unjust to mandate victims to intervention. Victims of crime in other contexts are not ordered to participate in court-mandated sanctions, however well-meaning such sanctions might be. Imagine burglary victims mandated to attend court-ordered seminars on how to make their homes less inviting to thieves. Few courts could or would mandate victims to participate in counseling. Critics of conjoint work argue that court supported couples counseling may be dangerous, even in seemingly voluntary situations, for example, when a victim has the choice to attend a court-ordered intervention with her abusive partner. In such situations, abusers may explicitly or implicitly coerce the victim to take part in the intervention. While proscribing conjoint work in standards protects victims from this type of coercion, setting this standard could limit a victim who voluntarily desires such an approach. Some standards have addressed this issue by permitting conjoint work in approved programs, not as an initial or primary intervention, but as an adjunctive intervention for use when a batterer has successfully completed other interventions.

Even if research clearly documented the effectiveness of some carefully conceived and implemented couples approaches, there is concern that intervention may not be implemented in the same way in other contexts. As the NIJ arrest replication studies suggest, even if the intervention were faithfully replicated, the specific ecology in a particular area may differ and produce different results. Framed from a scientific standpoint, this analysis emphasizes the need for attention to external validity. Viewed this way, drafters of standards can hardly be faulted for resisting implementation of an intervention they believe to be dangerous. This is true even when that intervention has been shown to be no worse than an alternative treatment in a setting (e.g., military base or university clinic) that may bear little resemblance to the contexts in which most providers in their states operate.

On the other hand, it is important to note that concerns about danger have not been leveled only against couple's treatment. Some authors have argued that approaches which are approved by many current standards may contain elements which are harmful. For example, Murphy and Baxter (1997) caution that highly confrontational approaches may be counterproductive and may lead to increased denial and noncompliance. Most standards do not address this issue, but Michigan's recently adopted standards (Governor's Task Force, 1998) specify that programs which use abusive or hostile confrontation techniques are contraindicated because such techniques may reinforce the use of abusive control in interpersonal relationships.

One potential solution to addressing the limitations of generalizability of studies is to encourage centralized outcome data collection from multiple program sites (Murphy, 1999). If data were gathered on individual programs, within their specific contexts, evidence for positive and negative effects would be available to guide practice.

Although this author firmly believes that research must be a primary source of information for making decisions about policy, there are some problems with dependence on research alone for setting standards for batterer intervention. If we cannot look exclusively to the research literature, what other knowledge bases can we draw upon? There are at least three sources of knowledge that have guided the development of standards to date, and can continue to play a role in the shaping of batterer intervention guidelines: (1) battered women's advocates, (2) best practices of experienced programs, and (3) shared values and community consensus. In addition, theory can be used to inform choices for standards. Theory can also guide practice; specifically, an ecological analysis yields some useful insights into directions for batterer intervention standards.

The shared knowledge of the battered women's movement must be considered a primary source of information for decisions about what should be included in standards for batterer programs. Battered women's advocates have worked most closely and extensively with survivors, and have developed strategies for helping survivors end or cope with violence and abuse in their lives. From this position, advocates have heard accounts from women which shed light on the potential for help and harm in batterer intervention. Advocates have initiated efforts to establish coordinated community responses to domestic violence and, thus, are often in positions of leadership. With the constant task of meeting the needs of battered women, advocates remain in the position of having ongoing information about the strengths and weaknesses of programs in their communities.

Another source of knowledge for standards development are the best practices of existing and experienced programs. While the practices of experienced programs may or may not have been evaluated by empirical research, the systematic gathering of practice knowledge can serve to guide the field. To the extent that standards are based on such systematic efforts, the guidelines derived are more likely to be helpful rather than hindrances to practice. Again this underscores the need for inclusive and comprehensive efforts in drafting standards. On the other hand, existing programs may have their own self-interests that may influence their involvement in setting standards. Programs may advocate for mandating of practices or procedures that promote their programs, and make it more difficult for programs with alternative procedures to thrive.

Standards can be set based on shared values and consensus within a community. For example, as discussed above, placing a strong value on victims' rights may lead a community to proscribe interventions that limit or diminish abused partners' choices, such as mandated conjoint counseling. Many issues covered in standards (e.g., confidentiality) are governed by issues of ethics and values rather than empirical evidence.

AN ECOLOGICAL FRAMEWORK: IMPLICATIONS FOR STANDARDS

Another source of knowledge to guide development of standards is theory. An ecological analysis can shed some light on the issue of standards. Briefly described, the ecological framework focuses on the understanding of human behavior at multiple levels of human ecology. Bronfenbrenner originally described four levels of ecology that influence human behavior: (1) the microsystem, (2) the mesosystem, (3) the exosystem, and (4) the macrosystem (Bronfenbrenner, 1972, 1975). The *microsystem* includes those interactions in a particular setting in which a person directly engages, as well as the subjective meanings assigned to them. For example, a batterer's family, work setting, or contact with the police are all microsystems. The *mesosystem* includes the linkages between microsystems in a person's social environment. When a probation officer contacts a batterer intervention program staff member to inquire about compliance, a mesosystem interaction has occurred. The *exosystem* includes those interactions in which others engage that have some type of impact on an individual. Applied to a domestic violence perpetrator, an example of an exosystem would be the decision-makers responsible for setting police arrest policy in the jurisdiction where he resides. The *macrosystem,* even more indirect than the exosystem, is the set of blueprints at a cultural, ethnic group, or social class level that dictate certain consistencies among similar settings. Macrosystem issues relevant to domestic violence would be the belief that issues within the family are private, or that men should not feel or express vulnerability. The ecological framework has been used by a number of authors in application to domestic violence (D. Dutton; 1995; M. A. Dutton, 1992; Edleson & Tolman, 1992; Rosenbaum, 1986).

Using the lens of the ecological approach draws our attention to aspects of standards that have been overlooked, and can generate questions and, ultimately, research that will better inform the drafting and revision of existing standards. Many standards guide the program microsystem (e.g., content, length, etc.) and most debates about standards center around microsystem issues, that is, what techniques and procedures will be used by batterer intervention programs. However, an ecological framework draws our attention to the other levels. Most importantly, standards may be viewed as mesosystems interventions. In other words, they are an attempt to bring greater coordination among relevant microsystems, generating greater consistency of philosophy and practice among important microsystems. In the case of the domestic violence perpetrator, relevant microsystems that standards might address are the court system, police, victims' intervention services, and probation. An important corollary of the ecological approach is that the greater the mesosystem linkages, and the greater the coordination between microsystems, the more powerful the influence on human behavior (Bronfenbrenner, 1979). By enhancing the coordination between systems addressing domestic violence perpetrators, standards may make those efforts more effective in reducing domestic violence.

An ecological analysis also draws attention to the need for improvement of practice in the ecology surrounding the batterer intervention program. If courts mandate attendance to programs but do not enforce attendance, compliance is likely to be low. Some proponents of batterer intervention standards base certain prescriptions on the assumption that batterer programs are likely to be the sole sanction that will be used by the courts. For example, termination from treatment programs for reoffense has been defended because it gives the message that further abuse will not be tolerated. If batterers were facing other meaningful sanctions from the courts (e.g., jail time, more intensive probation), programs would not need to dismiss participants to communicate such a message.

Having drawn attention to standards from an ecological framework, the next step is to use the framework to generate questions for further examination. Research that will inform the best practices in mesosystem coordination would be especially valuable. Consider the findings of Gondolf (1999) who examined four batterer programs in four different geographic areas. This study allowed for a comparative evaluation of multiple sites, using the same evaluation methods across sites. This permitted an examination of how differences in court referral, program duration, and extent of services impact recidivism. Gondolf (2000) also provided an informative example of how context issues may be examined. That study showed that rapid court review of cases appeared to increase substantially compliance with intakes to a mandated batterer intervention project. The program (a diversion program) had recidivism results comparable to those of programs using post-disposition mandates. The study examined the context of the batterer intervention project, and demonstrated how variations in arrest practices, as well as court review and dispositions, impact who attends and completes the batterer intervention project. Studies evaluating coordinated batterer intervention programs provide other examples of research examining context and mesosystem impact response (Murphy, Musser, & Maton, 1998; Steinman, 1988; Syers & Edleson, 1992).

CONCLUSIONS

The lack of substantive findings supporting specific intervention strategies suggest that standards that mandate specific program practices without variation are, as some critics have charged, overly prescriptive. Not only does the existing data not provide evidence for mandating a single approach to batterer intervention, it does not provide strong support for doing batterer intervention at all. Given this, we need standards that provide reasonable limitations on irresponsible practice, but also accommodate responsible innovation. For example, standards recently drafted in Michigan contain a clause providing for scientific and other innovation that varies from program standards when those variations are externally reviewed and safety issues are adequately addressed (Governor's Task Force, 1998). Variance from standards must be done under conditions that ensure that the highest standards for victim safety, participant rights, and other ethical concerns are met.

It is clear we need to act in a confusing and inconclusive research environment. If proliferation of potentially harmful and ineffective programs is to be controlled, standards can be one tool used to accomplish that goal. However, the tool cannot be used without some cost. We must also recognize that there is a growing climate of contentiousness about standards, and powerful stakeholders who oppose the current standards will gain creditability if standards appear overly rigid or prematurely prescriptive. The debate about standards is healthy if it pushes us to be clearer about assumptions, leads to proceduralization of best practices, and forces us to work together to form powerful partnerships in ending domestic violence. The debate will be counterproductive if a false dichotomy is strengthened, and critics and supporters of standards dig deeper into positions without acknowledging the legitimate concerns raised by both sides.

REFERENCES

Austin, J., & Dankwort, J. (1999). Standards for batterer programs: A review and analysis. *Journal of Interpersonal Violence, 14*, 152-168.

Bennett, L., & Piet, M. (1999). Standards for batterers intervention programs: In whose interest? *Violence Against Women, 5*(1), 6-24.

Berk, R. A. (1994, Summer). What the scientific evidence shows: On the average, we can do no better than arrest. *Domestic Abuse Project Research Update, 4.*

Berk, R. A., Campbell, A., Klap, R., & Western, B. (1992). The deterrent effect of arrest in incidents of domestic violence: A bayesian analysis of four field experiments. *American Sociological Review, 57,* 698-708.

Bronfenbrenner, U. (1972). *Influences on human development.* Hinsdale, IL: Dryden Press.

Bronfenbrenner, U. (1975). *Influences on human development* (2nd ed.). Hinsdale, IL: Dryden Press.

Bronfenbrenner, U. (1979). *The ecology of human development: Experiments by nature and design.* Cambridge, MA: Harvard University Press.

Dutton, D. G. (1995). *The domestic assault of women* (2nd ed.). Boston: Allynn-Bacon.

Dutton, M. A. (1992). *Empowering and healing the battered woman: A model for assessment and intervention.* New York: Springer.

Edleson, J., & Tolman, R. M. (1992). *Intervention for men who batter: An ecological approach.* Newbury Park, CA: Sage.

Fagan, J. (1995, July). *The criminalization of domestic violence: Promises and limits.* Paper presented at the annual conference on Research and Evaluation sponsored by the National Institute of Justice, the Bureau of Justice Assistance, and the Office of Juvenile Justice and Delinquency Prevention, Washington, DC.

Garner, J., Fagan, J., & Maxwell, C. (1995). Published findings from the NIJ Spouse Abuse Replication Program: A critical review. *Journal of Quantitative Criminology 8*(1), 1-29.

Geffner, R. (1995). Standards in the family violence field. *Family Violence and Sexual Assault Bulletin, 11*(3), 1-2.

Goldman, J. (1991). Protect us from the protectors. *Family Violence and Sexual Assault Bulletin, 7*(3),15-17.

Gondolf, E. W. (1999). A comparison of four batterer intervention systems–Do court referral, program length, and services matter? *Journal of Interpersonal Violence, 14,* 41-61.

Gondolf, E. W. (2000). Mandatory court review and batterer program compliance. *Journal of Interpersonal Violence, 15,* 428-437.

Governor's Task Force on Batterer Intervention. (1998). Batterer intervention standards for the State of Michigan.

Healy, K., Smith, C., & O'Sullivan, C. (1998). *Batterer intervention: Program approaches and criminal justice strategies.* U.S. Department of Justice.

Murphy, C. (1999). *Towards empirically based standards for abuser intervention: The Maryland model.* Unpublished manuscript. University of Maryland, Baltimore County.

Murphy, C. M., & Baxter, V. A. (1997). Motivating batterers to change in the treatment context. *Journal of Interpersonal Violence, 12,* 607-619.

Murphy, C. M., Musser, P. H., & Maton, K. I. (1998). Coordinated community intervention for domestic abusers: Intervention system involvement and criminal recidivism. *Journal of Family Violence, 13,* 263-284.

Pate, A. M., & Hamilton, E. E. (1992). Formal and informal deterrents to domestic violence: The Dade County Spouse Assault Experiment. *American Sociological Review, 57,* 691-697.

Pence, E. (1989). Batterer programs: Shifting from community collusion to community confrontation. In P. L. Caesar & L. K. Hamberger (Eds.), *Treating men who batter: Theory, practice and programs* (pp. 24-50). New York: Springer.

Rosenbaum, A. (1986). Group treatment for abusive men–Process and outcome. *Psychotherapy*, 23, 607-612.

Rosenbaum, A., & Stewart, T. P. (1994, September). Treatment standards for abuser programs. *Violence Update*, 5(1), 9 & 11.

Saunders, D. G. (1996). Interventions for men who batter: Do we know what works? *In Session-Psychotherapy In Practice*, 2(3), 81-93.

Sherman, L. W. (1992). *Policing domestic violence*. New York: Free Press.

Sherman, L. W., & Berk, R. A. (1984). The specific deterrent effects of arrest for domestic assault. *American Sociological Review*, 49, 261-272.

Sherman, L. W., Gottfredson, D., MacKenzie, D., Eck, J., Reuter, P., & Bushway, S. (1999). *Preventing crime: What works, what doesn't, what's promising*. Report to the United States Congress.

Sherman, L. W., Smith, D. A., Schmidt, J. D., & Rogan, D. P. (1992). Crime, punishment, and stake in conformity: Legal and informal control of domestic violence. *American Sociological Review*, 57, 680-690.

Steinman, M. (1988). Evaluating a system-wide response to domestic violence: Some initial findings. *Journal of Contemporary Criminal Justice*, 4, 172-186.

Syers, M., & Edleson, J. L. (1992). The combined effects of coordinated criminal justice intervention in woman abuse. *Journal of Interpersonal Violence*, 7, 490-502.

Tolman, R., & Edleson, J. (1995). Intervention for men who batter: A review of research. In S. Stith & M. Straus (Eds.), *Understanding partner violence: Prevalence, causes, consequences, and solutions* (pp. 262-274). Minneapolis, MN: National Council on Family Relations.

Developing Guidelines
for Domestic Violence Offender Programs:
What Can We Learn
from Related Fields and Current Research?

Daniel G. Saunders

SUMMARY. This article reviews research on domestic violence that can help inform the development of guidelines for programs for men who batter. It also illustrates some successes and problems in other fields that might be instructive for the domestic violence field. Firm conclusions about "best practice" guidelines for intervention seem to be premature because of flaws in evaluation studies. In addition, there is growing evidence of variability among men who batter on dimensions such as severity of violence, childhood traumas, generality of violence and personality traits. Programs also need to be able to respond to motivational and cultural difference among abusers. Existence of variability implies the need for multiple forms of interventions. *[Article copies available for a fee from The Haworth Document Delivery Service: 1-800-HAWORTH. E-mail address: <getinfo@haworthpressinc.com> Website: <http://www.HaworthPress.com> © 2001 by The Haworth Press, Inc. All rights reserved.]*

KEYWORDS. Domestic, violence, offender, programs, guidelines, research

[Haworth co-indexing entry note]: "Developing Guidelines for Domestic Violence Offender Programs: What Can We Learn from Related Fields and Current Research?" Saunders, Daniel G. Co-published simultaneously in *Journal of Aggression, Maltreatment & Trauma* (The Haworth Maltreatment & Trauma Press, an imprint of The Haworth Press, Inc.) Vol. 5, No. 2(#10), 2001, pp. 235-248; and: *Domestic Violence Offenders: Current Interventions, Research, and Implications for Policies and Standards* (ed: Robert A. Geffner, and Alan Rosenbaum) The Haworth Maltreatment & Trauma Press, an imprint of The Haworth Press, Inc., 2001, pp. 235-248. Single or multiple copies of this article are available for a fee from The Haworth Document Delivery Service [1-800-HAWORTH, 9:00 a.m. - 5:00 p.m. (EST). E-mail address: getinfo@haworthpressinc.com].

Although evaluations of programs for men who batter first appeared in the mid-1980s, the accumulation of knowledge about effective practice has been very slow. Firm conclusions are difficult to make because of methodological problems with the evaluation studies. For example, only a few evaluations have randomly assigned offenders to comparison groups and almost none have used no-treatment or minimal treatment control groups (for reviews see Gondolf, 1997a; Hamberger & Hastings, 1993; Holtzworth-Munroe, Beatty & Anglin, 1995; Rosenfeld, 1992; Saunders, 1996a; Tolman & Edleson, 1995). In addition, many evaluations used small samples, short follow-up periods, and had low follow-up interview rates. As a result, a number of issues are widely discussed and debated in the field without much guidance from research findings.

Despite the paucity of information on effective interventions, guidelines and standards for intervention programs are growing in number (Austin & Dankwort, 1997, 1999; Healy, Smith, & O'Sullivan, 1998). The general purpose of these standards is to make victim safety and offender accountability the highest priority (Austin & Dankwort, 1997). Among the secondary goals are setting minimal standards for training and enhancing the consistency of response across all of the systems in the community that are working with offenders and victims. Many standards are statewide, while others cover only cities or counties. Some standards are voluntary and others are mandatory for court-referred cases or government funded programs. Some of these standards offer general guidelines, but others specify the methods to be used, the methods that should not be used, the intervention format (usually group counseling), and the treatment length (Austin & Dankwort, 1997, 1999). Without being closely tied to research knowledge, however, standards run the risk of creating rigid paradigms. A "one size fits all" approach may result in less effective and efficient interventions, which means increased rates of re-victimization. Among the advantages of mandatory, highly specific standards is that community wide coordinated responses within and across law enforcement, survivor and other agencies will be more consistent (e.g., Tolman, in this volume). Men who batter, victims, and service providers know more completely what to expect from offender programs. Among the disadvantages is that motivational, cultural, personality and other differences might not be considered in fashioning the most effective treatment (Moore, Greenfield, Wilson, & Kok, 1997). Standards may also instill a false sense of confidence in the effectiveness of certified programs. Standards currently in place are not based on the same level of rigorous research as the practice guidelines and standards of many professional organizations, for example, the American Psychological Association, the American Professional Society on the Abuse of Children, and the International Society for Traumatic Stress Studies.

The purpose of this article is to present some evidence that indicates that the best intervention outcomes for men who batter may be obtained when the type of offender is matched to the type of treatment. As in other intervention outcome research, the answers are likely to be complex. The most fruitful lines of inquiry frequently go beyond the question "What works?" to the question "What works with what type of offender, and under what circumstances?" Quantitative outcome research, however, will not give us all of the answers (see Murphy & O'Leary, 1994). For example, our values about the extent to which couples should try to keep a marriage intact are likely to influence practitioners' choice of treatment methods and goals (Saunders, 1981). In addition to describing some domestic violence research relevant to practice guidelines, this article also describes some successes and failures in the development of practice models in related fields that may be provide useful insights.

INDIVIDUAL DIFFERENCES AND PARADIGM DEVELOPMENT

The notion of individual differences among men who batter, and their categorization into subtypes, is controversial because it suggests different etiological theories (Bennett, 1998; Moore et al., 1997). It is possible, however, to integrate individual level theories, including theories of subtypes, into macro, socio-cultural theories. For example, gender role socialization and reinforcement of male dominance can be viewed as factors influencing all men, and men who batter in particular, while at the same time viewing these macro factors as interacting with a variety of individual background factors. "Nested" ecological models provide useful frameworks because the variation in individual responses can be incorporated into a larger socio-cultural framework (Dutton, 1994).

Indeed, there is evidence for considerable variation among men who batter. For example, the frequency and severity of domestic violence varies dramatically (Straus & Gelles, 1990). There is also growing evidence for different types of men who batter along several dimensions, including childhood traumas, generalized versus family-only aggression, and personality type (Holtzworth-Munroe & Stuart, 1994; Saunders, 1993). The stage of motivation (Begun et al., this volume; Levesque, Gelles, & Velicer, in press) and level of moral development (Gondolf, 1987) are other individual variables that have implications for individualized interventions. Some speculate that matching men to interventions based on motivational level or moral development is more important than the theoretical model used by the program. These theories have yet to be tested in offender programs.

None of the research available today was available when abuser programs were developed. When a new social problem is identified, practitioners must provide services based on their clinical wisdom and beliefs about etiology and waiting for research results is not an option when lives are in danger. In the domestic violence field, it appears that what began as clinical intuition became elements of programs identified as "model programs." These model programs later became the basis for making absolute statements about effective and harmful approaches. It may be time to reconsider some of the common working assumptions in the field and to be aware of possible consequences of reifying practice methods.

Some of the questions needing further resolution are:

(a) Is an individual or group format best? A common assumption in the field is that group formats are most effective (Austin & Dankwort, 1997). Several plausible rationales are given for group rather than individual treatment, such as opportunities for peer confrontation, yet no comparative studies have been conducted on this question (Saunders, 1996a). On the negative side, there is some speculation that group settings may allow men to reinforce problem denial, and sexist and violent attitudes in ways that are not apparent to group leaders.

(b) How long should interventions last? Only a few studies have attempted to address this question and the results are not consistent (e.g., Davis, Taylor, & Maxwell, 1998; Edleson & Syers, 1991). Programs are generally becoming longer but only a few programs are placing men into different program tracks of different lengths based on an assessment that indicates their risk for recidivism (Healy et al., 1998). Current standards vary greatly in the number of sessions required, from 12 to 52 (Healy et al., 1998). We may eventually learn that some men require only 12 sessions and others will require a year to two years. Even if longer programs are not necessarily more effective, some argue that a benefit of lengthy programs is that they can monitor the offenders' behavior better than most probation departments (Adams, 1984).

(c) Is there a place for trauma-based or insight approaches? The reluctance to use "insight approaches" provides one example of how practice may have become reified. At least eight standards for batterers' treatment prohibit the use of "insight" or "psychodynamic" approaches (Healy et al., 1998). One standard states:

> Those batterer intervention services seeking to comply with the Program Standards employ the Profeminist Model and may supplement this approach with the Cognitive-Behavioral and Psychoeducational Model. The other theoretical models [insight, ventilation, interaction] are fundamentally flawed and should not be employed in intervention work with

batterers in Pennsylvania. (Pennsylvania Coalition Against Domestic Violence, 1992, p. 33)

Insight approaches seem to have been contraindicated out of a fear that a focus on stressors, emotional factors, or childhood traumas would provide the men with another excuse for battering (Adams, 1988). An association may also be made between ventilation methods, which are likely to increase aggression, with insight methods. When many programs were first developed, insight approaches were assumed to take too long and offenders were believed to need confrontation and concrete skills more than insight (Jennings, 1987). Some evidence will be given below to show that insight approaches hold promise for certain types of abusers.

(d) Is a conjoint or gender specific format best? This question is probably the most hotly debated in the field. The experimental comparisons of these two formats are few in number and not conclusive (O'Leary, in press). Anecdotal information over the years revealed that some women are battered immediately after conjoint sessions. As a result, many of us were cautious about conjoint approaches out of the concern that women would be abused for what they disclosed in sessions, in particular their intention to leave the relationship or their re-victimization (Saunders, 1985). We were also concerned about the "meta-message" that she is implicitly "part of the problem" by her mere attendance in a conjoint session. However, generalizations based on worst-case scenarios may push practice guidelines too far and prevent the development of effective interventions for carefully screened cases. Not all guidelines are rigid on this issue. Some standards include criteria for what they consider the safe use of couples counseling and some marital clinics include protocols for carefully screening out cases in which the woman is afraid or has suffered severe violence (Healey et al., 1998; O'Leary, 1996; Vivian & Heyman, 1996).

(e) Other issues. There are a number of other issues discussed in the field, with many standards explicitly addressing them. These include the level of confidentiality afforded to the offender, the gender of the leaders, whether a co-leader is needed, the size of groups, the use of confrontation, and input or oversight from advocate organizations (for discussion of some of these issues see Adams, 1994; Rosenbuam & Stewart, 1994).

As with the other issues, practice models and standards were developed without the benefit of research knowledge. In one state, co-leadership was at first encouraged by the state's standards and later mandated based on the experience of practitioners (Bennett & Piet, 1999). In another state, a program with an Afro-Centric curriculum and same-race groups was not sent court referrals and had to cease operation because it did not fit the dominant paradigm in the state (Healy et al., 1998). Some programs are learning that confrontation does not seem effective with some ethnic groups and thus standards may be too rigid on the use of confrontation (Healy et al., 1998).

Many more studies will be needed to answer the above questions with confidence. For all of these questions, however, recognition of the variability among abusers may help to provide the answers.

INNOVATIVE TREATMENTS AND TREATMENT MATCHING FOR MEN WHO BATTER

Programs for men who batter cannot be neatly categorized as "pro-feminist," "cognitive-behavioral," "anger management," "psychodynamic," "family systems," or other categories. Studies conducted in the 1980s showed that most programs were fairly eclectic and borrowed from different theories (e.g., Feazell, Myers, & Deschner, 1984). Most programs tend to be structured and focus on helping the men take responsibility for their abuse, broaden their definitions of abusive behavior, and learn skills to replace violent behavior (Gondolf, 1997a). Programs seem to differ most on the emphasis they place on several dimensions. Common etiological assumptions and the methods derived from them can be categorized on the following dimensions (adapted from Saunders, 1996a):

1. Skills training is based on social learning assumptions about the behavioral deficits and behavioral excesses of offenders. For example, men who batter are less skilled than other men in communicating with their partners (Holtzworth-Munroe, Bates, Smutzler, & Sandin, 1997). Modeling of positive behavior and behavioral rehearsal are used to enhance relationship skills that replace destructive behaviors.
2. Cognitive approaches assume that faulty patterns of thinking lead to negative emotions, which in turn lead to abusive behavior. For example, men who batter tend to make negative attributions about the intent of their partners' behaviors (Holtzworth-Munroe, Bates, Smutzler, & Sandin, 1997). Restructuring of these thoughts is likely to reduce anger and the fear and hurt that often underlies it. These approaches can also be used to help the men to become aware of their core belief systems developed in childhood, including rigid beliefs about gender roles.
3. Sex role re-socialization helps the men to see the negative effects of constricted male roles and the benefits of gender equality. Male dominance is viewed as one of the effects of this rigid socialization.
4. Building awareness of control tactics is designed to help the men take responsibility for their behavior. The men are urged by group leaders and group members to take ownership of their intentions to control others. The negative physical and emotional outcomes on victims may also be

pointed out. An emphasis is placed on expanding the definition of abuse to include isolation, demeaning language, control of finances and other means of control.

5. Family systems approaches assume that couples unknowingly engage in repeated cycles of interaction that may culminate in violence. The focus is on analyzing and changing communication patterns.

6. Trauma-based approaches rest on the assumption that the men need to re-experience and resolve their childhood traumas, in particular witnessing parental violence and physical abuse from their parents (Saunders, 1996b). One of the assumptions is that they cannot empathize well with others because they are cut off from their own painful memories.

The first four approaches seem to be the ones most commonly integrated into the same program (e.g., Ganley, 1987). Family systems approaches, not always used in conjoint sessions, are probably the most controversial and most likely to be prohibited in standards (Austin & Dankwort, 1999). Also, as noted earlier, practitioners have been reluctant to use trauma-based approaches for fear that they will provide an excuse for battering or will take too long. I will focus here on these approaches because recent research and discussion of these approaches is prompting their reconsideration. Jennings (1987) first argued for an unstructured, insight model, maintaining that men who batter are capable of insight and that a more naturalistic way of learning alternatives to violence was likely to last longer. Stozny (1994) developed a model to increase the men's compassion for their own childhood traumas. Such compassion is assumed to be incompatible with aggression. He showed higher rates of treatment involvement and treatment retention with this model in a controlled experiment.

In another experiment, five months of feminist-cognitive-behavioral group treatment were compared with five months of process-psychodynamic group treatment in a randomized experiment (n = 136; Saunders, 1996b). A high rate of victim interviews (79%) and evidence of treatment integrity were achieved. The two treatments did not differ on measures of violence, fear level, relationship equality, and general changes as reported by the men's partners an average of 22 months after treatment. However, antisocial and hypomanic men completing the highly structured feminist-cognitive-behavioral groups had significantly lower recidivism rates than these types of men in the process-psychodynamic groups. The reverse was the case for men with dependent personalities: They had significantly lower recidivism rates in the process-psychodynamic groups and higher rates in the feminist-cognitive-behavioral groups. There was also a finding that the process-psychodynamic group had a significantly lower attrition rate overall.

Another recent experimental comparison of abuser treatments also found an interaction effect between an abuser trait and the type of treatment (Brannen & Rubin, 1996). Conjoint group treatment was compared with gender specific group treatment. There were no differences in recidivism rates as reported by the women. However, the conjoint treatment was more effective than the gender specific treatment when the man was an alcoholic. One of the limitations of this study was its use of very small samples.

One argument for the use of standards is that they are often applied only to court-ordered men and since court-ordered men are likely to be the most anti-social they may need the most structured approaches, as the above evidence suggests. Standards may help ensure such structure. However, with the proliferation of mandatory arrest policies it can no longer be assumed that those arrested are the most likely to have anti-social traits and the most chronic and severe patterns of abuse. In the above study (Saunders, 1996b), no difference was found between deferred prosecution, court-ordered, and voluntary referrals on most personality measures (unpublished analysis), including no difference between court-ordered and voluntary men on antisocial personality (MCMI-I). Deferred prosecution men were the least antisocial of the three groups. Voluntary men scored higher on borderline and anxiety traits. In Gondolf's (1999) sample involving men from four different programs, the men voluntarily referred were more likely to be antisocial, depressed, borderline, and passive-aggressive. The mandatory referrals were more likely to be narcissistic and compulsive.

Individual differences can also be seen in the patterns emerging of factors related to recidivism after treatment. One of these factors is alcohol abuse (DeMaris & Jackson, 1987; Hamberger & Hastings, 1990; Jones & Gondolf, 1997). Severe personality disorders may also predispose men to re-abuse (Dutton, Bodnarchuk, Kropp, Hart, & Ogloff, 1997; Hamberger & Hastings, 1990; Jones & Gondolf, 1997). Not surprisingly, the chronicity (Tolman & Bhosley, 1991) and severity (Jones & Gondolf, 1997) of pre-treatment assaults are good predictors of assault after treatment. Therefore, if more research points to a consistent pattern of likely treatment failures, these high risk cases can be placed on a more intensive or longer term track, or as some would argue, they should be denied treatment altogether.

POSSIBLE LESSONS FROM OTHER FIELDS

In addition to research on domestic violence, the accounts of paradigm development from other fields may be relevant to this discussion. Brief examples from the fields of alcoholism, mental health, sexual aggression, and corrections are presented.

Alcoholism Field

The alcoholism field experienced an extremely heated "battle" over divergent paradigms that lasted for three decades and continues in diminished form today (Sobell & Sobell, 1995). The medical/disease models, prominent in state credentialing and training agencies, have been pitted against social learning models. Proponents of the medical model insist that abstinence is essential for recovery (Clarke & Saunders, 1988). Social learning theorists insist that controlled drinking is possible, at least for some alcoholics (Sobell & Sobell, 1995). Only recently have research findings begun to modify some cornerstone beliefs of the disease model. Today there is growing acceptance of different paradigms. For example, types of alcoholics are being identified and there is evidence for the effectiveness of matching types of clients with types of treatment (Mark, Babor, DelBoca, Kadden, & Cooney, 1992).

Those who went against the dominant paradigm in the alcoholism field paid a price. There were lawsuits and accusations of heresy, personal attacks, and challenges to their veracity and integrity as researchers (Clarke & Saunders, 1988). The Chair of the National Council on Alcoholism stated that only one intervention is effective (abstinence), and that we need "responsible" research and "judicious" publication of findings (Clarke & Saunders, 1988, p. 25). As a result, Congress directed the NIAAA to stop funding studies that found evidence for controlled drinking (Clarke & Saunders, 1988). An awareness of the history of debates in the alcoholism field may help keep the working assumptions in the domestic violence field more tentative and responsive to the development of new knowledge.

Mental Health Field

Generalizations from the most tragic cases in a field can sometimes dramatically shape policies and practices and lead to less effective and efficient practice in the long run. For example, the over-prediction of dangerousness seems to have driven practices and policies in the mental health field for many years (Monahan & Shah, 1989). The small percentage of mental patients who were violent (Monahan & Arnold, 1996) fueled the stereotype that all mental patients were violent or had a high potential for violence. Research on the over-prediction of dangerousness led to the development of more specific criteria and more care in committing patients involuntarily to long-term hospitalization (Monahan & Shah, 1989).

The overgeneralization from "worst cases" might be operating now in the domestic violence field. Although all men who batter have by definition been violent, they differ in their propensity for severe, frequent, or lethal violence

(Saunders, 1999). The profiles of domestic violence developed from shelter samples appear to differ substantively from the profiles developed from community samples and some clinic samples (Johnson, 1995). The tendency to react to "worst case outcomes" might be avoided in the domestic violence field in part through the development of measures for assessing dangerousness (Saunders, 1999). Some programs use procedures for distinguishing between low risk and high-risk offenders. They place the high-risk offenders into more intensive and longer-term tracks (Healy et al., 1998).

Sexual Aggression Field

Examples from this closely related field show that it is possible to integrate a focus on the victimization and trauma of offenders with a focus on accountability and cognitive-behavioral interventions. In one recent survey of sex offender programs involving 1,186 U.S. providers, 85% of the adult programs focused on the offenders' past victimization/trauma as part of comprehensive programming (Freeman-Longo, Bird, Stevenson, & Fiske, 1994). The links between childhood victimization and later perpetration may be clearer in this field. Practitioners in the sex offender field may also feel more comfortable focusing on offender trauma/victimization issues because the programs tend to be prison-based and longer term, which is rare in the treatment of domestic violence. Practitioners in this field might be able to help domestic violence practitioners resolve the apparent conflict between a dual focus on resolving childhood issues (as a determinant of abuse) and responsibility for behavior as an adult (free will). Insight approaches, when applied right, can increase accountability because the men see that they are at higher risk than other men of being perpetrators and that their anger and hurt are linked to childhood events and not current relationships.

General Offender Rehabilitation

Rehabilitation in the general field of corrections may be even more closely tied to the domestic violence field because of the overlap in characteristics and actual cases in the two offender groups. Fagan (1996) points out that the domestic violence field has much to learn from the field of criminology. These lessons include the limits of criminal justice sanctions and the benefits of matching abuser types with intervention types. There is evidence from the general field of offender rehabilitation for the ability to: (a) predict recidivism, (b) determine which cases are high risk cases and in need of longer treatment, and (c) match the needs of offenders with treatment type, a process known as "responsivity" (Andrews, Bonta, & Hoge, 1990). One meta-analysis included 154 coefficients from outcome studies in juvenile and adult corrections (Andrews, Zinger et al., 1990). Criminal sanctions were found to be largely ineffective, including the severity of judicial dispositions and the use of restitution. So called "appropriate" treatments, however, were effective. "Appropriate" service delivery was defined as: services to high risk cases, all behavioral approaches, specific matching between the offender's learning style and treatment, and a non-behavioral but structured focus on the "criminogenic needs" of the offender.

CONCLUSIONS

Debates over best practices in the field of abuser treatment have yet to benefit very much from outcome evaluations and domestic violence research in general. Perhaps the firmest conclusion to be drawn is that firm conclusions about best practice methods are premature. Accounts of the development of practice methods in other fields, such as alcoholism treatment and mental health, may provide the domestic violence field with some valuable lessons about the consequences of inflexible paradigms. In the closely related field of offender rehabilitation, there is good evidence for the benefits of matching offender types with types of interventions in reducing recidivism. Guidelines based on practice wisdom that simultaneously allow an openness to evidence that challenges any currently used paradigm are needed. In particular, guidelines need to account for differences in the motivational levels, cultural backgrounds, risk of severe violence, and other factors that recognize the individual characteristics of men who batter.

REFERENCES

Adams, D. (1988). Treatment models for men who batter: A profeminist analysis. In K. Yllo & M. Bograd (Eds.), *Feminist perspectives on wife abuse* (pp. 176-199). Thousand Oaks, CA: Sage.

Adams, D. (1994). Point/Counterpoint: Treatment standards for abuser programs. *Violence Update*, September, 5-6.

Andrews, D. A., Bonta, J., & Hoge, R. D. (1990). Classification for effective rehabilitation: Rediscovering psychology. *Criminal Justice and Behavior*, *17*(1), 19-52.

Andrews, D. A., Zinger, I., Hoge, R. D., Bonta, J., Gendreau, P., & Cullen, F. T. (1990). Does correctional treatment work? A clinically relevant and psychologically informed meta-analysis. *Criminology*, *28*(3), 369-404.

Austin, J., & Dankwort, J. (1997). A review of standards for batterer intervention programs. VAWnet, a project of the National Resource Center on Domestic Violence, <http://www.vaw.umn.edu/Vawnet/standard.htm>.

Austin, J., & Dankwort, J. (1999). Standards for batter programs: A review and analysis. *Journal of Interpersonal Violence, 14*(2), 152-168.

Begun, A., Shelley, G., Strodthoff, T., & Short, L. (2001). Adopting a stages of change approach for individuals who are violent with their intimate partners. *Journal of Aggression, Maltreatment, & Trauma, 5*(2) #10, 105-127.

Bennett, L. (1998). In defense of batterer-program standards. Families in Society: *The Journal of Contemporary Human Services*, (January-February), 93-97.

Bennett, L., & Piet, M. (1999). Standards for batterer intervention programs: In whose interest? *Violence Against Women, 5*, 6-24.

Brannen, S. J., & Rubin, A. (1996). Comparing the effectiveness of gender-specific and couples groups in a court-mandated spouse abuse treatment program. *Research on Social Work Practice, 6*(4), 405-424.

Clarke, J. C., & Saunders, J. (1988). *Alcoholism and problem drinking: Theories and treatment*. Elmsford, NY: Pergamon Press.

Davis, R. C., Taylor, B. G., & Maxwell, C. D. (1998). *Does batterer treatment reduce violence? A randomized experiment in Brooklyn*. Unpublished manuscript.

DeMaris, A. & Jackson, J. K. (1987). Batterers reports of recidivism after counseling. *Social Casework, 68*(8), 458-465.

Dutton, D. G. (1994). *The domestic assault of women: Psychological and criminal justice perspectives*. Vancouver: University of British Columbia Press.

Dutton, D. G., Bodnarchuk, M., Kropp, R., Hart, S. D., & Ogloff, J. P. (1997). Client personality disorders affecting wife assault post-treatment recidivism. *Violence & Victims, 12*(1), 37-50.

Edleson, J. L., & Syers, M. (1991). The effects of group treatment for men who batter: An 18-month follow-up study. *Research on Social Work Practice, 1*(3), 227-243.

Fagan, J. (1996). *Criminalization of domestic violence: Promises and limits*. Rockville, MD: National Institute of Justice.

Feazell, C. S., Myers, T., & Deschner, J. (1984). Services of men who batter: Implications for programs and policies. *Family Relations, 33*, 217-223.

Freeman-Longo, R. E., Bird, S., Stevenson, W. F., & Fiske, J. A. (1995). *1994 Nationwide survey of treatment programs and models*. (The Safer Society: P.O. Box 340, Brandon, VT 05733).

Ganley, A. L. (1989). Integrating feminist and social learning analyses of aggression: Creating multiple models for intervention with men who batter. In L. Caesar & L. K. Hamberger (Eds.), *Treating men who batter: Theory, practice, and programs* (pp. 196-235). New York: Springer.

Gondolf, E. W. (1987). Changing men who batter: A developmental model for integrated interventions. *Journal of Family Violence, 2*(4), 335-349.

Gondolf, E. W. (1997a). Batterer programs: What we know and need to know. *Journal of Interpersonal Violence, 12* (1), 83-98.

Gondolf, E. W. (1997b). Patterns of reassault in batterer programs. *Violence & Victims, 12*(4), (Winter 1997), 373-387.

Gondolf, E. W. (1999). MCMI-III results for batterer program participants in four cities: Less "pathological" than expected. *Journal of Family Violence, 14*, 1-18.

Hamberger, L., & Hastings, J. (1990). Recidivism following spouse abuse abatement counseling: Treatment program implications. *Violence & Victims, 5*, 131-147.

Hamberger, L., & Hastings, J. (1993). Court mandated treatment of men who assault their partner. In Z. Hilton (Ed.), *Legal responses to wife assault* (pp. 188-232). Thousand Oaks, CA: Sage.

Healy, K., Smith, C., & O'Sullivan, C. (1998). *Batterer intervention: Program approaches and criminal justice strategies.* Washington, DC: National Institute of Justice.

Holtzworth-Munroe, A., Bates, L., Smutzler, N., & Sandin, E. (1997). A brief review of the research on husband violence: Maritally violent versus nonviolent men. *Aggression & Violent Behavior, 2*(1), 65-99.

Holtzworth-Munroe, A., Beatty, S. B., & Anglin, K. (1995). The assessment and treatment of marital violence: An introduction for the marital therapist. In N. S. Jacobson & A. S. Gurman (Eds.), *Clinical handbook of couple therapy* (pp. 317-339). New York: Guilford Press.

Holtzworth-Munroe, A., & Stuart, G. L (1994). Typologies of male batterers: Three subtypes and the differences among them. *Psychological Bulletin, 116*(3), 476-497.

Jennings, J. L. (1987). History and issues in the treatment of battering men: A case for unstructured group therapy. *Journal of Family Violence, 2*(3), 193-213.

Johnson, M. P. (1995). Patriarchal terrorism and common couple violence: Two forms of violence against women. *Journal of Marriage and the Family, 57*, 283-294.

Jones, A. S., & Gondolf, E. W. (1997, June 29-July 2). *Post-program predictors of re-assault for batterer program participants.* Paper presented at the 5th International Family Violence Conference, University of New Hampshire.

Levesque, D. A., Gelles, R. J., & Velicer, W. F. (in press.) Development and validation of a stages of change measure for battering men. *Cognitive Therapy and Research.*

Mark, D. L., Babor, T. F., DelBoca, F. K., Kadden, R. M., & Cooney, N. L. (1992). Types of alcoholics, II: Application of an empirically derived typology to treatment matching. *Archives of General Psychiatry, 49*, 609-614.

Monahan, J., & Arnold, J. (1996). Violence by people with mental illness: A consensus statement by advocates and researchers. *Psychiatric Rehabilitation Journal, 19* (4), 67-70.

Monahan, J., & Shah, S. A. (1989). Dangerousness and commitment of the mentally disordered in the United States. *Schizophrenia Bulletin, 15*(4), 541-553.

Moore, K. J., Greenfield, W. L., Wilson, M., & Kok, A. C. (1997). Toward a taxonomy of batterers. *Families in Society, 78*, 352-360.

Murphy, C. M., & O'Leary, K. D. (1994). Research paradigms, values, and spouse abuse. *Journal of Interpersonal Violence, 9*(2), 207-223.

O'Leary, K. (2001). Conjoint therapy for partners who engage in physically aggressive behavior: Rationale and research. *Journal of Aggression, Maltreatment, & Trauma, 5*(2) #10, 145-164.

O'Leary, K. D., Heyman, R. E., & Neidig, P. H. (1999). Treatment of wife abuse: A comparison of gender-specific and conjoint approaches. *Behavior Therapy, 30*, 475-505.

Pennsylvania Coalition Against Domestic Violence. (1992). Accountability: Program Standards for Batterer Intervention Services. Author, 524 McKnight St., Reading PA 19601.

Rosenbaum, A., & Stewart, T. P. (1984). Point/Counterpoint: Treatment standards for abuser programs. *Violence Update*, *5*(1), 2, 9, 11.

Rosenfeld, B. D. (1992). Court-ordered treatment of spouse abuse. *Clinical Psychology Review*, *12*, 205-226.

Saunders, D. G. (1981). Treatment and value issues in helping battered women. In A. S. Gurman (Ed.), *Questions and answers in the practice of family therapy* (pp. 493-496). New York: Bruner/Mazel.

Saunders, D. G. (1985). Book review of *Spouse abuse: A treatment guide for couples* by P. H. Neidig & D. H. Freidman. *Journal of Marital and Family Therapy*, *11*(2), 216-218.

Saunders, D. G. (1993). Husbands who assault: Multiple profiles requiring multiple responses. In N. Z. Hilton (Ed.), *Legal responses to wife assault* (pp. 208-235). Newbury Park, CA: Sage.

Saunders, D. G. (1996a). Interventions for men who batter: Do we know what works? *In session: Psychotherapy In Practice, 2/3*, 81-94.

Saunders, D. G. (1996b). Feminist-cognitive-behavioral and process-psychodynamic treatments for men who batter: Interaction of abuser traits and treatment models. *Violence and Victims*, *11*, 393-414.

Saunders, D. G. (1999). Woman battering. In R. T. Ammerman & M. Hersen (Eds.), *Assessment of family violence, 2nd edition* (pp. 243-270). New York: John Wiley.

Sobell, M. B., & Sobell, L. C. (1995). Editorial: Controlled drinking after 25 years: How important was the great debate? *Addiction*, *90*, 1149-1153.

Stozny, S. (1994). *Treating attachment abuse: A compassionate approach*. New York: Springer.

Straus, M. A., & Gelles, R. J. (1990). *Physical violence in American families*. New Brunswick, NJ: Transaction.

Tolman, R. M. (2001). An ecological analysis of batterer intervention program standards. *Journal of Aggression, Maltreatment, & Trauma, 5*(2) #10, 221-233.

Tolman, R. M., & Bhosley, G. (1991). The outcome of participation in a shelter-sponsored program for men who batter. In D. Knudsen & J. Miller (Eds.), *Abused and battered: Social and legal responses* (pp. 113-122). New York: Aldine de Gruyter.

Tolman, R. M., & Edleson, J. L. (1995). Intervention for men who batter: A review of research. In S. Stith & M. A. Straus (Eds.), *Understanding partner violence: Prevalence, causes, consequences and solutions* (pp. 262-273). Minneapolis, MN: National Council on Family Relations.

Vivian, D., & Heyman, R. E. (1996). Is there a place for conjoint treatment of couple violence? *In Session: Psychotherapy, 2*, 25-48.

Toward Empirically Based Standards for Abuser Intervention: The Maryland Model

Christopher M. Murphy

SUMMARY. This article describes the development of operational guidelines for Abuser Intervention Programs in Maryland. Unlike in many states which have adopted quite specific standards regarding program format, duration, etc., the Maryland guidelines address a fairly narrow range of issues. These include outreach to victims, communication with the courts, and the need for intervention programs to address domestic abuse directly in their program content. Maryland has also established a research task force on Abuser Intervention Programs, whose

The author gratefully acknowledges the efforts of many people who were involved in developing and implementing Maryland's Operational Guidelines for Domestic Violence Abuser Intervention Programs, and who have established the Abuser Intervention Research Collaborative. Rachel Wohl, Eugene Morris and Alan Sun supplied reflections and recollections that were used in drafting this paper.

This work was supported, in part, through a grant administered by the Maryland Governor's Office of Crime Control and Prevention–Grant #VAWA-97-033-D, awarded by the Bureau of Justice Assistance, Office of Justice Programs, U.S. Department of Justice. The Assistant Attorney General, Office of Justice Programs, coordinates the activities of the following program offices and bureaus: Bureau of Justice Assistance, Bureau of Justice Statistics, National Institute of Justice, Office of Juvenile Justice and Delinquency Prevention, and the Office of Victims of Crime. Points of view or opinions contained within this document are those of the author and do not necessarily represent the official position or policies of the U.S. Department of Justice.

[Haworth co-indexing entry note]: "Toward Empirically Based Standards for Abuser Intervention: The Maryland Model." Murphy, Christopher M. Co-published simultaneously in *Journal of Aggression, Maltreatment & Trauma* (The Haworth Maltreatment & Trauma Press, an imprint of The Haworth Press, Inc.) Vol. 5, No. 2(#10), 2001, pp. 249-264; and: *Domestic Violence Offenders: Current Interventions, Research, and Implications for Policies and Standards* (ed: Robert A. Geffner, and Alan Rosenbaum) The Haworth Maltreatment & Trauma Press, an imprint of The Haworth Press, Inc., 2001, pp. 249-264. Single or multiple copies of this article are available for a fee from The Haworth Document Delivery Service [1-800-HAWORTH, 9:00 a.m. - 5:00 p.m. (EST). E-mail address: getinfo@haworthpressinc.com].

249

goal is to use empirical data to inform the use of best practices in the state, to facilitate empirical research at abuser intervention programs in Maryland, and to develop more detailed program standards in the future. *[Article copies available for a fee from The Haworth Document Delivery Service: 1-800-HAWORTH. E-mail address: <getinfo@haworthpressinc.com> Website: <http://www.HaworthPress.com> © 2001 by The Haworth Press, Inc. All rights reserved.]*

KEYWORDS. Domestic, violence, intervention, perpetrators, programs, guidelines

I. OVERVIEW

After two attempts to develop state standards for Abuser Intervention Programs (AIP's), and as a result of extensive debate and compromise, Maryland has settled on a modest set of operating guidelines with the goal of developing empirically based practice standards in the future. A group of AIP directors and academicians has established a research task force that has begun to review existing knowledge, design investigations, and disseminate information to inform program practices and to aid in the development of empirically-based program standards. The goal is to serve as a national model for a scientific approach to abuser intervention program practice and standards.

II. THE DEVELOPMENT OF OPERATING GUIDELINES FOR ABUSER INTERVENTION PROGRAMS

Maryland Batterers' Treatment Providers' Focus Group

Beginning in 1993, the Maryland Batterers' Treatment Providers' Focus Group, a working group of abuser intervention program directors and practitioners, developed a draft set of standards based primarily on the Massachusetts model. Concerns had developed among domestic violence programs in Maryland that unqualified practitioners, with little or no expertise in domestic violence, were irresponsibly treating court-ordered referrals. The working group meetings were well attended by batterer program personnel, and served as a vehicle for information sharing and discussion of program practice and philosophy. Once the standards were developed, the Maryland Network Against Domestic Violence set out to promote them, but the work stalled when it came time to develop a legislative strategy for official adoption and implementation of the standards.

Maryland Attorney General and Lt. Governor's Family Violence Council

In 1995, about a year after the original standards were proposed, the Post-Disposition Committee of the newly formed Maryland Attorney General and Lt. Governor's Family Violence Council took up the issue of Abuser Intervention Program standards. This committee contained a broad-based membership including policy makers, judges, prosecutors, parole and probation administrators, domestic violence victim and offender service providers, and sexual assault service providers. Their charge was to develop an agenda and action plan regarding probation and counseling for abuse perpetrators, and services for victims of abuse.

Abuser program standards proved to be the most controversial topic handled by the committee. The initial plan was to find a legislative or judicial strategy for implementing the draft of Maryland standards, which were based largely on those previously developed in Massachusetts. However, vocal opposition was raised by committee members who had not participated in drafting these standards. One member suggested and drafted an alternative model based on program outcomes. He argued that all programs should be required to assess outcomes in a standardized fashion, for example through a victim report on the Conflict Tactics Scale (Straus, 1979). In addition, he argued that if multiple programs were competing for the same court-mandated clients, an empirical trial should be required in which judges randomly assign batterers to the available programs. Alternatively, programs that failed to attain recidivism rates below a certain, empirically-derived, standard, could be denied referrals. The over-riding point was that clients should be assigned to programs on the basis of demonstrated outcomes, rather than pre-specified standards, and that program practices should not be specified in the absence of empirical support for their efficacy.

The attorney directing the state Family Violence Council forged a consensus between these divergent perspectives, one asserting a need for outcome-based standards with no specifications about program practices, and the other supporting the adoption of fairly strict practice standards in the absence of empirical support. The committee decided against adopting standards that rigidly prescribed program models or practices because there was insufficient evidence to support the efficacy of any specific approach, and because such standards might preclude research on innovative models. Extensive discussion of outcome-based standards, however, produced the conclusion that existing programs lacked sufficient funding, staffing, and training to collect outcome data in a rigorous fashion. Thus, the committee decided to adopt a modest set of operating guidelines that everyone could agree were sound and likely to promote the well-being and safety of victims. In addition, the committee recommended that "abuser intervention programs, together with research academicians, should create a Research Task Force that will serve as a national demonstration project to develop empirically-based standards for effective abuser intervention methods" (Maryland Family Violence Council, 1996, p. 42). The composition and activities of this research task force are described later in this paper.

Operating Guidelines. The operating guidelines (included as Appendix) represented a set of "bottom line" issues that received broad-based support from a committee of service providers and researchers. The committee was diverse in theoretical orientation, professional identity, and political perspective. Their deliberations involved existing practices in the state, empirical data on abuser intervention and related areas of behavior change, the potential impact of various proposed guidelines on future practice, and legislative and administrative strategies for implementing the guidelines. The stated goals of the operational guidelines for Maryland are to establish responsibility to victims and accountability to the courts, to ensure that abusers are referred to programs that focus on stopping abuse, to promote partnership with the legal community and victims' advocacy programs, and to ensure outreach to victims. The guidelines placed very few restrictions on intervention practices in the absence of a compelling scientific basis for favoring specific intervention models or procedures over others.

One specific goal of the guidelines is to ensure that abusers are referred "to intervention programs that focus on stopping abuse and preventing abusers from evading or minimizing their responsibility for abusive behavior." Likewise, the guidelines maintain that "the abuser bears sole responsibility for his or her actions" (Maryland Family Violence Council, 1996, p. 101). In deliberating these points, many committee members expressed concerns about traditional therapeutic approaches that explore psychodynamic or relationship issues thought to underlie violent behavior, without directly addressing violence or abuse (Adams, 1988; Bograd, 1984). Several members noted that credibility with the court system may be jeopardized by such approaches, given that individuals are referred specifically to address problems with domestic violence. The guidelines, however, do not preclude therapists from addressing family-of-origin issues, relationship dynamics, or other therapeutic or psychoeducational issues in abuser intervention programs, as long as such efforts include a focus on stopping abuse and encourage the assumption of personal responsibility for abusive acts.

A second area addressed by the guidelines involves maintaining effective communication with the referral sources for mandated clients. Programs are specifically directed to: (a) indicate to the court if the abuser is not amenable to services and to make appropriate recommendations if feasible; (b) report back to the court within one month on any clients who fail to follow-up on the initial referral; and (c) notify relevant referring parties about the abuser's attendance and participation in the program. These bottom line issues were geared to prevent practitioners from taking court referrals without arranging for appropriate communication and follow-up with the legal system. As stated in the general purpose of the guidelines, the broad intention is to ensure that counseling programs for abuse perpetrators remain part of a coordinated community response involving the legal system and services for victims.

A third general issue, which is addressed at some length in the guidelines, involves outreach and accountability to victims. More specifically, programs are instructed to: (a) conduct outreach to victims in order to inform them about services available to them in the community; (b) maintain victims' confidentiality; and (c) inform victims about the abuser's program attendance. Although some concerns were raised regarding the expense of victim outreach, and about whether contacting victims may negatively impact their safety, a broad consensus was eventually achieved on the requirement of victim contact. Most of the arguments against victim outreach involved inappropriate disclosure to abusers by program staff of information provided by victims. A requirement that programs maintain victim confidentiality and keep separate victim files was therefore included in the operational guidelines in an effort to limit the chance that outreach would place victims at risk. In the final analysis, the potential benefits to victims from receiving service outreach and information about the abuser's compliance with court-ordered counseling, along with the potential benefit of improved assessment of the abuser's difficulties from collateral victim reports, were deemed to far outweigh potential safety risks associated with routine victim contact.

The operating guidelines also address several other basic issues. A standard set of definitions is provided for abusive behavior in order to outline the scope of the problem addressed by abuser programs. The guidelines specify background information that should be obtained from abusive clients. The need for confidentiality waivers to communicate with victims and other mental health professionals is indicated, and the need for screening and referrals associated with substance abuse or mental health problems are addressed. The guidelines require programs to obtain a signed treatment contract with the offender that specifies criteria for successful completion of the court order to counseling. Finally, the guidelines address the importance of employing staff members who are culturally sensitive, representative of the client populations served, and free from violence and impairment due to substance abuse in their own lives.

A variety of topics were considered for inclusion in the operating guidelines and dropped because a sufficient consensus could not be garnered to support them. A requirement that abuser program staff be licensed in one of the traditional mental health professions was briefly considered, and then dropped by broad consensus. Committee deliberations revealed that traditional mental health professionals, unlike activists in the battered women's movement, had no special knowledge of, or experience with, domestic violence and had a spotty record in responding to battered women's safety and service needs. In addition, the empirical literature on behavior change, despite its methodological limitations, indicated that paraprofessionals achieve equivalent results when compared to professional counselors (Berman & Norton, 1985; Christensen & Jacobson, 1994). Representatives from several area programs argued that their paraprofessional counselors were highly competent and often more similar than mental health professionals in social background to the client population. Further deliberations revealed a potential safety concern regarding victim confidentiality arising from the fact that courts do not recognize confidentiality privileges for paraprofessionals. Therefore, a clause was added to the guidelines indicating that programs should not maintain files on victims unless they can be protected by the confidentiality privilege of a licensed supervisor.

Also dropped was a requirement for specific program length. Deliberations revealed that programs varied considerably in length, and the available empirical evidence, despite suggesting that longer treatment tends to produce higher success rates in individual psychotherapy (Howard, Kopta, Krause & Orlinsky, 1986), did not support the notion that longer abuser intervention programs were more effective than relatively brief (e.g., 12-session) programs (Edleson & Syers, 1990; 1991). Likewise, any requirement that programs adopt a specific intervention model, or adhere to a specific program philosophy, was dropped due to a lack of consensus about best approaches, difficulty in precisely defining program philosophy, a high level of eclecticism in actual practice, and the absence of clear empirical evidence to support the efficacy of any specific approach over others in the area of batterer intervention. The report by the American Psychological Association Presidential Task Force on Violence and the Family (APA, 1996) was helpful in these deliberations. The report urged caution in providing only one form of standard batterer treatment and encouraged a range of treatment options be made available to work with domestic violence offenders.

Self-Certification Process. The committee spent considerable time exploring options for legislating and/or administering the operating guidelines. There was relatively little support for legislation to enact the guidelines, given their limited scope, the preliminary state of knowledge about best practices for abuser intervention, and given other legislative priorities related to domestic violence. Policy makers who were involved in developing the guidelines argued that the absence of empirical support for the efficacy of abuser intervention programs in general would undermine legislative support for mandating relevant standards. Subsequently, the Maryland Department of Human Resources, which oversees the local Departments of Social Services, was approached to serve as the licensing or certification body for abuser intervention programs. This, and other state agencies, however, were either deemed inappropriate to administer the operating guidelines, or were unwilling to assume the administrative burden and costs.

Therefore, the committee pursued a judicial strategy for implementing the guidelines, along with a self-certification process. They obtained the support of the administrative (chief) judges of the district and circuit courts, who crafted a policy requiring judges to refer domestic abusers only to programs that self-certify compliance with the operational guidelines. In order to self-certify compliance, abuser programs were asked to complete a detailed questionnaire explaining their procedures or plans for addressing each issue covered by the operational guidelines, and to provide relevant documentation such as intake forms, confidentiality waivers, treatment contracts, and treatment protocols. They were also asked to provide basic information that might be of interest to prosecutors and referring judges, including fees, length of services, enrollment procedures, and discharge procedures. This self-certification process is fairly rigorous, and was designed to dissuade practitioners or mental health agencies who have only a casual interest in domestic violence from obtaining court referrals, while allowing access for any legitimate program or provider who has a serious commitment to this work.

III. THE MARYLAND DOMESTIC VIOLENCE ABUSER RESEARCH COLLABORATIVE

A collaborative group of practitioners and researchers was formed in early 1997. The original committee charge from the Family Violence Council's 1996 report is as follows:

> Maryland abuser intervention programs, together with research academicians, should create a Research Task Force that will serve as a national demonstration project to develop empirically-based standards for effective abuser intervention methods. The task force should identify gaps in knowledge about the effectiveness of abuser intervention, facilitate uniform outcome data collection by all intervention programs, and conduct

controlled scientific studies of various intervention methods. This will
be a collaborative effort and research results are to be used to assist all
programs to increase their effectiveness. (Maryland Family Violence
Council Report, p. 41)

Since its inception, the Research Collaborative has focused on building the
capacity to conduct collaborative research through the development of mutually beneficial working alliances between practitioners and researchers. The
collaborative meets monthly, and, at present, has active representation from
eight Maryland abuser intervention programs and three universities. The collaborative has academic and practitioner co-chairs, a consultant from outside
the state who is a prominent domestic violence researcher, and active representation from the Maryland Attorney General's and Lt. Governor's Family Violence Council. Service providers and treatment program administrators have
been centrally involved in all aspects of this effort, and, by all indications, are
deeply committed to the use of empirical research to enhance abuser intervention practices and develop standards.

Over time, the goals of the collaborative have evolved into a three-pronged
strategy. The first prong involves the development of a research agenda that is
highly relevant to practice. The goal is to use collaborative dialogue in order to
formulate research questions that generate strong interest among both treatment providers and investigators (Murphy & Dienemann, in press). The second
prong involves building the capacity for research at participating programs by
establishing standard intake data collection procedures, standard agreements regarding the use of human subjects and the reporting of research results, a strategy for estimating program costs associated with research, and standard
methods for assessing program effects. The idea is to create a highly
"user-friendly" context for investigators from both within and outside the state
to collaborate on research with participating programs. The third prong involves a consistent feedback loop whereby information about research can be
communicated to Maryland AIP's, can encourage the use of best practices in
the state, and can inform the eventual development of practice standards.

The activities of the collaborative thus far reflect these three goals. Regarding the development of a research agenda, the group organized a
roundtable meeting in November, 1997, attended by practitioners, administrators, policy makers, and researchers. Presentations and group discussions
were used to elicit broad-based input into the development of a research
agenda for the collaborative. The organizers produced a report that contains
recommendations for practice-relevant investigations of abuser intervention
programs. The key points of these dialogues were summarized in a recent paper (Murphy & Dienemann, in press). Interestingly, one conclusion was that

Maryland AIP practitioners, in general, are more interested in enhancing overall program efficacy and in reaching difficult, treatment-resistant abusers than in finding the "best model" or in proving that one intervention theory is better than another.

Regarding capacity-building for research, the group has secured funding for a study investigating the feasibility and cost of a centralized outcome data collection process for Maryland AIP's that relies on victim phone interviews. A number of vexing technical problems remain in assessing outcomes this way, however, including the ascertainment of accurate and complete victim contact information from abusers, limited willingness by court-mandated abusers to provide voluntary informed consent to participate in research, and mixed reactions from victims regarding the completion of research assessments with interviewers who are not affiliated with the treatment program. The research collaborative has also secured funding for a part-time administrator who facilitates the efforts of the collaborative, including the development of standard intake data collection procedures for participating programs.

Regarding the communication of research findings to practitioners, the collaborative has established a quarterly newsletter that contains readable summaries of research on abuser intervention along with companion pieces describing relevant practice information. A second, evolving aspect of this communication involves the preparation of more detailed and extensive research summaries related to specific topics that are targeted for review by a program standards committee. For example, the issues of couples' therapy and program length have been targeted for detailed analysis and review, with the prospect of including related provisions in an updated version of the operating guidelines.

IV. FUTURE EFFORTS

The collaborative is working hard to create a greater integration of science and practice that meets the needs of both researchers and practitioners. The collaborative will continue to use existing knowledge to inform best practices and standards in Maryland. In addition, the group is striving to create the capacity for multi-site investigations that are sensitive to the criminal justice system, and community, contexts in which abuser counseling is provided, have the capacity to enhance program practices, and can inform the development of empirically-based program standards.

Many challenges remain for Maryland to become a model for the application of empirical knowledge in developing best practices and standards for abuser intervention programs. Perhaps these initial efforts will help others around the country to see the utility of research-practice partnerships oriented toward a common goal of developing and disseminating effective interventions to reduce domestic violence.

REFERENCES

Adams, D. (1988). Treatment models of men who batter: A profeminist analysis. In K. Yllo, & M. Bograd (Eds.), *Feminist perspectives on wife abuse* (pp. 176-199). Newbury Park, CA: Sage.

American Psychological Association (1996). *Violence and the family: Report of the American Psychological Association Presidential Task Force on Violence and the Family*. Washington, DC: American Psychological Association.

Berman, J.S., & Norton, N.C. (1985). Does professional training make a therapist more effective? *Psychological Bulletin, 98*, 401-407.

Bograd, M. (1984). Family systems approaches to wife battering: A feminist critique. *American Journal of Orthopsychiatry, 54*, 558-568.

Christensen, A., & Jacobson, N.S. (1994). Who (or what) can do psychotherapy: The status and challenge of nonprofessional therapies. *Psychological Science, 5*, 8-14.

Edleson, J.L., & Syers, M. (1990). Relative effectiveness of group treatments for men who batter. *Social Work Research and Abstracts, 26*, 10-17.

Edleson, J.L., & Syers, M. (1991). The effects of group treatment for men who batter: An 18-month follow-up study. *Research on Social Work Practice, 1*, 227-243.

Howard, K.I., Kopta, S.M., Krause, M.S., & Orlinsky, D.E. (1986). The dose-effect relationship in psychotherapy. *American Psychologist, 41*, 159-164.

Maryland Family Violence Council (1996). *Stop the violence: A call to action*. Recommendations and action plan, available from the Maryland Attorney General's and Lt. Governor's Family Violence Council, 200 St. Paul Place, 16th Floor, Baltimore, MD 21202.

Murphy, C.M., & Dienemann, J. A. (in press). Informing the research agenda on domestic abuser intervention through practitioner-researcher dialogues. *Journal of Interpersonal Violence*.

Straus, M.A. (1979). Measuring intrafamily conflict and violence: The Conflict Tactics Scales. *Journal of Marriage and the Family, 41*, 75-88.

APPENDIX

THE ATTORNEY GENERAL'S AND LT. GOVERNOR'S FAMILY VIOLENCE COUNCIL

Operational Guidelines
for Domestic Violence
Abuser Intervention Programs in Maryland

PURPOSE

The purpose of these Guidelines is to promote victim safety by establishing minimum operating standards for Abuser Intervention Programs (AIP). In order to receive court-ordered referrals AIPs must certify to local courts their compliance with these Guidelines.

Minimum operating standards contained in these Guidelines are intended to accomplish the following:

- establish program responsibility to victims and accountability to courts;
- ensure referral of abusers to intervention programs that focus on stopping abuse and preventing abusers from evading or minimizing their responsibility for abusive behavior;
- ensure AIPs participate in a coordinated approach to ending domestic violence that involves a partnership with the legal community and victim advocacy programs at the local and state level; and
- ensure outreach to victims.

1.0 PROGRAM CERTIFICATION

An AIP seeking court-ordered referrals shall certify to the local court, on an annual basis, compliance with these Guidelines.

The Family Violence Council recommends that administrative offices of local courts develop a process to receive certification from AIPs and, on an annual basis, compile and distribute to judges within the jurisdiction a list of AIPs that have so certified.

2.0 DEFINITION OF ABUSIVE BEHAVIOR AS IT OCCURS IN DOMESTIC VIOLENCE

For the purpose of these Guidelines and as a reference for AIPs, abusive behavior occurring in intimate relationships is defined as follows:

- Abuse is a pattern of coercive control directed toward the victim.
- Abusive behavior involves the use of physical harm, emotional harm, or intimidation to control the victim's thoughts, feelings or actions.
- Abusive behavior results in a living environment of fear which impinges upon the victim's basic rights and freedoms.

2.1 Abusive Behavior May Consist of the Following:

A. Deliberate use of physical force or threat to use physical force to harm another.

Specific behaviors include, but are not limited to: hitting, pushing, choking, scratching, pinching, restraining, slapping, pulling, hitting with weapons or objects, shooting, stabbing, damaging property or pets, or threatening to do one of these acts.

B. Verbal and emotional forms of assault and control, such as stalking, intimidation, coercion, threats, or degradation.

Specific behaviors include, but are not limited to: name calling, insults, labeling, threats, blaming, and humiliating actions to diminish the victim's sense of self-worth.

C. Economic forms of control.

Specific behaviors include but are not limited to: withholding or denying access to money or other basic resources, and sabotaging employment, housing or educational opportunities.

D. Sexual abuse, assault or coercion.

Specific behaviors are those intended to have the effect of intimidation or harm in a sexual manner, including but not limited to: unwanted touching, voyeurism, sexual degradation, and rape.

E. Social isolation.

Specific behaviors include, but are not limited to: denying communication with friends or family members, prohibiting access to transportation and telephone, and other possessive or jealous behaviors.

F. Failure to comply with immigration requirements, making an immigrant spouse unable to work and vulnerable to deportation and/or loss of child custody.

2.2 Responsibility for Abusive Behavior

The abuser bears sole responsibility for his or her actions. Substance abuse or emotional problems do not diminish responsibility for abusive behavior.

3.0 OPERATING STANDARDS

AIPs must certify compliance with the following standards in order to receive court-ordered referrals of domestic violence abusers for program intervention.

3.1 Victim Confidentiality

A. The AIP shall maintain the confidentiality of victims unless specifically waived by the victim or it is determined by the AIP that there is reason to believe the victim may be in imminent danger.

B. The AIP shall inform victims upon initial contact that they are required by law to report incidents of child abuse to local authorities and to inform the police if they have reason to believe there is imminent danger to others as a result of the abuser's violent behavior.

C. Files on victims shall be maintained separately from files on abusers. AIPs should not maintain files on victims unless the files are protected by the confidentiality privilege of a licensed supervisor.

3.2 Intake Process

A. The AIP shall indicate to the court or court monitor if the abuser is assessed as not being amenable to the program's services and, to the extent feasible, make appropriate recommendations.

B. The AIP shall submit a report to the court or the court monitor if a court-ordered abuser fails to contact the program, within either one month or the response time ordered by the court, whichever is shorter.

C. The AIP shall, under ordinary circumstances, offer a screening and intake appointment within ten (10) business days of the abuser's contact with the program.

D. The AIP shall develop a history and profile of the abuser's violent behavior based on descriptions from criminal justice agencies, the victim(s), treatment programs, and other relevant persons or agencies. The AIP shall require the abuser to provide the following information:

- abuser's name, Social Security number, address, and employer;
- partner and/or victim's name;
- abuser's history of substance abuse;
- abuser's history of psychiatric illness, including but not limited to threats or ideation of homicide or suicide, history of depression or paranoia;
- history of abusive behavior as defined in Section 2.0;
- whether the abuser possesses or has access to weapons, and any history of threat or actual use of weapons against the victim;
- degree of possessiveness by the abuser toward the victim, including forced periods of isolation; and
- abuser's compliance with court-ordered child support and/or family maintenance payments.

E. The AIP is encouraged to obtain the following information from the victim(s), court(s), and/or abuser:

- copy of the criminal or civil domestic violence record; and
- copy of the police report, statement of charges, petition for ex-parte protection and/or protective order.

F. The AIP shall secure a waiver of confidentiality from the abuser to allow communication with the victim and/or current partner about incidents of abuse and the abuser's participation in the program. The AIP will attempt to provide information to victims about services available to maintain safety, as well as educational and counseling resources.

G. The AIP shall either provide or refer abusers for treatment services to address factors contributing to the abusive behavior. The AIP will secure from the abuser a reciprocal release of information to allow for an exchange of information with relevant service providers.

H. A contract, specifying the responsibilities of both the AIP and the abuser shall be signed once the client is determined to be suitable for the program. The contract shall, at a minimum, reflect the following:

- duration of the program;
- agreement on fee rate and payment requirements;
- agreement to stop all forms of violence;
- agreement to refrain from drug and alcohol use while in attendance at group meetings; and
- conditions resulting in program non-compliance and the consequences thereof.

3.3 Victim Safety

A. The AIP shall inform the victim about the abuser's attendance at the program unless the victim requests not to be informed.

B. The AIP shall evaluate the abuser's lethality and warn victims determined to be at high risk. The AIP shall establish a "duty to warn" procedure directing staff to warn the victim and/or notify the police if a direct threat is made against the victim or other person.

4.0 DISCHARGE CRITERIA

The contract signed by the abuser and the AIP shall specify criteria for discharge from the program.

4.1 Program Completion

The abuser shall be deemed to have completed the program upon fulfilling the requirements set forth in the program contract.

4.2 Program Responsibilities

A. The AIP shall notify the referring court, corrections, probation or other court monitor of the abuser's attendance and participation and, to the extent feasible, make appropriate recommendations.

B. The AIP shall notify the victim of the abuser's completion of or termination from the program, unless the victim requests not to be informed. Notification shall include, at a minimum, whether the abuser has complied with the court order. The AIP shall advise the victim that program completion cannot guarantee her safety.

5.0 PROGRAM STAFFING

A. Staff employed by the AIP shall be violence free in their own lives. No AIP shall hire an individual who has been a domestic violence abuser unless the program director is satisfied that the prospective staff member has successfully completed a certified AIP and has since remained violence free for a reasonable period of time, as determined by the program.

B. Staff employed by the AIP shall not use alcohol or drugs to an extent or in a manner that is determined to impair the individual's ability to function in a responsible, professional manner.

C. The AIP shall strive to employ staff who represent the cultural diversity reflected in the community being served, provide services to culturally diverse groups, and comply with the requirements of the Americans with Disabilities Act.

Musings of a State Standards Committee Chair

L. Kevin Hamberger

SUMMARY. The movement among states to promulgate, publish, and implement treatment standards for programs and providers of treatment for men who batter has gained increasing momentum in recent years. This movement, in turn, has created controversy. On the one hand, there are those who view the process of standards development, as well as the products, as essentially good and evolving. On the other hand, there are those who have argued that the process has been flawed, exclusionary, and the products based more on philosophy than sound science. The present paper describes the thoughts of a researcher who also served as chair of a state standards committee. The role of research in standards development and evolution is discussed. The role and contribution of researchers to a collaborative process of standards development and implementation is discussed. Suggestions for enhancing the collaborative process are provided. *[Article copies available for a fee from The Haworth Document Delivery Service: 1-800-HAWORTH. E-mail address: <getinfo@haworthpressinc.com> Website: <http://www.HaworthPress.com> © 2001 by The Haworth Press, Inc. All rights reserved.]*

The views expressed in this paper are entirely those of the author, and not necessarily those of the Governor's Council on Domestic Abuse, or the Wisconsin Committee on Abuser Treatment Standards.

[Haworth co-indexing entry note]: "Musings of a State Standards Committee Chair." Hamberger, L. Kevin. Co-published simultaneously in *Journal of Aggression, Maltreatment & Trauma* (The Haworth Maltreatment & Trauma Press, an imprint of The Haworth Press, Inc.) Vol. 5, No. 2(#10), 2001, pp. 265-286; and: *Domestic Violence Offenders: Current Interventions, Research, and Implications for Policies and Standards* (ed: Robert A. Geffner, and Alan Rosenbaum) The Haworth Maltreatment & Trauma Press, an imprint of The Haworth Press, Inc., 2001, pp. 265-286. Single or multiple copies of this article are available for a fee from The Haworth Document Delivery Service [1-800-HAWORTH, 9:00 a.m. - 5:00 p.m. (EST). E-mail address: getinfo@haworthpressinc.com].

265

KEYWORDS. Abuser treatment standards, researchers, collaboration, multidisciplinary, research-based, politics

The rationale for developing standards for programs and providers of services to perpetrators of family violence is compelling. As pointed out by Geffner (1990), as well as by Holtzworth-Munroe (1997), without appropriate standards, potential for doing *more* damage is great. Geffner (1990) argues that working in the area of partner violence requires specialized skill, training, and experience. It seems almost ironic, then, that the issue of developing, implementing and enforcing standards for treatment of men who batter their partners has been a volatile and controversial topic since the first state, Colorado, did so in 1988. Indeed, the tone of debate and discussion can be characterized as passionate, polemical, even bitter (Goldman, 1991; Hessmiller-Trego, 1991; Segel-Evans, 1991). Accusations have been made about the exclusionary nature of many state standards, which bar the use of certain treatment approaches for working with court-ordered batterers (Geffner, 1995; Goldman, 1991). It has also been argued that the very *process* of development of state standards has often excluded key stakeholders from the research community, as well as those who favor treatment approaches that are controversial among battered women's advocates and others in the mainstream of the battered women's movement (Geffner, 1995). Those who are concerned about the current state of affairs in development and implementation of standards have often argued that politics has played a larger role than science in the development and implementation of standards (Geffner, 1995). Indeed, some in the domestic violence scientific community have argued that scientists have had no voice in the standards development process (Geffner, 1995). Proponents of treatment standards as they are currently written have argued that the process of standards development has been fair and open (Gondolf, 1995), including careful study of scientific literature and commencement of symposia as part of the standards development process.

This author plays multiple roles in the field of partner violence, including researcher/scientist, advocate and policy maker, working as a volunteer in shelter settings and serving on the Governor's Council on Domestic Abuse. It was in the context of these various (and, at times, competing) roles that I took on the mantle of Chair of the Standards Committee for the State of Wisconsin. This essay contains a number of thoughts that a standards committee chair might ponder in considering the role of research and researchers in the development of treatment standards. The essay will consider the researcher's role in informing discussion about the current "state of knowledge" related to the many issues that standards committees consider. Prior to discussing the researcher's role, however, an overall context is provided within which to understand the current debate about standards, their value and form. The first contextual facet will consider whether the current debate about abuse abatement program and provider treatment standards is new or unique. The second facet will consider why standards may have developed and evolved in the manner in which they did. Within this context, difficulties with standards, from a scientific/empirical perspective will be discussed. The essay will conclude with consideration of what researchers can contribute to development of treatment standards, and recommendations for both researcher and nonresearcher committee members to enhance collaboration to develop the most appropriate standards.

THE CURRENT DEBATE: IS IT NEW OR UNIQUE?

In 1993, the Agency for Health Care Policy and Research (ACHPR) published clinical practice guidelines for the detection and treatment of depression (Depression Guideline Panel, 1993). Broadly summarized, the AHCPR guidelines encouraged primary care physicians to increase the rate and accuracy with which they identify depressed patients in primary care settings. The guidelines also recommended pharmacotherapy as the first line of treatment for primary care physicians. The AHCPR guidelines are based on extensive and detailed reviews of the scientific literature on detection, diagnosis, and treatment of depression. Nevertheless, the guidelines, and their empirical bases, have been subject to criticism, particularly from the clinical psychology establishment (Munoz, Hollon, McGrath, Rehm, & VandenBos, 1994). These eminent psychologists took issue with the methodological rigor of some of the research underlying the guidelines. The tendency of the guidelines to downplay methodological limitations of underlying research was also noted. The panel of psychologists also disagreed with the primary emphasis of the guidelines on recommending pharmacotherapy as a first-line treatment approach. In addition, some of the publications emanating from the major guidelines documents were criticized as having a distinct biomedical bias, and failed to present a balanced discussion about the role of both medications and psychotherapeutic approaches to treatment of depression. Many other criticisms and concerns were also raised by this group. The above summary should suffice, however, to illustrate that, even in areas of psychosocial treatment that appear to have a solid empirical base, deep disagreements and divisions can occur when guidelines for best treatment approaches are developed.

Nathan (1998) reviewed the issues of treatment standards for mental health professionals, and pointed out that, in every area of attempts to create clinical guidelines, controversy exists. Proponents of guidelines typically view them as good for the profession and for consumers, and argue that sufficient data exist to support their development. Those critical of guidelines typically argue that (1) there is insufficient empirical evidence to support them, (2) most guidelines are biased in some manner, (3) guidelines restrict professional judgement and flexibility. Also, guidelines in the area of mental health have been criticized as containing overly strong language, and implying greater knowledge in the field than currently exists. Despite such controversies, Nathan asserts that practice guidelines are here to stay, and a return to the pre-guideline era is neither likely nor desirable.

Nathan's (1998) analysis illustrates that, within any given area of treatment, the establishment of treatment or professional guidelines is likely to be controversial. In the case of depression, a massive body of empirical literature was reviewed to develop guidelines for diagnosis and treatment. Even so, critics of the guidelines were able to marshal cogent arguments related to the weaknesses of underlying research, as well as the philosophical biases of the guidelines, despite reliance on a strong empirical base.

Now consider the case of abuse abatement treatment programming. The field is only a little more than two decades old. As a treatment field, the basis of abuse abatement has been characterized more by philosophical and political analysis than by empirical analysis and systematically collected data. Research on men who batter their partners, as well as research on treatment, has been published for little more than fifteen years. Hence, research in the area of treatment of abusive men is still in a relative infancy. Most studies have assessed only a narrow range of possible treatment approaches (Hamberger & Hastings, 1993), and the type of research to date has been primarily descriptive or quasi-experimental. Very few experimental studies of abuse abatement treatment have been conducted and completed. Therefore, it should not be surprising that the emergence of treatment standards in the field of abuse abatement counseling has sparked such a high level of controversy and debate. The youthfulness of the field, the relative paucity of solid research, and the heavy reliance on political and philosophical analysis create a situation ripe for contention. Therefore, members of the research, treatment, and advocacy communities should not despair at the current level of debate and discussion. Rather, it could be viewed as an opportunity to test the limits of our knowledge, determine gaps and develop methods and processes for maximum inclusion of all relevant stakeholders in continuing discussions and subsequent iterations of treatment standards.

WHY DID BATTERER TREATMENT STANDARDS DEVELOP?

There is no available systematic history of the development and evolution of the movement to establish abuse abatement treatment standards. Nathan (1998) suggests that the movement to develop treatment guidelines is related to ongoing empirical advances in a given field, pressure on providers to use empirically supported methods, demands of society for treatment providers to be accountable for their actions, and the need to show treatment efficacy for reimbursement. In the field of partner violence, there appear to be four primary reasons behind the movement to establish treatment standards. Though somewhat similar to the reasons provided by Nathan, some reasons for establishing abuse abatement program standards have evolved directly from the battered women's movement.

Program Accountability. The first reason for developing treatment standards is to ensure accountability of batterer treatment programs to battered women and to the community, in general. Partner violence is a serious problem, which not only affects quality of life for everyone involved, but can also lead to serious injury, disability, and even death. In addition, partner violence is an epidemic, affecting a significant proportion of any given community. Further, community resources expended to intervene include law enforcement, criminal justice, medicine, and social services. Partner violence also results in lost worker productivity, costing business and industry millions of dollars per year. In addition, courts and departments of corrections increasingly rely on the promise of treatment programs to help perpetrators mend their ways as an alternative to costly incarceration in already overcrowded jails. Given then the community context, within which batterer treatment programs exist and work, as well as the faith instilled in such programming by key community stakeholders such as judges and community corrections personnel, it makes sense that programs and providers which purport to be experts in ameliorating partner violence should be able to account for their practices and back up their claims of effectiveness. They should also be accountable to support battered women in meeting needs for safety.

The issue of batterer program accountability to battered women, while somewhat different than accountability to the community, is especially important. Most women who are battered do not want their intimate relationship to end. Rather, they want the violence to end. Many battered women are cautious in their optimism about their partners ending violence from going through batterer treatment. Indeed, many such women express reservations to providers about whether treatment will "work." Others have acknowledged that program effectiveness will be at least, in part, related to the dedication and resolve of the perpetrator/client. Yet others are hopeful that their partner will benefit from abuse abatement treatment so the relationship can move on and grow. So powerful is this hope, that the perpetrator's involvement in abuse abatement counseling is an important predictor of the woman ending marital separation (Gondolf, 1988). Therefore, given the importance that perpetrator counseling plays in the decisions of battered women, it also seems natural and reasonable that those who hold themselves out as experts in the treatment and amelioration of partner violence are also accountable to battered women.

Protection of Victims. Although it is impossible for treatment programs to guarantee safety to the battered victim through working with her partner, batterer treatment standards may enhance victim safety in a number of ways. First, by having the perpetrator involved in a treatment program that meets minimal standards, there is assurance about the types of anti-violence messages he will be exposed to, minimal training level of the therapists, therapeutic modalities used to achieve non-abusiveness, and consequences for failure. There may also be assurances related to the communication and feedback loops and networks between treatment programs and other concerned agencies (e.g., shelter, corrections) to facilitate perpetrator compliance and accountability and victim safety. Finally, standards may require program communications with the victim. Such communications could include providing her with information on such matters as safety resources for her, and treatment program limitations. In addition, she may be informed of her partner's compliance with treatment, involvement in treatment, completion of/termination from treatment, and, if possible, projections of risk for reoffending and prognosis. To the extent that standards require (a) treatment methods known to be effective, (b) perpetrator accountability, and (c) communication between the treatment provider and the victim and relevant community resources, safety may be enhanced.

Abuser Accountability. Men who batter their partners are well-known to minimize, deny, and blame their violence on factors external to themselves (Ganley, 1987). This can occur at any time and point in the perpetrator's life, including prior to, during, and after an assault. It can occur in discussion with workmates, or in his own quiet moments of thought about his relationship. Denial, minimization, and externalization can also be evident in police investigations, during arraignment, and at trial. Treatment providers typically witness denial and minimization during various points in treatment, but most typically at the beginning. Indeed, it is a maxim of treatment that change cannot occur, either in part or in whole, as long as the client is minimizing, in denial, or blaming others for their actions. A major part of treatment, then, is to work to facilitate client ownership of his violent and abusive behavior.

A major concern, among battered women's advocates and others (Adams, 1989; Pence, 1989) is that abuser treatment programs can easily become centers where abusive men are provided both subtle and overt reinforcement for their defensiveness and failure to accept total responsibility for their behavior and for changing it. Therefore, it is believed by standards proponents that language can be built into treatment standards that unambiguously require treatment programs to be aware of the risks of collusion with perpetrators, and have written policies in place for avoiding it altogether, or addressing such collusion when it is evident. Other standards provisions for facilitating client accountability include policy and procedures requirements for dealing with noncompliance with treatment regimens, attendance policies, consequences for reoffending, and confidentiality limitations. With such provisions in place, standards create a set of minimal procedural requirements that batterer-clients must successfully negotiate to either complete treatment programming, or pay consequences for failure to do so.

End "Questionable" Practices for Treating Perpetrators. The primary purpose of abuse abatement treatment is to protect battered women through holding abusive men accountable and helping them end violence. Hence, any treatment approach that does not place responsibility for the violence, and for stopping it, squarely on the perpetrator, is typically viewed as questionable or inappropriate. Other criteria for determining therapy approaches to be inappropriate include evidence, within the treatment approach, of victim-blaming, or diffusing responsibility for the violence to the relationship or communication patterns, or requiring the victim to participate in the treatment.

Adams (1988) reviewed a number of approaches to treatment, together with a feminist analysis of their strengths, weaknesses, and acceptability as treatments for men who batter their partners. Adams identified five primary approaches to treating partner assaulters: ventilation, psychodynamic/insight-oriented, systems/interactional, cognitive-behavioral and profeminist. On the basis of his analysis, Adams ruled out three of the five approaches as inappropriate for treatment of batterers: ventilation, psychodynamic/insight-oriented, and systems/interactional. One approach, cognitive-behavioral, was interpreted as appropriate, if combined with feminist power analysis of relevant cognitions and behaviors, rather than focusing strictly on anger management. Gondolf and Russell (1986) also analyzed anger management approaches and concluded that, without the addition of feminist-based power and control analyses, such approaches were inappropriate as a treatment of choice for abusive men.

In general, those treatment approaches deemed inappropriate for use with abusive men were determined to, variously, blame the victim or, at least, hold her partially responsible for the violence, place the victim at risk by having her present with the perpetrator and disclose information without adequate safeguards. Other criticisms included focusing therapeutic effort on underlying problems within the abusive man or within the relationship rather than directly targeting violence, power, and control. At the time of Adams' (1988) analysis, there was almost no empirical evidence for or against any of the treatment methods reviewed. His conclusions were based almost entirely on a philosophical, sociopolitical analysis. Nevertheless, the review came to have a profound impact on the field of abuse abatement program evaluation, and has been widely cited.

Given this brief history and rationale for development of standards for the treatment of partner-abusive men, it is clear that the ultimate goal of batterer treatment standards is to provide some measure of protection to victims, and require treatment programs to adopt this view as an overarching philosophy of treatment of abusive men. However noble, the establishment of such standards, and their codification into policy and law does create some problems, both intended and unintended.

PROBLEMS WITH STANDARDS

One major problem with treatment standards is with the term, itself. According to *Webster's New Collegiate Dictionary* (1973), "standard" is synonymous with the words "criterion," "gauge," "yardstick," "touchstone," with a shared meaning element of "a means of determining what a thing should be." As a noun, the meaning of "standard" for present purposes is further defined as "something set up and established by authority as a rule for measure of quantity, weight, extent, value, or quality." Hence, use of the term "standards" to define how abuse abatement treatment should best be done suggests that we, as a field, know what *is* best. However, as pointed out by a number of reviews of abuse abatement treatment, the state of the art is such that (a) firm assertions about the efficacy of such treatment cannot be made (Hamberger & Hastings, 1993; Rosenfield, 1992), (b) it is not known for whom certain types of treatment will work best (Saunders, 1996), and (c) there is little empirical basis for much of what is done to help abusive men change (Eisokovitz & Edleson, 1989). Therefore, a danger of developing abuse abatement treatment standards, and codifying them into policy and law, is that they suggest a level of knowledge that may not yet exist.

At the same time standards may suggest greater authority and knowledge than actually exist, they raise the bar of expectations held by key stakeholders. For example, referral sources such as judges and probation agents may rely on standards to determine whether to refer an abusive man to treatment, and to whom he should be referred. Such referral sources may expect, therefore, that any program meeting the standards is operating within accepted levels of quality, and that there is a suitable knowledge base against which program and provider behavior can be measured to determine that acceptability.

Treatment standards also raise the bar of expectations in terms of professional liability. Prior to published, state-endorsed standards, there was little to argue for or against any particular approach to treatment. A lone exception to this is the work of Hart (1988). Hence, while adverse outcomes could still lead to assignment of liability, in the absence of standards, various practices could be defended on other grounds. The emergence of published standards, as noted above, suggests an accepted, empirical base supporting accepted practices. As pointed out by Nathan (1998), despite problems with treatment standards, one effect of them is that, to reduce liability risk, providers will be reluctant to stray too far from the limits imposed by standards. To the extent that a provider deviates from accepted practice standards in providing abuse abatement services, she/he may be increasing liability risk, particularly if things go wrong. Even for those who do meet standards requirements, however, liability risk is also increased, in that adverse outcomes may now be investigated and judged against accepted, published standards, with increased frequency. Hence, one effect of standards, then, is to create a narrow range of "accepted" treatment methods, even if their empirical base is weak. This may have an unintended effect of "locking in " a treatment approach that is minimally effective, and excluding innovative approaches that may actually be more effective.

In summary, the movement to develop treatment standards for programs and providers of services to men who batter their partners has gained much momentum. This momentum has occurred with battered women's advocates, as well as many treatment providers. There are many good reasons for the development of treatment standards. These include protection of battered women, particularly from inappropriate methods of treatment, holding perpetrators accountable for actively participating in quality treatment programs which use approved treatment methods, and holding treatment programs accountable to both the community and battered women which rely on them to organize all they do in working with abusive men around the central value of protecting battered women, and ending violence in all its forms.

On the other hand, while a noble cause, abuse abatement treatment programs today have a relatively small, if growing, empirical base. Little is known about the efficacy of predominant models of treatment, and research on new and innovative treatment approaches is in a veritable infancy. Hence, treatment standards as they now exist may promise more than is possible to deliver in terms of expectations to consumers, as well as of treatment providers. In turn, raised expectations of treatment program quality and provider competence creates new and increased risks of liability for adverse outcomes.

In addition to the above potential problems with imposition of treatment standards for treatment of men who batter, another set of problems also accrues, particularly in the area of innovation and scientific inquiry. Specifically, since standards are codified into public policy, professional codes of conduct and, in many instances, law, they assume a level of rigidity and orthodoxy of approach to treatment. Parameters of operation are typically narrowly defined. Deviations from those parameters are considered violations, the consequences of which can include loss of certification and qualification to provide services to abusive men. Hence, regardless of one's theoretical perspective or preferred treatment approach in general, to participate as a treatment provider to abusive men means adopting and accepting requirements of associated treatment standards.

An associated problem is that the narrow definitions of approved and accepted clinical approaches to treating abusive men imposed by standards, stunts development of creative and innovative treatment approaches. This is particularly so in the field of abuse abatement treatment. There appear to be two predominant treatment approaches that have characterized abuse abatement treatment to date, profeminist education and cognitive-behavioral, separately and in various combinations. In a best-case scenario, there is little empirical data to support the effectiveness of either of these approaches, and none to support their superiority to any other approach. However, in any state with defined standards that mandate a specific treatment approach, efforts by a provider to explore alternative treatment approaches such as examining underlying dynamic issues related to early trauma as a way to help men end violence may result in disqualification from certification.

In addition to stunting clinical innovations, abuse abatement program and provider treatment standards can have a chilling effect on scientific inquiry to develop and determine the most effective, safe and appropriate treatment approaches. Clinical innovation and treatment efficacy research are interdependent and often work hand-in-hand. However, since standards often codify those treatment approaches that are *not* allowed, as well as those that are, research on the disapproved approaches is made prohibitively difficult.

SHOULD TREATMENT STANDARDS BE UNDONE?

The standards movement has swept the nation. According to Austin and Dankwort (1997), as of November, 1997, twenty-four states have created and promulgated either state or county standards. Another seven states have developed drafts of treatment standards. Thirteen states and the District of Columbia are in the process of developing standards. Given the momentum of the movement, it is not reasonable to suggest that standards can be repealed. Moreover, as noted above, despite the disadvantages of treatment standards, there are many good reasons for having them, as well. Requiring treatment programs and providers to function as part of the broader community of workers to stop partner violence is a good thing. It is also desirable to require treatment programs that purport to be effective to also be accountable to both the broader community and to battered women. This includes using appropriate caution in extolling the virtues of abuse abatement treatment, helping victims access resources that empower them and promote safety, and holding perpetrators accountable for their actions.

Nevertheless, there are some aspects of treatment standards that should be open to examination and change. In particular, as new research is published, leading to advances in our knowledge, standards need to be re-examined and modified in light of such advances. Ideas and beliefs that appear valid today may be reinforced and validated as new research emerges. For example, a typical component of treatment standards require programs to focus on and analyze abusive behavior in light of power and control, and the need to share power. Programs are also to avoid victim blaming, and confront it when it emerges in group sessions. Recent research has provided validation for the idea that most men who batter do so to achieve power and control over their partners, whereas most women who use violence do so to defend themselves or retaliate against prior violence (Barnett, Lee, & Thelen, 1997; Hamberger, Lohr, & Bonge, 1994; Hamberger, Lohr, Bonge, & Tolin, 1997). Future research may further refine and extend these concepts, thus providing impetus for modification of standards.

On the other hand, ideas and practices that are held up today as both undisputed fact and state-of-the-art knowledge may need to be re-examined in light of new research. In general, there are a number of areas and components of abuse abatement treatment standards that will need to be re-examined as new research emerges. Holtzworth-Munroe (1997) identified a number of such areas and issues, including (a) the utility of conjoint treatment approaches that are sensitive to partner violence issues, (b) the possibility that multiple forms of treatment will be effective with different types of perpetrators, (c) men who batter, as a group, are heterogeneous, not "all the same," (d) development and role of motivational interviewing to enhance treatment acceptance, (e) relapse-prevention programs to facilitate maintenance of gains. Another area that lacks a solid empirical base is duration of treatment. Early writers (e.g., Sonkin, Martin, & Walker, 1985) recommended, for probation mandated clients, that treatment last for the entire duration of probation, which could extend to five years. More recently, California standards mandate 52 weeks of treatment, and Massachusetts mandates 80 hours of treatment. These recommendations and mandates suggest a belief that "more is better" when it comes to treatment duration. Little research has addressed the issue, however. Edleson and Syres (1990) found that, compared to a 32-session program, participants in a 12-session program showed higher completion rates, and lower recidivism rates. In addition, in a quasi-experimental analysis, Rosenbaum, Gearan, and Ondovic (1997) found that participants in 10- and 20-session treatment programs had lower rates of post-treatment recidivism than participants in a 7-week program. However, participants in the two longer program formats did not differ from each other, suggesting diminishing returns from participating in longer programs, beyond a certain threshold. Obviously, more work needs to be done to answer the question of treatment duration. However, these studies are provided here as examples of how research can challenge long and deeply held beliefs. Hence, although it is important to recognize those aspects of treatment standards that are valuable and valid, it is also important to acknowledge that future iterations of standards need to be informed by the body of research that is relevant to the issues at hand.

The question may legitimately be asked, "How do we do research if we are locked into certification of treatment and treatment programs?" Under such circumstances, conducting certain types of research, such as comparing treatment methods, may be difficult. Such a question, and the accompanying concern is most likely to occur in those states with standards which clearly prescribe a specific treatment approach. In such states, an appropriate action would be to modify standards to allow exemptions for research that tests alternative treatment models and approaches. Another approach, illustrated by the Maryland standards, requires certain operational guidelines, but proscribes little in the way of technique or treatment length. Such flexibility allows for the study of alternative approaches, and actually invites development of treatment approaches based on outcomes. In other states, such as Wisconsin, standards apply to programs accepting court-mandated clients. Hence, research programs that rely on non-mandated, community-referred clients can continue to develop. Data from outcome and comparison studies can be used to educate standards committees about the importance of research and research exemptions.

THE ROLE OF RESEARCH
IN INFORMING STANDARDS DEVELOPMENT

Research in the field of partner violence and about men who batter and their treatment can make valuable contributions to the development of treatment standards. In fact, it is safe to assert that to remain viable and credible, it will be necessary to incorporate research findings into deliberations and decisions about standards of care and treatment for men who batter. The primary functions of research are to discover new knowledge, validate existing or prior observations, and synthesize current knowledge into new concepts and ways of understanding. In essence, at any given point in time, research informs the field of what is known. In addition, since research is a perpetual, ongoing process, each study or literature review conducted also raises a number of new questions, thus informing the field of gaps in knowledge. Awareness of such gaps points the way to new research in an effort to close them, while raising new questions. Hence, through the process of research, knowledge is never complete. As areas of study evolve, research can become more sophisticated in terms of questions asked, methods used to answer them, and methods used to analyze the resultant data. Through this process, though ultimate questions are rarely answered, a field draws closer to a sense of certainty, while at the same time developing increasing appreciation for the qualifiers that surround the answers. Thus, for example, in the field of abuse abatement treatment, we are just beginning to move away from early, general questions about "Does treatment work?" to "What type of treatment works best with what type of perpetrator?" Similarly, methodology in treatment outcome is beginning to move away from single group designs, looking only at outcome among treatment completers, or at most comparing outcome among treatment completers and dropouts, or comparison of nonrandomized groups of treated and untreated men (e.g., Dutton, 1986; Hamberger & Hastings, 1988). More recent research has utilized randomized assignment of perpetrators to different treatment conditions (O'Leary, 1997; O'Leary & Neidig, 1993; Saunders, 1996). Outcome measures have begun to include both completers and dropouts within different treatment conditions (Davis & Taylor, 1999). These methodological improvements move the field closer to answering questions related to treatment efficacy with different types of abusive men.

In addition to increasing our knowledge of the field, as noted above, research can also inform us of the limitations of knowledge, (i.e., what we do not know). For example, there are very few published reports of treatment studies that directly and experimentally compare treatment of abusive men with no treatment. Hence, it is not well known whether treatment of abusive men is effective in helping such men stop their abusive and violent behavior. In addition, very few studies have actually directly compared different types of treatment with each other to determine the comparability or superiority of different treatment approaches. Saunders (1996) compared a cognitive-behavioral/feminist approach with a process-psychodynamic group approach, and found few differences in overall outcome. The study did find that men with dependent personality traits did better with the process-psychodynamic approach, and men with antisocial traits fared better in the cognitive-behavioral/feminist approach. Brannen and Rubin (1996) published a study comparing gender-specific group treatment for abusive men and victims with a couples group approach in a court-mandated treatment context. Results showed no overall differences between treatment approaches except for alcoholic men. Men with histories of alcohol abuse showed greater violence reductions in the couple's format than similar men in gender-specific group formats.

These and other studies in the field of treatment outcome are beginning to provide answers, preliminary as they are, to many questions about which treatments work best, which treatments are safe, and under which circumstances such treatments are best administered. However, as noted above, research is an ongoing enterprise, and no single study can be taken as providing ultimate answers. But, studies do provide information that can be helpful in informing discussion and decision-making in policy-making areas such as development and promulgation of treatment standards. As studies are replicated across settings, with different research samples, a body of literature develops, which adds confidence in their use in such discussions.

Are There Other Ways of "Knowing?" The systematic gathering of empirical data is a highly valued method of gaining and advancing knowledge in our society. However, in the domestic violence movement, other ways of knowing and communicating knowledge have predominated. In particular, a time-honored method of teaching and imparting knowledge is for formerly battered women to present their personal stories of abuse, adaptation, resistance, and triumph. From these accounts of lived reality, one learns a great deal about the dynamics of abuse, the impact of abuse on victims and children. One also learns a great deal about what types of community interventions have been helpful and those that have been unhelpful, or even harmful. The stories of battered women are compelling and moving, to novice and experienced, alike. In addition, battered women's stories and accounts are useful. Indeed, researchers have wondered about the validity of victims' reports, and have subjected them to systematic research. In general, battered women's accounts of violence against them have been found to be unrelated to social desirability response biases (Arias & Beach, 1987; Dutton & Hemphill, 1992). In addition, detailed, carefully conceived records of personal accounts and experiences, as well as clinical experiences and observations constitute case studies, which occupy a valuable place in the field of applied research (Kratochwill, Mott, & Dodson, 1984).

Hence, in the context of the work of abuse abatement treatment standards committees, the accounts of battered women will likely have similar status to that of published research. Take, for example, the case of deciding where couples counseling fits into the picture. A committee is likely to place at least as much weight on battered women's personal accounts of being endangered or harmed as a result of participating in couples counseling, as on a published report demonstrating that couples counseling is no more likely to result in recidivism than is gender-specific counseling. Similarly, the reports and accounts of experienced battered women's advocates and perpetrator treatment services providers will also likely be accorded considerable attention and face validity by standards committees.

Limitations of Forms of Knowing. The limitations of individual stories, or even collective stories, no matter how compelling and truthful, are obvious. In particular, such accounts are not representative of the general population, and may, in some instances, represent extreme selection bias, which severely limits generalizability. In addition, sometimes personal accounts are transmitted through third parties, i.e., "I knew a person who. . . . " Hence, by themselves, personal stories may be of limited use when considering large scale, broad-based policy of the type represented by treatment standards.

Systematic, empirical research is also not without limitations. Questions of sample representativeness and generalizability also exist with this mode of learning and knowing. For example, a study may report a decrease in violence among court-mandated participants versus court-involved men not mandated to treatment. Such a study is limited in generalizability to men who are court-ordered to treatment. Whether the treatment will be equally effective with men not involved with the court system remains to be seen. Similarly, some treatment outcome studies have specific exclusion criteria which severely limits generalizability of findings (e.g., Dutton, 1986). Many outcome studies have reported only on those who have completed treatment, thus limiting generalization of findings only to treatment completers (e.g., Davis & Taylor, 1999), and inflating the outcome rates.

Another aspect of systematic research that can be problematic is difficulty in replication. Although an initial study may show great promise, it is necessary to replicate it in different settings, with different types of individuals to assess the validity and reliability of the phenomenon. Premature acceptance of findings of a single study could lead to ineffective and even harmful policy development. Therefore, before research is embraced in the development of treatment standards, it will be necessary to demonstrate that the study has replicated. In addition, it will be important for researchers to be appropriately critical and scientifically pessimistic about early and preliminary studies, and take a leadership role in calling for, and conducting, replications.

These few, brief examples of limitations demonstrate that there is no perfect way of knowing, although there may be a "best" way. Both forms of knowledge gathering and knowing have limitations. Both, however, can and do contribute to the process of developing standards for treating abusive men. The important point for researchers participating in such deliberations is to understand these differences, and develop a niche for making substantive contributions. Both researchers and nonresearchers alike must understand limitations of different types of knowledge gathering, and take these into consideration during deliberation of issues.

THE RESEARCHER'S ROLE WORKING
ON A STANDARDS COMMITTEE

It should be apparent, from the above discussion, that researchers have vital contributions to make to the development of treatment standards for work with abusive men. In particular, researchers bring to the table a specialized knowledge and unique experiences in the field of partner violence. Advanced and specialized training in research and research methodology qualifies researchers to evaluate the empirical literature on the topic for standards committees. Researchers can also help evaluate whether research being considered in deliberations is current or outdated. This leads to another role of translating and interpreting relevant empirical literature to nonacademic and nonresearcher committee members. In addition, researchers in the field of partner violence are, in general, sympathetic to the primary tenets of the domestic violence movement, wanting, ultimately, to end violence toward women. Many researchers have worked in advocacy in the field, as well. As pointed out by Gondolf, Yllo, and Campbell (1997), researchers are in a unique position to act as a type of mediator or translator between numerous and competing perspectives. In this position, the researcher can help identify multiple perspectives and contributions of different committee members, and tie these together, conceptually. The researcher can "translate" ideas and concepts from one position into language that is relevant and understandable to representatives of different disciplines. To accomplish this role effectively, the researcher must be conversant in both scientific ideas and the goals and methods of activists and others involved in developing standards.

To function effectively on standards committees, however, researchers must be cognizant of a number of factors. First, researchers must recognize that they are but one part of the total effort mobilized to end domestic violence. As important as research is to researchers, it sometimes appears to have little bearing on the activities of advocates and others working in the trenches on a daily basis. Policymakers may have an interest in research, but it may be inaccessible to them on a regular basis. Hence, researchers who join standards committees will need to approach their tasks from a perspective of mutual appreciation and respect for the perspectives and experiences of their advocacy colleagues. Through honoring the history, traditions, and methods of their col-

leagues, researchers can acknowledge differences in values and goals, and negotiate with their interdisciplinary colleagues about how to achieve common
goals.

While this would ideally be a two-way street, it is advisable to not expect it,
at least initially. As pointed out by Hamberger (1998), researchers have not
historically had a natural trusting relationship with community advocates.
Hence, conscious initiative to nurture such relationships will be necessary in
many cases.

Keep Doing Research. Perhaps the major contribution researchers can
make to treatment standards committees, and the process of developing treatment standards, is to continue doing research relevant to the issue at hand. As a
committee chair, and a researcher, one of the most frustrating aspects of committee deliberations was discovering the number of gaps in empirical knowledge of a wide array of issues, many of which have been summarized above.

In addition to knowledge gaps, another frustration is the unavailability or
inaccessibility of much research to those not in the research field. Since the
vast majority of standards committee members are not academic, social science researchers, they are not aware of, nor regular subscribers to the major archival journals devoted to the topic of partner violence. Further, many studies
are presented and discussed at national conferences long before they are published. Hence, these studies, while accessible to those in the research community, are even more inaccessible to nonresearchers. Therefore, it will be
important for researchers, once again, to work to make such information available to facilitate informed deliberation of key issues.

Establish Alliances with Domestic Violence Advocates. Researchers are frequently viewed with some suspicion by advocates, who may view researchers
as being more interested in ivory-tower, esoteric issues than issues that impact
real-life concerns of victims and advocates (Gondolf et al., 1997). Further, researchers may be viewed as a type of intellectual carpetbagger by some, using
advocates and victims to collect data which enhances the researcher's career,
but giving little or nothing back in a way that enhances the safety and lives of
the people they study (Hamberger & Ambuel, 1996).

One practical way for researchers to overcome these deficits and develop
alliances with advocates and other nonresearchers is to involve them in the research process from the beginning. This could be informal, as in the case of
discussing research ideas with local advocates, or asking for feedback on a research protocol that has already been developed, showing willingness to make
modifications to the satisfaction of the nonresearcher stakeholders. Yet another method for developing alliances and increasing credibility with community-based groups is for researchers to proactively share their work and
findings with local and state-level groups. Keeping such groups abreast of the

latest work facilitates ongoing discussion of key issues, rather than ignoring them until times of critical discussions, such as during development of treatment standards.

A more formal manner to develop alliances is to develop community advisory groups to provide input and feedback when developing research projects. Such groups can guide the researcher in developing research projects that are sensitive to the safety and welfare of research participants, and, where possible, responsive to the needs of the community. Another approach would be to join local domestic violence task forces, assuming roles that are not directly research-oriented. This approach requires the researcher to function from the perspective of an advocate or policymaker, thus enhancing appreciation of issues faced by nonresearchers.

Development of Standards Inevitably Involves Politics. As alluded to above, an important process of developing treatment standards involves political processes. The work of stopping domestic violence is interdisciplinary, with each group bringing unique perspectives and experiences to the process. Therefore, perspectives will differ, goals will differ, objectives will also differ. This would be true even if standards committees were made up entirely of researchers. Therefore, to develop consensus on an ultimate product (i.e., a treatment standards document) will require discussion, debate and, at times, compromise. The key question for researchers and nonresearchers alike, in this context, is to decide what elements of treatment standards are absolutely necessary, and which ones are preferable.

CONCLUSION AND RECOMMENDATIONS

The movement by many states to develop and implement standards for the treatment of men who batter their partners has gained considerable momentum in the past several years. Researchers have recently expressed considerable concern that not enough attention has been paid by standards committees to empirical research and the input of researchers to the standards promulgation process. Reasons for this lack of researcher involvement could be related to local committee selection processes that may have excluded researchers. It could also be related to researcher characteristics, as well. Some of these researcher characteristics include lack of involvement with day-to-day work with victims and perpetrators, lack of understanding of the "culture" of advocates and policymakers. On the other hand, advocates and policymakers may not view researchers as sufficiently committed to the movement to end partner violence. Research may be viewed as not sufficiently related to the practical needs of the field. There are a number of things researchers can do to develop more effective working relationships with community and advocacy groups:

1. Work actively with community groups and workers on both research and nonresearch-related activities.
2. Provide information and education on the value of research for domestic violence programs.
3. Become educated about community and advocacy concerns and responsibilities in the area of family violence.
4. Recognize and acknowledge the sensitive nature of domestic violence research, and its implications for both victims and perpetrators.
5. Develop research programs via community-collaborative efforts.
6. Make research results more readily accessible to community workers and policymakers.

Researchers can also do much to build bridges that lead to greater research involvement in the treatment standards process:

1. Share specialized knowledge and expertise with committee members in an educative manner that facilitates discussion and decision-making.
2. Continue development and sharing of their own research programs.

Several interpersonal strategies can help researchers and nonresearchers work together more effectively on standards committees:

1. Both groups must acknowledge the interdisciplinary nature of standards committees.
2. Acknowledge differences honestly, but respectfully.
3. Identify common goals and values.
4. Identify and acknowledge mutual contributions to the field.

Finally, treatment standards committees can and should do many things to integrate research and researchers into the standards development process:

1. Family violence researchers should be explicitly included on standards committees.
2. Standards documents should be reviewed at regular intervals and, if warranted, modified in light of new knowledge.
3. Standards should include explicit provisions for research on current and innovative approaches to abuse abatement treatment.

REFERENCES

Adams, D. (1988). Counseling men who batter: A profeminist analysis. In M. Bograd & K. Yllo (Eds.), *Feminist perspectives on wife abuse* (pp. 176-199). Newbury Park, CA: Sage.

Adams, D.(1989). Feminist-based intervention for battering men. In P.L. Caesar & L. K. Hamberger (Eds.), *Treating men who batter: Theory, practice, and programs* (pp. 3-23). New York: Springer.

Arias, I., & Beach, S.R. (1987). Validity of self-reports of marital violence. *Journal of Family Violence, 2,* 139-149.

Austin, J., & Dankwort, J. (1997). A review of standards for batterer intervention programs. *VAWNET Electronic Resources for Those Working to End Violence Against Women* [on-line]. Available: <http://www.vaw.umn.edu/Vawnet/standard.htm>.

Barnett, O.W., Lee, C.Y., & Thelen, R. (1997). Gender differences in attributions of self-defense and control in interpartner aggression. *Violence Against Women, 3,* 462-481.

Brannen, S., & Rubin, A. (1996). Comparing the effectiveness of gender-specific and couples groups in a court-mandated spouse abuse treatment program. *Research and Social Work Practice, 6,* 405-424.

Davis, R.C., & Taylor, B.G. (1999). Does batterer treatment reduce violence? A synthesis of the literature. *Women & Criminal Justice, 10,* 69-93.

Depression Guideline Panel (1993). *Depression in primary care: Detection, diagnosis, and treatment: Quick reference guide for clinicians* (Clinical Practice Guideline No. 5, AHCPR Publication No. 93-0552). Rockville, MD: Dept of Health and Human Services, Public Health Services, Agency for Health Care Policy and Research.

Dutton, D. (1986). The outcome for court-mandated treatment for wife assault: A quasi-experimental evaluation. *Violence and Victims, 1,* 163-176.

Dutton, D.G., & Hemphill, K.J. (1992). Patterns of socially desirable responding among perpetrators and victims of wife assault. *Violence and Victims, 7,* 29-40.

Edleson, J., & Syres, M. (1990). Relative effectiveness of group treatments for men who batter. *Social Work Research and Abstracts, 26,* 10-17.

Eisokovitz, Z.C., & Edleson, J.L. (1989). Intervening with men who batter: A critical review of the literature. *Social Service Review, 37,* 384-414.

Ganley, A. (1987). Perpetrators of domestic violence: An overview of counseling the court-mandated client. In D. J. Sonkin (Ed.), *Domestic violence on trial: Psychological and legal dimensions of family violence* (pp.155-173). New York: Springer.

Geffner, B. (1990). Family abuse, the judicial system, and politics. *Family Violence and Sexual Assault Bulletin, 6,* 1.

Geffner, R. (1995). Standards in the family violence field. *Family Violence and Sexual Assault Bulletin, 11,* 3.

Goldman, J. (1991). Protect us from the protectors. *Family Violence and Sexual Assault Bulletin, 7,* 15-17.

Gondolf, E.W. (1988). The effect of batterer counseling on shelter outcome. *Journal of Interpersonal Violence, 3,* 275-289.

Gondolf, E.W. (1995). Gains and process in state batterer programs and standards. *Family Violence and Sexual Assault Bulletin, 11,* 27-28.

Gondolf, E.W., & Russell, D. (1986). The case against anger control treatment programs for batterers. *Response, 9*, 2-5.

Gondolf, E.W., Yllo, K., & Campbell, J. (1997). Collaboration between researchers and advocates. In G.K. Kaufman-Kantor, D. Finkelhor, & M.A. Straus (Eds.), *Family violence research* (pp. 261-555). Newbury Park, CA: Sage.

Hamberger, L.K. (June, 1998). *Community collaboration to develop research programs in partner violence.* Paper presented at Program Evaluation and Family Violence Research: An International Conference. Durham, NH.

Hamberger, L.K., & Ambuel, B. (November, 1996). *Community collaboration to develop clinical and research programs in partner violence.* Paper presented at the meeting of the Association for the Advancement of Behavior Therapy, New York, NY.

Hamberger, L.K., & Hastings, J.E. (1988). Skills training for treatment of spouse abusers: An outcome study. *Journal of Family Violence, 3*, 121-130.

Hamberger, L.K., & Hastings, J.E. (1993). Court-mandated treatment of men who assault their partners: Issues, controversies, and outcomes. In N.Z. Hilton (Ed.), *Legal responses to wife assault: Current trends and evaluation* (pp. 188-229). Newbury Park, CA: Sage.

Hamberger, L.K., Lohr, J.M., & Bonge, D. (1994). The intended function of domestic violence is different for arrested male and female perpetrators. *Family Violence and Sexual Assault Bulletin, 10*, 40-44.

Hamberger, L.K., Lohr, J.M., Bonge, D., & Tolin, D. (1997). An empirical classification of motivation for domestic violence. *Violence Against Women, 3*, 401-423.

Hart, B. (1988). *Safety for women: Monitoring batterer's programs.* Harrisburg, PA: Pennsylvania Coalition Against Domestic Violence.

Hellmiller-Trego, J. (1991). Letter to the editor. *Family Violence and Sexual Assault Bulletin, 7*, 5.

Hessmiller-Trego, J. (1991). Letter to the editor. *Family Violence and Sexual Assault Bulletin, 7*, 24-25.

Holtzworth-Munroe, A. (July, 1997). Mandated batterer treatment standards. Paper presented at the Fifth International Family Violence Research Conference, Durham, NH.

Kratochwill, T., Mott, S., & Dodson, S. (1984). Case study and single case research in clinical and applied psychology. In A.S. Bellack & M. Hersen (Eds.), *Research methods in clinical psychology* (pp. 55-99). New York: Pergamon.

Munoz, R.F., Hollon, S.D., McGrath, E., Rehm, L.P., & VandenBos, G.R. (1994). On the AHCPR Depression in Primary Care Guidelines: Further considerations for practitioners. *American Psychologist, 49*, 42-61.

Nathan, P.E. (1998). Practice guidelines: Not yet ideal. *American Psychologist, 53*, 290-299.

O'Leary, K.D. (July, 1997). *Guidelines for treatment of partner abuse in a couple format.* Paper presented at the Fifth International Family Violence Research Conference, Durham, NH.

O'Leary, K.D., & Neidig, P.H. (November, 1993). *Treatment of spouse abuse.* Paper presented at the meeting of the Association for the Advancement of Behavior Therapy, Atlanta, Georgia.

Pence, E. (1989). Batterer programs: Shifting from community collusion to community confrontation. In P.L. Caesar & L.K. Hamberger (Eds.), *Treating men who batter: Theory, practice, and programs* (pp. 24-50). New York: Springer.

Rosenbaum, A., Gearan, P.J., & Ondovic, C. (July, 1997). *Completion and recidivism among court- and self-referred batterers in a psychoeducational group treatment program: Implications for intervention and public policy.* Paper presented at the Fifth International Family Violence Research Conference, Durham, NH.

Rosenfield, B.D. (1992). Court-ordered treatment of spouse abuse. *Clinical Psychology Review, 12*, 205-226.

Saunders, D.G. (1996). Feminist-cognitive-behavioral and process psychodynamic treatments for men who batter: Interaction of abuser traits and treatment model. *Violence and Victims, 11*, 393-414.

Segel-Evans, K. (1991). Letter to the editor. *Family Violence and Sexual Assault Bulletin, 7*, 25-26.

Sonkin, D.J., Martin, D., & Walker, L.E.A. (1985). *The male batterer: A treatment approach.* New York: Springer.

Webster's New Collegiate Dictionary. (1973). Springfield, MA: G. & C. Merriam Company.

CONCLUSION

Future Directions in Mandated Standards for Domestic Violence Offenders

Alan Rosenbaum
Robert A. Geffner

SUMMARY. Over the past decade, states have been enacting domestic violence legislation, which often empowers judges to mandate batterers into intervention programs. To insure that these programs meet reasonable standards and that there is some homogeneity among programs, collateral laws mandating the development of batterer treatment standards are also common. The standards that have emerged have become a source of controversy. The current volume was developed in order to examine the issues and evidence, and to suggest some guidelines, if not for the standards themselves, then for the process that states might use in developing rational, useful standards, or in reevaluating and revising existing standards. To that end, this article offers a synthesis of the selections in this special volume and a suggested set of recommendations that committees might consider as they engage in the difficult processes of standard development or revision. *[Article copies available for a fee from The Haworth Document Delivery Service: 1-800-HAWORTH. E-mail address: <getinfo@haworthpressinc.com> Website: <http://www.HaworthPress.com> © 2001 by The Haworth Press, Inc. All rights reserved.]*

[Haworth co-indexing entry note]: "Future Directions in Mandated Standards for Domestic Violence Offenders." Rosenbaum, Alan and Robert A. Geffner. Co-published simultaneously in *Journal of Aggression, Maltreatment & Trauma* (The Haworth Maltreatment & Trauma Press, an imprint of The Haworth Press, Inc.) Vol. 5, No. 2(#10), 2001, pp. 287-293; and: *Domestic Violence Offenders: Current Interventions, Research, and Implications for Policies and Standards* (ed: Robert A. Geffner, and Alan Rosenbaum) The Haworth Maltreatment & Trauma Press, an imprint of The Haworth Press, Inc., 2001, pp. 287-293. Single or multiple copies of this article are available for a fee from The Haworth Document Delivery Service [1-800-HAWORTH, 9:00 a.m. - 5:00 p.m. (EST). E-mail address: getinfo@haworthpressinc.com].

KEYWORDS. Domestic violence, standards, batterer intervention, batterer treatment, certification, court mandated

The Massachusetts Body of Liberties of 1641 provided that "Everie marryed woeman shall be free from bodilie correction or stripes by her husband, unlesse it be in his owne defence upon her assault." Massachusetts was one of only two American colonies to pass laws making spouse abuse illegal and, in fact, these were the first such laws to be enacted anywhere in the Western world (Pleck, 1987). Massachusetts continues its leadership in domestic violence legislation by becoming one of the first states to enact standards for batterer treatment programs. The Massachusetts standards, authorized by law in 1991, have served as a model in the standard development process in many other states. As Murphy (in this volume) notes, the drafted set of standards in Maryland was "based primarily on the Massachusetts model"; however, they were eventually discarded because they lacked empirical support and might preclude research and the development of more effective interventions. The Massachusetts standards have achieved "model" stature as a result of what Jukes (1999) refers to as the "waffle factor," which refers to the fact that repetition confers validity, and that because of the politics of abuse, people are afraid to question the validity of a "fact" which has been so established.

The liabilities of the Massachusetts model become apparent if we contrast its procedures and provisions with those of the Maryland model, as described by Murphy (in this volume). The Maryland Family Violence Council created a task force consisting of researchers, academicians, representatives of abuser intervention programs, the Maryland Attorney General's office, and the Family Violence Council. The objective of this task force was to "develop empirically based standards for effective abuser intervention methods." In contrast, the Massachusetts standards were developed under the auspices of the Department of Public Health by a committee of 12, which included neither researchers nor academicians, and representatives of only two philosophically similar batterer treatment programs. Input from individuals with diverse opinions was neither invited, nor accepted. This has sometimes been the situation in other states as well (e.g., Florida).

The Maryland committee decided against adopting standards that rigidly prescribed specific program models "because there was insufficient evidence to support the efficacy of any specific approach." Five years earlier, the Massachusetts committee apparently felt there was sufficient justification to proscribe couple's counseling approaches, and declare certain methods as "inappropriate." These included psychodynamic individual or group therapy, which centers causality of violence in the past; communication or anger management techniques, which lay primary causality on anger; systems theory approaches, which treat the violence as a mutually circular process; theories or techniques which identify poor impulse control as the primary cause of violence; and methods which identify psychopathology on either parties' part as a primary cause of violence.

The Maryland committee, noting the absence of evidence supporting any specific treatment length, dropped any length requirements. The Massachusetts standards originally required that programs be no less than 40 hours in duration, and further, that no session be shorter than 90 minutes. In 1994, the Massachusetts standards were changed and the minimum treatment length was arbitrarily doubled to 80 hours. Shortly thereafter, other states also adopted duration requirements without empirical support (e.g., California mandated 52 weeks, which is the equivalent to 104 hours).

The discrepancies between these two models and the methods by which they were developed dramatize the importance of the present volume. The process of establishing standards for batterer treatment is ongoing. Many states have not enacted standards and may either be in the process of doing so, or will engage in the process in the near future. Arbitrary adoption of models simply because they have been around the longest, have the most surface appeal, and have capitalized on the "waffle effect," (Jukes, 1999) is potentially dangerous. Gelles (in this volume) makes the important point that support for the efficacy of current incarnations of domestic violence offender interventions is lacking. The Levesque and Gelles (1998) meta-analysis suggests that effect sizes are small, and they are not alone in questioning whether batterer interventions are worth the price of admission. One thing is more than clear from the contributions in this volume: Domestic violence offender treatment is a work in progress. At this point, we simply do not know which treatment works best.

It is also clear that a single intervention strategy may not address the needs of what we now know to be a very diverse population. Holtzworth-Munroe and others (Holtzworth-Munroe & Stuart, 1994; Holtzworth-Munroe, Meehan, Herron, Rehman, & Stuart, in press) have argued for a typology of batterers and have further suggested that treatment may be subtype specific. Some support for this comes from a study by Saunders (1996), which found that psychodynamic approaches were more effective with dependent batterers, while cognitive-behavioral approaches were more effective with antisocial batterers. So, not only do we not know which treatments are the most effective, we do not know which treatments are most (and least) effective with whom. Another wrinkle concerns Prochaska's transtheoretical model (Prochaska & DiClemente, 1984; Prochaska et al., 1994), which has been applied to batterers (Levesque, Gelles, & Velicer, 1999) and is addressed in this volume by Begun et al. This model suggests that batterers may also differentially respond to

treatment based on their stage of readiness for change, which again emphasizes the potential value of stage-matched interventions. We cannot answer the
question "Does batterer treatment work?" without first asking the question,
"Which type of treatment works best with which type of offender, and under
what circumstances?" We cannot answer any of these questions without research, and we cannot do the research unless treatment standards are flexible
and permissive of innovation.

Standards may have to be flexible in other ways, as well. The article by
Dowd (in this volume) was intended to draw attention to the fact that women
are increasingly being prosecuted for partner aggression and, as with male
batterers, are being mandated into batterer treatment programs. The term
"batterer" continues to be a male gendered term, and there is controversy regarding whether it should be applied to women who are aggressive to their
male intimate partners. Regardless of how they are labeled, treatment programs for partner-aggressive women are becoming more common and states
need to consider whether they should be subjected to the same standards as
programs for men. Existing standards do not specifically address programs for
women. While separate certification standards for programs dealing with
women may be unnecessary, the framers of state standards should include language regarding the special treatment needs of partner-aggressive women.

It is also important to remain mindful of the purposes of batterer treatment
in the first place, namely, protection of women and the prevention of woman
abuse. Such a major task requires a coalition, which includes practitioners, researchers, victim advocates, and the legal system. All of these interests must be
represented in the development of reasonable standards. The processes described by Hamberger and Murphy in this volume are characterized by inclusion and cooperation, and should be viewed as models for the process, if not
the content, of batterer treatment standards. Too often, in-fighting and compe-
tition among batterer treatment providers, battered women's advocates, shelter
personnel, researchers, and academicians obscures the fact that they have a
common mission, which is the elimination of domestic aggression in all of its
forms. Unfortunately, in the development of standards, these diverse stakeholders have often functioned like special interest groups rather than as partners, resulting in standards that are more a political statement than an
insurance against substandard treatment.

The impetus for the present volume was the growing dissatisfaction among
a diverse group of researchers, academicians, advocates and service providers
with the standards that were being adopted in states across the country. The
concerns were first addressed in a series of discussions, presentations, and
seminars at the Fifth International Family Violence Research Conference in
Durham, New Hampshire in 1997. The objective, at that time, was to develop a

set of model standards, which were sensitive to the concerns of all the interests that were represented. It quickly became apparent that there was too much divisiveness and too little trust among the various stakeholders to even hope to reach any consensus regarding standards. The conclusion we draw from the works in the present volume is that what is needed is not a set of model standards, but a set of guidelines for the process of developing standards. We therefore close by offering a set of considerations derived from this volume for individuals, committees, and legislative bodies charged with writing or revising standards.

1. Specification of the content of therapy is premature and without empirical foundation. Evidence for the efficacy of any form of batterer treatment is inconclusive at this time. Specification of specific models in standards without justification will impede the development of new, innovative, and potentially more effective approaches. Similarly, the absolute exclusion of specific approaches, such as abuse-specific couple's counseling or psychodynamic therapy, is arbitrary and inconsistent with clinical evidence. The use of scare tactics, such as identifying specific strategies as dangerous or unethical in the absence of supporting evidence, is not appropriate.

2. Evidence for any specific treatment length is lacking. Clinically, it makes sense that longstanding behavioral and characterological problems are not quickly or easily resolved, and the longer a client remains in treatment, the more confident we may be that any changes made will be maintained. However, in the area of batterer treatment, longer programs often have lower completion rates and the empirical evidence does not support the superiority of longer programs across the board for all offenders. On the other hand, we must also remain mindful of the intent of standards, which is to protect against substandard, profit-driven programs. We must therefore continue to conduct research that will provide an empirical basis for setting minimal treatment length for different types of offenders.

3. Standards must not preclude the conduct of research. This might be accomplished by setting standards that are flexible with regard to such elements as program content or length. It might also be accomplished by providing exemptions to the standards for research purposes. The articles in the present volume speak not only to what we do know, but also to how much we do not know. The inclusion of researchers and academicians in the standards development process is essential to insure that research interests will be protected.

4. Batterer treatment subsumes a diverse set of interventions and service providers. It may be approached from a therapeutic perspective, a didactic perspective, or a combination. It may be confrontational or supportive. Providers may be mental health professionals, non-professionals,

law enforcement workers, shelter workers, and in rare cases, ex-batterers. This diversity must be represented in the development of the standards. The committee that develops the standards should have representation from all interested parties. The development of the Maryland standards provides a good model for insuring representation of the various stakeholders.

5. In most disciplines, the standards for providers specify the education and training requirements for practice rather than the specifics of the practice itself. Quality control is attained by ensuring that practitioners have been adequately trained and have at least a minimum amount of experience. Applied to batterers' treatment, this would mean that state standards would specify the minimum credentials of practitioners but would leave them free to define the parameters of treatment. It might also suggest that the field begin to consider establishing a credential to certify specialized training in batterers' intervention.

6. Batterers' intervention is a work in progress. As intervention strategies evolve, we expect that subtype-specific, or stage-matched interventions may begin to replace the more general ones that are currently popular. State standards need to be regularly revisited, revised, and updated to reflect changes in our empirical knowledge regarding treatment outcome, and developments in intervention technology and practice. State standards should include mechanisms to protect them against obsolescence.

7. Standards should include some requirement for outcome evaluation. As Maiuro et al. (in this volume) note, only 30% of states have evaluation requirements incorporated into their standards. One potential way of protecting against substandard care is basing ongoing certification on empirically demonstrated effectiveness.

We believe that effective treatment for spouse/partner abuse offenders offers the best hope of protecting victims of relationship aggression. If we are to have batterer treatment standards, they must be practical, reasonable, empirically informed, and flexible. Standards must facilitate rather than impede the development of effective interventions.

REFERENCES

Dowd, L. (this volume). Female perpetrators of partner aggression: Relevant issues and treatment. *Journal of Aggression, Maltreatment & Trauma.*

Gelles, R. J. (this volume). Standards for programs for men who batter? Not yet. *Journal of Aggression, Maltreatment & Trauma.*

Hamberger, L. K. (this volume). Musings of a state standards committee chair. *Journal of Aggression, Maltreatment & Trauma.*

Holtzworth-Munroe, A., & Stuart, G. L. (1994). Typologies of male batterers: Three subtypes and the differences among them. *Psychological Bulletin, 116*, 476-479.

Holtzworth-Munroe, A., Meehan, J. C., Herron K., Rehman, U., & Stuart, G. L. (in press). Testing the Holtzworth-Munroe and Stuart batterer typology. *Journal of Consulting and Clinical Psychology*.

Jukes, A. E. (1999). *Men who batter women*. New York: Routledge.

Levesque, D. A., & Gelles, R. J. (1998, July). *Does treatment reduce violent recidivism in men who batter? Meta-analytic evaluation of treatment outcome research*. Paper presented at the Program Evaluation and Family Violence Research Conference, Durham, New Hampshire.

Maiuro, R. D., Hagar, T. S., Lin, H., & Olson, N. (this volume). Are current state standards for domestic violence perpetrator treatment adequately informed by research? A question of questions. *Journal of Aggression, Maltreatment & Trauma*.

Murphy, C. M. (this volume). Toward empirically based standards for abuser intervention: The Maryland model. *Journal of Aggression, Maltreatment & Trauma*.

Pleck, E. (1987). *Domestic tyranny*. New York: Oxford University Press.

Prochaska, J. O., & DiClemente, C. C. (1984). *The transtheoretical approach: Crossing traditional boundaries of therapy*. Homewood, IL: Dorsey Press.

Prochaska, J. O., Velicer, W. F., Rossi, J. S., Goldstein, M. G., Marcus, B. H., Rakowski, W., Fiore, C., Harlow, L. L., Redding, C. A., Rosenbloom, D., & Rossi, S. R. (1994). Stages of change and decisional balance for 12 problem behaviors. *Health Psychology, 13*, 39-46.

Saunders, D. G. (1996). Feminist-cognitive-behavioral and process-psychodynamic treatments for men who batter: Interaction of abuser traits and treatment models. *Violence and Victims, 11*, 393-414.

Index